# *Later Life*
## *Third Edition*

# Later Life
## Third Edition

## Lewis R. Aiken
*Pepperdine University*

LAWRENCE ERLBAUM ASSOCIATES, PUBLISHERS

1989    Hillsdale, New Jersey                    Hove and London

Lawrence Erlbaum Associates, Inc., Publishers
365 Broadway
Hillsdale, New Jersey 07642


Production, interior and cover
design by Robin Marks Weisberg




**Library of Congress Cataloging-in-Publication Data**
Aiken, Lewis R., 1931–
    Later life.
    Bibliography: p.
    Includes indexes.
    1. Aging. 2. Aged. 3. Gerontology. I. Title.
QP86.A38    1989         362.6         88-24293
ISBN 0-8058-0259-2


Printed in the United States of America
10  9  8  7  6  5  4  3  2

# Contents

# *Preface*

There are many reasons why a particular group of people is singled out for special study. The seriousness of the problems posed or the benefits offered by the group to society as a whole and an increase in the power of the group by virtue of its size and influence are two related reasons why it should be of particular interest to researchers and other scholars. One such group that has gained in prominence and hence interest during the past three decades consists of those whose characteristics and circumstances constitute the subject matter of *gerontology*—the study of later life.

Old age is both costly and beneficial to society. All too often the societal benefits of long life, such as continuing productivity and the role of the experienced elderly as teachers and guides of the young, are minimized while the costs of old age are emphasized. These costs, in terms of health care, retirement payments, housing, and social services for the elderly, are, of course, real enough. For example, people who are 65 years of age and older constitute 12% of the American population but account for 30% of all hospital stays and over 40% of all days of hospital care. Because of the growing power of the elderly and their spokespersons, Medicare and Medicaid may eventually give way to some form of national health insurance, which may well be even more costly to American society.

In spite of recent improvements in services for the elderly, many continue to be treated as second-class citizens who are waiting on the shelf for death to overtake them. Furthermore, costs are assessed not only in monetary units. It is costly to the young and middle-aged as human beings, both now and in the years ahead when they will be the aged, to treat older people as anything other than respected, valuable members of society. The elderly can offer skills, wisdom, and psychological support to younger age groups, and the results of surveys and other research investigations reveal that most older people desire to be productive, contributing members of society and are capable of being so.

If for no other reason, the sheer magnitude of the elderly population is forcing society to take greater notice of this age group. Today, over 28 million Americans are 65 years of age or older, a figure that is projected to rise to over 32 million by the end of the century. Not only are the elderly increasing in numbers, but the proportion of the over-65 group in the total population is growing even faster. These facts translate into political power for the elderly, power that has resulted in better medical care, increased housing subsidies, larger retirement incomes, and expanded social services for this age group.

During the 7 years since the second edition of this book was published, significant changes in the demographic characteristics and status of the elderly population have occurred. In addition, research on the biology, psychology, and sociology of aging have provided new insights and findings concerning the problems and possibilities of aging. Of special interest in this regard are research on the diagnosis, causation, and treatment of Alzheimer's disease and depression in the elderly. Progress in the psychological assessment of older persons and research on increasing the life span are other noteworthy developments. Finally, new legislation and civil and private programs for older citizens, such as changes in retirement and health-care programs, have provided additional information that is incorporated into this edition of *Later Life*.

One purpose in writing this book was to identify and to review what is known about later life and the methods by which the information was obtained. I have attempted to accomplish this goal in a fairly nontechnical manner, but a certain amount of specialized language has proved necessary. Appendix B contains definitions of most of the technical terms used in the book; the subject index and Appendix A should also prove helpful. Another, perhaps even more important, purpose in writing the book was to motivate and direct further study and research on this most interesting and increasingly influential stage of human development. Many readers may also be interested in providing services to the elderly or in intervention on their behalf. To assist in this process, suggestions and guidelines for action and interaction with elderly people are provided.

Like its predecessors, the third edition of *Later Life* is an interdisciplinary treatise, designed as a textbook on gerontology or geropsychology and a reference source on aging. Although it emphasizes psychological factors in aging, biological, sociological, economic, legal, and other perspectives are also considered at length. Consequently, the reader will encounter many facts and concepts from biology, sociology, economics, philosophy, and even a few literary quotations. Some information about earlier stages of life and how they help prepare a person for old age has also been included. Stressed throughout the text is the

interpersonal variability of the aged population and the aging process and consequently that elderly people, who are at least as diverse as other age groups,
should be viewed and treated as unique individuals.

*Lewis R. Aiken*

*Tho' much is taken, much abides; and tho'*
*We are not now that strength which in old days*
*Moved earth and heaven, that which we are, we are,*
*One equal temper of heroic hearts,*
*Made weak by time and fate, but strong in will*
*To strive, to seek, to find, and not to yield.*
                    —Tennyson, *Ulysses*

# The Study of Aging

Human life, as with the lives of all animals, begins with a single cell and progresses through a series of developmental stages. The human fetus becomes an infant; the infant, a child; the child, an adolescent; and the adolescent, an adult. The final stage of human development is old age, which, depending on health, financial circumstances, and psychosocial factors, can be the best or the worst time of life.

## PERSPECTIVES ON OLD AGE

Traditionally, old age has been perceived as the stage of one's life when decrements outweigh increments, when capacities and opportunities are declining rather than expanding. The definition of old age depends, or course, on the characteristics of older people, who are at least as diverse in their physical and psychological attributes as their younger contemporaries. In addition, the meaning of *old age* varies with the attitudes and needs of society. In some societies, for example, the elderly are more respected and their skills more effectively utilized than in others. Furthermore, any society is a collection of individuals whose ages and stages of development affect their perceptions and definitions of "old." A person of 30 or 40 may seem old to a young child, a middle-aged adult may consider 75 years as the beginning of old age, whereas a particular 75-year-old views himself as only "middle-aged."[1]

---

[1]Attitudes toward aging and old age are not discussed at length until chapter 8. However, the reader may wish to assess his or her own attitude and knowledge about aging right now by taking the "Facts on Aging" quiz on p. 190.

Also important in determining whether a person is considered "old" is his or her attitude toward life and aging. A constructive attitude toward aging is one that recognizes advantages as well as disadvantages to growing old. Among the advantages, or at least possibilities, of later life are decreased responsibilities, increased discretionary time, an ability to attend less to trivial matters and focus more on matters of greater importance, less suceptibility to the anxieties, vanities, and social pressures of youth and middle age, less preoccupation with what other people think about oneself, and an increased acceptance of life and death (Kalish, 1982).

Influenced to a great extent by retirement legislation, society as as whole has come to accept a definition of *old age* as a period beginning sometime during the seventh decade of life. This somewhat arbitrary benchmark, most often considered to be age 65 but gradually being revised upward, is a chronological definition of old age. But chronological age by itself is rarely an accurate indicator of a person's biological, psychological, or social age. In defining *biological age,* features such as posture, skin texture, hair color and thickness, strength, speed, and sensory acuity are taken into account. On the other hand, *psychological age* is defined by one's feelings, attitudes, and way of looking at things. Finally, *social age* is determined by social roles and activities and whether they are considered appropriate for a person of a particular age or stage of maturity.

From a strictly medical viewpoint, age is assessed in terms of functional capacity—the ability to engage in purposeful activity. This viewpoint is consistent with the notion that a person can be old at 40 or 80 years of age, depending on his or her overall health, attitude, and other circumstances. Physicians also distinguish between primary aging, or senescence, and secondary aging, or senility. *Senescence* refers to the period of life when a person is growing old, when there is a natural decline in bodily functioning. Although it is age-related, senescence is different from aging in that *aging* is a lifelong process and senescence begins at different times for different people. Also different, although related to aging and senescence, is *senility,* a term that, until fairly recently, has been used to label an organic brain disorder in older people characterized by confusion and orientation. Because of its impreciseness and negative connotations of aging, *senility* is a term that gerontologists now use sparingly if at all.

Biological, psychological, and social age all interact in defining *age norms*— the physical and behavioral characteristics displayed by the majority of people at a particular stage of development. Age norms, and therefore the stage of an individual's development, are a function of certain developmental milestones, ceremonies, or rites of passage, such as entering school, graduating, getting married, and retiring from employment. Viewed from this developmental perspective, aging is a continuous, lifelong process, and hence there is no specific point at which one can be said to be "old" for the first time. The developmental perspective also recognizes that the process of aging or growing old is the result of a complex interaction of biological, psychological, and socioeconomic factors. Consequently, the study of aging must be an interdisciplinary enterprise, involving a variety of subjects and professions.

## LONGEVITY AND LIFE EXPECTANCY

Biological organisms vary greatly in their rate and pattern of development, and the life span of an organism is related to its particular developmental rate and pattern. Length of life, the *longevity* of an animal, varies from a few hours in adult mayflies and a few days in fruit flies and houseflies[2] to over a hundred years in some humans, large birds, and Galapagos turtles. Even greater longevity is found in the plant kingdom, where giant redwoods and bristlecone pines live for thousands of years.

### Very Old Humans

On the human level, the unofficial longevity record is held by Methuselah, who is reported to have lived for 969 years. The 1988 *Guiness Book of World Records* lists the greatest authenticated age as 120, the age of Shigechiyo Izumi of Japan before his death in 1986. The record for authenticated longevity in the United States is 114 years, the age of Martha Graham when she died in 1959. The oldest American listed on the Social Security rolls was a former slave named Charlie Smith, who was reputed to be 136 years old at the time of his death a few years ago.

Other famous, presumably exaggerated, accounts of very old people are the cases of Thomas Parr, who was presented to Charles I of England as a 152-year-old curiosity, and Javier Pereira, a Colombian Indian who claimed to be 167 years old. Physicians who examined Pereira when he visited the United States in 1956 concluded that he was indeed "very old," but exactly how old they could not determine. Shirali Mislimov, a native of the Caucasus region of the Soviet Union, is said to have been 168 when he died in 1973. Another Soviet citizen, Rustam Mamedov, who in 1977 stated that he clearly recalled the Crimean War of 1854 and the Turkish War of 1878, maintained that he was 142. A little detective work has revealed, however, that these men actually did not know their correct ages and undoubtedly exaggerated them. During the 19th and early 20th centuries, birth records in the Caucasus region were kept by the local church. By arranging with church authorities to add 40 or 50 years to his age or by assuming the identity of an older man, a young man of draft age (18–55 years) could deceive Tsarist inspectors into believing that he was much older than his actual chronological age. Some men even appropriated the birth dates of their fathers.

---

[2]The immature larvae and pupae of these insects may live for months or even years.

During Stalin's time the myth of the ancient Russians was kept alive because the great ages of these men presumably demonstrated the superiority of life under communism (Longworth, 1978). Similarly, another long-lived group—the Villacabambans of Ecuador, reputedly celebrate three or four birthdays each year (Rosenblatt, 1986).

## Life Expectancy and Longevity Throughout History

Human *life expectancy,* the average length of time in years that a person born during a certain year can be expected to live, has increased throughout history. From an estimated 20–30 years during the days of ancient Greece and Rome, life expectancy at birth rose very slowly to 35 years in the Middle Ages and Renaissance, to 45 years in mid-19th century American, 47 years in 1900, and 75 years in 1988 (see Fig. 1.1). It is estimated that life expectancy at birth will be approximately 80 years by the year 2000.[3]

The figures just given, however, do not tell the whole story. Because of the shorter life expectancies in former times, a 20th century time traveler would be surprised by the small numbers of elderly people to be found in earlier historical periods. But the time traveler might very well encounter a few very old people even in ancient times. These rare individuals would be people of sound constitution and adaptability who had survived the many diseases, wars, and other dangers that were commonplace and took a heavy toll of the child and adult populations. Furthermore, the oldest people in former times were approximately the same ages as those living today. For example, although inscriptions on tombs suggest that life expectancy was 20 to 30 years in ancient Greece, Sophocles wrote *Oedipus Rex* at the age of 75 and won a prize for drama at 85. Not to be outdone by his Greek predecessor, Marcus Seneca, a renowned Roman orator, lived for 93 years (53 BC to 39 AD). In summary, there are more older people today than in earlier times, but they do not live much longer than their historical counterparts. Average life span has increased, but maximum life span appears to have remained essentially the same.

Relative to the world population as a whole, there were no substantial increases in the number of old people until the 19th century. Associated with this increase in the elderly population were the first dramatic breakthroughs in medicine and public health. It was also during the 19th century that the large numbers, and consequently the increasing needs, of this age group prompted certain European governments to institute reforms and social service programs for the aged.

The chronological age distribution in a population is determined by both the birth rate (*fertility rate*) and the death rate (*mortality rate*). In earlier times, both

---

[3]A computer program for calculating your life expectancy may be obtained by writing to Lewis R. Aiken, PhD, Social Science and Teacher Education Division, Pepperdine University, Malibu, CA 90265.

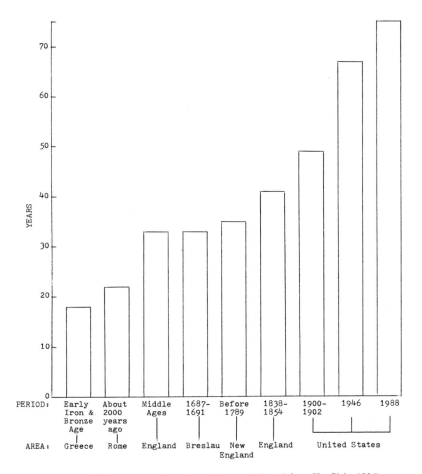

FIG. 1.1.   Life expectancy throughout history. (Adapted from Hayflick, 1984).

rates were high for most societies, maintaining a rather constant age distribution. But advances in medicine, nutrition, and protection against the elements and accidents have altered that distribution considerably in recent years.

One of the major causes of shorter life expectancy during previous centuries was the high rate of infant mortality. But in 20th century America, *infant mortality,* defined as death before the age of 1 year, decreased from almost 100 (per 1,000 births) in 1915 to 30 in 1930 and 9.9 in 1987 (National Center for Health Statistics, 1988a). Next to infancy, the greatest decline in mortality rate has occurred in early childhood, followed by a smaller decrease in the 5- to 55-year age range and an even smaller decline in the 55+ age group. Advances in the treatment of influenza, pneumonia, tuberculosis, diphtheria, typhoid fever, and scarlet fever by the use of sulfa drugs, antibiotics, and other medicines and public health measures (e.g., mass immunizations) have greatly reduced the frequency of death during infancy and early childhood in particular.

## The Elderly Population in 20th Century America

Demographic statistics show that the percentage increase in the population of the United States during this century has been two and one-half times as great in the 65-and-over bracket as in the under-65 bracket. The number of Americans who are 65 or over has increased from 3.1 million in 1900 to 16.7 million in 1960 and 29.2 million in 1986 (see Fig. 1.2). Every day there are approximately 1,750 more Americans over 65 than the day before, and on the average those who reach 65 can look forward to 17 additional years of life. Population projections indicate that the number of Americans 65 and over will rise to 35 million by the year 2000 and reach a possible 65 million by 2030, at which time people born in the post-World War II baby boom will be over 65. From 12% of the national population in 1986 and a projected 13% in the year 2000[4] it is estimated that over 21% of the American population will be 65 or over in the year 2030 (American Association of Retired Persons, 1987). Furthermore, the population of the very old (75 years and over) has increased steadily since 1900 and is expected to continue rising.

In the United States and other developed countries, both the fertility and mortality rates have declined since the late 1950s. One result of these declining rates, and especially that of the fertility rate, has been an increasing proportion of older people in the population. A consequence of a declining *fertility rate,* defined as the number of children per woman of childbearing age, is a lower proportion of younger people and a higher proportion of older people in the population as a whole. The U.S. fertility rate declined from 1.23 children in 1957 to .65 in 1986, resulting in nearly zero population growth (ZPG) in the United States and many other developed countries. If this continues, it is estimated that by the year 2030 the percentage of people below 20 years of age will have decreased by approximately the same percentage as the increase among those 55 years and older.

Also indicative of the growing elderly population is an increase in the median age of the total American population. The median age was 16 years in 1790, when the first U.S. Census was taken. It had risen to 28 years by the 1970 census and to 30 years by the 1980 census (U.S. Bureau of the Census, 1981). If the present trend continues it will approach 35 years by the year 2000 and 40 years by 2030. In addition to declines in infant mortality and the fertility rate, the steady rise in the median age and the proportion of elderly people can be attributed in some measure to the decline in deaths caused by heart disorders,

---

[4]The projected increase in the number of older Americans of 20% from 1986–2000 compared with an increase of 86% from 2000 to 2030 is due to the lower fertility rate during the Great Depression years of the 1930s and the higher fertility rates of the post World War II era.

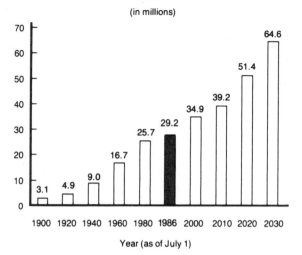

(in millions)

FIG. 1.2. Number of persons 65 and over from 1900 to 2030. (Copyright 1988 by the American Association of Retired Persons. Reprinted with permission. Based on data from U.S. Bureau of the Census.)

cancer, and other killer diseases among those in the 45 to 75 year age bracket. It is likely that cures for heart disease and possibly cancer will be found during the next 20 years, and that these disorders will be replaced by accidents, kidney diseases, pneumonia, and Alzheimer's disease as major causes of death among the elderly (Peterson & Rosenblatt, 1986b).

## The Graying of America

The marked increase in elderly Americans documented by the preceding statistics amply attests to what gerontologist Robert Butler has called "the graying of America." This growth is expected to have a pronounced effect on our economic and social institutions during the years ahead and has already begun to create problems. For one thing, it has increased the *dependency ratio*—the ratio of the number of dependent (incapacitated and retired) persons to the number of active wage earners in the population. Understandably, the rising dependency ratio has caused difficulties for the social security system in particular.

The graying of America also carries with it the challenge that the addition of "years to life" not be wasted and that new opportunities for personal development, which will add "life to years," also be provided. The growing political power of the aged, which promises to surpass that of the Black power and women's movements of the past quarter century, is exerting a great deal of influence in realizing this challenge. In particular, compared with their counterparts of today, the "young–old" group of people aged 55–75 years, who have retired from a first career but desire to remain active and involved, are expected to be healthier, better educated, and more demanding of a greater variety of options in life than their age-mates of yesteryear (Neugarten, 1975).

## GROUP DIFFERENCES AND OTHER FACTORS IN LONGEVITY

Human longevity and the proportion of older people in a population vary with demographic variables such as sex, marital status, ethnicity, nationality, and geography, as well as individual differences in exercise, diet, personality, and particularly heredity. Studies relating these variables to longevity have, of necessity, been primarily correlational rather than experimental, but the findings are interesting and pose intriguing questions.

### Sex Differences

Longevity varies considerably with the sex of the person, although the difference has not always been of the same magnitude as it is today. Statistics on aging among women during different historical periods are more difficult to obtain than those on men, but it is estimated that the average life span of women in the pre-Christian era was approximately 25 years and had reached only 30 years by the 15th century. Death during childbirth was a major cause of the difference in longevity between the sexes in earlier times.

In 1900 life expectancy was 51.1 years for White American women and 48.2 years for White American men, but by the year 1986 these figures had risen to 78.9 and 72.0 years. The sex difference in longevity is, of course, not limited to Americans. With the exception of a few countries in South Asia and the Middle East women outlive men throughout the world, a superiority that they share with other female mammals (Rosenblatt, 1987a).

Although the ratio of males to females in the human species is 130 : 100 at conception, by the time of birth the ratio has declined to 105 : 100, by age 40 to 96 : 100, by age 65 to 82 : 100, and by age 85 to 40 : 100 (American Association of Retired Persons, 1987). In the United States and several European countries, women now live on the average approximately 7 years longer than men. Not only do newborn girls have a greater life expectancy than newborn boys (78.9 to 72.0 in 1986), but the sex difference in life expectancy persists through age 65 (18.6 to 14.6 years) and even age 85 (6.4 to 5.2 years) (Rosenblatt, 1987a).

Correlated with the greater longevity of women is the fact that the major killer diseases—heart attacks, cancer, and stroke—are more common in men. Heredity and hormones undoubtedly contribute to the greater susceptibility of males to these disorders, but lifestyle differences are also seen as important. Compared with men, women tend to smoke less, consult physicians and follow their instructions more frequently, experience less exposure to industrial pollutants and hazards, handle stress more effectively, and have better social supports. As women's lifestyles become more similar to those of men, the sex difference in longevity should become smaller—as witnessed by the decrease in the male/female gap in average life expectancy (from 8 to 7 years) in the United States during the 1980s.

## Marital Status

It is a statistical fact that, on the average, married people live longer than unmarried people, but the reasons are not clear. One plausible explanation is that marrieds eat better and take better care of their health than unmarrieds. Other reasons that have been offered for the greater longevity of married people are (Kobrin & Hendershot, 1977): (a) marriage selects rather than protects, in that longer-living people are also more likely to marry or stay married; (b) society views unmarried people as odd or unusual, a circumstance that places them under social stress and consequently wears them down physically; and (c) close interpersonal ties, which are more likely to be absent among the unmarried, are important in maintaining a sense of well-being, which, in turn, promotes longevity.

The relationship between marriage and longevity is not a simple one, because the effects of marriage interact with those of biological gender. Women live longer than men, but the difference is much less for married than for unmarried people. Gove (1973) interpreted this statistic in terms of social ties. He noted that unmarried women tend to have stronger ties than unmarried men to family and friends but that, compared with those of married men, the roles of married women are more confining and frustrating. Consequently, from a psychological viewpoint women are seen as benefiting less from marriage and suffering less from being single than men.[5]

Kobrin and Hendershot (1977) tested Gove's (1973) thesis concerning the importance of social ties to longevity in a national sample of people who had died between the ages of 35 and 74. They found a complex interaction in the relationships of sex, marital status, and living arrangements to mortality rates. Among men, those who were heads of families lived longest, followed by those who were living in families but not as heads. Men who lived alone had the lowest average longevity. Among women, those who were heads of families lived longest, but, in contrast with men, women who lived alone had the second highest longevity. Lowest of all women in average longevity were those who lived in families but not as heads.

---

[5]Interestingly enough, women who have borne children tend to live longer than those who are childless. The greater longevity of childbearing women has been attributed to increased secretion of the female hormone estrogen (see Woodruff, 1977).

The findings of Kobrin and Hendershot are, in general, consistent with those of Gove: Close social ties and higher social status, which are more likely to be found in marriage than outside it, favor greater longevity. This is truer for men, however, than for women. Unmarried men typically have fewer social ties and lower social status than married men, but unmarried women usually retain their interpersonal ties and may have even higher social status than they would as dominated members of families.

## Ethnic Group Differences

Another important variable related to longevity and life expectancy is ethnicity. Asian-Americans, Blacks, Hispanics, and Native Americans, in order of decreasing life expectancy, have shorter life spans than White Americans (U.S. Bureau of the Census, 1981). On the average, the lives of Black men are more than 6 years shorter than those of White men, and the lives of Black women more than 5 years shorter than those of White women (see Table 1.1). Similar differences between Blacks and Whites have been reported for median ages. The 1980 U.S. Census found the median age to be 24.9 years for Blacks and 31.3 years for Whites.

One reason for the shorter life expectancy of Blacks is that hypertension is more than twice as common among Black Americans as among White Americans. On the other hand, the life expectancy of Black men who reach age 65 is nearly equal to that of their White counterparts. Similarly, the life expectancy of Black women who reach age 65 is almost equal to that of 65-year-old White women.

The life expectancies of several other ethnic minorities in the United States are even lower than that of Blacks. For example, Mexican-Americans have a life expectancy of approximately 57 years, and American Indians, of about 44 years. The 1980 U.S. Census found the median age to be 23.2 years for Hispanics, 23 years for American Indians, Eskimos, and Aleuts, and 28.6 years for Asians and Pacific Islanders (U.S. Bureau of the Census, 1981). But, due undoubtedly to improved nutrition and medical care, gains in life expectancy for American

TABLE 1.1
Life Expectancy of Americans at Birth in 1900 and 1986*

| Group | 1900 | 1986 |
|-------|------|------|
| Black men | 32.5 | 65.5 |
| Black women | 35 | 73.6 |
| White men | 48.2 | 72 |
| White women | 51.1 | 78.9 |

*Data from U.S. Bureau of the Census, *Current Population Reports*, 1986.

minorities have been even greater than those for American Whites during recent years.

Some environmental factors that are associated with ethnic group differences in life expectancy are poverty, lack of education, and the related conditions of poor housing, sanitation, and nutrition, and health care. Improved social and economic conditions and the resulting greater availability of life's necessities—good housing and working conditions, clean water and nourishing food, adequate medical care—have certainly contributed to the fact that, although life expectancy for White persons has increased by 50% since 1900 it has doubled for minority groups.

## Nationality

Statistics reported by the Population Reference Bureau (1987) indicate that, of the estimated 5.03 billion people in the entire world in 1987, approximately 290 million were 65 years of age or over. As shown in Table 1.2, over 58% of the world population but 49% of the persons 65 and over live in Asia. Another 12% of the world population lives in Africa, but only 6% of those 65 and over live on that continent. The relatively small percentage of elderly people living in the less-developed countries of Asia and Africa can be contrasted with the situation in Europe and North America, where 15% of the world population but 32% of those 65-and-over lived in 1987. Tables 1.2 and 1.3 paint a similar picture in

TABLE 1.2
Some Demographic Statistics for Eight World Regions*

| Region | Total Population (millions) 1987 | Total Population (millions) 2000ᵃ | Percent of Population 65 and Over (1987) | Life Expectancy at birth in years (1987) |
|---|---|---|---|---|
| Africa | 601 | 880 | 3 | 51 |
| Asia | 2930 | 3598 | 5 | 61 |
|   East Asia | 1275 | 1435 | 5 | 67 |
|   Southeast Asia | 421 | 544 | 3 | 60 |
|   Southern Asia | 1112 | 1448 | 4 | 54 |
|   Western Asia | 121 | 171 | 4 | 62 |
| Europe | 495 | 507 | 13 | 74 |
| Latin America | 421 | 537 | 4 | 66 |
| North America | 270 | 296 | 12 | 75 |
| Oceania | 25 | 29 | 8 | 72 |
| USSR | 284 | 312 | 9 | 69 |
| Entire World | 5026 | 6158 | 6 | 63 |

ᵃProjected population figures.
*Source: Population Reference Bureau, 1987.

TABLE 1.3
Life Expectancy at Birth in Selected Countries in 1985*

| Country | Life Expectancy (years) |
| --- | --- |
| Australia | 75.4 |
| Austria | 73.4 |
| Bangladesh | 48.7 |
| Belgium | 73.9 |
| Brazil | 64.2 |
| Bulgaria | 72.1 |
| Canada | 76 |
| China | 65.4 |
| Denmark | 74.8 |
| France | 74.8 |
| Germany, Federal Republic | 74.1 |
| Greece | 74.4 |
| Guatemala | 60.5 |
| Hong Kong | 75.6 |
| Hungary | 70.8 |
| India | 56.8 |
| Indonesia | 54.8 |
| Israel | 74.8 |
| Italy | 74.8 |
| Japan | 77.1 |
| Luxembourg | 71.4 |
| Mexico | 66.4 |
| New Zealand | 74.2 |
| Norway | 76.2 |
| Philippines | 62.7 |
| Poland | 71.8 |
| Singapore | 72.3 |
| Sweden | 76.6 |
| United Kingdom | 74.1 |
| United States | 74.6 |
| Uruguay | 70.6 |

*Based on data from Torrey, Kinsella, and Taeuber, 1987.

terms of longer life expectancies in developed than in developing countries. Life expectancy is highest of all countries in Sweden (76.6 years), where 17% of the population in 1985 was 65 and over (Torrey, Kinsella, & Taeuber, 1987).

Although North America and Europe are similar in possessing large elderly populations, during the 20th century the annual rate of increase in the number of people 65 and over has been greater in the United States and Canada than in most European countries. In addition to being proportionally larger, the elderly population has grown faster in highly industrialized Western countries than in the developing countries of Africa, Asia, and Latin America. It is projected, however, that the underdeveloped nations of the world will manifest substantial gains in the proportions of elderly people during the remainder of this century. By the year 2000, 59% of the world's projected 410 million elderly people will reside in developing countries and 41% in developed countries. Improvements in economic and social conditions, changes in living conditions and health care, combined with a previously high fertility rate, are expected to result in dramatic increases in life expectancy in the developing nations of the world. It is predicted that life expectancy and the proportion of elderly people will increase dramatically in China and India in particular, reaching over 80 million in each country shortly after turn of the century (Torrey et al., 1987).

Obviously, even today not everyone in less technologically advanced societies dies at an early age. Individuals having very long life spans are found in sizable numbers among the Hunza people in the Karakoram Range of the Himalayas, the Abkhasians of the Soviet Republic of Georgia, and the Vilcabambans of Ecuador. Nearly 50 out of every 100,000 people in the Caucasus region of the Soviet Union, contrasted with about 5 in 100,000 Americans, reportedly live to be 100 or more. Birth records of the Hunza are more difficult to obtain than those of the Abkhasians and Vilcabambans, but UNESCO data indicate that the Hunza are the only people in the entire world who are completely free of cancer.

## State and Climate

The distribution of older people in the United States varies with geographical location (see Fig. 1.3). The most populous states—California and New York—also contain the largest numbers of people 65 and older. Florida, Pennsylvania, Texas, Illinois, Ohio, and Michigan also have elderly populations of over 1 million. In fact, almost half the elderly population of the United States lives in these 8 states. A substantial majority (71%) of the elderly live in urban areas and towns, with only 5% residing in rural areas and the remainder in fringe areas (American Association of Retired Persons, 1987).

The higher percentage of elderly people in certain states, Florida, for example, can be explained by the greater migration of older people to those states. On the other hand, the high percentage residing in many other states is the result of a larger number of young people moving out of state to seek opportunity and adventure. Data showing that life expectancy varies with state may be explained in a similar fashion as being due to age-related immigration and emigration. Differences in ethnic composition, nutrition, climate, sanitation, and health resources also play a role. A combination of several of these factors may explain why life expectancy is highest in Hawaii and lowest in Washington DC (U.S. Bureau of the Census, 1981).

Specific types of climate have often been prescribed for patients with certain disorders. For example, a warm dry climate that is relatively free of air pollutants is prescribed in certain cases of emphysema and other respiratory conditions.

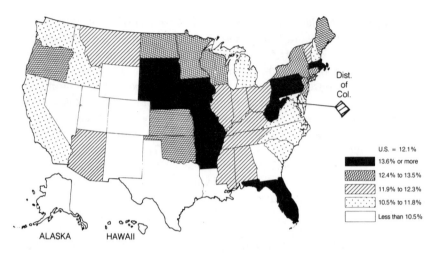

FIG. 1.3.   Persons 65 and over as percentage of total U.S. population in 1986.
(Copyright 1988 by the American Association of Retired Persons. Reprinted with
permission. Based on data from U.S. Bureau of the Census.)

Tuberculosis sanitaria are frequently located at high altitudes, and altitude has
also been associated with heart disease. It is also noteworthy that all three of the
world's longest-living peoples—the Hunza, Abkhasians, and Vilcabambans—
reside in mountainous regions.

   More systematic data on the relationship between longevity and altitude were
obtained by Mortimer, Monson, and MacMahon (1977). Reviewing deaths in
New Mexico from 1957–1970, they found 403 deaths from coronary heart
disease per 100,000 men who were living at the lowest altitude but only 291
deaths from the same cause per 100,000 men living at the highest altitude.

## Exercise and Diet

The importance of regular physical exercise at any stage of life cannot be overemphasized. Many people who do not realize that immobility can cause serious
physical disorders are stricken by serious illness at a time of life when they are
not even thinking about old age. The fact that enforced limitations on one's
activities can increase the rate of both physical and mental deterioration is clearly
demonstrated by the results of studies conducted by N. D. Mankovsky of the
Soviet Institute of Gerontology. Mankovsky found that 50- to 60-year-old people
who were put to bed for 3 weeks and prevented from moving showed many of the
same symptoms as heart attack patients. From the results of these experiments
and interviews with very old people, Mankovsky concluded that work is a
valuable remedy against premature aging (''Soviets Say. . .,'' 1977).

Exercise, especially at high altitudes, causes the heart to work harder and thus become conditioned for emergencies. The long-living people of the Caucasus, Himalayas, and Andes are all agrarians who get plenty of exercise. The Vilcabambans in particular are quite explicit in attributing their longevity and good health to walking a great deal. Somewhat closer to home, research has shown that U.S. mail delivery men, who walk a great deal, live 2 years longer on the average than mail sorters and other postal employees whose jobs do not take them away from the post office (Simmons, 1977).

Regular exercise is a contributing factor to health and longevity, but too much exercise may be just as bad as too little. Furthermore, it is difficult in nonexperimental studies to isolate the effects of exercise from those of nutrition. Gots (1977) argued that perhaps even more important than altitude and exercise in contributing to a long, healthy life is what one eats. This is not a surprising conclusion, because it is well known that being overweight is associated with a shorter life span. Less well known is the fact that underweight people also have shorter life spans than people of average weight ("Study Finds. . . ," 1980).

Granting that nutrition is correlated with longevity, what is the best diet? One plan has been offered by the long-living Abkhasians—a diet low in calories, meat, eggs, and salt. Reduced food intake, and especially a diet low in fats and calories, has also been found to be related to a healthier, longer life in technologically more advanced societies. In any event, certain nutritionists recommend the following diet for those who wish to increase their chances of living a long time:

1. Lower protein intake and more protein from vegetables (grains, legumes, cereals), and less from animal products (red meat, whole milk, eggs).
2. Less fat, especially animal fat.
3. Fewer calories—enough to satisfy energy requirements but no more.
4. Skim-milk instead of whole-milk products.
5. Chicken and fish more often and red meats only three or four times a week.
6. Greater portions of whole grains, beans, rice, nuts, fresh fruits, and vegetables that provide essential vitamins, minerals, and fiber.

It is generally agreed that moderation in eating, smoking, and drinking (alcoholic beverages), combined with regular moderate exercise, are associated with a lower incidence of disorders of the heart, brain, and liver. Relative freedom from the pressures and worries of civilization, as in the case of the Abkhasians, Hunza, and Vilcabambans, may also contribute to longevity. Psychological factors, such as maintaining an interest in one's surroundings and feeling useful and accepted by others, can be just as important as exercise, diet, and nonsmoking (see Report 1.1). From a study of factors promoting the long lives of the Abkha-

## Report 1.1 CENTENARIANS TELL SECRET: EXERCISE MIND AND BODY*

JOHN H. AVERILL, *Times Staff Writer*

WASHINGTON—A congressional committee listened in fascination and admiration Wednesday as a panel of eight centenarians, two of them in wheelchairs, passed along some secrets on how to live beyond age 100.

Their advice boiled down to this: remain active and have a hobby.

"Teach people to have a hobby," said Harry Lieberman of Great Neck, N.Y., who took up painting when he was 80 and now has his work exhibited in 10 museums around the world.

Lieberman, who will be 103 today, told the House Select Committee on Aging that unless old people have something to do "they become bitter."

Lieberman, who wears his sparse whitish hair in a ponytail and sports a mustache and goatee, said he spent six years in idleness after retiring from a confectionary business at age 74—"and those were the worst six years of my life."

"You make the laws," Lieberman said to the congressmen as he urged them to find ways to help old people remain active. "You have to have something in your hands, and not be torn up as an old man," he added.

Rep. Claude Pepper (D-Fla.), the committee chairman, said the purpose of the hearing was to look into the "centenarian explosion."

"Only 3,200 Americans lived past their centennial in 1969," he explained. "Today that number exceeds 13,000."

Pepper, who at 79 is the oldest member of the House, said that when he was born in 1900 the life expectancy of children born that year was 49. Today it is 72.

He called the eight centenarian witnesses arrayed along a table in front of the committee "living evidence of whole new horizons for life extension."

Two witnesses punctured any belief that use of alcohol and tobacco are insurmountable barriers to a person's living a century.

"I enjoy chewing tobacco, and my father taught me how to drink whiskey when I was a boy," said 111-year-old George Washington White, who use to be a fireman on the Southern Railway's famous No. 97 Crescent Limited. Since losing his teeth, White said, he eats raw eggs and oatmeal.

L. Perry West, a 101-year-old retired brick manufacturer, attributed his longevity to a life of physical fitness. But he also said he enjoyed cigars and pipes until he turned 100 and that he still indulges in "alcoholic drinks and beverages in moderation."

A Los Angeles centenarian, Maria Majar de Quiroz, who is 100, addressed the committee in Spanish with her granddaughter interpreting. Mrs. Quiroz and her husband moved to Los Angeles from Mexico in 1919, and when her husband died in 1924 she cleaned houses and did sewing to support her eight children. She took her first airplane ride when she flew to Washington for the hearing. She attributed her long life to "hard work."

Remaining active also was the prescription offered by Dr. W. L. Pannell, 100, who still practices medicine in East Orange, N.J. "Try to keep up activities," Pannell told the committee in a firm voice, "exercise your mind and body."

Three elderly black women—Lizzie Dickens, 103, of Whitakers, N.C.; Ida Johnson, 102, of Anderson, S.C.; and Nanreen Walton, 104, of Hickory, N.C.—credited their long life to hard work and prayer.

"The Lord has taken care of me," said Mrs. Dickens, who is now confined to a wheelchair.

*From Averill (1979). Copyright, 1979, *Los Angeles Times*. Reprinted by permission.

sians, Benet (1974, 1976) concluded that equal in importance to work and diet is a social structure that permits a meaningful old age and a sense of group belongingness.

## Heredity

Many different biological factors can have an influence on longevity. Children born of older mothers, for example, have a higher incidence of congenital disorders that shorten their lives. Of particular importance, however, is the genetic makeup of the individual. Although certain authorities feel that the role of heredity in longevity has been overemphasized, length of life does tend to run in families. Gerontologists admit that smoking, environmental pollution, diet, exercise, and health care are related to longevity, but they would undoubtedly agree that the rate of aging, to a marked extent, depends on genetic endowment.

Evidence of a hereditary basis for longevity comes from casual observations as well as from scientific studies of the life spans of people with different genetic relationships. One conclusion from such investigations is that correlations between the life spans of different groups of people vary directly with the degree of genetic relationship. Parents who live long tend to have children who also live long. Fraternal twins generally live to much the same age, but, as expected with a characteristic influenced by heredity, the ages at death of identical twins are even closer (Kallmann & Jarvik, 1959).

From the results of a study of identical twins who were 60 years and older, Kallman and Sander (1963) concluded that there is a substantial degree of stability in both physical and mental traits over a lifetime. Despite pronounced differences in environment in some instances (e.g., New York doctor vs. Western rancher, English-speaking vs. foreign-language-speaking), elderly identical twins were just as difficult to distinguish as when they were younger: They had similar hair patterns and wrinkle patterns, and their energy levels were approximately equal. A particularly dramatic example of biological similarity persisting throughout a lifetime is that of a pair of twin sisters. Both became blind and deaf in the same month, both became mentally ill, and they died within a few days of each other.

Heredity is important, perhaps the most important of all factors affecting longevity. But neither heredity nor environment by itself determines how rapidly a person ages. Constitutional makeup interacts with the physical and psychosocial environment of an individual in determing how well he or she copes with and survives the stresses of life and how gradually aging takes place.

It is as though, at birth, each individual inherited a certain amount of adaptation energy, the magnitude of which is determined by his genetic background, his parents. He can draw upon this capital thriftily for a long but monotonously uneventful existence, or he can spend it lavishly in the course of a stressful, intense, but perhaps more colorful and exciting life. In any case, there is just so much of it, and he must budget accordingly. (Selye, 1976, p. 72)

## PROFESSIONAL INTEREST AND RESEARCH IN AGING

As is true today, people in ancient times were aware of the effects of aging on physical and mental abilities. Attempting to reverse or postpone these effects, they consulted magicians, priests, physicians, or anyone purporting to have a remedy or palliative to combat the ravages of time.

The ancient Romans looked upon old age itself as a disease, and stemming from this belief was the search for a way to "cure" the disease and discover the secret of eternal life. Efforts to find this secret, and the related searches for the philosopher's stone and the fountain of youth, occupied the time and energies of many brave and intelligent men. No fountain of youth was discovered, but antidotes for aging ranged from shedding one's skin like a snake to inhaling the breath of young girls. Seemingly fantastic from a modern point of view, these procedures have their counterparts in the goat gland surgery, ground sheep embryo treatments, and elixirs of life (e.g., Gerovital) that have been recommended for prolonging life in the 20th century. Although no one has discovered a miraculous cure for aging, the quest has not been abandoned even today. Public attention and support have shifted, however, to attempts to make old age more pleasant rather than indefinite in length. Researchers and practitioners in many disciplines and professions, notably geriatrics and gerontology, are combining their efforts to make this goal a reality.

### Geriatrics

*Geriatrics* (from the Greek *geras,* meaning old age) is a branch of medicine dealing with the health problems of the aged, including both the treatment and prevention of disease and injury. During the 19th and early 20th centuries, scientific pioneers in many countries conducted research and wrote about health problems associated with aging. Noteworthy among these pioneers were several Russians, including I. Fisher, P. Yengalytchev, S. P. Botkin, E. Metchnikoff, and V. Korenchevsky. However, the medical specialty of geriatrics was founded by an American, Ignaz Nascher, who in 1914 coined the term *geriatrics* for that branch of medicine that deals with the health problems of the elderly. Responding to the fact that older people constitute one of the major groups requiring medical care, the first geriatric clinic in the United States was opened in Boston in 1940, and today many hospitals have special medical clinics for the aged.

According to Robert Butler (1975), only a small percentage of medical school faculty are experts in problems of the aged. Butler, who has continually stressed the need for greater interest and research in geriatric medicine, believes that medical schools have failed to motivate students toward careers in this specialty because they are not exposed to healthy older people. He maintains that if a sufficient number of trained geriatricians were available, the diseases of old age could be made less debilitating, less burdensome, and hence less costly.

In any event, medical schools have expanded their research and training programs in this area as professional interest in later life has grown. The growth of interest in problems of the aged is witnessed by the increasing membership of professional organizations and the growing number of publications on geriatrics. The major professional organization of physicians who specialize in geriatrics is the American Geriatrics Society. From its beginnings in 1950 as a society of only 352 members, it has grown to over 7,000 today. Three major American journals in the field of geriatrics are the *Journal of the American Geriatrics Society; Geriatrics;* and the *Journal of Geriatric Psychiatry.*

Being practical people, medical scientists will probably discover additional ways to slow down aging long before they understand the process itself. To date, they have succeeded in increasing the average life span, but as indicated earlier in this chapter, this has been accomplished primarily by saving the lives of infants and young people rather than by prolonging the lives of the very old. Some years ago, Brown (1966) cited a number of research directions that may help prolong life; among these are organ transplants, control of cells and tissues so damaged organs and limbs can be regenerated, and the development of virus cells or cells with special inhibitors or stimulator substances. As we see in the next two chapters, this list has been expanded during the intervening years.

## Gerontology

Many renowned philosophers and scientific pioneers, including Roger Bacon, Francis Bacon, Benjamin Franklin, and Francis Galton, wrote about aging during the 13th–19th centuries. Sir Edmund Halley, an 18th century British astronomer, was the first to conduct a scientific analysis of life expectancy. Interest in sociological and psychological research on aging was encouraged by other writings and activities during the 19th century. Noteworthy among these were the writings of the Frenchman Frederic Le Play, the surveys of the Britisher Charles Booth, and statistical studies of birthrates, death rates, and the relationships of age to crime rates and suicide that were initiated by the Belgian, Adolphe Quetelet.

Two significant books on aging, Minot's *The Problems of Age, Growth, and Death* and Metchnikoff's *The Prolongation of Life* were published in 1908. In 1922, the psychologist G. Stanley Hall wrote the first important American book on aging, *Senescence: The Second Half of Life,* when Hall himself was in his eighth decade of life and attempting to understand what was happening to him.

The science and profession of *gerontology,* which grew out of these early efforts, is the study of biological, psychological, medical, sociological, and economic factors having a bearing on old age. Gerontology is an interdisciplinary field, based on the premise that solutions to the problems of aging require the cooperative efforts of specialists in many fields. Biologists contribute their knowledge and research concerning the biological processes involved in aging; psychologists, who may refer to themselves as *geropsychologists,* study changes in mental abilities, personality, and behavior with age; sociologists, and in particular *social gerontologists,* study the social roles and status of older people and other aspects of group behavior in old age and how social and cultural factors influence the aging process. Obviously, there is considerable overlap among the activities of various specialists, a fact that is recognized and accepted in the multi- or interdisciplinary approach. In addition to being concerned with research, gerontology is an applied discipline dedicated to improving the health and well-being of older people.

Some authorities consider a Russian, V. Korenchevsky, who, with Lord Nuffield founded the International Club for Research on Aging, to be the father of gerontology. Others reserve that honor for the American E. V. Cowdry. Cowdry certainly made important contributions to the field, among which are his pioneering book on *Problems of Aging* (1939) and his efforts in establishing the International Association of Gerontology (IAG) in 1948. The IAG, a worldwide organization of gerontologists with branches in many countries, originally focused on medicine and biology but expanded its professional activities during the 1950s to include the social sciences.

The primary professional association of gerontologists in the United States is the Gerontological Society, a multidisciplinary organization founded in 1945, which has divisions of Biological Sciences, Clinical Medicine, Psychological and Social Sciences, Social Research, and Planning and Practice. Together with several other professional and governmental organizations, the Gerontological Society promotes interdisciplinary research on aging. Research studies and position papers on topics in gerontology are presented at annual meetings and published in the *Journal of Gerontology* and *The Gerontologist,* the official journals of the Gerontological Society. There are, of course, many other periodicals in gerontology and geriatrics that researchers and practitioners read, a number of which are listed in Table 1.4.

More than 1,300 colleges and universities in the United States offer courses, special certificates, or degree programs in aging (Paul, 1986). Training in gerontology is, like the field itself, multidisciplinary. Larger, well-established training and educational programs, such as those at the University of Southern California, Duke University, and the University of Chicago, have been complemented in recent years by dozens of smaller programs at colleges and universities throughout the United States. Students who enroll in these programs take courses in sociology, psychology, social work, and education. They may also study medicine, biology, physiology, economics, home economics, anthropology, the-

TABLE 1.4
Selected Periodicals on Aging and for the Elderly

*AAHA Action Bulletin*
*Activities, Adaptation, and Aging*
*Advances in Gerontological Research*
*Age*
*Aging and Work* (Industrial Gerontology)
*Aging International*
*Aging Magazine*
*Aging News/Research and Training*
*Current Literature on Aging*
*Death Education*
*Educational Gerontology*
*Experimental Aging Research*
*Facts on Aging*
*Gerontologist*
*Gerontology and Geriatrics Education*
*International Journal of Aging and Human Development*
*Journal of Aging Studies*
*Journal of Clinical and Experimental Gerontology*
*Journal of Gerontological Nursing*
*Journal of Gerontological Social Work*
*Journal of Gerontology*
*Journal of Long-Term Care Administration*
*Journal of Minority Aging*
*Journal of Nutrition for the Elderly*
*Journal of the American Geriatrics Society*
*Long Life Magazine*
*Modern Maturity*
*Older American Reports*
*OMEGA, The International Journal of Death and Dying*
*Prime Time Magazine*
*Psychology and Aging*
*Research on Aging*
*Retirement Life*
*Social Security Bulletin*

*Other Journals Reporting Research on Aging*

*Developmental Psychology*
*Human Development*
*International Journal of Behavioral Development*
*Journal of Marriage and the Family*

ology, public administration, and hospital administration. It is just as well that training programs in gerontology are interdisciplinary, because the professional and paraprofessional occupations related to aging and the aged are also quite varied. Job listings at meetings of national and regional gerontological societies include work in hospitals, nursing homes, community recreation programs, counseling, housing, nutrition, research, and teaching. As indicated by the kinds of jobs available, gerontology is primarily an applied field. Be that as it may, research on aging and old age is also quite active.

## Research Methods

Because of the high cost of research and the many methodological problems facing researchers in gerontology, advances in scientific knowledge of aging are often difficult to achieve. The problem of financial support is perhaps easier to solve than methodological problems, although budget cuts during the 1980s have resulted in a decrease in federal support of research and programs for the elderly.

Psychologists and other social scientists who receive substantial training in research methodology have devoted considerable attention to developmental research methods. Among the many methodological questions that they must face are those concerning instrumentation, sampling, and the reliability, validity, and standardization of psychological tests and other measuring instruments. Unfortunately, tests and inventories that possess satisfactory reliability and validity when administered to children or young adults are often less reliable and valid when used with older groups. Consequently, results obtained when these instruments are employed in research on the psychological and social characteristics of the elderly are often inaccurate. It is becoming more generally recognized that the norms and other psychometric characteristics of a standardized test or inventory must be determined on samples of older people if the instrument is to be used in gerontological research and diagnosis.

Another serious methodological problem in research on the aged involves the representativeness of the group of older individuals sampled. For example, grossly incorrect conclusions pertaining to the elderly in general may be drawn from studies conducted on samples of institutionalized or segregated older people. All too often gerontological researchers have limited their samples to readily available groups in nursing homes or retirement communities, who are not representative of the elderly in general.

Assuming that problems of instrumentation and sampling have been dealt with, the gerontological researcher must next decide what scientific procedures to employ. Although it is the method of choice for investigating cause–effect questions, experimentation is used infrequently in gerontological research. Because of their greater social acceptability and ease of implementation, biographical or life-history studies, controlled or uncontrolled observations, surveys, and correlational methods have been more popular. Application of such nonexperimental methods may yield interesting descriptions and conclusions regarding the interrelationships of personal characteristics and events, but the findings cannot be interpreted in cause–effect terminology.

The most popular of all procedures in developmental research employing chronological age as the independent variable and some measure of physical or behavioral change as the dependent variable are longitudinal and cross-sectional research methods. These methods involve the collection of observational, psychometric, and survey-type data on different age groups or on the same age group (cohort) followed over time. Although causal interpretations are seldom warranted by the findings of developmental investigations, the time-related changes in physical and behavioral characteristics observed in longitudinal and cross-sectional studies often help to narrow the list of possible causes of such changes.

In a *longitudinal study,* the same individuals are followed up and reexamined over a period of several months or years. An example is retesting the same group of people every 5 years for a period of 25 to 50 years to investigate changes in mental abilities across the life span. Among the most extensive ongoing longitudinal studies of elderly people are those being conducted by the Center for the Study of Aging and Human Development at Duke University and the Baltimore Longitudinal Study of Aging sponsored by the National Institute on Aging.

Longitudinal studies might appear to be the best way to study age-related changes in human characteristics, but most developmental research on aging is based on the cross-sectional method. Adolphe Quetelet is credited with being the first scientist, in 1838, to apply this method to the study of human development. A *cross-sectional study* involves comparing different age groups on some characteristic. For example, a cross-sectional study of changes in mental abilities during adulthood might involve administering appropriate tests of mental abilities to samples of 20-, 30-, 40-, 50-, 60-, 70-, and 80-year-olds and statistically comparing the mean scores of the seven groups.

Cross-sectional studies are less expensive than longitudinal studies and, with some effort, can be completed in a relatively short period of time. They do not require long-term commitments by researchers, and subjects are not so easily lost as a result of moving, dying, or refusing to participate further in the study. A possible shortcoming of cross-sectional studies is that they necessitate some kind of initial matching of the different age groups. For example, in studying the relationships of mental ability to age, the investigator should match the various age groups on education before comparing their mental abilities. The problem is that adequate matching is often difficult to achieve, and even so, differences in other variables, such as educational opportunity, can still affect the results. A major problem in interpreting the results of a cross-sectional study is that the researcher cannot be certain whether the observed differences among age groups are produced by the aging process itself, by generational or cultural differences (*cohort differences*), or by time-related changes in the attitudes and values of society.

With regard to the validity of research findings, both cross-sectional and longitudinal studies have limitations. Because a person's age is related to the cultural context in which he or she was brought up, cross-sectional studies confound (i.e., mix up) the effects of age and cohort differences. Longitudinal studies, on the other hand, tend to confound the age of the person with the time at which the behavioral or other measurements are made. Time of measurement is also an important variable because the physical, social, and psychological context in which the measurement takes place changes with time. Furthermore, changes in scores on the same tests administered to the same individuals at different times may be attributable to practice effects or increased familiarity with the test material rather than to age per se.

What is needed in order to obtain a clearer picture of the effects of age, apart from cohort and time-of-measurement effects, is a combination of the cross-sectional and longitudinal approaches. Arguing in this vein, Schaie (1967) proposed a three-component model that includes three types of comparisons (Table 1.5). A simple cross-sectional study would involve the three times of birth (cohort) comparisons in any column of the table (cells A-D-G, B-E-H, or C-F-I). A simple longitudinal study would involve the three comparisons in any row of the table (cells A-B-C, D-E-F, or G-H-I). In a third type of age-related comparison, the *time-lag design,* several cohorts are examined, each at a different time period. As depicted by cells G-E-C in the table, the subjects in a study employing a time-lag design are all of the same age when they are measured, but they were born at different times (i.e., they belong to different cohorts) and are measured or examined at different times.

Unfortunately, a cross-sectional design confounds age-related differences with cohort differences, a longitudinal design confounds age-related differences with differences due to time of measurement, and a time-lag design confounds cohort differences with differences related to time of measurement. Consequently, none of the designs by itself enables the researcher to unravel the true

TABLE 1.5
Representation of Cross-Sectional, Longitudinal, and
Time-Lag Designs for Developmental Research*

| Time of Birth (Cohort) | Time of Measurement | | |
|---|---|---|---|
| | 1970 | 1980 | 1990 |
| 1930 | 40 A | 50 B | 60 C |
| 1920 | 50 D | 60 E | 70 F |
| 1910 | 60 G | 70 H | 80 I |
| Time-Lag | Ages in years are above letters in table | | |

*Adapted from Botwinick, 1978. Used by permission. (See text for explanation of table.)

effects of aging, free of the confounding effects of cohort differences and the time at which the measurements were made.

Further efforts to design approaches to separate differences in behavior due to age, cohort, and time of measurement have been suggested by Baltes (1968) and Schaie (1977). Schaie (1977) proposed a *most efficient design* involving a combination of cohort-sequential, cross-sequential, and time-sequential research strategies. Beginning with a cross-sectional study of two or more age groups measured at the same point in time, the researcher then retests these groups after several years to provide longitudinal data on several cohorts. Two or more new age-groups are also tested to form a second cross-sectional study. The process can be repeated every 5 to 10 years, retesting previously tested age groups to add to the longitudinal data and testing new age groups to add to the cross-sectional data.

The data from a study employing a most efficient design can be analyzed in three ways—cohort-sequentially, cross-sequentially, and time-sequentially. A *cohort-sequential analysis* is concerned with the interaction of cohort and age in their effects on the dependent variable. For example, changes in attitude or ability from age 60 to 70 in a group born in 1910 may be compared with such changes from age 60 to 70 in a group born in 1920. Referring to Table 1.5, the difference in attitude or ability between G and H is compared with the difference between E and F. On the other hand, a *cross-sectional analysis* is concerned with the interaction between cohort and time of measurement. For example, the change in attitude or ability from 1970 to 1980 in a group born in 1930 is compared with the change during the same period in a group born in 1910. Referring to Table 1.5, the A-B difference is compared with the G-H difference. Finally, a *time-sequential analysis* is concerned with the interaction between age and time of measurement. For example, the attitudes or abilities of 50-year-olds are compared with those of 60-year-olds, both in 1970 and 1980. In other words, in Table 1.5 the D-B difference is compared with the G-E difference.

## Research Agencies

Private foundations provide some financial support for research on aging, but the greatest amounts of money and other assistance come from governmental organizations and agencies. Federal support for research and research training concerned with the biological, medical, psychological, and sociological aspects of aging was formerly the responsibility of the Adult Development and Aging Branch of the National Institute of Child Health and Human Development. A very small percentage of the budget of the National Institute of Mental Health was also allocated to research on the psychiatric and psychological problems of old age.

Currently, a number of federal agencies are involved in research and training programs that benefit the elderly; these agencies include the Administration on Aging, the Office of Nursing Home Affairs, the National Institute on Aging, and the Department of Education. One of the newest federal agencies, and the one concerned primarily with research on aging, is the National Institute on Aging. In 1975 this agency took over the Gerontology Research Center in Baltimore as its internal program and assumed the aging grants functions of the National Institute of Child Health and Human Development. Robert Butler, whose eminent career in gerontology was reportedly motivated to some extent by the fact that he was reared by his grandparents, became the first director of the National Institute on Aging (NIA) in 1976.

Among the activities that have been pursued by NIA in the area of biology are research on Alzheimer's disease, untoward drug reactions in the elderly, osteoporosis (see chapter 4), and prosthetic devices for the elderly. The institute's research support is, of course, not limited to biology, and an effort has been made to strike a balance between support of biological and behavioral science research on aging.

Other nations have followed the lead of the United States in supporting research in gerontology and geriatrics. The British Council for Aging, for example, has enlisted the cooperative efforts of experimental and behavioral gerontologists, geriatricians, and caring agencies in conducting basic research on aging. The growing numbers and influence of older people should ensure that such efforts receive continuing support and that the outcomes of these efforts improve the condition and circumstances of the elderly, and hence society as a whole.

## SUMMARY

Old age is generally considered to begin in the early to middle 60s, a viewpoint that neglects the fact that people age at different rates and that both biological and psychological factors must be taken into account in defining old age. For a number of reasons, primary among which are the decline in infant mortality and a reduction in deaths caused by certain disorders of adulthood, life expectancy has risen steadily during the 20th century. The increase in average longevity has resulted in a greater proportion of elderly people in the population and an attendant shift in the social status of and concern about this group. Of course, not all people age at the same rate. Many different factors—marital status, ethnicity, nationality, geographical area, exercise, diet, smoking, pollution, and especially heredity—have been found to be related to longevity.

The two professions that are most concerned with the processes and problems of aging are geriatrics and gerontology. Geriatrics is a medical specialty that deals with health and disease in old age; gerontology is an interdisciplinary field encompassing all aspects of knowledge about aging.

A variety of methodological approaches—longitudinal, cross-sectional, time lag, cohort-sequential, cross-sequential, and time-sequential—have been used in developmental research on aging. These different research strategies are necessitated by the fact that many variables other than the process of aging itself, such as differences in cohorts and times of the measurement of the dependent variable, affect the outcomes of developmental research investigations.

Research and training programs to benefit the elderly have received substantial support from the public and private sectors during the past two decades, although governmental support declined somewhat in the 1980s. A federal agency that is concerned exclusively with screening and supporting research and projects on aging and the aged is the National Institute on Aging. Interest in the biological, psychological, and sociological problems of aging is international in scope, and research on these problems is being actively pursued throughout the world.

## SUGGESTED READINGS

Benet, S. (1974). *Abkhasians: The long-living people of the Caucasus.* New York: Holt, Rinehart & Winston.

Birren, J. E., & Cunningham, W. R. (1985). Research on the psychology of aging: Principles, concepts and theory. In J. E. Birren & K. W. Schaie (Eds.), *Handbook of the psychology of aging* (2nd ed., pp. 3–34). New York: Van Nostrand Reinhold.

Birren, J. E., & Woodruff, D. S. (1983). Aging: Past and future. In J. E. Birren & D. S. Woodruff (Eds.), *Aging: Scientific perspectives and social issues* (pp. 1–15). Monterey, CA: Brooks/Cole.

Deming, M. B., & Cutler, N. E. (1983). Demography of the aged. In J. E. Birren & D. S. Woodruff (Eds.), *Aging: Scientific perspectives and social issues* (pp. 17–51). Monterey, CA: Brooks/Cole.

Freeman, J. T. (1979). *Aging: Its history and literature.* New York: Human Sciences Press.

Hagestad, G. O., & Neugarten, B. L. (1985). Age and the life course. In R. Binstock & E. Shanas (Eds.), *Handbook of aging and the social sciences* (2nd ed., pp. 35–81). New York: Van Nostrand Reinhold.

Schaie, K. W., & Hertzog, C. (1982). Longitudinal methods. In B. B. Wolman (Ed.), *Handbook of developmental psychology.* Englewood Cliffs, NJ: Prentice-Hall.

Swenson, C. F. (1983). A respectable old age. *American Psychologist, 38,* 327–333.

Woodruff, D. S. (1977). *Can you live to be one hundred?* New York: Chatham Square.

# 2

# Physical Structure and Functioning

Although inevitable in living things, aging is not a uniform biological process. As described in the last chapter, there are marked inter- and intraspecies differences in the rate of aging and in longevity. The kinds and magnitudes of changes with aging, which occur gradually over a long time period, vary greatly from individual to individual. Furthermore, biological factors do not act alone in affecting the process of aging: psychological, social, and even economic factors interact with biology to determine the nature and rapidity of aging. Age-related decrements in the sensory and motor systems of the body, for example, affect a person's attitude and activities, which in turn influence the rates at which these systems decline in their functioning. It is well substantiated that the progress of a disease and the decline in general health are affected by the joint action of biological and psychological variables. In addition, psychological variables such as attitude and personality determine the extent to which the individual is able to cope with the physiological changes that occur with aging.

Not only does aging vary from species to species and among different members of a species, but there are also differences within a single individual at which various bodily structures age. For example, the reproductive system of humans usually ages more rapidly than the nervous system. Even here, however, psychological and other experiential variables affect the rate and degree of decline. Researchers have found that certain conditions thought to be due to aging are caused in large measure by poor nutrition, disease, and disuse. "Use it or you'll lose it" is a slogan that applies not only to motor skills and sex, but to mental abilities and many other functions of the human organism as well. Furthermore, the loss of a loved one, a friend, and meaningful roles and activities—events that are more likely to occur in old age—can precipitate a physical and

28

psychological decline or can exacerbate an existing illness at any time of life. Thus, when we read about or otherwise become aware of the physical and mental decline associated with old age, it should be emphasized that such marked changes are not inevitable or irreversible. People can do something about disabilities—they can exercise, eat the right foods, seek intellectual stimulation, and engage in social interaction with other people. These activities make the decrements associated with aging less pronounced and less debilitating.

## PHYSICAL APPEARANCE

The thriving mass market for skin creams, scalp and hair preparations, dental adhesives, cleansers, and assorted cosmetics is a testimony to the concern with changes in physical appearance that accompany aging. The preoccupation in our culture with staving off the ravages of time and retaining a youthful appearance is motivated by the same desire as yesteryear's search for the fountain of youth. Although people gulp vitamins and go on crash diets to maintain a younger appearance in a society that glorifies youth, nowhere is more money and effort spent than on the skin. This is due not only to the fact that a person's skin is highly visible to other people, but also because it is possible to do something to improve the appearance of the skin—at least temporarily.

### The Skin

With aging, the amount of collagen in the skin decreases. Because collagen, a fibrous protein material, is the primary ingredient of skin, the loss of collagen causes a decline in the total amount of skin. In fact, the structure of the skin is so affected by aging that a dermatologist can usually estimate a person's age within a range of 5 years by examining a 2-millimeter section of the skin. You can demonstrate one effect of aging on your skin, that of elasticity, by conducting the following simple test:

> Place your wrist and palm down on a flat surface with the fingers stretched as widely as possible. Take a pinch of skin on the back of the hand between the thumb and forefinger and pull it up as far as you comfortably can. Hold the pinched skin for five seconds, release it, and then count the number of seconds it takes for the skin to become smooth again. In a healthy teenager the skin usually falls back very rapidly. Between the teenage years and age 45 two or three seconds are usually required, but after this the time increases rapidly. For a 65-year-old, the pinched skin may still form a visible ridge 5 minutes later. (Turner & Helms, 1987; Walford, 1983)

To a casual observer, the skin of an older person is more wrinkled, rougher, less resilient, paler, and splotchier than that of a younger person. The decrease in subcutaneous fat and muscle tissue causes the skin to lose its elasticity, develop wrinkles, and sag into folds or jowls. The emaciated look of many older persons is also affected by the loss of subcutaneous fat. The ability of the skin to retain fluids declines in old age, causing it to become less flexible and dry, a dryness that is also affected by the fact that older people perspire less than when they were younger. Skin cells also live less long and are replaced more slowly in the old than in the young.

Other changes in the skin that are related to aging are the various spots and growths frequently seen on older hands and faces. Quite common are "liver spots" (*lentigo senilis*), darkly pigmented areas that appear on the backs of hands and wrists but actually have nothing to do with the liver. The skin of an older person is more easily broken and heals less rapidly than when he or she was younger. Consequently, purplish spots (*senile purpura*) caused by cutaneous bleeding are also found on older skin, as well as small red benign tumors (*cherry angiomas*) and various malignant skin cancers (*basal cell carcinoma*).

Many people attempt to retard or at least to disguise the age-related changes in the skin by use of cosmetics, face lifts, and other treatments. Greater concern is usually expressed over the appearance of the face, hands, and other exposed parts because of their visibility and tendency to show age changes more readily than areas of the body that are usually covered. Treatments for aging, wrinkling skin are fairly expensive and only temporarily effective. These include such processes as injection of silicone or collagen preparations under the skin or mildly wounding the skin to induce it to lay down more collagen.

## Other Changes in Appearance

Another noticeable sign of aging is graying or whitening hair, which occurs more slowly in certain ethnic groups (e.g., Asians) than in others (Caucasians). The hair also tends to lose its luster and becomes sparser in most men and women. Although men's beards usually become thinner with age, a sometimes disturbing growth of hair is observed in their nostrils, ears, and eyebrows (in all the wrong places!). Changes in the androgen–estrogen ratio produces considerable facial hair in women, especially on the chin and upper lip. Aging also brings an increase in the incidence of varicose veins, peridontal disease, and a loss of teeth. The loss of teeth, coupled with a decrease in subcutaneous fat, leads to pronounced wrinkling around the mouth.

The structural appearance of the face in old age is affected by the loss of bone mass in the jaw, which tends to recede while the nose protrudes. Facial appearance is also affected by changes in the eyes. The eyelids thicken with age, the eye sockets develop a hollowlike appearance, and a cloudy ring (*arcus senilis*) forms around the cornea. The occurrence of cataracts, which are more common in old age, can also affect a person's appearance.

The effects of aging on overall body shape and stature are found in broadening of the hips and narrowing of the shoulders. Loss of collagen between the spinal vertebrae causes the spine to bow and the height to shrink, and the tendency of older people to stoop makes them appear even shorter than they are. Postural changes are especially noticeable in older women who develop a widow's or dowager's "hump" at the back of the neck. This "widow's hump" is the result of osteoporosis, a disorder, common in older women, which results in a gradual loss of bone mass.

The magnitude of age-related changes in appearance varies with each individual and is influenced by diet, health care, and environmental conditions (prolonged exposure to sunlight, air and water pollution, etc.). Inadequate diet and poor health care, combined with air and water pollutants, cause certain groups of people to be more susceptible to the physical signs of old age than other groups. Thus, many women of lower socioeconomic status, lacking hormonal treatments during menopause, tend to manifest symptoms of aging sooner than middle-class women. In addition, laborers who work in unhealthful environments age more rapidly than those who spend their days in clean offices (Perry, 1974).

Age changes in health and physical appearance are overwhelming and even disastrous to the self-images and security of some individuals, whereas others are able to transcend their physical disabilities and be content in spite of an altered appearance and declining health. Because of the greater cultural expectations of beauty in the female sex, physical manifestations of aging appear to be of greater concern to women in general than to men (Nowak, 1974). The cultural stereotype that men become more distinguished looking as they age but women merely look older reinforces this concern. Furthermore, changes in bodily appearance can affect a person's social and occupational, and hence economic, status. This is especially true when an aging individual continues to pursue an occupation in which physical attractiveness is very important.

## INTERNAL ORGANS AND SYSTEMS

The modifications in appearance that accompany aging are the results of both external and internal changes in the human body. The structure of all organs and organ systems gradually deteriorates, and consequently their functioning becomes less efficient in old age. Loss occurs at all levels—cellular, organ, and systemic, and especially in functions involving several different systems.

The effects of age-related physical deterioration and disease are seen in the older person's lessened ability to cope with stress, in particular multiple stresses, and adapt to environmental changes. Any change, including aging itself, can be stressful, and consequently can create adjustment problems for the elderly. This is particularly true of people in the "old–old" category of 75 to 85 years—the age group in which the loss of reserve capacity and deterioration of internal and external organs is especially pronounced.

Even in the very old, however, reduction in the efficiency of functioning and adaptability are neither uniform nor inevitable. Furthermore, changes in organismic structure are far from perfectly correlated with decrements in functioning. A person's previous history of disease and injury and the kind of life he or she has lived play important roles in determining the magnitude and rate of functional deterioration with age. Psychological factors also affect the individual's responses to physical deterioration and the ability to cope with or compensate for declines in the structure and functions of the body's vital systems.

## Cardiovascular System

No organ is more vital than the heart, and failure of this organ is responsible for the deaths of thousands of people each year. Contrary to the general rule that most body structures decrease in weight as a person ages, although heart tissue may atrophy and cardiac muscle cell size decrease, fat and calcium deposits cause the weight of the heart to remain the same or even increase. The heart loses some of its resiliency, however, making the number of heartbeats fewer and more irregular and the blood volume output substantially less. The aorta and blood vessels of the heart harden and shrink. Coupled with the loss of cardiac muscle strength, this makes the heart work more and accomplish less in pumping blood to the body. The stroke volume and heartbeat decrease, blood pressure increases, and the blood supply of the heart itself may be reduced. Common results of these changes are chest pains (*angina*), shortness of breath, and sometimes heart attack and stroke.

As indicated in Table 2.1, the amount of blood pumped by the resting heart (*cardiac output*) in a typical 75-year-old man is only about 70% and the blood flow to the brain only about 80% of that of a 30-year-old. It also takes longer for the heart of an older person to return to its normal pumping and beating levels after excitement or exercise. However, the picture of cardiovascular functioning in later life is not all bleak. Research conducted by the Baltimore Longitudinal Study of Aging has shown that, when free of disease, the hearts of many older persons pump about as well as the hearts of younger people.

As noted previously, the total amount of collagen, a protein substance that is the chief component of connective tissue fiber, decreases with aging in the skin and between spinal vertebrae. But the number of cross-linkages in collagen molecules increases with age in certain internal organs. The elasticity of blood vessels is so affected by the building up and altering of collagen molecules that the arteries of an octogenarian may be as solid as metal. Unfortunately, medical science has not yet found a way to reverse these age-related changes in collagen, and the resulting loss of elasticity in body tissues.

TABLE 2.1
Physical Characteristics of an Average 75-Year-Old Man
Compared to a 30-Year-Old Man*

| Physical Characteristic | Comparative Percentage |
|---|---|
| Nerve conduction velocity | 90 |
| Body weight for males | 88 |
| Basal metabolic rate | 84 |
| Body water content | 82 |
| Blood flow to brain | 80 |
| Maximum work rate | 70 |
| Cardiac output (at rest) | 70 |
| Glomerular filtration rate | 69 |
| Number of nerve trunk fibers | 63 |
| Brain weight | 56 |
| Number of glomeruli in kidney | 56 |
| Vital capacity | 56 |
| Hand grip | 55 |
| Maximum ventilation volume (during exercise) | 53 |
| Kidney plasma flow | 50 |
| Maximum breathing capacity (voluntary) | 43 |
| Maximum oxygen uptake (during exercise) | 40 |
| Number of taste buds | 36 |
| Speed of return to equilibrum of blood acidity | 17 |
| Also: | |
|    Less adrenal and gonadal activity | |
|    Slower speed of response | |
|    Some memory loss | |

*From Shock (1962) Copyright © 1962 by Scientific American, Inc.
All rights reserved.

In any event, collagen is responsible for the increased sluggishness of an old heart and the hardening of the arteries. These changes in the heart and coronary arteries result in reduced blood flow through the body. Consequently, the rate at which oxygen and nutrients are transported to the cells and waste products are carried away is reduced. The reduction in oxygen supply to the body tissues is one reason why older people usually tire more rapidly than the young.

## Respiratory System

The functioning of other internal organs is also affected by aging, but not all of them age at the same rate. The heart and blood vessels age at one rate, the liver at another, the nervous system at a third rate, and so on. The effectiveness of the lungs diminishes even more rapidly than that of the heart; maximum one-breath capacity (*vital capacity*), total capacity, residual lung volume, and basal oxygen consumption decline markedly in old age. As indicated in Table 2.1, the vital capacity of the lungs is only 56% and the maximum oxygen uptake during exercise only 40% at age 75 of what they were at age 30.

The age-related structural changes that are responsible for the decline in functioning of the lungs include weakening of the muscles lining the rib cage and reduced expansion of the lungs, resulting primarily from changes in collagen in the tissue of the lungs and the walls of the blood vessels (Weg, 1983). Combined with the increased sluggishness of the heart, these structural decrements cause older people to experience shortness of breath and to take longer to return to normal breathing after exerting themselves to an unusual degree.

## Musculoskeletal System

Among the more noticeable changes produced by aging are a loss of several inches in height, a stooped posture, and knobby knees. Loss of collagen between the spinal vertebrae causes the spine to bow, and, coupled with the tendency of the elderly to stoop, makes them look even shorter than they are. A curved posture (head down, back and knees bent, forward pitch in walking) is common.

As a person ages, deposits of mineral salts in the bones increase and the dense part of the bones becomes spongier and more fragile. In addition to changes in stature and posture, stiffness and pain in the joints of the lower spine, hips, and knees limit their range of movement and mobility. For example, McCracken (1976) described his elderly father getting out of a chair in this manner:

> He'd sit in his chair just thinking about getting up. He'd run his hands up the arms of the chair a little way, brace, and push. And he'd stand up. Well, he was up. He'd stand for a moment, put his hands on the back of his hips. He'd still be bent over a little bit. But then he'd straighten up and be off about his business. (p. 21)

The quantity of synovial fluid, which serves to lubricate the joints and hence reduce friction, decreases and may lead to arthritic pain during later life. The flexibility and extent of movement of the joints also decline, effects that are contributed to by changes in muscles. Because the bones are more brittle, fractures of the vertebrae, ribs, and hips—which are slow to heal—often occur.

The loss in overall body weight that usually accompanies aging is due in part to a decrease in the total amount of muscle tissue, which also leads to a decline in strength. For example, the hand grip strength of an average 75-year-old man is only 56% of that of a 30-year-old (see Table 2.1). Muscular strength actually begins to decline in the late 20s, the rate of decline varying with the particular muscle group and the extent to which a person exercises. But effort, especially when exerted in short, intense bursts, does not depend on the muscles alone. Decrements in the functioning of the heart and lungs, as well as the mobility of the tissues and joints, also affect a person's maximum strength.

It is now believed that many symptoms of decline in the musculoskeletal system (stiffness in joints, muscle weakness, osteoporosis or thinning of bones, etc.) are greatly affected by disuse, being "out of shape," and related lifestyle factors. Goodchilds and Huddy (Tavris, 1987) have even suggested that osteoporosis is a generational artifact characteristic of older women who rarely exercised and failed to develop full bone strength when they were young.

## Gastrointestinal System

Although digestive difficulties are not the most serious problems of later life, digestive and eliminative processes typically function less well in the old than in the young. Among the age-related changes in the gastrointestinal system are declines in: digestive enzymes, esophageal peristalsis, stomach motility, intestinal peristalsis, and secretions of the intestinal mucosa. The glands of the stomach wall begin to atrophy, and the slower movement of food through the digestive tract, which results from the smaller number of contractions, increases the likelihood of constipation. At one end of the alimentary canal, the loss of teeth, ill-fitting dentures, and gum disorders such as gingivitis cause difficulties in chewing. Due in part to a lifetime of poor dental hygiene and malnutrition, over 50% of older people lose their teeth. And at the other end of the alimentary canal, the appearance of hemorrhoids creates problems of elimination.

Efficient functioning of the gastrointestinal system in old age is important, because what a person eats and how well the food is digested can influence his or her sense of well-being and rate of aging. Older people usually exercise less than when they were young, so those who want to keep from gaining weight must reduce their caloric intake as they age. On the other hand, the elderly require more rather than less protein in the diet. Because meat, a major source of protein, is more expensive than other foods, alternative protein-rich foods such as peas must be eaten more frequently to keep costs down.

Whether or not an older person selects a nutritious, balanced diet is affected by declines in the acuity of the senses of taste and smell. A 50% decline in the number of taste buds during old age contributes to the fact that appetites are usually not as keen and almost all foods are less appealing. Perhaps less obvious is the fact that declines in the senses of vision, feeling, and even hearing can also influence eating habits. The appearance and texture of foods, as well as the sounds that one makes when preparing and chewing them, affect their palatability. Finally, psychosocial factors such as whether one eats alone or with companions play a role in nutrition and the enjoyment of eating.

## Genitourinary System

The effectiveness of the kidneys, like that of the lungs, diminishes even more rapidly that than of the heart as a person ages. By age 75 the number of functioning excretory units (*glomeruli*) has declined by 56% and the glomerular filtration rate to 69% of the age 30 values (see Table 2.1), causing body toxins and wastes to be excreted less efficiently. Older people excrete less urine and there is also less creatine in the urine. The decrease in the elasticity of the bladder and a decline in its capacity to less than one-half that of a young adult, coupled with enlargement of the prostate gland, is responsible for many of the urinary problems of older men. Among these problems are frequent urination and loss of bladder control, which are sources of concern and embarassment to many elderly individuals.

With respect to the sex organs, age-related changes are less distinctive in men than in women. There is a decrease in the volume and force of the ejaculate, and the testes show some shrinkage. Severe testicular atrophy, however, is uncommon. In contrast, reduction in the size of the cervix and uterus is quite pronounced in older women. Atrophy of the vagina mucosa also occurs unless estrogen replacement therapy is used.

## Hormones and the Immune System

The decrease in both male and female sex hormones is a part of age-related changes in the endocrine system as a whole. Declines are observed in steroid and thyroid hormones, as well as in ACTH. Impairment of the body's regulatory devices also affects homeostatic functions such as temperature control.

The influence of aging on the immune system can be seen in the declining effectiveness of the body in eliminating foreign substances. Failure of the immune system occurs in diseases such as pneumonia, tuberculosis, and cancer, which are much more common among the elderly than in young adults. In addition, a loss of effectiveness in the immune system can result in an autoimmune reaction, in which the body turns against itself and produces disorders such as arthritis.

## Nervous System

There is some dispute over the matter, but it is a generally accepted fact that human beings are born with essentially all the brain neurons they will ever have. The size and complexity of these neurons increase as the individual matures, but neurons in the brain and spinal cord, unlike those outside the central nervous system, do not regenerate when destroyed by injury or disease. Due to a decrease in number and size of neurons, by age 75 the brain weight of an average man has declined to 56% and the number of nerve trunk fibers to 63% of the age 30 values. Cerebral blood flow as well as oxygen and glucose consumption by the brain also decline with aging.

Despite these losses, most authorities agree that in the absence of disease the brain's ability to function does not appear to be greatly impaired in old age. It is noteworthy that mental abilities improve during childhood and adolescence despite the fact that brain cells are lost regularly from birth onward. Nevertheless, it is generally agreed that the ability of the brain to process information is affected by a decrease in the number of neurons, a measurable loss in the velocity of nerve impulses, and a reduction with aging in the blood supply to the brain. It is estimated, for example, that the cerebral blood supply of a 75-year-old man is only 80% of that of a 30-year-old.

Age-related changes in the brain have an effect on the sleeping–waking cycle, although environmental and psychological factors also play important roles in sleep. By ages 60 to 70 the daily amount of sleep has decreased by an average of 1 to 2 hours. Elderly people tend to sleep less, and their sleep is neither as deep nor as refreshing as the sleep of the young. Insomnia is very common, especially in older women. Many sleep poorly at night but catch up by means of "cat naps" during the day.

William Dement and his associates have shown that sleep actually consists of four stages, ranging from light to very deep sleep. The cycle from light to deep sleep and back again to light sleep takes about $1\frac{1}{2}$ hours on the average. It is during Stage 1, the stage of lightest sleep, that rapid eye movements (REMs) indicative of dreaming occur. The intermediate stages, Stages 2 and 3, comprise about 60% of sleep time and Stage 4—the stage of deepest sleep—about 20% of sleep time. Some dreaming without REM sleep does occur in Stages 2, 3, and 4, but much less than in Stage 1. It has been found that the REM period of sleep (Stage 1) shortens somewhat and Stage 4 (deepest sleep) shortens appreciably in old age. During the later hours of night sleep, old people typically alternate between Stage 2 and REM (Roffwarg, Muzio & Dement, 1966).

## SENSATION, PERCEPTION, AND MOVEMENT

Aging is accompanied by modifications in the structure and functioning of all the sense organs. Due in part to decrements in the sensory receptors themselves and in part to changes in the peripheral nerve pathways and the central nervous system, the thresholds for vision, hearing, taste, smell, and the skin senses all become higher. A general effect of aging is to dull sensations and to slow down responses to sensory stimuli. As a consequence, the average elderly person tends to receive and to react to sensory information more slowly if at all. Declines in sensory and motor abilities usually occur gradually, beginning in the 30s and 40s but becoming more pronounced after age 60 or so. Furthermore, as is the case with age-related changes in internal organs and systems, the magnitude and quality of the decline vary with the particular person and the sensory modality. Older persons in whom sensorimotor deficits are particularly severe may be considered stubborn, strange, or even mentally ill, rather than simply less perceptive or reactive. But, by relying on past experience and exercising good judgment, the majority of elderly people are able to adapt to or compensate for normal age-related declines in sensory and motor abilities. Hopefully, as Plato suggested, spiritual eyesight improves as physical eyesight declines.

## Vision

The two most important senses, vision and hearing, are the ones that show the greatest degeneration with age. Visual acuity, however, does not suddenly deteriorate at age 45 or 50. The ability to see details is actually relatively poor in young children, improving gradually to about age 20 and then remaining fairly constant until it begins declining in the early 40s. Part of the loss in visual acuity during middle and late life is caused by a decrease in the size of the pupil, resulting in less light reaching the retina. Sagging eyelids can also obstruct vision in some elderly people. Consequently, brighter lighting is needed for reading or other close work. Slower constriction and dilation of the iris in old age also affect the ability to adjust to sudden changes in brightness.

Decreased sensitivity of the retina in old age affects not only the ability to see under low illumination but also the ability to differentiate colors of objects. Because the yellowing lenses of older eyes act as filters for greens, blues, and violets, these colors are particularly difficult to distinguish. A reduction in the transparency of the lenses also causes a scattering of light within the eyes, creating glare. Glare and decreased sensitivity to light, combined with the poorer peripheral vision of older adults, make certain activities, such as night driving, particularly hazardous.

Another change that contributes to poor detail vision, especially at near distances, is hardening of the lenses of the eyes and resulting problems of accommodation. This disorder, known as *presbyopia,* is correctable with prescription lenses and is not considered a severe impairment. More severe losses of vision in old age are produced by cataracts, glaucoma, and retinal disease. The most common of these is a pronounced clouding of the lenses known as *cataracts,* a condition that is almost "normal" in very old people. Even more severe than cataracts is *glaucoma*—damage to the optic nerve resulting from increased intraocular pressure. People with glaucoma initially experience a reduction in the size of the visual field, and eventually blindness. A number of other diseases (e.g., diabetes) can produce degeneration of the retina and hence a gradual loss of vision, but only about 1% of older adults are legally blind.

The rapidity with which visual stimuli are sensed, especially when presented in rapid succession, also declines in old age. The reduced speed with which the pupils of the eye react to light increases the time needed to detect visual stimuli. Small changes in the environment become quite difficult to see and must be repeated or intensified if the individual is to respond to them.

More complex than elementary sensations are *perceptions,* consisting of sense impressions plus the meanings or interpretations given to them by the observer. Of particular interest to developmental psychologists who study perception are illusions. Older people tend to be less receptive than young adults to certain perceptual illusions and aftereffects (e.g., Necker cube illusion, Ebbinghaus illusion) but are more receptive to other illusions (e.g., Müller-Lyer illusion; see Fig. 2.1). The on–off rate at which a flickering light is seen to fuse into a steady beam (*critical fusion frequency* or CFF) is also lower for older than for younger adults.

Certain age-related differences in the susceptibility to visual illusions (e.g., the CFF) may be attributed to changes in the lenses or pupils of the eyes. Other perceptual changes seem to require interpretation in terms of central nervous

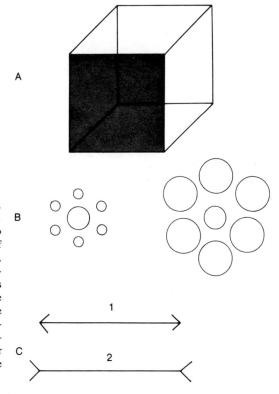

FIG. 2.1.   (A) Necker cube illusion, devised by L. A. Necker in 1832. The shaded surface can be made to appear on the front or back surface of the cube. (B) Ebbinghaus illusion, devised by H. Ebbinghaus. The circles in the middle of the two patterns are of equal size, but the one in the left pattern appears larger than the one in the right pattern. (C) Müller-Lyer illusion, devised by F. Müller-Lyer in 1889. Line 1 appears shorter than line 2, although they are the same physical length.

system dynamics. One attempt to provide a general principle to account for age-related changes in perceptual abilities is *stimulus persistence theory,* (Axelrod, Thompson, & Cohen, 1968):

> In the senescent nervous system, there may be an increased persistence of the activity evoked by a stimulus, i.e., . . . the rate of recovery from the short-term effects of stimulation may be slowed. On the assumption that perception of the second stimulus as a discrete event depends on the degree to which the neural effects of the first have subsided, the poorer temporal resolution in senescence would then follow. (p. 193)

Stimulus persistence theory has been used to explain why older people react more slowly than younger ones to a series of stimuli presented in quick succession. According to the theory, it takes longer for an older person to recover from the effects of one stimulus before another stimulus can be detected.

Although it is true that older adults are usually unable to evaluate and respond to stimuli as quickly as younger adults, stimulus persistence theory does not explain all research findings on perception in the aged. Furthermore, other psychologists point to the greater cautiousness of older people as an explanation of their slower responses to visual stimuli. In any event, visual losses in later life can be compensated for to a great extent by eyeglasses, larger print, intensified lighting, and the use of colors that can be seen more readily (more yellow, orange, and red; less green, blue, and violet). Providing for sufficient time to adapt and make decisions based on visual information is also essential.

## Hearing

Because of gradual atrophy of the auditory nerve and end organs within the inner ear, the ability to hear actually starts declining in early adulthood. Thus, sensitivity to sounds, particularly high frequency sounds, begins to diminish as early as age 20. Referred to as *presbycusis,* this disorder is even more common in the aged than visual impairment. A decline in the number and strength of muscle fibers that support the eardrum also contributes to hearing loss as the individual ages. A hearing aid can help many elderly people hear better, but some individuals react negatively to such prosthetic devices.

Deterioration in hearing is due to the aging process and also to structural damage inflicted by years of noise bombardment and accidents involving the ears. The loss may be so gradual that a person is not even aware that anything is wrong, other than the fact that for some reason people do not speak as clearly as they used to. Because men tend to lose their hearing sooner than women, the older husband who turns up the radio or television set can easily blast his wife out of the house. This sex difference may be the result of greater exposure of men to loud noises on the job.

Presbycusis has a greater effect on the hearing of sibilants such as *s, sh,* and *ch,* which are carried by speech frequencies of over 3,520 hertz (Shock, 1952b; also see Fig. 2.2). Consequently, an older person may hear "ave" instead of "save" and "alk" instead of "chalk." Because the discrimination of speech sounds is particularly affected by presbycusis, it is recommended that one speak in a lower or deeper tone of voice and enunciate clearly when talking to an elderly person. Older people also experience difficulty in understanding rapidly spoken words, a disability perhaps caused by a combination of problems in hearing and processing information rapidly. Therefore it is wise to speak more slowly than normal when talking to a very old person. Background noise also has a greater disruptive effect on the hearing of elderly people, so understanding tends to be better in a quiet room than in a noisy street or social gathering. On the other hand, background noise of low volume may not be heard, causing elderly people to experience a sense of "deadness" in the environment.

Hearing, like vision, is not simply a matter of sensation. It is a perceptual experience produced by the interaction of auditory sense impressions and past experience. For example, a hearing loss does not necessarily affect an older person's appreciation of familiar music, because auditory memory can fill in tonal gaps and lead one to "hear" frequencies to which he or she is no longer sensitive. But some people, who are either unaware of or reluctant to admit they have a hearing problem, pretend to hear well when their hearing, and hence their understanding of what they hear, is incomplete.

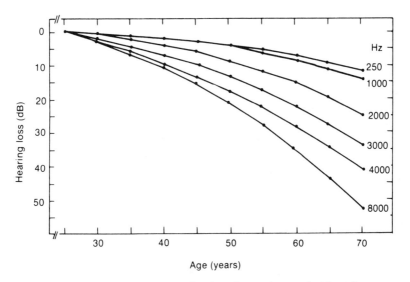

FIG. 2.2.   Hearing loss for tones of various frequencies as a function of age. (From Botwinick, 1978. Copyright © 1978 by Springer Publishing Company, Inc., New York. Used by permission.)

Semantics, or the meanings that words have for speakers and listeners, also affects the perception of auditory messages. As people grow older they appear to lose some of their ability to stretch the meanings of words, impairing their understanding of the total idea that the speaker is attempting to communicate. Consequently, speech therapists recommend that special care be taken to make certain that very old people understand what is said to them.

Other sense modalities interact with hearing to facilitate the understanding of auditory messages. Vision and hearing can compensate for each other to some extent, so the speaker should make certain to face an older listener. Getting an older person's attention by touch or gesture is also helpful in communicating with him or her.

Loss of hearing, even more than loss of sight, can produce a sense of isolation, loneliness, and emotional distrust. People with hearing disorders may avoid social interaction because they fear they will say or do something inappropriate. A more serious effect on personality occurs when a hard-of-hearing person becomes chronically suspicious of what other people are saying and develops a paranoid disorder.[1] The results of a study by Cooper, Curry, Kay, Garside, and Roth (1974), which was conducted on 132 mental patients with an average age of 68 years, are interesting in this regard. None of the patients had been mentally ill before the age of 50, but at the time of the study 65 were paranoid and 67 (the "control group") had other psychiatric problems. Over 46% of the paranoid patients had a hearing loss, compared to 38% of the controls—a small but statistically significant difference. Because the deafness of the paranoid patients was of a long-standing, bilateral nature, usually produced by chronic middle-ear problems, deafness had begun long before the onset of the mental disorder.

## Taste and Smell

Both taste and smell decline to some extent with aging. A decrease in the number and functioning of taste buds begins at about age 50, and by age 70 a typical man has less than half as many taste buds as he had in his 20s. There is some loss in olfactory cells as well, which, combined with the greater hairiness of the nostrils in old age, affects the sense of smell.

Taste sensitivity begins to decline appreciably at age 60, particularly in men. All four tastes—sweet, salt, sour, and bitter are affected, but the loss of sensitivity is greatest for sweet. Consequently, foods that seem sickeningly sweet to

---

[1]Paranoid conditions are mental disorders characterized by systematic delusions of grandeur or persecution, or by ideas of reference. Delusions are firmly held beliefs that the patient will not relinquish even in the face of contrary evidence.

younger people are often quite palatable to the elderly. Older people also tend to use greater amounts of salt, pepper, and other seasonings. The preference for sweet, spicy foods shown by many elderly people must be monitored carefully if nutritional requirements are to be met and digestive upsets avoided.

The taste of food is affected by the sense of smell, which also becomes less keen with aging. Older adults tend to prefer stronger essences and may not be bothered by odors that are unbearable to younger adults (e.g., the odor of strong urine). A number of other factors play a role in taste and smell. As is generally known, serious respiratory illness affects the sense of smell, and consequently the sense of taste. In addition, experience can at least partially compensate for a loss of taste and smell receptors. It is noteworthy, for example, that wine tasters and gourmets are often elderly.

## Cutaneous (Skin) Senses

The traditional four cutaneous senses are touch (or pressure), pain, warmth, and cold. A variety of receptors are involved in the sense of touch, but their functioning is not well understood. Touch sensitivity appears to increase from birth to middle age, but becomes less acute in later life. The decrease in touch sensitivity is associated with a decline in the number of nerve cells enervating the skin.

The ability to experience pain also declines with age, being only about one third as great in an average 70-year-old as in an average 20-year-old (Arehart-Treichel, 1972). Older adults do not seem to be as sensitive as younger adults to pain, which can be a serious deficit when an elderly person is unaware of an injury that requires attention. Loss of pain sensitivity is not, however, uniform across the body. For example, the decline is greater in the arms and face than in the legs. Cultural and personality factors also influence the perception of pain and probably the rate at which it diminishes in old age.

Concerning temperature sensitivity, older people usually adapt less well to extremes of heat and cold and cannot tolerate them as well as the young. The elderly frequently have feelings of discomfort—sensations of being either too hot or too cold—even when the external temperature remains constant. The ability to sweat freely is affected by the decrease in sweat glands in old age, increasing susceptibility to heat exhaustion. And the loss of subcutaneous fat, combined with poor blood circulation, increases susceptibility to cold. Because of their vulnerability to accidental hypothermia—a loss of body heat that is potentially fatal, it is recommended that temperatures in homes and facilities for the elderly be kept higher than 65°F, even as high as 83°, if it is not uncomfortable. This is especially true when the residents are over 75 years old, have arteriosclerosis or some other vascular disorder, or are taking certain medications.

## Vestibular Senses

Receptors for the vestibular senses, or senses of posture and balance, are located in the semicircular canals and otolith organs of the inner ear. Of particular significance in maintaining one's balance are the small calcite crystals known as *otoliths*. Deterioration of these microscopic structures appears to be one reason why many old people fall so easily and have greater difficulty reorienting themselves than the young. They may sway when standing still, and become dizzy when rising, climbing, or viewing heights.

The growth in number and size of the otoliths from the fetal stage until the late teens is correlated with improvement in the sense of balance. But beginning at about age 50, the otoliths show signs of deterioration, a structural change that signals a decline in the sense of balance. And by age 70, the number of otoliths in the inner ear has decreased substantially and balance sensitivity has followed suit (Ross, 1977).

## Motor Abilities

Owing to decreased strength and energy and increased stiffness in the joints, movement becomes more difficult with age. Older people are less able to do hard work, especially if it must be done rapidly, and it takes them longer to recuperate from strenuous effort. On visits to the doctor, the elderly frequently complain of weakness and fatigue, but 80% of those over 65 manage to get around from place to place fairly satisfactorily. They may have to walk slowly, "shuffling" along, and use a cane, but they usually get where they want to go. Physical activity can, however, be quite troublesome to individuals who suffer from arthritis or other chronic disorders. Personal grooming tasks (bathing, dressing, trimming one's toenails, etc.) can be difficult even in the case of mild disorders, and getting about the house and going outside may be impossible when one's health is very poor.

Speed of responding on tasks requiring fast reflexes or reactions, especially reaction time situations in which the person must choose among several alternatives, shows an age decrement (Fig. 2.3). The ability to coordinate various movements, fine muscle movements in particular, are also affected (Botwinick, 1978; Shock, 1952a). Although some slowing of movement always occurs in old age, practice, motivation, and physical exercise can improve the speed and skill with which psychomotor tasks are performed. Furthermore, the range of individual differences in the motor abilities of older people is quite large. For example, it has been found that superbly healthy men in their 70s and 80s perform as well as normal men of 20 (Birren, Butler, Greenhouse, Sokoloff, & Yarrow, 1963; Botwinick & Thompson, 1968). The study by Birren et al. (1963) compared the physical and mental abilities of healthy men in the 65- to 91-year

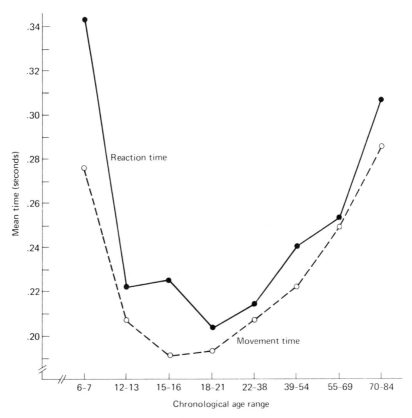

FIG. 2.3. Age changes in reaction time and movement time (data from Hodgkins, 1962)

age range with those of a group of young men whose average age was 21. It was found that the older men were as good as the younger ones on several physiological measures. For example, there were no differences between the two groups of men in blood flow to the brain and the consumption of oxygen during exercise.

In spite of declining sensorimotor abilities, nearly 60% of older Americans have valid driver's licenses. Unfortunately, drivers over age 65 tend to have more accidents per distance driven and to be at fault in the accidents more often. Recognizing that many older people must travel by car but that those with certain diseases or disabilities pose a danger to themselves and others, a special screening examination for the aged has been proposed (Butler, 1975). The examination, which would have to be passed every year after age 50, would consist of visual, auditory, and reaction time tests, as well as measures of judgment in driving situations. Combined with certification that the person is in good physical condition, such an examination could appreciably lower the high accident rate of elderly drivers. Because losing a driver's license is discouraging to anyone who values the speed and convenience of automobile transportation, a person who failed any part of the test battery would be given an opportunity to make up the deficiency. Refresher courses, such as the one developed at the University of Michigan's Institute of Gerontology, have been designed to assist older people in overcoming such driving deficiencies.

## The Empathic Model

Except in the rare case of a completely age-segregated society, people of different chronological ages must interact and cope with each other. Because social interactions are usually enhanced by understanding, procedures for helping one age group develop an understanding and appreciation of the problems and motivations of another age group could be of practical value (Kastenbaum, 1971; Pastalan, 1974). To help younger people experience the relative slowness of older people, Kastenbaum (1971) contrived a procedure by which a younger person is placed in an accelerated environment and is forced to deal with it in the same way as an old person must deal with the real world.

Even more comprehensive is the research of Pastalan (1974) and his coworkers at the University of Michigan's Institute of Gerontology. They devised a special method for studying the sensorimotor problems associated with old age and creating understanding in younger people. Labeled the *Empathic Model,* the method involves using mechanical devises to simulate the loss of sensation and movement experienced by aging people. Some of these devices are coated lenses, noseplugs and earplugs, and fixatives or gloves to desensitize touch. Among the lessons learned by a young person who dons these gadgets are that old people often experience difficulties in seeing traffic signs and distinguishing words from background noise (see Report 2.1).

Using the Empathic Model, researchers have identified several sources and types of perceptual problems in elderly people: difficulty seeing in natural and unbalanced artificial light because of glare; fading of colors, greens and blues most and reds least; poorer depth perception and slower visual recovery in moving between brighter and darker places; and blurring of sounds, especially sounds containing high frequencies, by background noise. Other sensory and motor problems revealed by the Empathic Model are the facts that food does not taste as good as it formerly did (consequently many people do not eat well), temperature differences are more difficult to distinguish (posing potential hazards in bathing and washing dishes), and fine muscular control declines (making the turning of pages and dials difficult).

As a result of findings employing the Empathic Model, changes in lighting, color combinations, and other features of the environment that take into account the sensory abilities and motor skills of older people have been recommended.

## Report 2.1*

SAGINAW, Mich. (AP)—Four junior high students became old people for a day to see how they felt and how others acted toward them.

"I found myself getting very irritable because I couldn't get around as well as I normally do," said 13-year-old Mike Russell of Zilwaukee.

He and others are students at Saginaw's North Intermediate School. Their health education teacher, Albert Garcia, helped apply the bandages, earplugs and splints to simulate physical handicaps.

The experiment was similar to those conducted at the University by Dr. Tamerra Moeller's students in her class on the psychology of aging.

"We tend to forget all of the adjustments a person must make as a result of the physical processes of aging," Dr. Moeller said. "Declining vision or hearing, chronic illness, memory loss—these processes are painful and unnerving."

Armed with this information, the students and their teacher devised ways to experience for a few hours some of those same physical ailments.

They used earplugs to reduce hearing, noseplugs to stifle smell, gloves to make hands slow and awkward, as they might be with arthritis, and bandages or splints to make arm and leg movements difficult.

A couple of them also put patches on one eye. They had first tried to use crinkled plastic wrap to get the impression of eyesight blurred by cataracts, but the paper kept slipping.

"The eyepatch was the biggest problem," said Mike. "I kept misjudging distance. The first surprise was that I couldn't catch a table tennis ball. Then I tried to pick up a pencil and missed. I even misjudged steps."

Terry Colby, 13, said: "When I went home at noon my mother said, 'You're not coming to the table with those gloves on.'

"I told her I had to, it was part of an experiment for health class. The gloves really cut down on movement, and even though I was slow and careful, I still spilled my glass of Kool-Aid."

Thirteen-year-old Holly Neuman had a plastic bag over her right hand and a bandage on the left eye.

"I couldn't turn the pages of my books," she said. "I also found the eye that wasn't covered got tired."

Ray Lucas, 13, spent the day with tape across his nose, and that helped him discover how closely the sense of taste is linked to the sense of smell.

"At noon, I had a deviled egg sandwich that tasted blah," he said. "Even the water tasted funny. My candy bar wasn't too good either."

*Used with permission of the Associated Press.

The purposes of these recommendations, which are made to designers and administrators of housing and other facilities for the elderly and to workers in agencies or institutions serving the aged, are to increase both the safety and pleasurability of the environment. Illustrative of the kinds of recommendations that have been made are those pertaining to driving: make road signs larger and more distinctive; remove unnecessary lights, signs, and other roadside distractions.

## THEORIES AND RESEARCH
## ON THE AGING PROCESS

As is true of different body organs and systems, the rate of aging varies from person to person. At one end of the continuum are the centenarians of the Caucasus, Himalayas, and Andes; at the other end are the victims of a disease known as *progeria*. One extremely rare form of this disease that has its onset in childhood is *Cockayne's syndrome* (see Report 2.2). A victim of this disorder shows signs of premature senescence and appears to "die of old age" while still a child or young teenager. Another type of progeria, *Werner's syndrome,* has its

---

### Report 2.2    SHE'S AN 'OLD WOMAN' AT ONLY 5*

SAN DIEGO (AP)—Penny Vantine appears to have sipped from the fountain of old age. She's going deaf, has arthritis, high blood pressure, cataracts in both eyes, blue mottled skin on her arms—and she's only 5 years old.

Penny doesn't just look old, she is old. Doctors say she is aging at the rate of 15 to 20 years every year. She has the looks and many of the ailments of a woman in her 80s, doctors say.

She has been losing weight and now weighs only 9 pounds and stands 29 inches tall.

Before long, she will probably die—essentially of old age, says her doctor, Harold M. Sterling.

"She is probably going to have a cardiac or respiratory illness she can't handle," says Sterling. "She will either have a heart attack or pneumonia."

Sterling fears it will happen this year. He says nothing can be done for her.

Penny suffers from a rare disorder called Cockayne's Syndrome. Many doctors have never heard of it and there are only a handful of cases in all medical literature.

It is believed to be caused by some metabolic or endocrine defect that places the victim irretrievably into a kind of time machine capable of suddenly bringing on old age and senility.

"She reminds me of a cranky, little old lady," said Susy Kaplan, recreation director at Children's Convalescent Hospital, where Penny lives. But she said the aged child is loved by everyone.

Penny's mother, Jeanne Mitchell, lives in Olympia, Wash., where there are no facilities for her daughter.

Penny has been cared for here at skilled nursing homes and came to Children's Hospital when nursing homes could no longer give her proper medical care.

Some Cockayne patients are mentally retarded, but because Penny no longer talks, Sterling said he can't tell. She had a speaking vocabulary of about 15 words when she came to Children's, but Sterling thinks Penny has become so depressed she refuses to talk.

She has been a medical curiosity among physicians, nurses, therapists, and other professionals. Hundreds of them have been to Children's to view her.

They talked in front of her, often commenting on her frightful condition and Sterling believes the comments have had their effect on her.

"After they left, you would find her all curled up in a ball like this," he said, covering his head with his arms. "When a child doesn't answer back when she is spoken to, everybody thinks she doesn't know what is going on."

*Used with permission of the Associated Press.

onset in the late teens. People with Werner's syndrome develop many of the signs of aging—graying and falling hair, deteriorating skin, cataracts, tumors, and arteriosclerosis—between the ages of 20 and 40. Cockayne's and Werner's syndromes, however, are considered to be caricatures of aging rather than true aging. Thus, the victims of these disorders show many external signs of aging but not the changes in age pigment and collagen of true aging.

There has been much speculation and hypothesizing about the biological basis of aging and why one species or one person lives longer than another. Although a comprehensive explanation of why and how biological aging occurs has not yet been formulated, research and theorizing concerned with the causes of aging and related issues—why organs and organ systems decline with age, why women live longer than men, why certain diseases are more common in old age—is an ongoing activity.

## Theories of Aging

In an effort to discover clues to the biology of aging, scientists who study the aging process have taken a special interest in both long- and short-lived people. Perhaps the first medical researcher to study the problem was Hippocrates, who considered the cause of aging to be a decline in body heat. Other explanations of aging advanced in pre-20th century times were Erasmus Darwin's notion that it is due to a loss of irritability in neural and muscular tissue and Eli Metchnikoff's concept of "autointoxication" (Wallace, 1977).

One set of modern theories of aging may be termed *breakdown* theories, according to which aging is the result of wear and tear, stress, or exhaustion of organs and cells. At the organic or systemic level are theories that purport to explain aging in terms of the effects of wear-and-tear or stress on the body: Body organs are seen to wear out with usage and exposure to various types of environmental stress. One argument against a wear-and-tear theory is the fact that exercise (at least within limits), which constitutes active usage of body organs, enhances physiological functioning and longevity rather than the reverse. Hans Selye's (1976) *stress theory* that every person inherits a certain amount of adaptation energy at birth and that the rate of aging varies directly with how liberally this energy is expended can be criticized on similar grounds.

Another "breakdown" explanation of aging is *homeostatic imbalance theory,* which attributes aging to the breakdown in homeostatic, or self-regulatory, mechanisms that control the internal environment of the body. Alex Comfort (1964) viewed aging as the result of an accumulation of homeostatic errors or faults and a consequent loss of the ability to maintain a steady, homeostatic internal balance. Support for this idea is found in the fact that as humans age, they take progressively longer to readjust after physical exertion.

Other examples of breakdown theories are immunological theory and autoimmunity theory. *Immunological theory* views aging as due to the gradual deterioration of the immune system, so that the body can no longer protect itself adequately against injury, disease, and mutant or foreign cells. The fact that hormones secreted by the thymus gland, which controls the immune system, diminish with aging (Zatz & Goldstein, 1985) is consistent with an immunological theory. On the other hand, *autoimmunity theory* emphasizes the fact that the aging body becomes unable to differentiate between normal and abnormal cells; consequently it creates antibodies to attack both and thereby rejects its own tissues.

Substance theories at the tissue level emphasize changes in collagen and the proliferation of mutant cells. The strands of the connective tissue protein known as collagen change with aging, resulting in less elasticity or resilience in visceral organs, slower healing, and other bodily changes. The number of mutant cells also increases with aging, raising the likelihood of cancerous growths.

Other examples of "substance theories" are cross-linkage theory, free-radical theory, and hormonal theory. *Cross-linkage* is the inadvertent coupling of large intracellular and extracellular molecules that cause connective tissue to stiffen. It has been suggested that cross-linkages of DNA molecules prevent the cell from reading genetic information properly (see Shock, 1977). As a consequence, enzymes that are sufficiently active to maintain the body and its functions are not produced. Some researchers maintain, however, that although cross-linkage is associated with aging, it is an effect or correlate of the process rather than a cause of it. Another substance theory of aging at the cellular level points to the accumulation of chemical "garbage" such as free radicals as the primary agent. *Free radicals,* which are highly reactive molecules or parts of molecules produced by the adverse reactions of body cells to radiation, air pollution, and even some of the oxygen in the air, may connect to and damage other cells or their DNA.

Illustrative of *hormonal theories* is Denckla's (1974) conception of aging as being caused by the release of antithyroid hormones by the hypothalamus. These "blocking hormones" presumably inhibit the absorption of thyroxin, which is necessary for cell metabolism and functioning. It is also possible that another hormone, referred to as DECO (decreased consumption of oxygen), is secreted by the pituitary gland and acts to block or keep cells from using the thyroid hormones in the blood.

As a person ages, waste products of body metabolism, many of which are poisonous and can interfere with normal cell functioning, build up. Cell deterioration also occurs when, as is true in cases of atherosclerosis, there are failures in the delivery of oxygen and nutrients to the cells. Within the cytoplasm of the cell are little energy "machines" known as *mitochondria,* which are composed of highly unsaturated fats combined with sugar and protein molecules. According to one theory, aging is caused by oxidation of the fat molecules in the mitochondria, which interferes with the energy-releasing function of these structures.

Noting the great similarity in length of life among genetically related persons, many researchers have become convinced that there is an "aging clock"—a pre-wired, genetically determined aging program—somewhere in the body. The aging clock presumably dictates the rate and time at which, barring physical mishap, one can expect to age and die. Some authorities believe that the aging clock is in the brain, perhaps in the hypothalamus. Others interpret the evidence as pointing to the existence of aging clocks in the individual body cells. A proponent of the individual cell theory is Leonard Hayflick (1980), whose experiments have demonstrated that there is a built-in limit to the number of times individual cells can subdivide before they die. Tortoise cells divide 90 to 125 times, human cells 40 to 60 times, and chicken cells 15 to 35 times (Hayflick, 1977). Hayflick estimated that because of genetically based limits on cell division, the maximum life expectancy obtainable if cancer, cardiovascular disorders, and all other diseases were eradicated is 110–120 years.

All of the preceding theories of aging have adherents, but the various positions are obviously not mutually exclusive. This is not necessarily a shortcoming, because there is evidence of multiple sites or causes of aging. Aging can occur at the tissue level, the cellular level, or in the cell nucleus. At the tissue level, aging is related to a decrease in collagen; at the cellular level, to a deterioration of mitochondria—the little energy machines in the cytoplasm of the cell; and at the nuclear level, to mutations of DNA and the cross-linkage of molecules within the cell nucleus (Anderson, 1974).

In addition to multiple sites, the evidence points to at least two kinds of aging processes: (a) accidental damage to the molecules, membranes, or parts of the body; and (b) the previously mentioned "wired-in," genetically programmed "aging clock." Such a clock presumably consists of a series of special on–off gene "switches," which, when the organism has reached maturity, turn off certain cell activities while turning on new cells that cause the destruction of the body's protein building blocks. Belief in the existence of such a genetic program has resulted in research directed at the DNA and RNA molecules responsible for cell replication. In addition, research on the role of the hypothalamus and endocrine glands—the pituitary and thymus glands in particular—continues.

## Prolonging Life

Whether the socioeconomic problems that would be created by a greatly extended average life span could be solved is a concern of gerontologists, but scientists and laypersons alike remain quite receptive to efforts to prolong life. C. S. Lewis once asked: "Why this preoccupation with squeezing out more spatiotemporal existence? Could it be a lack of confidence in what comes hereafter?" Whatever the answer to this question may be, the number of diets, drugs, surgical procedures, and other methods that have been tried in a search for greater longevity is legion.

One approach that works to a degree in lengthening the lives of small animals is calorie restriction beginning about the time of birth. Roy Walford, a UCLA professor, believes that marked restriction of food intake combined with vitamin supplements can increase human life span appreciably. A practitioner of his own theory, Walford goes without eating 2 days a week and on every other day limits himself to 1,500 calories (see Batten, 1984; Rosenblatt, 1986). Although under-feeding lengthens the lives of small animals, it has been found that is also results in animals that are less resistant to stress than normally fed ones (Anderson, 1974). Rather than advocating a drastic decrease in food intake on the part of humans, other scientists advise decreasing the intake of certain foods (saturated fats, salt, refined sugar) while increasing the intake of other foods (green leafy vegetables, whole grains).

It is a sensible idea to eat lightly and nutritiously at any age, but severe restriction of caloric intake, when initiated after puberty, does not seem to have dramatic effects on human longevity. Consequently, most people who are concerned with living a long life, as well as looking and feeling better, have turned to other methods. One possibility is hypothermia—lowering the body temperature to 2–3 degrees Celsius, a procedure that has been shown to extend the lives of small animals by 20%–25%. However, it is doubtful whether humans would be willing to subject themselves to this treatment. Other methods also have mixed blessings. For example, many people who were concerned about the role of cholesterol in arteriosclerosis and heart attacks switched from saturated to polyunsaturated fats. Unfortunately, polyunsaturated fats increase oxidation reactions in cells, thereby creating more free radicals and hence more cellular damage of the sort associated with aging (Rosenfeld, 1976a).

The situation with drugs and vitamins is not much more hopeful. One drug—Gerovital—has been purported to be able to treat a host of physical afflictions, including angina pectoris, arteriosclerosis, arthritis, gray hair, high blood pressure, and wrinkled skin, as well as depression and other psychological disorders. The problem is that Gerovital is prepared from procaine hydrochloride, commonly known as Novocain, which has not been demonstrated to have a significant effect on the physical or psychological problems related to aging.

Reasoning that aging is associated with too much tissue or cellular oxygen, researchers have reported some success in prolonging life spans of animals by the use of dietary supplements of antioxidants such as vitamins C and E. Summarizing the results of experiments with vitamin E, Harman, Heidrick, and Eddy (1976) concluded that, because the decline in the immune system with age is the result of the degrading action of free radicals on the body cells, the antioxidant abilities of vitamin E can help retard the decline of the immune system by protecting the cells from free radicals. But as discovered by Packer and Smith (1977), vitamin E, in its role as an antioxidant, does not always increase the life

TABLE 2.2
Modifiable Aspects of Aging

| Aging Marker | Personal Decision(s) Required |
| --- | --- |
| Cardiac reserve | Exercise, nonsmoking |
| Dental decay | Prophylaxis, diet |
| Glucose tolerance | Weight control, exercise, diet |
| Intelligence tests | Training, practice |
| Memory | Training, practice |
| Osteoporosis | Weight-bearing exercise, diet |
| Physical endurance | Exercise, weight control |
| Physical strength | Exercise |
| Pulmonary reserve | Exercise, nonsmoking |
| Reaction time | Training, practice |
| Serum cholesterol | Diet, weight control, exercise |
| Social ability | Practice |
| Skin aging | Sun avoidance |
| Systolic blood pressure | Salt limitation, weight control, exercise |

Source: Fries & Crapo 1981.

span of cells. Rather, they speculate, when vitamin E does extend cellular life span, the results are produced by the interaction of vitamin E and some yet unidentified chemical or chemicals.

Finally, it can be argued that at least some of the physical disabilities that occur with aging are the results of disuse or physical inactivity rather than age itself. Therefore, many authorities recommend a schedule of regular exercise, which older adults appear to need even more than younger people. Good advice is, of course, important, but ultimately people must decide for themselves whether they are willing to do what is required to experience a healthier and happier existence in later life. Table 2.2 lists some of the markers of aging and the personal decisions required to modify them. The way is clear, but how many people possess enough self-discipline to take it?

## SUMMARY

Age-related changes in the skin, muscles, and bones of the hur____ body, and the consequent altered appearance of the individual, represent a source of stress that may be weathered well or poorly. Changes in the internal and external organs and systems of the body are also associated with old age. There is a general decrement in the cells and tissues of all internal organs, resulting in declines in functional efficiency of the cardiovascular, respiratory, musculoskeletal, gastrointestinal, and genitourinary systems. The infiltration of collagen into body tissues is associated with reduced functioning of the heart in particular. Reductions in the number of brain neurons, the blood flow to the brain, and the speed of nerve impulses affect the capacity of the brain to process information in old age. The sleeping pattern is also affected; elderly people sleep less and not as soundly as younger people.

Presbyopia is the most common visual disorder of aging, but cataracts and glaucoma are more serious. Age-related changes in the eyes require using glasses, stronger light, and larger print, especially for close work. A gradual loss of sensitivity to high and middle pitches (presbycusis) also occurs in later life. Declining sensitivity to sounds can usually be helped by a hearing aid, although psychological factors play a role in the understanding of speech and the appreciation of music. Taste, smell, touch, pain, temperature sensitivity, and the sense of balance also decline with age.

Movement becomes more difficult and reaction time slower as a person ages, but individual differences in motoric functioning are extensive. The use of mechanical devices worn by younger observers (the Empathic Model) can assist them in understanding deficits in sensation and movement associated with aging and consequently to empathize with the elderly. The results of such experiments have also contributed to the design of facilities and prosthetic devices for older people.

Among various explanations that have been offered to account for biological aging are "breakdown" theories, such as homeostatic imbalance theory and autoimmunity theory, and "substance" theories such as cross-linkage theory and the accumulation of free radicals in cells. A comprehensive theory of aging must take into account at least two processes: accidental damage to molecules, tissues, or organs, and the functioning of a wired-in, genetically programmed "aging clock."

Experiments on lengthening the lives of animals have involved caloric restriction, hypothermia, and various drugs. Antioxidants such as vitamins C and E have received particular attention. The overall results of such experiments, however, permit no definitive conclusions regarding the effects of vitamins or other chemicals on the aging process in humans.

## SUGGESTED READINGS

Costa, P. T., Jr., & McCrae, R. R. (1985). Concepts of functional or biological age: A critical view. In R. Andres, E. L. Bierman, & W. R. Hazzard (Eds.), *Principles of geriatric medicine* (pp. 30–37). New York: McGraw-Hill.

Denny, P. (1983). The biological basis of aging. In D. S. Woodruff & J. E. Birren (Eds.), *Aging: Scientific perspective and social issues* (2nd ed., pp. 226–241). Monterey, CA: Brooks/Cole.

deVries, H. A. (1983). Physiology of exercise and aging. In D. S. Woodruff & J. E. Birren (Eds.), *Aging: Scientific perspectives and social issues* (2nd ed., pp. 285–304). Monterey, CA: Brooks/Cole.

Hayflick, L. (1985). Theories of biological aging. In R. Andres, E. L. Bierman, & W. R. Hazzard (Eds.), *Principles of geriatric medicine* (pp. 9–21). New York: McGraw-Hill.

Kline, D. W., & Scheiber, F. (1985). Vision and aging. In J. E. Birren & K. W. Schaie (Eds.), *Handbook of the psychology of aging* (2nd ed., pp. 296–331). New York: Van Nostrand Reinhold.

Ostrow, A. C. (1984). *Physical activity and the older adult. Psychological perspectives.* Princeton, NJ: Princeton Book Co.

Weg, R. B. (1983). Changing physiology of aging. In D. S. Woodruff & J. E. Birren (Eds.), *Aging: Scientific perspectives and social issues* (2nd ed., pp. 242–284). Monterey, CA: Brooks/Cole.

Woodruff, D. S. (1983). Physiology and behavior relationships in aging. In D. S. Woodruff & J. E. Birren (Eds.), *Aging: Scientific perspectives and social issues* (2nd ed., pp. 178–201). Monterey, CA: Brooks/Cole.

# Health and Disease

# 3

People who are fortunate enough to live long lives do not "die of old age," as the saying goes. Although aging makes them more susceptible to physical illness, like everyone else they die of some disease or accident. The prevalence of physical disorders in older Americans is witnessed by the fact that in 1986 people in this age group, who constitute 12% of the population of the United States, accounted for 31% of all hospital stays and 42% of all days of hospital care in this country (American Association of Retired Persons, 1987). As impressive as these statistics may be, they are not an accurate indicator of the extensiveness of health problems in old age.

Far from "running" to doctors' offices or checking into hospitals whenever they are ill, most elderly people stay at home and try to cope with health problems that might appear insurmountable to a younger person. Such health problems are frequently made even worse by a lack of money. Despite financial support for treatment and care through Medicare, Medicaid, and other programs, health costs are a major expense for older people, who typically spend a higher percentage of their incomes for this purpose than their younger contemporaries. Also, unlike most younger adults, even when elderly people recover from accidents or illnesses they are usually not as healthy as they were before.

Physical and financial hardships are not the only consequences of illness during old age. Although almost everyone must cope with disease or disability at some time or other, persistent health problems invariably have an effect on one's sense of well-being and attitude toward life. Despite the age-related physical changes described in the last chapter, for a healthy individual old age can be another interesting and challenging time of life. But for the chronically ill, it can be painful and depressing.

## DEMOGRAPHICS OF DISEASE

The type and incidence of health problems in old age are related to a number of demographic factors. Compared with older women, older men tend to be more vulnerable to disease, especially to heart disorders, lung cancer, respiratory conditions, and accidents. Older men are also more often the victims of homicide and suicide: approximately four times as many men as women committed suicide in 1985 (National Center for Health Statistics, 1987c).

Two other demographic variables related to illness and death are socioeconomic status and ethnicity. Working-class people have poorer health and a shorter life span than those higher up the socioeconomic ladder (Dingle, 1973), and a similar, undoubtedly related, difference exists between Blacks and Whites. Forty-five percent of the elderly Black respondents in a 1986 survey rated their health as fair or poor, but only 29% of the elderly White respondents gave the same report. Significant age differences were also found: compared with 7% of persons under 65, 30% of those 65 and over assessed their health as fair or poor (American Association of Retired Persons, 1987).

Many of the sex, socioeconomic, and ethnic-group differences in disease and longevity are the results of environmental conditions such as pollution, diet, and sanitation rather than heredity. Thus, men are more likely than women to encounter pollution on the job, and poorer people usually eat less nutritious food and have less adequate medical care than their more affluent contemporaries.

Because of advances in medicine and improved living conditions during this century, it would seem that older people today would be healthier than those of yesteryear. It is certainly true that, because of more sanitary living conditions, better nutrition, mass immunization, and antibiotics, the types of diseases that have the most debilitating effects on the elderly have changed. Measles, diphtheria, influenza, pneumonia, and tuberculosis are not as threatening to the aged as they once were. Be that as it may, despite medical successes in combatting these diseases and the fact that most older people today are fairly healthy, as a group the elderly continue to have a significantly higher rate of illness than other age groups. Although the gains in average longevity during this century have been remarkable, the rates of heart disease, cancer, and cerebrovascular disease (stroke) remain high. As shown in Table 3.1, nearly three-fourths of all older Americans die of one of these three disorders. A large percentage also suffer from respiratory disorders, diabetes, atherosclerosis, kidney diseases, and less fatal conditions such as arthritis, osteoporosis, cataracts, and deafness. Consequently, it is arguable whether older people of today are actually healthier than their age-mates of former times. It has even been suggested that, by interfering with the Darwinian principle of survival of the fittest, medical science has succeeded in creating a larger but weaker human population.

As indicated in chapter 1, the expected life span of a 65-year-old American today is close to what it was in 1900. At that time, a 65-year-old could expect to

TABLE 3.1

Numbers and Rates for the 10 Leading Causes of Death
Among Americans 65 Years and Over in 1985*

| Rank | Cause of Death | Number | Rate[a] |
|------|----------------|--------|------|
| 1 | Diseases of the heart | 620,082 | 2,173 |
| 2 | Malignant neoplasms, including neoplasms of lymphatic and hematopoietic tissues | 298,683 | 1,046.7 |
| 3 | Cerebrovascular diseases | 132,341 | 463.8 |
| 4 | Chronic obstructive pulmonary diseases and allied conditions | 60,634 | 212.5 |
| 5 | Pneumonia and influenza | 58,829 | 206.2 |
| 6 | Diabetes mellitus | 27,284 | 95.6 |
| 7 | Accidents and adverse effects | 24,971 | 87.5 |
|   | Motor vehicle accidents | 6,156 | 21.6 |
|   | All other accidents and adverse effects | 18,815 | 65.9 |
| 8 | Atherosclerosis | 22,770 | 79.8 |
| 9 | Nephritis, nephrotic syndrome, and nephrosis | 17,393 | 61 |
| 10 | Septicemia | 13,402 | 47 |
|   | All other causes | 194,156 | 680.5 |
|   | All causes | 1,470,545 | 5,153.3 |

*Source: National Center for Health Statistics, 1987c.
[a]Per 100,000 population in 65 years and over age group.

live 13 more years, compared to 16 more years now—an increase of only 3 years. If cancer, the second major cause of death among the elderly, were completely eliminated, the average life span would rise by only 1.2 to 2.3 years. But if all cardiovascular and kidney diseases were conquered, the average life span would increase by approximately 10 years (Butler, 1975). This dramatic, if not world-shaking, increase in longevity is already underway. Thus, the results of a study by the Mayo Clinic indicate that the number of cerebrovascular accidents ("strokes"), especially among the elderly, has declined appreciably during the past 30 years. Possible causes of the decline are better treatment of high blood pressure, a decrease in smoking since the Surgeon General's report of 1964, and dietary changes ("Reports Show . . . ," 1979).

## CHRONIC DISORDERS

In contrast to acute disorders, which are of relatively short duration, chronic disorders are long-standing conditions such as cardiovascular disorders, hypertension, various respiratory aliments, arthritis, diabetes, rheumatism, and gastrointestinal disorders. Although young people have more acute illnesses, older people are more susceptible to chronic disorders, which constitute the most prevalent health problem for them. In addition, both the number and severity of chronic and acute illnesses increase with aging. However, the conditions are not merely the results of aging; they often have their origins in childhood and earlier adulthood—and the habits of a lifetime.

Although only about 25% of men and 10% of women over age 65 are seriously handicapped by illness, approximately 75% have one or more chronic conditions that restrict their activities. The incidence of these chronic diseases, and the likelihood of being disabled by them, rises progressively with age during later life. The most common chronic conditions among the elderly and the approximate percentages of elderly people affected by each are: arthritis (48%), hypertension (39%), hearing impairments (29%), heart disease (30%), orthopedic impairments and sinusitis (17% each), cataracts (14%), diabetes and visual impairments (19% each), and tinnitus (9%) (American Association of Retired Persons, 1987). Although these diseases do not kill, they can make life extremely unpleasant for oneself and others and increase one's susceptibility to more lethal conditions.

## Arthritis

*Arthritis,* an inflammation of the joints accompanied by pain, stiffness, and movement difficulties, is especially common among older individuals. This disorder usually affects large joints such as those of the hips and knees, but it can also affect the ankles, fingers, and vertebrae. Arthritic individuals experience pain and stiffness, difficulty moving the afflicted joints, and problems getting around and engaging in formerly routine activities.

*Osteoarthritis,* a painful disorder of the knees and wrists in particular, is the most common crippler of the aged; an estimated 85% of persons over age 70 are afflicted with this disorder (Mannik & Gilliland, 1980). It is characterized by degeneration and loss of cartilage at the ends of bones and the formation of sharp "spurs" in the joints.

Although there is no known cure for arthritis, the symptoms can be relieved by drugs (aspirin and other analgesics), range-of-motion exercises for the affected joints, weight reduction, and, in extreme cases, replacement of a crippled joint with a prosthesis.

## Diabetes

Other less serious chronic conditions that respond well to treatment are cataracts, hernias, hemorrhoids, and varicose veins. More serious chronic problems include prostate disorders, chronic respiratory illness, and diabetes mellitus. The symptoms of *diabetes,* which is common among the elderly, are weight loss, abnormal thirst, and frequent urination. Caused by a breakdown in the ability of the body to use glucose, diabetes in the aged is often fatal without strict adherence to treatment and diet. In 1985, it was the sixth leading cause of death in the 65-and-over age group (National Center for Health Statistics, 1987c).

## Respiratory Disorders

The most common acute disorders among the elderly are respiratory ailments, but respiratory problems may also be chronic. Chronic respiratory disorders such as bronchitis, emphysema, and fibrosis are especially common in older men, presumably because of their greater exposure to cigarette smoke and air pollutants. Other respiratory disorders that are potentially fatal to elderly patients are tuberculosis, influenza, and pneumonia. Chronic obstructive pulmonary diseases (bronchitis, emphysema, asthma, etc.) are the fourth leading cause, and pneumonia and influenza the fifth leading cause of death in the 65-and-over age group (National Center for Health Statistics, 1987c). Influenza and pneumonia are usually acute illnesses that may accompany other physical disorders. In fact, pneumonia was once so common that it was referred to as the "old man's friend" because of its frequent association with death in members of that age-sex group who were suffering from other disorders. The name may still be appropriate in the case of a patient who has arthritis, heart disease, influenza, and rheumatism at the same time and eventually dies of pneumonia.

The decreased responsiveness of the immune system during later life may lead to a common cold becoming complicated by bronchitis and pneumonia before it runs its course. For this reason, and the greater susceptibility of elderly people to lower respiratory tract infections in particular, it is advisable for all individuals who are 65 or older to be immunized with pneumococcal vaccine once and with influenza vaccine every year. In addition, booster dosages of diphtheria and tetanus toxoids should be received every 10 years from age 65 on (American College of Physicians, 1985).

## Osteoporosis

With aging, a demineralization process takes place in the bones, reducing bone mass and making the dense part of bone structure spongier and more brittle. The effects of these changes are pain in the joints of the lower spine and hips, a loss of several inches in height, and a greater danger of fractures of the vertebrae, ribs, hips, and wrists. A common cause of these changes is *osteoporosis,* a gradual long-term loss of the mass of the bones.

Osteoporosis is four times as common in women as in men in the 45–70 year age group, affecting as many as 50% of all American women older than 50 and perhaps 90% of those older than 70. The disorder is also more common in Whites (especially those originating in Northern Europe) and Asians than in Blacks.

Although it is doubtful whether osteoporosis is simply a calcium-deficiency disease, 1,500 milligrams of calcium is prescribed to control for the demineralization in osteoporosis. Also prescribed are 400 units of vitamin D per day and sometimes flouride and growth hormones, are prescribed. Women who have gone through the menopause are often given estrogens ("estrogen-replacement therapy" or ERT). However, the use of ERT, which can reduce osteoporotic fractures but may also contribute to cancer or cardiovascular disease, is debatable. A program of regular exercises designed for women with osteoporosis has also been reported to be helpful in stabilizing or partially reversing some of the deleterious effects of this disease (Smith, Khairi, Norton, & Johnston, 1976). In addition to lack of exercise, alcohol and certain drugs (cortisone, diuretics, tetracycline, thyroid hormone, antiepileptics), phosphorated carbonated beverages, cigarette smoking, and chronic hyperthyroidism may contribute to osteoporosis; heredity also seems to be a factor.

## Accidents

Chronic degenerative musculoskeletal diseases such as osteoporosis and arthritis, and the resulting orthopedic impairments, are worsened by accidents. Every year, some 200,000 persons over 65—the majority of them women, fracture a hip in a fall. Half of these victims die within 12 months, frequently from pneumonia (Peterson & Rosenblatt, 1986a). As shown in Table 3.1, accidents are the seventh leading cause of death among older Americans. Injuries incurred by a fall at home or during a traffic accident in which an older pedestrian is hit by a vehicle are especially common (see Fig. 3.1).

The causes of accidents involving elderly drivers include failing to yield, signaling or changing lanes incorrectly, making a wrong turn, missing a stop sign or stop light, and parking incorrectly. Accidental falls are caused by waxed floors, loose carpets, slippery bathtubs, high beds, misplaced furniture and stairs that make older people trip and fall (Freiberg, 1987). Such accidents are more likely to occur when the victim has poor vision, poor hearing, an impaired sense of balance, or a neurological disorder. And because healing and recuperation are slower in older people, an accident that represents only a temporary setback to a younger person may require long-term hospital or home care and result in a permanent disability in an elderly individual. Recognizing that good safety habits, combined with good mental and physical health, can help prevent accidents, the National Institute on Aging (1980) has recommended the preventive measures listed in Table 3.2. Attention to these simple suggestions can help prevent many of the more than 800,000 injuries and nearly 25,000 deaths in elderly Americans caused by accidents each year.

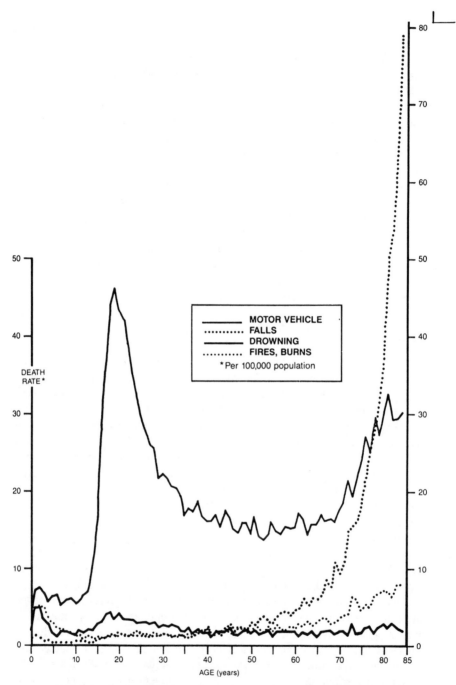

FIG. 3.1. Accidental death rate by age in the United States in 1986. (Source: National Safety Council tabulations of National Center for Health Statistics ICD codes are E810-E825 for motor vehicles, E880-E888 for falls, E832, E910 for drowning, E890-E899 for fires and burns.)

TABLE 3.2
Recommended Precautions Against Accidents in Old Age*

To help prevent falls:

1. Illuminate all stairways and provide light switches at both the bottom and the top.
2. Provide night lights or bedside remote-control light switches.
3. Be sure both sides of stairways have sturdy handrails.
4. Tack down carpeting on stairs and use nonskid treads.
5. Remove throw rugs that tend to slide.
6. Arrange furniture and other objects so that they are not obstacles.
7. Use grab bars on bathroom walls and nonskid mats or strips in the bathtub.
8. Keep outdoor steps and walkways in good repair.

To help prevent burns:

1. Never smoke in bed or when drowsy.
2. When cooking, don't wear loosely fitting flammable clothing; bathrobes, nightgowns, and pajamas catch fire.
3. Set water heater thermostats or faucets so that water does not scald the skin.
4. Plan which emergency exits to use in case of fire.

To help prevent injuries when riding public transportation:

1. Remain alert and brace yourself when a bus is slowing down or turning.
2. Watch for slippery pavement and other hazards when entering or leaving a vehicle.
3. Have fare ready to prevent losing your balance while fumbling for change.
4. Do not carry too many packages, and leave one hand free to grasp railings.
5. Allow extra time to cross streets, especially in bad weather.
6. At night wear light-colored or fluorescent clothing and carry a flashlight.

*Source: National Institute on Aging (1980).

## Cancer

Malignant neoplasms, or cancer, are second only to cardiovascular disease as a cause of death in later life. The death rate for all types of cancer is greater among the elderly than in younger people, increasing gradually to middle age and then rapidly accelerating into old age. Among the different types of cancer, those involving the digestive tract (stomach, colon, liver), respiratory organs (lungs, etc.), genital and urinary organs, and breast (women) account for over half the deaths due to cancer in this age group. However, cancer of the kidneys and skin are also common.

Cancer has often been referred to as the "silent killer," in that it frequently remains undetected until well advanced. Because treatment is usually more effective in the beginning stages of the disease, early detection and diagnosis are emphasized and encouraged. All adults, and those over 40 in particular, are urged to be aware of the following seven warning signs of cancer:

A sore that does not heal.

A change in a wart or mole.

A lump or thickening in the breast or elsewhere.

Persisting hoarseness or cough.

Chronic indigestion or difficulty swallowing.

Unusual bleeding or discharge.

A change in bowel or bladder habits.

Individuals having one or more of these symptoms should consult a physician immediately.

The results of observation and research suggest that psychological variables, such as an attitude of passivity and hopelessness in the face of stress, can affect the growth, if not the genesis, of cancer cells (Schmale, 1971). Convinced of the importance of psychological factors in the prognosis of cancer, Carl and Stephanie Simonton (Simonton, Matthews-Simonton, & Creighton, 1978) have supplemented physical treatment methods (surgery, radiation, chemotherapy) with psychological techniques. Their purpose is to get patients to think positively and confidently about their ability to control the illness and to stimulate the immune system by their thoughts. Relaxation to control anxiety and visual imagery, in which patients imagine their white blood cells attacking and destroying cancer cells, are among the techniques employed. Significant results have been reported using these methods, but most physicians remain skeptical. In general, oncologists (physicians who specialize in the treatment of cancer) seem to feel that psychological treatment in conjunction with physiochemical treatment is worth trying, but they caution against the danger and cruelty of unduly raising the hopes of cancer patients.

## Heart Disease

Included in the category *cardiovascular diseases* are diseases of the heart, hypertension, cerebrovascular diseases or stroke, and atherosclerosis. The first and third of these disorders are the first and third causes of death among the elderly. Heart disease, although a common chronic condition and the ranking cause of death among elderly Americans, is, of course, not limited to this age group.

However, the probability of death from heart disease is 150 times greater in a 75-year-old than in a 35-year-old.

In addition to age, the incidence of cardiovascular diseases is related to heredity, sex, race, geography or nationality, and lifestyle. The significance of heredity is seen in the fact that people with a family history of cardiovascular disorders are more likely to develop a condition in this category. With regard to sex and race, mortality due to heart disease and stroke is higher in men than women and higher in Blacks than Whites. Hypertension (high blood pressure), a frequent accompanier of heart failure and cerebral hemorrhage, is also more prevalent in men and Blacks than in women and Whites.

Among the lifestyle factors linked to heart disorders are lack of exercise, heavy smoking, psychological stress, and high blood cholesterol level. Lifestyle is, of course, related to nationality. People in Asian and African cultures, where typical diets includes higher amounts of vegetables and lower amounts of animal fats than the diets of people in most North American and Western European countries, have a lower incidence of heart disease than North Americans and Western Europeans. The situation among the Japanese, who eat a lot of salted fish but little meat, is enlightening. The heavy vegetarian diet of the Japanese keeps their blood cholesterol, and hence the incidence of heart disease, low. But a high salt intake raises their blood pressure, increasing the likelihood of hypertension.

Another lifestyle factor related to heart disease is marital status. It has been found that death rates due to heart attacks are greater among single, widowed, and divorced people than among married people, regardless of age, sex, or race. Although not absolutely guaranteed, it can be presumed that a marital relationship usually creates a healthier, more therapeutic environment by providing emotional support, feelings of belonging, and a sense of control over one's life, and hence promotes greater recuperative power after a heart attack (Lynch, 1977).

Although somewhat controversial, the results of research on the relationship of coronary heart disease to a behavioral pattern designated as Type A have been widely cited (Rosenman et al., 1975). Type A individuals are characterized as "driven, aggressive, ambitious, competitive, preoccupied with achievement, impatient, restless in their movements, and staccato-like in their speech." The contrasting behavioral pattern is that of a Type B individual, who is described as more relaxed, easy-going and patient, speaking and acting more slowly and evenly. Compared with Type B's, Type A individuals reportedly manifest a significantly higher incidence of heart attacks, even when differences in age, serum cholesterol level, smoking frequency, and blood pressure are taken into account.

Whatever its causes may be, a heart attack is an anxiety-arousing experience at any age and can have a profound psychological effect on the victim. Consequently, heart attack patients require not only drugs, a special diet, and an appropriate combination of rest and exercise, but often psychotherapeutic assistance as well. Some heart patients develop a condition known as *angor anima,* a fear of impending death, which can precipitate another attack if not dealt with. In any event, there are important physical and psychological reasons for keeping heart patients relaxed and untroubled.

During the past few decades significant advances have been made in the treatment of heart disease and other cardiovascular disorders. These include a variety of surgical and mechanical procedures such as coronary bypasses, heart valve replacements, arterial ''cleaning,'' the installation of electronic pacemakers and mechanical pumps, and (rarely) heart transplants. These procedures have enabled many heart-attack victims, who might have once been condemned to a life in bed, to live relatively normal, productive lives (see Report 3.1).

## ORGANIC BRAIN DISORDERS

Organic brain disorders are a common cause of death in old age, but many people who are diagnosed as having a brain disorder live for years, manifesting gradual, declining abilities and insidious changes in personality. These are the *chronic brain syndrome* cases, which can be treated symptomatically but not ''cured.'' On the other hand, the symptoms of *acute brain syndrome,* although frequently severe, are transient and reversible.

Elderly patients comprise more than half of the first admissions to mental hospitals, and most of them are suffering from chronic brain syndrome. One chronic condition that is found more often in the ''young–old'' than in the ''old–old'' is alcoholism. When untreated, chronic alcoholism can result in a brain disorder known as Korsakoff's syndrome, a relatively rare condition occuring most often in people in their 50s and 60s. The symptoms of Korsakoff's syndrome include disorientation, impulsiveness, loss of memory, confabulation,[1] and inflammation of the peripheral nerves of the body. More common in later life, however, are cerebral arteriosclerosis, multi-infarct dementia, and Alzheimer's disease.

### Cerebral Arteriosclerosis

Cerebral arteriosclerosis (hardening of the arteries of the brain) usually has its onset in the mid-60s, and the victim dies of a heart attack or stroke within 3 to 4 years. In old age the walls of the arteries of the brain become thickened, and the diameter of the vessels is reduced owing to fatty deposits. These accumulations of fatty tissue and calcified material, known as *plaque,* clog the arterial channels

---

[1]A person who confabulates tries to fill in gaps in his or her memory by guessing or lying.

---

**Report 3.1    AGE, HEART ATTACK NO DETERRENT**
*Clarence C. Chaffee, at 80, Is Still Winning Tennis Titles\**

WILLIAMSTOWN, Mass. (AP)—Doctors were skeptical when Clarence C. Chaffee resumed training for the national Super Seniors tennis championships a few weeks after suffering a heart attack.

"They made me cut out the jogging, but doctors can't tell how I feel. Only I can do that," said the 80-year-old former Williams College coach.

Five months later he had captured seven of the eight national tennis titles in his age class, including a "Grand Slam" of the singles competition, with hardcourt victories indoors and out plus the grass and clay court titles.

After his heart attack April 29, a pacemaker was implanted in Chaffee's chest, but he said recently, "I don't even know it is there. If I thought about it during a tournament, I'd have too many (mental) blockages."

**A Former Coach at Brown**
Chaffee, an all-around athlete at Brown University, coached tennis, squash and soccer for 33 years at Williams. He didn't begin competing nationally until he was 70. Since then he has collected 41 national seniors titles.

"I never had the time to play around when I was young, because I had a job and family," he said. "And later on I wasn't eligible for the amateur tournaments. They called me a professional, because I was a coach. I lost 10 years of my best play because of that rule."

But a relaxation of the U.S. Tennis Assn.'s eligibility rules for amateurs in the 1970s turned Chaffee loose. And Super Senior tennis, a special category for those over age 55, hasn't been the same since.

**Won in Los Angeles**
In mid-August, Chaffee, ranked fourth in the country, took the USTA hardcourt singles championship in Los Angeles for players 80 to 85. A week later he won the U.S. indoor hard court title in San Francisco.

In the next two weekends he took the national grass court championships in East Providence, R.I., and the clay court championships in Charlottesville, Va.

With partner Clarke Kaye, 80, of Louisville, Ky., he also won the national doubles crown on three of the surfaces and finished second in the indoor doubles.

*\*Used by permission of The Associated Press.*

---

and interfere with blood circulation. As a result the vessels are unable to carry enough nutrients, vitamins, and oxygen in the blood to the brain, and the probability of a blockage or rupture increases.

A blockage of a blood vessel is called a *thrombosis* (or when mobile, an *embolism*), and a rupture is called a *hemorrhage*. Either a thrombosis or a hemorrhage in a cerebral blood vessel is referred to as a *cerebrovascular accident (CVA)*, or *stroke*, a condition that can produce heart failure. Blockage of a small blood vessel is technically known as a "small stroke," and blockage of a large vessel as a "major stroke," or CVA. The warning signs of a CVA include dizziness, temporary dimness or loss of vision (one eye, in particular), sudden falling, temporary speech loss or difficulty speaking or understanding speech, and sudden weakness or numbness in the arm, leg, or face on one side of the body (American Heart Association, 1985).

Cerebral arteriosclerosis affects over 3 million people and kills nearly 200,000 people in the United States annually. A typical patient is in his early 70s and manifests the organic syndrome symptoms of confusion, disorientation, incoherence, restlessness, and occasionally hallucinations. Complaints of headaches, dizziness, and fatigue also occur, with some patients becoming paralyzed on one side of the body (hemiplegia) and having seizures. Superimposed on these physical symptoms are the anxiety and depression resulting from the severe stress occasioned by the disorder. As with any stress situation, maladaptive personality characteristics and behaviors that were present before the physical trauma are accentuated.

## Multi-infarct Dementia

The revised third edition of the *Diagnostic and Statistical Manual of the American Psychiatric Association* (American Psychiatric Association, 1987) groups organic mental disorders into three categories: multi-infarct dementia, dementia of the Alzheimer type, and psychoactive substance-induced organic mental disorders. The first two disorders are associated with neuronal degeneration, which leads to atrophy (shrinking) and related degenerative changes in the brain during old age. The shrinkage, which can reduce the brain to 15% to 30% of its previous weight, occurs primarily in the frontal cortex, the temporal cortex, and the associated white matter. The condition becomes more apparent after age 65, peaking in frequency at about age 70, and then begins to decline. Over 33% of the people who live past age 80 and an estimated 50% of all nursing-home patients are suffering from senile dementia.

The most common subcategory of senile dementia, *multi-infarct dementia,* is due to cerebrovascular disease associated with hypertension and vascular damage. This condition was formerly labeled *psychosis with cerebral arteriosclerosis,* but the name was changed when it became apparent that the symptoms are related not to arteriosclerosis but rather to localized areas of dying or dead cerebral tissue (infarcts). Extensive and localized softened areas in the brain, presumably caused by blood-supply deprivation due to a thrombosis or embolism, as well as changes in the cerebral blood vessels, are found on autopsy.

The course of multi-infarct dementia is erratic and the pattern of deficits "patchy"; certain cognitive functions are affected early, whereas others remain relatively untouched. When the onset of the disorder is gradual, the early physical symptoms include headache, dizziness, weakness, and fatigue. Among the changes in cognition and personality that are noted are memory defect, periods of confusion, and lowered work efficiency. Disturbances of abstract thinking, judgment, and impulse control may also occur. Patients may have episodes of laughing and crying (sham emotion), trouble swallowing, confusion or disorientation, and difficulty assimilating new experiences. As the disorder progresses, memory, confusion, and disorientation in time and place become progressively worse. For example, patients may be unable to remember when they ate last, whether or not they took their medicine, and whether the stove was turned off. They may lose the ability to perform certain routine tasks, manifest little interest in external events, remain untidy, and become preoccupied with eating, eliminating, and other bodily functions. Memory, speech, and personal habits deteriorate even further as time progresses. At an advanced stage, the symptoms of multi-infarct dementia are very much like those of Alzheimer's disease.

## Alzheimer's Disease

An organic brain syndrome that has received a great deal of research and media attention during recent years is Alzheimer's disease, which affects an estimated $1-2\frac{1}{2}$ million Americans. In this condition, the brain atrophies and postmortem microscopic examination reveals the presence of senile plaques, neurofibrillary tangles, and degenerated neurons in the brain. More than 75% of the neurons in the basal forebrain may be lost. Although its onset is usually after age 65, Alzheimer's patients may manifest progressive cognitive and emotional changes as early as the fifth or sixth decade of life. The onset of the disorder is insidious and its course progressive. The psychological changes associated with it are gradual, usually beginning with simple memory failure (e.g., difficulty remembering names). Intellectual abilities (memory, judgment, abstract thinking, etc.), personality, and behavior gradually deteriorate, with the changes becoming steadily worse over time (see Report 3.2). There is a decline in mental alertness, adaptability, sociability, and tolerance for new things or changes in routine. Patients may become more self-centered in their thoughts and activities, untidy, agitated, preoccupied with natural functions (eating, digestion, excretion), and in certain cases manifest paranoid symptoms. The rate at which the disorder progresses and the particular symptoms vary with the individual, but in the terminal stages all patients are reduced to a vegetative level of functioning. In rare instances, the symptoms are reversed and a partial recovery occurs.

The exact cause of Alzheimer's disease is not known, although a variety of substances or conditions have been reported to be association with the disorder. These include biochemical deficiencies (of certain enzymes, neurotransmitters such as acetylcholine, or minerals), deposits of certain proteins (beta amyloid, A68), excessive amounts of aluminum and a shortage of the hormone somatostatin in the brains of Alzheimer's patients (Kevles, 1986; Schmeck, 1987). Other suggested causes are a slow-growing virus, cerebral trauma, an immune system defect, and a chromosomal defect. The fact that Alzheimer's tends to run in families suggests a genetic basis, or at least an inherited susceptibility (see

---

### Report 3.2    ALZHEIMER'S DISEASE: A CASE HISTORY*

A good friend of mine, a woman then in her middle 50s, asked me to evaluate her increasing forgetfulness. She was a highly successful executive and an amateur artist, and I told her that my own forgetfulness was nearly as bad as hers, and I was ten years younger.

But I erred greatly. She later sought a diagnosis from a neurologist, then from another neurologist, both of whom told her what I had: that nothing was wrong and that she had to "expect those things at your age." Finally a neuropsychologist found definite indications of Alzheimer's disease. In the meantime my friend had noted increasing confusion and forgetfulness, and she was becoming very anxious and severely depressed. Having married late in life, she had two teenage sons, and her husband had recently retired due to severe arthritis, so she was deeply concerned about what their fate would be if her condition continued to worsen. She was able to accept death, although she hardly welcomed it, but the thought of extensive deterioration put her in an understandable state of panic.

About three years later she left the management-consulting firm she had helped organize and took a position as an administrator with the local school system, where her symptoms would be less noticeable and she could enroll in an excellent health-care plan. She became less sociable and outgoing, and her sexual interests, which apparently had always been strong, diminished considerably, although I never knew how much of this decrease was due to her depression and how much to her disease.

By the time she was 61, her episodes of forgetfulness were frequent, and the changes had led to tension in her marriage. Her husband was torn by his love for her and his fear that he would spend years caring for a confused and deteriorating woman when he himself was having serious health problems. He was also embarrassed by his wife's confusion and forgetfulness when they were out with other people, and she was made even more anxious by his embarrassment.

There is no known cure for my friend's Alzheimer's disease, but this does not mean that she and her husband need to wait passively for her to deteriorate further and eventually die. I encouraged them to go for family therapy, with their now young-adult sons, in the hope that such treatment would diminish the depression and anxiety that accompanied the disorder. I don't know whether they did seek psychotherapy, and I also don't know many psychotherapists who have had any experience or training in working with families facing these problems.

My friend's situation is familiar to those who work with older people, but very few resources are available for helping either the victim or the victim's family. It is important to note that, even though nothing can be done about the organic symptoms of the disease, a great deal can be done through counseling and psychotherapy to help the family face what is likely to come. Yet such services are very difficult to find.

*Source: After Kalish, 1982, p. 54. Reproduced with permission.

---

Sargent, 1982). That Down's syndrome individuals who live into adulthood develop Alzheimer's disease suggests the presence of a defective gene on the 21st chromosome pair (Sinex & Myers, 1982).

## Diagnosis and Treatment of Brain Disorders

Although chronic brain disease is considered irreversible, many patients who manifest symptoms of brain disorder can be treated. If a brain scan reveals little or no atrophy, it may be that the patient is suffering from a disorder such as thyroid deficiency, anemia, diabetic coma, or even a heart attack rather than brain deterioration. Butler (1975) reported that physicians often fail to distinguish between reversible and irreversible brain disorders; they misdiagnose malnutrition, anemia, heart failure, drug overdoses (tranquilizers and barbiturates in particular), alcoholic stupor, CVAs, and reactions to dehydration as irreversible brain disease. Severe depression, the clinical picture of which includes forgetfulness, difficulty concentrating, and helplessness, has also been mislabeled as senile brain disease.

Among the symptoms of reversible brain disorder listed by Butler (1975), of which medical diagnosticians should be aware, are: a fluctuating level of awareness (from mild confusion to stupor to delirium), disorientation, misidentification of people, and impairment of intellectual functions. Hallucinations, unusual aggressiveness, and a dazed expression may also be present. Many of these same symptoms, of course, occur in irreversible brain diseases, but they may go untreated if physicians do not recognize the possibility of a treatable, reversible disorder.

Other than custodial care and medication for the control of emotions, little is done to treat patients who are accurately diagnosed as having an organic brain disease. Severely deteriorated patients usually while away the time in nursing homes or other institutions, remaining there and receiving minimal care for the rest of their lives. Because senile dementia patients tend to accumulate in mental hospitals, which are supposed to be treatment centers, relatives are advised to move them to less expensive facilities that are expressly custodial in nature.

## HEALTH CARE AND TREATMENT

Good health is undeniably an important factor in feeling happy and satisfied with life. To a limited extent, discomfort and disease in old age can be combated with medical treatment, but attention to preventive health measures before and during old age is a more effective defense. The associations between specific diseases and lifestyle factors, as listed in Table 3.3, underscore the fact that there are measures that both older and younger people can take to preserve their health and prevent overwhelming, debilitating illness.

### Preventive Health Measures

The truth of the proverb that "an ounce of prevention is worth a pound of cure" is particularly evident in respect to health in old age. As the body's ability to ward off the effects of diseases, accidents, and other stressors declines with aging, it becomes essential to take precautions against accidents, to exercise and eat sensibly, and to receive periodic medical checkups. The wellness movement

TABLE 3.3
Disease Conditions and Lifestyles*

| Disorders/Disease | Lifestyle Factors |
|---|---|
| Arteriosclerosis, atherosclerosis, coronary disease, and hypertension | High fat, highly refined carbohydrate diet, high salt; obesity; sedentary lifestyle; cigarette smoking; heavy drinking, alcoholism; unresolved, continual stress; personality type |
| Cerebrovascular accidents | Sedentary lifestyle; low fiber, high fat or high salt diet; heavy drinking, alcoholism (which contribute to atherosclerosis, arteriosclerosis, and hypertension, risk factors for cerebrovascular accidents) |
| Osteoporosis and periodonitis | Malnutrition—inadequate calcium, protein, vitamin K, fluoride, magnesium and vitamin D metabolite, lack of exercise; immobility; for women, sex steroid starvation |
| Chronic pulmonary disease | Cigarette smoking; air pollution; stress; sedentary habits |
| Obesity | Low caloric output (sedentary), high caloric intake; high stress levels; heavy drinking, alcoholism; low self-esteem |
| Cancer | Possible correlation with personality type; stress; exposure to environmental carcinogens over a long period of time; nutritional deficiencies and excesses; radiation; sex steroid hormones; food additives; cigarette smoking; occupational carcinogens (for example, asbestos); occult viruses; diminution of immune response (immune surveillance) |
| Dementia and pseudodementia | Malnutrition; long illness and bed rest; drug abuse (polypharmacy, iatrogenesis); anemia; other organ system disease; bereavement; social isolation |
| Sexual dysfunction | Ignorance (the older individual and society at large); societal stereotypic attitudes; early socialization; inappropriate or no partner; drug effects (for example, antihypertensive drugs); psychogenic origin; long periods of abstinence; serious systemic disease |

*Source: From Weg, 1983 (Reproduced by permission)

and related programs aimed at helping people become more physically fit, nutritionally aware, and adept at managing stress have improved the health and well-being of many younger and older individuals in recent years. The preventive measures emphasized by these programs, such as stopping smoking, reducing consumption of red meat and alcohol and increasing consumption of fiber, and learning how to manage stress, would, if adhered to rigorously, significantly reduce the incidence of many killer diseases in later life.

**Exercise.**    Regular exercise of an appropriate kind has general salutary effects, both physical and psychological, on human beings. In particular, exercise reduces the incidence of cardiovascular disease and hence promotes longevity.

Walking, calisthenics, swimming, and jogging in moderation increase oxygen consumption, ventilation capacity, cardiac output, blood flow, muscle tonus and strength, and joint flexibility. In addition, regular exercise results in decreases in body fats and poisons, as well as reductions in blood pressure and the response times of body cells and organs. By reducing nervous tension and enhancing the sense of well-being, physical exercise also improves the ability to cope with psychologically stressful situations (deVries, 1983; deVries & Hales, 1982).

**Nutrition.** Eating alone or from loneliness and skipping meals because food is too expensive or because of a loss of interest in cooking or eating can create serious nutritional problems for the elderly. Dietary restrictions, dental and digestive problems, reductions in the sensitivity of taste and smell, as well as depression can interfere with the enjoyment of food. Good nutrition is also hampered by the high cost of food and the unavailability of transportation for many of the elderly. Lacking the social stimuli traditionally associated with meals, isolated older people frequently end by eating unplanned snacks or "picking" at their food. Actually, it is generally recommended that the aged eat four or five light meals per day instead of a smaller number of heavier meals. In most cases these meals should include less carbohydrate and more protein than was appropriate for the individual prior to old age.

Realizing that a large percentage of elderly people either fail to select a nutritionally balanced diet or cannot afford one, the federal government provides funds for several tax-supported nutrition programs. The Nutrition Program for Older Americans makes available, through state agencies, low-cost group meals and home-delivered meals to persons 60 years of age and older. A part of this program known as "Meals on Wheels" provides for the delivery of hot food to the homes of older people, and another section of the program arranges for transportation to nutrition sites in the community. Even more extensive than the Nutrition Program for Older Americans because it involves all age groups, is the Food Stamp Program. Under this program, individuals or families with low incomes are eligible for stamps, which can be exchanged for footstuffs. Homebound or handicapped people over 60 years can also exchange food stamps for home-delivered meals. Finally, emergency foodstuffs and related supplies and services are available to low-income elderly under several federally sponsored programs.

**Drugs.** Approximately one third of all the drugs sold in the United States are consumed by elderly people. Many of these are medications prescribed for chronic conditions such as cardiovascular disorders and degenerative joint diseases. Sedatives and tranquilizers are taken in quantity by elderly people to control the anxiety, depression, and insomnia that are commonplace in old age. Many over-the-counter, nonprescription drugs are bought for self-treatment of respiratory disorders, gastrointestinal disorders, general aches and pains, and sleeping problems.

Improper usage of drugs may occur when elderly people forget to take their medicine or take an incorrect dosage, are unable to read the labels or open drug containers, or lack the funds or transportation to obtain needed drugs. However, drug misuse or abuse is also caused in no small part by the overreadiness of physicians to write prescriptions. Physicians frequently prescribe both too much medication and combinations of medications that produce bad reactions in older patients. When prescribing drugs to elderly patients, it must be kept in mind that what was an appropriate dosage in early or middle adulthood may not be right or safe in old age. The increasing ratio of fat to lean body mass in later life and the decline in kidney functioning with age result in drugs being absorbed differently by body tissues and remaining in the body longer. Consequently, drug dosage must be carefully monitored by the physician and changed when necessary.

Adverse drug reactions account for approximately 5% of all hospitalizations and often occur as a result of medications given in the hospital itself. Drug reactions such as confusion and depression are sometimes misdiagnosed and attributed to "senility." With respect to bad reactions produced by improper dosage or other problems, the drugs that give the most trouble to elderly people are sedatives, digitalis drugs, diuretics, antihypertensives, antidepressants, and the major tranquilizers. The synergistic effects of combining alcohol with sleeping pills, tranquilizers, allergy medicines, or depressants produces stupor, coma, and even death in some cases.

***Physicians' Attitudes.***    One of the cornerstones of modern medicine is that the attitude of the patient plays a significant role in the progress of an illness. The attitude of the attending physician may also be crucial to the health of an elderly patient. Unfortunately, physicians and other health professionals tend to be significantly more negative in their attitudes toward treating elderly patients than toward treating younger people (Spence, Feigenbaum, Fitzgerald, & Roth, 1968). Butler (1975) noted that future physicians, whose first encounter with an older patient in medical school is in the form of a cadaver, may engage in gallows humor and refer to older patients as "crocks," "turkeys," and "dirtballs." In addition, Comfort (1976) reported knowing licensed physicians who ridiculed and humiliated older patients whom they viewed as insulting to their medical skills.

It is hoped that these attitudes are uncommon and changing, because the elderly average significantly more physician visits than persons under 65. In 1986, older Americans averaged nine visits to the doctor compared with an average of five visits for those under age 65 (American Association of Retired Persons, 1987). But even well-meaning physicians are sometimes inadvertently condescending to older patients, calling them by their first names and in other ways treating them as inferiors. Furthermore, doctors report having more difficulty in communicating with older patients and of insufficient time to treat them ("Docs Find. . . ," 1978). Rather than making time-consuming and expensive tests to evaluate the causes of an elderly patient's symptoms, the doctor may inaccurately diagnose the patient as ''senile.''

To some extent one may sympathize with doctors who find that treating elderly patients is less satisfying than treating younger patients. However, the problem of physician attitudes needs to be dealt with. Certainly, more adequate medical education designed to assist future physicians in dealing with elderly patients is a prescription with which Robert Butler and other geriatric physicians would undoubtedly concur. In addition, it would help if more medical students were attracted to geriatrics and family medicine as specialties. But geriatrics is both a difficult and unprofitable specialty, and specialists in family medicine usually prefer to work with younger patients who are more likely to get well and hence reward their efforts.

## Nursing Homes

Although a ''typical'' elderly person is not likely to be found in a nursing home, approximately 1.3 million older Americans reside in nursing home facilities (Peterson & Rosenblatt, 1986a). The great majority of these individuals are White, with Blacks and other minorities contributing a much smaller proportion of residents than their numbers in the general population might warrant. Approximately 70% of nursing home residents are women, the majority of whom suffer from cardiovascular diseases, cancer, or chronic brain disorders. They have been placed in these homes because they became disoriented and confused, wandered away from home, were incontinent, and/or in other ways manifested a need for extensive nursing care (Butler & Lewis, 1982).

Only about 5% of Americans over 65 reside in nursing homes at any given time, but when psychiatric and other extended care medical facilities are included over 20% of the elderly American population is institutionalized at some point (Kastenbaum & Candy, 1973). Some experts argue that 10%–15% of the elderly population should be placed in nursing homes, whereas others feel that only about 2% actually need this kind of care (Butler, 1975).

Although being placed in an institution, where new friends are made and competition is not so keen, can occasionally restore a person's taste for life (de Beauvoir, 1972), being moved to the new surroundings with new people usually creates problems of adjustment. Institutional conditions that must be adjusted to include a lack of privacy, new rules and regulations, staff and roommates or floormates of different background from one's own, and being cut off from friends and relatives on the outside.

The reputation of nursing homes as being ''houses of death'' comes from the high mortality rate in these institutions. Up to 20% of all deaths among elderly Americans occur in nursing homes (Kastenbaum & Candy, 1973), frequently during the first weeks or months of residence; over one third of the residents die within the first year. In fact, doctors and nurses often make little or no effort or take no "heroic measures" to prolong the lives of terminally ill patients, simply letting them die (Brown & Thompson, 1979).

One factor related to survival in a nursing home is the attitude of the patient. A depressed attitude suggests a poor prognosis, and an angry or hostile attitude a good prognosis for living more than a few months after admission (Ferrare, 1962). A related variable is the degree of control that the patient feels he or she has over the situation: Patients who feel that they can exert some control over the environment tend to have more positive attitudes and hence tend to survive longer.

Illustrative of the relationship between degree of control and the attitudes of patients are the results of an experiment by Langer and Rodin (1976). The subjects, nursing home patients between the ages of 65 and 90, were divided into three groups. The home administrator told the members of one group (experimental group) that they still had a great deal of control over their own lives and should therefore decide how to spend their time. For example, they were encouraged to decide whether or not they wanted to see a movie that was being shown and were given the responsibility of taking care of a plant. A second (comparison) group of patients was assured that the nursing home staff was concerned about their well-being, but the patients were not encouraged to assume greater control over their own lives. They were told that the staff would inform them when to see the movie, and although they were also given a plant they were told that the nurses would take care of it. A third (control) group of patients was given no special treatment. Subsequent ratings of the happiness, alertness, and activity of the residents were obtained from the nurses and the residents themselves. The results revealed significant increases in the happiness, alertness, and activity of the experimental group, whereas the ratings of the comparison group on these variables declined. Follow-up data obtained 18 months later (Rodin & Langer, 1977) showed even more impressive results. Not only did the patients in the experimental group continue to be more vigorous, sociable, and self-initiating than those in the comparison and control groups, but the death rate in the first group was only half that of the other two groups.

As the results of these investigations suggest, the deaths of nursing home patients and other ill or otherwise desperate people are sometimes attributable to feelings of helplessness, hopelessness, and simply "giving up." For example, being forced to move from a more familiar environment to a less familiar one, such as a different hospital ward or institution, is commonly associated with increased rates of illness and mortality in elderly people (see Report 3.3).

Despite a general reputation for being unpleasant and dehumanizing, nursing homes vary greatly in facilities and care that is offered. On the one extreme are the large, proprietary homes of a "tender-loving greed" character, and on the other are small convalescent homes run by religious organizations. Some homes resemble prisons, whereas others are more like country clubs. Some homes are

Report 3.3    PARASYMPATHETIC DEATH IN A PSYCHIATRIC
HOSPITAL*

A female patient who had remained in a mute stage for nearly 10 years was shifted to a different floor of her building along with her floor mates, while her unit was being redecorated. The third floor of this psychiatric unit where the patient in question had been living was known among the patients as the chronic, hopeless floor. In contrast, the first floor was most commonly occupied by patients who held privileges, including the freedom to come and go on the hospital grounds and to the surrounding streets. In short, the first floor was an exit ward from which patients could anticipate discharge fairly rapidly. All patients who were temporarily moved from the third floor were given medical examinations prior to the move, and the patient in question was judged to be in excellent medical health although still mute and withdrawn. Shortly after moving to the first floor, this chronic psychiatric patient surprised the ward staff by becoming socially responsive such that within a 2-week period she ceased being mute and was actually becoming gregarious. As fate would have it, the redecoration of the third-floor unit was soon completed and all previous residents were returned to it. Within a week after she had returned to the ''hopeless'' unit, this patient, who like the legendary Snow White had been aroused from a living torpor, collapsed and died. The subsequent autopsy revealed no pathology of note, and it was whimsically suggested at the time that the patient had died of despair.

*Source: Lefcourt, 1973, p. 422.

reminiscent of yesteryear's ''poorhouses,'' whereas residents in other homes pay as much as $3,000 a month or more (Brodzinsky, Gormly, & Ambron, 1986).

The quality of nursing homes depends to some degree on whether the home is a skilled nursing facility, an intermediate care facility, or a nonskilled institutional or private home facility. Los Angeles's Keiro (''Home for Respected Elders''), for example, is a nursing home in which members of the Japanese-American community have no misgivings about placing their aged parents. On the other hand, nursing care in many private homes is so poor that a number of experts have advocated replacing all existing private nursing homes with government-owned and professionally staffed facilities. People who entrust their parents to a nursing home should be concerned about such matters as nurse–patient ratio, the availability of creative facilities and physical therapy equipment, and the frequency of physicians' visits (Jacoby, 1974).

The federal government began paying for nursing home care through Medicaid in 1966, and the result has been quite profitable for many business people. Money invested in a private nursing home may yield 40% or more interest on one's investment in a single year. Unfortunately, the quality of the home typically fails to keep pace with investors' profits. Ideally, a nursing home should provide excellent medical and convalescent care in a homelike atmosphere. It should be run by a trained hospital administrator who recognizes the need for both liveliness and quietness, depending on the patient and the situation, and makes provisions for them. This picture is reportedly truer of homes in England, Holland, and Scandinavia than in the United States and many other Western countries, where institutions for the aged too often merit the title of "deathbed dormitories" (de Beauvoir, 1972; see Report 3.4).

Surveys by the National Academy of Sciences and the Senate Committee on Aging during the early 1980s found extensive abuses and inadequate care, and consequently a failure to meet federal standards, in a sizable percentage of nursing homes. In response to the survey findings, the Nursing Home Quality Reform Act was passed, establishing stricter federal standards for nursing homes and a patients' bill of rights. Not only does the Reform Act expand the authority of the Department of Health and Human Services to discipline nursing homes that violate federal standards, but it guarantees a patient's rights to privacy and to voice grievances and to have them addressed promptly. Patients are also guaranteed a role in selecting physicians and planning their medical care, as well as freedom from physical and mental abuse. More specifically, the Nursing Home Quality Reform Act gives residents and their families the following: the right to 30 days notice before a transfer; the right to up-to-date information on diagnosis, treatment, and prognosis; the right to a written explanation of services provided; the right to privacy in medical examinations and treatment; the right to privacy with visitors; the right to receive and send unopened mail and untapped telephone calls; and the right to present grievances to the state agency that protects the rights of nursing home residents (Freiberg, 1987).

Because of scandals involving nursing homes and the increased cost of institutional treatment, health care of the elderly has begun to move away from hospi-

---

**Report 3.4    A GRANDAUGHTER'S FIRST VISIT TO A NURSING HOME***

The smell of the place was so strong that I stepped back, trying to fight it off. . . . We stood for a moment looking at the recreation room. . . . A few of the residents chatted together. Several of them looked up hungrily at us, and one old lady in a wheelchair beckoned to me with a clawlike hand. Two bored attendants exchanged laconic comments, and a nurse in a starched white cap wiped the face of a sweating, palsied old man. A few old people had visitors, and, jealously guarding them in inescapable clusters of chairs, they leaned forward to grab onto every word. The visitors looked guilty and uncomfortable and miserably self-conscious.

After the visit in the car, my mother turned to me. The brittle smile was gone from her face and she looked exhausted. "Well, Deb, what did you think?" I looked out at the street. "It's awful," I said flatly. "It's horrible and ugly and smelly and I can't understand," my voice rose, "how you can let Gram be so miserable!" My mother turned her head slightly so I couldn't look directly into her eyes. My father glanced away from the icy street long enough to give Mom a look of compassion.

"We know, Deb," he said mildly. "We know. But there's really nothing else to do."

*After Saul, 1974, pp. 63, 68. Reproduced with permission.

tal-based and nursing home treatment to home health care, day-care centers, and preventive medicine clinics. These alternatives are potentially less costly than hospitals and nursing homes and are also less likely to foster feelings of depersonalization and dependency that occur so often among residents of institutions.

Among the alternatives to institutionalization that have been proposed is the multigenerational household. One investigator (Sussman, 1977) reported that members of 60% of the 365 households interviewed by him indicated that they would be willing to care for elderly relatives in their homes, particularly if the family were financially reimbursed. Only about 20% of the respondents stated that they would not accept an older person in their home under any circumstances, primarily because of a bad experience with an aged relative.

## Health Costs and Insurance

Compared with people under age 65, the elderly spend many more days in bed, visit doctors a greater number of times, have longer and more frequent stays in the hospital, and consume more medications. In 1984 expenditures represented by these activities averaged $4,202 per person for Americans 65 and over, compared with $1,300 for those under 65. Such costs would be impossible for the elderly and their families to meet without turning to federal and state governmental agencies for assistance (American Association of Retired Persons, 1987)

Expenditures for health care are the second largest item in the federal budget, outranking even appropriations for defense. In 1984, the federal government paid an estimated $59 billion for Medicare, $15 billion for Medicaid, and $7 billion for other health-care programs for the elderly. Be that as it may, these combined figures account for only 67% of the health-care costs for elderly Americans (American Association of Retired Persons, 1987).

The best-known and most widely applicable of the federal health-care programs benefiting the elderly are Medicare and Medicaid, both of which are administered by the Health Care Financing Administration. Medicare, which since 1966 has covered all people who are eligible for social security benefits (31 million Americans in 1987), is divided into two parts: Part A (Health Insurance for the Aged—Hospital Insurance) and Part B (Supplemental Medical Insurance). Part A, after a $400 deductible paid by the patient, covers the full cost of hospital care up to 60 days for any episode of an illness and all over $100 a day from the 61st to 90th day in the hospital. There is also a "lifetime reserve" of 60 days for more than 90 days of hospitalization, but the patient must pay $200 a day when using that reserve. Part A also pays for certain posthospitalization services, including up to 100 days in an extended care facility (20 days complete coverage, 80 days copayment of $50 per day).

Coverage under Part A of Medicare is automatic, being financed by a portion of the social security tax. But individuals must apply for Part B (Supplemental

Medical Insurance) and pay for it by a deduction from their social security checks. These premiums rose from $3 per month in 1966, when the program was instituted, to $24.80 per month in 1988. The premiums, however, take care of less than 30% of the cost of Part B; the federal government pays the remainder from general tax revenues. After a $75 deductible amount, Part B pays for 80% of the costs of outpatient physician services, certain types of therapy, home health services, and other services and supplies. Not covered are medical check-ups, prescription drugs, eyeglasses, dentures, and hearing aids.

Despite its apparent high cost, the Medicare program pays only about half the hospital and doctor bills of the elderly. The remainder comes from personal savings, private medical insurance, or other sources. Worried senior citizens, 55% of whom carry some sort of private medical insurance, sometimes pay for more insurance than they need. Added to the overhead costs and the profits made by private insurance companies, such unusable policies make the overall cost of insurance from private companies substantially higher than that from nonprofit agencies such as Blue Cross and Blue Shield.

Elderly poor people who cannot afford even the monthly premium of Part B of Medicare must look elsewhere for health-care funds. Medicaid (Medical Assistance Program), a comprehensive health-care program administered by local welfare departments using federal and state funds, was designed for just such people. Medicaid covers the same services and supplies as Medicare, in addition to drugs, eyeglasses, long-term care in licensed nursing homes, and other services depending on the particular state. Anyone who is eligible for old-age assistance or welfare is usually eligible for Medicaid, but the applicant must demonstrate a financial need ("means test").

There have been many criticisms of federal health-care programs for the elderly, by both the elderly themselves and health-care professionals. For example, older people often object to the requirement that they pay the first $75 and 20% of the remaining portion of their medical expenses in each calendar year. Furthermore, people who cannot afford Part B of Medicare may be humiliated by the Medicaid "means test." Health-care professionals may object to the paperwork involved in filing health insurance claims, government "control" of medical services, and the Medicare definition of "reasonable charge." Both doctors and patients may object to the apparent unfairness of other Medicare provisions. As an illustration, when an elderly patient who has been hospitalized with an acute medical condition (e.g., a broken leg) is transferred to a nursing home for convalescence, Medicare will pay most of the bill. But when he or she is sent directly home or judged unlikely to recover, Medicare will pay none of the posthospitalization bill. Furthermore, Medicare does not cover the cost of spectacles, dental work, hearing aids, foot care, or drugs prescribed outside the hospital. Many elderly patients learn, however, that even when only part of a claim is paid initially by Medicare, filing an appeal will often result in at least a portion of the unpaid balance being reimbursed (Porter, 1980).

In an attempt to control the costs of health care, a payment system for hospital charges based on 23 major diagnostic categories divided into 467 Diagnostic Related Groups (DRGs) was implemented by Medicare in 1983. The 23 diagnostic groups represent the major organs of the body; the DRGs derived from these groups are differentiated according to principal diagnosis, procedures usually performed, secondary diagnosis, discharge disposition, and age of the patient. Hospital reimbursement under Medicare is determined by the average length of stay and the treatment procedures employed, as indicated by the DRG category in which the patient was placed. Unfortunately, it has been alleged that the DRG system is self-defeating: Patients are leaving the hospital more quickly, but the costs of hospital readmission and nursing home care cancel out the savings from discharging patients "quicker but sicker" (Atchley, 1987).

Added to the ever-increasing cost of medical bills, the criticisms and shortcomings of the current system indicate a need for other changes in the federal government's approach to health care for the elderly. Particularly debilitating, both financially and physically, are catastrophic and long-term illnesses. During the late 1980s, Congress and the Reagan Administration were attempting to reach agreement on a bill that would put a ceiling on out-of-pocket cost to the patient of short-term catastrophic illness. Another bill that would provide long-term, home-based care, which is much less costly than nursing home residency, was also being considered by Congress.

Whatever legislative changes occur in Medicare, it is hoped that they represent simplifications rather than an ever-increasing complexity of its provisions. Even more ambitious changes in the health-care system in the United States are foreseen by Robert Butler (1975), who maintains that current federal programs will eventually be extended to some form of national health insurance. Beyond national health insurance, Butler envisages that it may even be necessary for medicine in the United States to become a public utility. Although Butler's vision will probably go unrealized for a while, during the coming decades more emphasis will certainly be placed on preventive medicine and perhaps less emphasis on organ transplants and other spectacular medical achievements that make headlines but cost a great deal of money while benefiting relatively few people.

## SUMMARY

Disease and disability are related not only to age, but to sex, socioeconomic status, and ethnicity as well. Although the maximum life span has not increased significantly during the present century, the disorders that are the most common causes of death have changed. Many infectious diseases, such as influenza, pneumonia, and tuberculosis, which took a heavy toll of lives earlier in the century, have been relegated to lower lethality ranks. Less progress, however, has been made in conquering cardiovascular disorders and cancer. Furthermore, with extended life expectancy, more people are now reaching old age and suffering from various chronic disorders associated with this period of life. The most common chronic illnesses in old age are arthritis, respiratory disorders, digestive and eliminative problems, and osteoporosis. Osteoporosis, a gradual loss of bone mass which is four times as common in women as in men, can lead to painful fractures of the spine, hips, ribs, wrists, and other bones. Traffic accidents and falls also contribute to substantial numbers of injuries and deaths among older people.

Heart diseases, cancer, and stroke are the three most prominent killers of older people. Obesity, lack of exercise, heavy smoking, psychological stress, and high blood cholesterol level are all related to the incidence of cardiovascular disorders. Great strides have been made in treating heart disease, and there is evidence that its incidence is declining. Progress in the treatment of cancer has not been as dramatic, but cancer research continues and knowledge is accumulating.

Organic brain damage in old age is caused by cerebral arteriosclerosis, tumors, CVAs, and age-related changes in brain tissue and neurons. The two major categories of senile dementia are multi-infarct dementia and Alzheimer's disease. The former is associated with localized areas of dying or dead brain tissue (infarcts), and the latter with the presence of senile plaques, neurofibrillary tangles, and degenerated neurons in the brain. Among the psychological symptoms of organic brain damage are confusion, disorientation, difficulty assimilating new experiences, incoherence, restlessness, childish emotionality, and sometimes self-centeredness and hallucinations. Disturbances of memory, abstract thinking, judgment, and impulse control are observed in multiinfarct dementia. In Alzheimer's disease, cognitive functions (memory, judgment, abstract thinking ability), personality and behavior deteriorate gradually over time. A great deal of research is currently being conducted on Alzheimer's disease, but the cause(s) and effective treatment(s) of this disorder remain uncertain.

Preventive health measures recommended for elderly people include regular exercise, good nutrition, judicious usage of both prescribed and nonprescribed drugs, periodic medical checkups by a physician who has a positive attitude toward older patients, and freedom from severe psychological stress. Unfortunately, lack of exercise, poor nutrition, drug abuse, and treatment by unsupportive physicians are all too common in later life. Nutrition programs for the elderly such as "Meals on Wheels" have been prompted by the recognition that many older people are unable or unwilling to eat nutritionally balanced meals.

The quality of nursing homes and other extended care facilities for elderly Americans varies greatly and is a source of continuing national concern. A number of alternatives to institutional care have been proposed, including home health care, day-care centers, and preventive medicine clinics. At the very least, closer supervision of the facilities, staff, and practices of nursing homes needs to be maintained and corrective measures applied by official agencies.

Despite billions of dollars appropriated each year by the federal government for Medicare and Medicaid, medical and dental bills continue to deplete the savings and income of many elderly people. Combined with the ever-increasing cost of health care, the complexity and apparent inequity of many Medicare provisions necessitates continued reevaluation and effective change.

## SUGGESTED READINGS

Avioli, L. V. (1986, February). Osteoporosis: A guide to detection. *Modern Medicine,* pp. 28–42.

Bierman, E. L. (1985). Aging and atherosclerosis. In R. Andres, E. L. Bierman, & W. R. Hazzard (Eds.), *Principles of geriatric medicine* (pp. 42–50). New York: McGraw-Hill.

Gerstenblith, G. M., Weisfeldt, L., & Lakatta, E. G. (1985). Disorders of the heart. In R. Andres, E. L. Bierman, & W. R. Hazzard (Eds.), *Principles of geriatric medicine* (pp. 525–526). New York: McGraw-Hill.

Jokl, E. (1983). Physical activity and aging. *Annals of Sports Medicine, 1*(2), 43–48.

Kannel, W. B., & Brand, F. N. (1985). Cardiovascular risk factors in the elderly. In R. Andres, E. L. Bierman, & W. R. Hazzard (Eds.), *Principles of geriatric medicine* (pp. 104–119). New York: McGraw-Hill.

Rowe, J. W. (1985, March 28). Health care of the elderly. *The New England Journal of Medicine, 312,* 827–835.

Salzman, R. T. (1983). Management of rheumatoid arthritis and osteoarthritis. *American Journal of Medicine, 75*(48), 91.

Siegler, I. C., & Costa, P. T., Jr. (1985). Health behavior relationships. In J. E. Birren & K. W. Schaie (Eds.), *Handbook of the psychology of aging* (2nd ed., pp. 144–166). New York: Van Nostrand Reinhold.

Sloane, B. (1983). Health care: Physical and mental. In D. S. Woodruff & J. E. Birren (Eds.), *Aging: Scientific perspectives and social issues* (pp. 306–332). Monterey, CA: Brooks/Cole.

# 4

# *Mental Abilities*

A popular view of old age is that of a time when abilities decline, activities are more restricted, and dependence on others becomes necessary. A common belief is that older people have poor memories, cannot think clearly, and experience a general decline in mentality. Sensory and motor abilities usually show some decrement in old age, but as we see here, mental abilities do not deteriorate quite so rapidly. In any event, judgment and wisdom can compensate for the losses in physical and mental abilities that do occur. Many very old people remain independent and active almost until the time of death, adapting successfully and maintaining their mental alertness and capabilities.

## CREATIVITY

Evidence that creative productivity does not necessarily decline in old age can be found in the lives of famous artists, scholars, and scientists. Pianist Artur Rubinstein was still playing brilliantly at age 89, some say with greater sensitivity and skill than ever. Many well-known geniuses, such as Pablo Picasso, Thomas Edison, and Luther Burbank, continued their highly creative endeavors into the ninth decade of life. Giuseppe Verdi produced the joyous, exuberant opera "Falstaff" at age 80, and Justice Oliver Wendell Holmes, Jr. formulated many of his most impressive legal opinions while in his 90s.

> Cato learned Greek at eighty; Sophocles
> Wrote his grand Oedipus, and Simonides
> Bore off the prize of verse from his compeers,

When each had numbered more than four score years.
And Theophrastus, at four score and ten
Had just begun his *Characters of Men.*
Chaucer, at Woodstock with the nightingales,
At sixty wrote the Canterbury Tales;
Goethe at Weimar, toiling to the last,
Completed Faust when eighty years were past.

—Longfellow, *Morituri Salutamus*

Older people learn new things, develop new skills, and may become truly creative for the first time during later life. Grandma Moses was 73 when she started painting, and held her first exhibition at age 80. By the time of her death at 101 she had achieved international fame as an artist. One may argue, however, that she was an exception, and that creative performance typically peaks much sooner than old age.

In one of the earliest scientific studies of the relationship of age to creativity, Lehman (1953) found that the period of peak productivity among artists was 30 to 39 years and that productivity declined thereafter. A similar pattern of an early peak and a decline with age was also found in a sample of scientists (Lehman, 1962, 1966). Likewise, chess masters tend to reach a performance peak in their 30s, although they typically show little decline until their 50s. A dramatic illustration of a persistently high level of mental functioning in chess is that the chess master Blackburne, who gave nine exhibitions between the ages of 76 and 79, averaging 21 games at each exhibition and winning 86% of them (Buttenwieser, 1935; see Report 4.1).

One difficulty with Lehman's (1953) conclusion that creativity usually peaks in the 20s and 30s is that many of the people whom he studied died when they were still fairly young. This circumstance produced a bias favoring early peak creativity, a methodological shortcoming that Dennis (1966) attempted to correct. In a study of 738 people who lived to age 79 or beyond, Dennis (1966) collected comparative longitudinal data on the productivity of three major groups: scholars, scientists, and artists (art, music, and literature). He found that although people in the fine arts and literature tended to produce more in their 20s than scholars and scientists, the period of greatest productivity for all three groups was in their 40s or shortly thereafter. The performance of scholars declined little after age 40, but the output of artists and scientists decreased appreciably after age 60. Similar findings pertaining to the creative productivity of scientific researchers were reported by Cole (1979). Using the number of research papers published during a particular 5-year span as a measure of productivity and how often each paper had been cited as a measure of quality, Cole found that chronological age had a curvilinear relationship with both productivity and quality in samples of chemists, geologists, mathematicians, physicists, psychologists, and sociologists. Productivity and quality for these scientists peaked in their early 40s, being lower at both earlier and later ages. Although important

---

Report 4.1    AT AGE 75, CHESS MASTER IS STILL A BLINDFOLDED WHIZ*

Chess master George Koltanowski set a world's record Saturday in San Francisco—at age 75—by playing and beating four opponents at once without looking at the boards.

Koltanowski, the chess editor of The Chronicle, thus became the oldest player to hold what chess players call a blindfold simultaneous exhibition.

His four opponents had full use of chessmen and boards as they called their moves out in turn to the master, who sat in a corner of his apartment with his eyes shut and his arm propped on a television.

The first player was checkmated in 13 moves and the other three resigned shortly thereafter. Mike Duncan of San Mateo lasted 26 moves before moving his rook to the wrong square and falling into a trap.

"I knew I'd lose," said Duncan, "but it's fascinating to find out just when the blow is going to come."

Koltanowski said he was nervous before the exhibition began but, as his opponents began to slip up, he sat back, cracked an occasional joke and nibbled cookies.

"It was like the good old days," said the master, who, in 1937, took on 34 opponents in a simultaneous blindfold exhibition in Scotland, winning 24 games and drawing ten.

"I'm back on the warpath," he added. "Next month I'm going to play six at once."

His wife, Leah, who witnessed the exhibition but who does not know how to play chess, smiled when asked if Koltanowski remembers such things as bringing home items from the market.

"George remembers what he wants to remember," she said.

*From San Francisco Chronicle, Feb. 26, 1979, p. 39. © San Francisco Chronicle, 1979. Reprinted by permission.

---

breakthroughs in mathematics and science are often associated with people in their 20s, the output of ordinary scientists such as those studied by Cole appears to remain stable in quantity and quality through their early 40s at least.

Differences in the period of peak productivity of various groups depend on individual creativity, as well as on the length of the training period. Productivity in the arts seems to depend more on individual creativity than experience and therefore peaks early. On the other hand, creative performance in scholarly or scientific endeavors requires a longer period of preparation and training and consequently shows a later peak.

The results of the aforementioned studies and the examples of numerous creative people indicate that creative performance is not limited to a particular chronological age range. Given adequate ability, good health, sufficient encouragement, and an opportunity, a person can be creative at any age. However, potentially creative people who are not properly stimulated or rewarded, or who are not provided with a chance to demonstrate their abilities, will, all too often, settle into a routine existence in which their potentials remain unfulfilled and may even deteriorate. Only a society that recognizes the wide variations in individuals, regardless of age, and provides opportunities for these differences to be manifested can hope to make optimal use of its older citizens.

## MEASUREMENT AND CHANGES OF INTELLIGENCE WITH AGE

In addition to curiosity, motivation, and flexibility, an extremely important factor in creativity at any age is mental ability. Of the many efforts made by psychologists to measure general and specific mental abilities, research and applications in the area of intelligence testing have been in the forefront. Unlike creative performance, which is actually a criterion variable, measures of general intelligence and specific mental abilities have been used primarily as predictors of future performance. The instruments employed to measure these variables attempt to assess maximum mental performance—what a person is capable of achieving with adequate motivation and opportunity.

### Wechsler Adult Intelligence Scale

Traditional intelligence tests, which are loaded with school-type tasks, were not designed originally to assess the abilities of older people. Early tests such as the Stanford–Binet Intelligence Scale were directed primarily at school-age children, the major purpose of the tests being to determine the abilities of children to profit from scholastic work. The first individual tests of intelligence constructed specifically for adults were the Wechsler Bellevue Intelligence Tests, published originally in 1939 and revised as the Wechsler Adult Intelligence Scale (WAIS) in 1955 and the Wechsler Adult Intelligence Scale-Revised (WAIS-R) in 1981.

The WAIS-R, which consists of 11 subtests and is scored for Verbal, Performance, and Full Scale intelligence quotients (IQs), was standardized on nine carefully selected age groups of "normal" American adults: 16–17, 18–19, 20–24, 25–34, 35–44, 45–54, 55–64, 65–69, and 70–74-year-olds. The sample in each age category was stratified by sex, geographic region, ethnicity (White vs. nonWhite), education, and occupation. The standardization of the WAIS-R, with respect to older adults, was a distinct improvement over that of its predecessor in that the samples of older adults were more representative of the respective age groups in the U.S. population.

In scoring the WAIS-R, raw scores on each subtest are converted to scaled scores based on the performance of the 25- to 34-year age group. Scaled scores on the six Verbal subtests are then summed to yield a "sum of Verbal scaled scores," scaled scores on the five Performance subtests are summed to yield a "sum of Performance scaled scores," and the Verbal and Performance scaled score sums are added to yield a "Total sum of scaled scores." Finally, the three

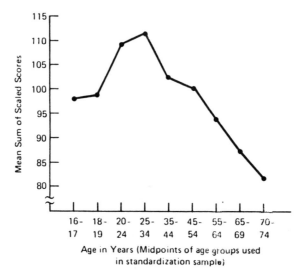

FIG. 4.1.   Decline in WAIS-R Full Scale scaled scores across age cohorts. (From Anastasi, 1988; Data from Wechsler Adult Intelligence Scale-Revised. Copyright © 1981, 1955 by The Psychological Corporation. Reprinted by permission. All rights reserved.)

scaled score sums are converted to "age-adjusted" IQs by referring to an age table in the WAIS-R manual. These "age-adjusted" IQs do not give a clear picture of changes in test performance with age, but a plot of the mean Total sum of scaled scores against age is more revealing. Figure 4.1 shows that these scores increase until the 25 to 34 year age range and then decline markedly through ages 70–74. Data such as these are the source of the much-discussed age decline in intelligence.

## Testing Older Adults

With the exception of the WAIS-R, the Schaie–Thurstone Mental Abilities Test (STAMAT), and one or two other instruments, intelligence tests norms have been inadequate for interpreting the performance of older adults. In addition to difficulties of score interpretation caused by inadequate norms, there are special problems in administering intelligence tests to older people. To begin with, older people, whose behavior is less susceptible to control by psychologists and educators, are frequently reluctant to be tested. Among the reasons for the uncooperativeness of elderly examinees are: lack of time, perception of the test tasks as trivial or meaningless, and fear of doing badly or appearing foolish (Welford, 1958). Older adults, to an even greater extent than more test-conscious younger adults, do not relish performing tasks that make them appear stupid or that they perceive as having no bearing on their affairs. They are also more susceptible to external distractions and fatiguing test materials.

Because of the lower motivation of the elderly to be tested, it obviously requires sensitivity and tact on the part of psychological examiners to obtain valid responses from persons in this age group. Unfortunately, it is often questionable whether a technically proficient but young examiner can establish sufficient rapport with an elderly examinee to communicate the test directions adequately and stimulate the examinee to do his or her best (Fletcher, 1972). Relatively few mental testers possess sufficient training and experience in psychological examination of the elderly to do a credible job. Most examiners find, however, that once elderly examinees have agreed to be tested, they are just as cooperative and motivated to do well as are younger examinees (Welford, 1958). They are, however, usually not as "testwise" as younger adults, who have had greater and more recent experience with tests than their senior contemporaries.

Even when older examinees try to do their best, the time limitations on tests, the presence of sensory defects, and the distractibility and easy fatigability of many elderly people make it difficult for them to perform satisfactorily. For example, one of the most characteristic things about being older is that one's reflexes and physical movements tend to slow down. For this reason, explanations of the declining scores of the elderly on tests of learning and memory must take into account the fact that most older people do not respond as rapidly as younger people. Although older people are usually at a disadvantage on timed tests, their performance improves significantly when they are given sufficient time in which to react. Consequently, the aged show little or no inferiority in comparison with younger people on untimed tests.

Sensory defects, especially in the visual and auditory modalities, can also interfere with performance in old age. Special test materials such as large-face type and experienced examiners who are alert to the presence of sensory defects can be of help. Occasionally, however, an alleged sensory defect may actually be a mask for a problem in reading and auditory comprehension. The author has had the experience of preparing to test an elderly man who, according to his wife, was embarrassed by his poor reading ability and therefore conveniently "forgot" his glasses and was unable to read the test materials.

Assuming that all goes well with the test procedure, the examiner must still avoid confusing scholastic intelligence with everyday mental functioning. The questions on the WAIS-R, for example, are concerned in large measure with academic subjects and are not especially relevant to the knowledge and interests of older people. Many older (and younger) people who do poorly on intelligence tests manage to cope satisfactorily with the demands of daily living. From a practical standpoint, how well a person functions in everyday life is the best indicator of his or her abilities. This fact had led some authorities to suggest that intelligence tests would be more valid for older examinees if the items consisted of problem situations specific to the lives of this age group.

Because the materials and method of administration affect performance on a test, more extensive research needs to be conducted to determine the effects of adjusting the test materials and administration procedure to the characteristics of the elderly. Whether or not such adjustments are advisable depends on what is being measured and the context in which the test results are interpreted. For example, timed tests measure different functions and serve different purposes from untimed tests. It seems reasonable, however, that special procedures of test administration, coupled with sensitivity and patience on the part of the examiner, can afford a better opportunity for elderly examinees to demonstrate their capabilities. Among these suggested procedures, which have been adapted from well-known instructional techniques, are (Aiken, 1980, p. 123):

1. Provide ample time for the examinee to respond to the test material.
2. Allow sufficient practice on sample items.
3. Use shorter testing periods than with younger adults.
4. Watch out for fatigue and take it into consideration.
5. Be aware of and make provisions for visual, auditory, and other sensory defects.
6. Arrange for the examination room to be as free as possible from distractions.
7. Employ a generous amount of encouragement and positive reinforcement.
8. Do not overstress or force examinees to respond to test items when they repeatedly decline to do so.

## Cross-Sectional and Longitudinal Studies of Age Changes in Intelligence

Conclusions from earlier studies of changes in general intelligence with age were almost always based on cross-sectional data (Doppelt & Wallace, 1955; Jones & Conrad, 1933; Yerkes, 1921). From his analysis of scores on the Army Examination Alpha administered to American soldiers during World War I, Yerkes (1921) found that average scores on this early group-administered test of intelligence declined steadily from the late teens through the sixth decade of life. In another early study, Jones and Conrad (1933) administered the Army Alpha to 1,200 New Englanders between the ages of 10 and 60 years. The general form of the curve relating mental ability to age in this investigation was a linear increase in scores from age 10 to 16, followed by a gradual decline to the 14-year level by age 55. Wechsler's (1958) analysis of the relationship of age to mean Full Scale scores on the Wechsler–Bellevue Form I reinforced these findings: Mean standard scores peaked in late adolescence, remained fairly constant from that point until the late 20s or early 30s, and subsequently showed a steady decline through old age.

The problems encountered in attempting to interpret the results of cross-sectional studies were discussed in chapter 1. Cross-sectional investigations compare people of different cohorts, that is, groups of people brought up in different sociocultural milieus. Differences among cohorts in factors such as educational opportunity, which is closely related to intelligence test scores, make it difficult to match people of different ages. Consequently, it is impossible to compare different age groups on intelligence without the confounding effects of education and other test-related experiences.

The steady rise in the average educational and socioeconomic levels of Americans during the current century must be taken into account when interpreting the apparent age decline in mental abilities. Because intelligence test scores are positively related to both educational level and socioeconomic status, it is understandable how older adults, who grew up during less intellectually stimulating times and had less formal education, might make significantly lower test scores than younger adults. Several longitudinal investigations have found that, although intelligence test scores tend to remain fairly stable or to decrease slightly after early adulthood, in some cases they may increase. It can be argued that because longitudinal studies of intelligence have most often been conducted on college graduates or other intellectually favored groups, the age-related changes do not necessarily apply to the general population (Bayley & Oden, 1955; Campbell, 1965; Nisbet, 1957; Owens, 1953, 1966). However, longitudinal investigations with people of average intelligence (Charles & James, 1964; Eisdorfer, 1963; Tuddenham, Blumenkrantz, & Wilkin, 1968) and with noninstitutionalized mentally retarded adults (Baller, Charles, & Miller, 1967; Bell & Zubek, 1960) have yielded similar findings. Botwinick (1977) interpreted these results as suggesting that intelligence continues to increase by small amounts during early adulthood and reaches a plateau between the ages of 25 and 30. Subsequently, people who are below average or fail to use their abilities decline somewhat in intelligence, but individuals of above-average intelligence show no decline or may even improve until age 50. Although the results of both cross-sectional and longitudinal studies reveal substantial declines in mental abilities during the 70s and 80s, Baltes and Schaie (1974) found that such abilities may continue to increase even after age 70. As these findings make clear, intellectual decline with aging is by no means inevitable, varying with the task and the individual.

## Psychosocial and Biological Variables

Whether a rise or fall in mental ability is observed during later life appears to depend on the kinds of experiences relevant to test performance that a person has during the adult years. Poor health, lack of education, slower responding, and personality variables such as greater cautiousness and anxiety, can also hinder the intellectual performance of older people (Reese & Rodeheaver, 1985). With respect to test experience, Wesman (1968) argued that older adults are not necessarily less intelligent than younger adults simply because the former sometimes do poorly on tests designed for the latter. Older adults may possess highly specialized knowledge and abilities not covered by conventional intelligence tests, abilities that enable them to be more competent than younger adults in dealing with the problems of everyday living.

Unfortunately, skills that older people can perform as proficiently as they did when they were young may have become obsolete in a rapidly changing, technologically based society. What is required, however, is not merely sympathy for elderly people whose cognitive abilities are outmoded or inadequate but retraining and compensatory education that will enable such individuals to function more effectively. Research by Schaie and Willis (1986a) suggests that it is possible to arrest, or even reverse, declines in mental functioning through special training and changes in attitude. This is a topic to which we return later in the chapter.

Experiential variables such as social isolation resulting from retirement, the deaths of family members and friends, and the increased "interiority" or withdrawal associated with old age can have a pronounced effect on functioning intelligence in later life. In addition, biological variables such as heredity, nutrition, and health affect intelligence. Studies of people in their 70s, 80s, and 90s have found a higher correlation between health and intelligence than between age and intelligence (Birren, Cunningham, & Yamamoto, 1983; Palmore, 1970; Schaie & Gribbin, 1975). Generally speaking, brighter people are healthier in old age and live longer than the less bright. It has also been suggested that the relationship between mental ability and health in old age may be reflective of personality adjustment, with better-adjusted people being both brighter and healthier (Neugarten, 1976).

One health-related factor that affects only a small percentage of older people but interferes with efficiency of intellectual functioning is chronic brain syndrome (Ben-Yishay, Diller, Mandelberg, Gordon, & Gertsman, 1971; Overall & Gorham, 1972). A more common condition is high blood pressure (hypertension), which may be accompanied by cardiovascular disease and stroke. The effects of chronic cardiovascular disease on mental functioning in old age has been demonstrated in a number of research investigations (e.g., Hertzog, Schaie, & Gribbin, 1978). And a serious stroke, which is related to insufficient oxygen flow to the brain, can affect both intellectual functioning and the motor skills required for speaking and walking.

The results of an investigation by Wilkie and Eisdorfer (1971) suggest that when intelligence does decline during old age, it may be caused not by aging itself but rather by high blood pressure. Over a 10-year period, these researchers observed 202 men and women in their 60s and 70s. The participants were divided into three groups according to their blood pressure—normal, borderline, and high—and were given a complete battery of psychological tests. The functional relationship between blood pressure and intellectual changes was seen by the end of the 10th year to be complex. Participants whose blood pressure was normal showed no significant changes in intelligence, whereas those with high blood pressure showed a drop of almost 10 points on the intelligence test. The test scores of the third group, those with borderline blood pressure, actually increased by an average of several points. The last finding was interpreted as support for the theory that slightly elevated blood pressure is needed to maintain good circulation in the brains of older people.

In addition to hypertension and cardiovascular disease, emphysema, acute infection, poor nutrition, injuries, and surgery can temporarily or permanently affect intelligence in later life by reducing the blood supply to the brain. Decreases in the speed and accuracy with which information is transmitted, coded, and stored in the brain occurs with aging of neurons in the central nervous system. "Loss of neuronal tissue, change in the metabolic rate of the brain, loss of circulatory capacity, all lead to a level of primary change (in intellectual and cognitive function)" (Eisdorfer, 1969, p. 247). According to Horn (1982), these biological changes take place gradually during adulthood as a person ages and place limits on intellectual functioning.

With respect to remediation of intellectual decline, there is evidence for a causal connection between physical exercise and intelligence. In one investigation, a battery of cognitive tests was administered to groups of young and old men before and after they participated in a program of physical exercise. Significant increases were found for both groups on measures of "fluid ability" but not on measures of "crystallized ability" (Elsayed, Ismail, & Young, 1980).

## Schaie Versus Horn: The Debate Continues

Deciding whether the research evidence permits any firm conclusions regarding the alleged decline in intelligence during later life is not a simple matter. There is some, although not necessarily marked, disagreement among psychologists such as John Horn and Warner Schaie regarding the magnitude, quality, and generality of age changes in intelligence. For example, Horn and Donaldson (1976) concluded that decrements in at least some of the important abilities constituting intelligence are likely to occur if one lives long enough. In fact, Horn maintained that intelligence may begin declining as early as the 20s and 30s.

Schaie (1983) recognized that there are differences between the mental abilities of older and younger adults, but he felt that such differences are related more to variations in the experiences of young and old cohorts than to age or time of measurement. Although some age-related decline does occur, Schaie believed that it is much less than Horn and his colleagues have asserted. To Schaie, the existence of interindividual variations in intelligence and its growth and decline, together with its multidimensionality, modifiability, and the interaction between age and cohort, lead to the conclusion that intelligence is a very plastic variable. He pointed out that a favorable environment, one with varied opportunities for intellectual stimulation and the maintenance of a flexible lifestyle, can help to maintain a high level of functioning intelligence in later life (Schaie, 1983; Schaie & Hertzog, 1986). Schaie recommended that, rather than simply becoming resigned to the seeming fixity or inevitable decline of intelligence in later life, psychologists should devote more attention to the subject of changing intelligence in a changing world and make an effort to modify cognitive behavior.

## Terminal Drop

An apparent exception to the conclusion that intellectual abilities do not invariably decline in old age is a phenomenon referred to as the *terminal drop*. The terminal drop is a decline in mental functioning (IQ, memory, cognitive organization), sensorimotor abilities such as reaction time, and personality characteristics such as assertiveness during the last few months or years of life. Prompting the initial research on the terminal drop was the claim made by a nurse in a home for the aged that she could predict which patients were going to die soon merely by observing that they "seem to act differently" (Lieberman, 1965). Subsequent research findings revealed declines in various areas of cognitive and sensorimotor functioning and general ability to cope with environmental demands in patients who died within a year after being tested (Granick & Patterson, 1972; Lieberman & Coplan, 1969; Reimanis & Green, 1971; Riegel & Riegel, 1972). Studies of deceased men who had participated in the Duke University longitudinal studies of aging found no terminal drop on tests of physical functioning, but scores on intelligence tests tended to drop sharply a few months or years before death (Palmore, 1982; Palmore & Cleveland, 1976; Siegler, McCarty, & Logue, 1982). The terminal drop was more likely to occur on nonspeeded tests such as vocabulary than on speeded tests of a perceptual or problem-solving nature. On the other hand, patients who did not show such declines in intellectual functioning and behavior did not die until a significantly longer period after being tested.

To the extent that it is genuine and not merely an artifact of inadequate research methodology (Palmore & Cleveland, 1976), a terminal drop in cognitive functioning is probably caused by cerebrovascular and other physiological changes during the terminal phase of life. Lieberman (1965) also noted that people who are approaching death become more preoccupied with themselves, not because of any conceit or egocentricity, but rather as a desperate effort to keep from falling apart psychologically. Realizing that they are no longer able to organize and integrate complex sensory inputs efficiently and cannot cope with environmental demands adequately, they may experience feelings of chaos and impending doom and be less willing or able to exert themselves to perform up to their potential on psychological tests.

## Specific Mental Abilities

General intelligence tests measure a combination of several mental abilities, and the pattern of change in performance with age depends on the specific ability being measured. For example, cross-sectional data reveal that scaled scores on the Verbal subtests of the Wechsler Adult Intelligence Scale remain fairly constant but that scaled scores on the Performance subtests decrease significantly with age (Wechsler, 1958). The findings of other cross-sectional studies are similar: Scores on vocabulary and information tests typically show no appreciable changes with aging, but perceptual-integrative abilities and comprehension of numerical symbols decline more rapidly.[1]

A frequently cited longitudinal study of age changes in mental abilities was conducted by Owens (1953), who compared the Army Examination Alpha scores of a group of middle-aged men with their performance on the same test 30 years earlier. It was found that the men scored higher in middle age than as youths on every Army Alpha subtest except arithmetic. The results of related investigations lead to the conclusion that an older person's verbal ability remains fairly constant and may even improve as long as he or she is in good health. Experience undoubtedly plays a role in determining which abilities decline and which do not: well-rehearsed verbal abilities involving vocabulary usage and verbal comprehension show little or no decrease with age (Arenberg, 1973).

As one ages it may become increasingly more difficult to understand new ideas, make complex decisions, master new concepts, or solve laboratory-type problems. But whether these changes are due to a decline in mental aptitude, the interfering effects of prior learning, physical and mental inactivity, loss of motivation to perform various tasks, or some other factor is not clear. Gergen and Back (1966) maintained that as a result of a limited time perspective, old people prefer short-range to long-range solutions to problems. Furthermore, the limited time perspective of the elderly may be accompanied by a limited space perspective, in which individuals consider only those factors that are physically close to them.

Also related to problem solving is the shift in sex differences in some abilities with aging. The superiority of young men to young women on laboratory-type problems undergoes a change with aging, in that there is no sex difference in this skill during the 50s and women are superior to men in the 60s (Young, 1971). In fact, the data point to a greater overall age-related decline in the mental abilities

---

[1]An exception is the task of detecting a simple figure in a complex one, a skill that appears to improve with age.

of men than in those of women (Neugarten, 1976). However, just how much of this difference is due to the highly verbal nature of the tests employed is not clear. Certainly, throughout the life span males tend to score lower than females on verbal-type tasks.

The most comprehensive studies of the differential effects of aging on mental abilities have been conducted by Schaie and his associates (Baltes & Schaie, 1974; Schaie, 1983; Schaie & Labouvie-Vief, 1974, Schaie & Strother, 1968). The results of the investigation by Schaie and Strother (1968), which employed both cross-sectional and longitudinal research methods, are illustrated in Fig. 4.2. Fifty people in each 5-year age interval from 20 to 70 years were tested with the SRA Mental Abilities Test, and as many as could be located were retested 7 years later. The results varied with specific abilities, but some decline was noted using both cross-sectional and longitudinal approaches. Figure 4.2 indicates that the cross-sectional approach revealed the greatest decline in abilities with aging, and the decline began at an earlier age than with the longitudinal approach.

A later longitudinal study (Baltes & Schaie, 1974) found a decline in the mental factor of "visuo-motor flexibility" but no significant change in "cog-nitive flexibility" with age. However, increases in the factors of "crystallized intelligence" and "visualization" were observed in the later years. *Crystallized*

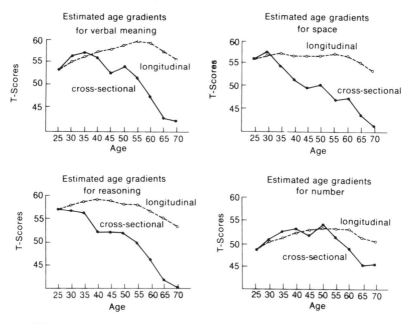

FIG. 4.2.   Standard scores on four subtests of the SRA Mental Abilities Test as a function of age in cross-sectional and longitudinal studies. (From Schaie & Stro-ther, 1968, pp. 675–676. Copyright 1968 by the American Psychological Asso-ciation. Reprinted by permission.)

*intelligence* is Raymond Cattell's term for intelligence that is specific to certain fields, such as school learning or other tasks in which habits have become relatively fixed. In contrast to *fluid intelligence,* which is general to many different fields and depends primarily on heredity, crystallized intelligence depends more on environment.

## Stages in Adult Intellectual Development

According to Jean Piaget (1952), cognitive development takes place in a series of four stages, beginning with a *sensorimotor stage* (0–2 years), when the child learns to exercise simple reflexes and coordinate various perceptions, and culminating in a *formal operations stage* (11–15 years), when the adolescent uses logic and verbal reasoning and can perform higher level, more abstract operations. According to Piaget, the entire sequence of four stages is normally completed by age 15, and what increases thereafter is not intelligence but achievement. Intelligence, which Piaget defined as the ability to solve new problems, supposedly declines slowly after age 15. However, certain theorists have taken issue with this conclusion and have suggested that cognitive development continues in adulthood and is accompanied by qualitatively different modes of thinking from the more formal thought processes of logical reasoning and problem solving. Research support for these theories is scanty, but the theories are intriguing and indicate the direction in which the issue of age changes in intelligence is being pursued.

Following Riegel's (1973) argument that mature thought is characterized not by a search for a single "correct" solution but by the understanding that, paradoxically, things can be true and not true at the same time, Pascual-Leone (1983) and Basseches (1984) have argued for an additional stage of reasoning in adulthood. This stage of *dialectical thought* involves movement or change and is made up of a continuous chain of thesis, antithesis, and synthesis:

> Dialectical thinking is an organized approach to analyzing and making sense of the world one experiences that differs fundamentally from formal analysis. Whereas the latter involves the effort to find fundamental fixed realities—basic elements and immutable laws—the former attempts to describe fundamental process of change and the dynamic relationships through which this change occurs. (Basseches, 1984, p. 24)

An example of the dialectical thinking of adulthood is the realization that an altercation may be nobody's "fault" and must be resolved by both opponents changing and adapting their demands to the situation.

Schaie (1977–1978) has also argued for the continuous qualitative change in cognition during adulthood. Beginning with the achieving stage of young adulthood, adult cognitive development progresses to the responsible stage of middle age and culminates with the reintegrative stage of old age. There is a transition from the childhood question ("What should I know?") through the adult question ("How should I use what I know?") to the later life question ("Why should I know?"). The type of intelligence exhibited in the *achieving stage,* considers the context of problem solving as well as the problem to be solved. This stage, which represents the application of term goals such as those involved in career and marriage decisions, is similar to that involved in school-type tasks but requires greater focus on the possible consequences of the problem-solving process. The second, or *responsible stage,* which requires applying cognitive skills in situations involving social responsibility, is typically manifested when the adult establishes a family and pays attention to the needs of his or her spouse and offspring. The last period in the development of adult intelligence, the *reintegration stage,* occurs when elderly people acquire information and apply knowledge that is more a function of their interests, attitudes, and values than it was in earlier years. Thus, elderly people are reluctant to waste time on meaningless test questions that are irrelevant to their lives and are unwilling to make a great effort to solve a problem unless it is one that they face in their everyday lives.

## MEMORY AND AGING

*Old age* has been defined as "the mother of forgetfulness," or alternatively, "the time when a man still finds women interesting but can't remember why." Another comment, reportedly made by one elderly person to another, is also relevant: "Three things are happening to me as I become older: I'm beginning to lose my memory. . . and the other two I've forgotten." Aphorisms and humor aside, a common complaint of older people is loss of memory, but to what extent and why aging affects the ability to remember is not entirely clear.

### Memory Processes

Most psychologists agree that there are at least three processes or phases in learning and remembering: acquisition or learning, encoding or storage, and recall or retrieval. *Acquisition* is concerned with acquiring information by means of one's senses, a process that is more likely to occur if the individual is motivated and attentive. One aspect of acquisition is establishing a sensory impression of the material to be remembered. This *sensory memory,* or sensory store, lasts only a few seconds, until the impression is registered in *short-term memory.* An example of short-term, or primary, memory is when you remember a telephone number until you have dialed it. The memory lasts only a few seconds or minutes at most, and then it is gone.

In order to have a chance of being remembered for an extended period of time, the to-be-remembered material must get out of short-term storage and into long-term storage. *Long-term memory,* or secondary memory, is defined as retention for at least 10 to 20 minutes. Very long-term memory was involved in Kastenbaum's (1966) study of the earliest memories of 276 centenarians. Like Maurice Chevalier in "Gigi," many of these individuals were much more engrossed in their memories of the distant past than their memories of more recent events. Another illustrative study, conducted on a single person, involved an attempt to recall verbal materials that had been learned 30, 40, and 50 years before (Smith, 1963). It was found that forgetting was most rapid after 63 years of age, and that hardest to recall was more difficult material that had not been overlearned originally or practiced subsequently.

Beginning with the classic work of Hermann Ebbinghaus, who also conducted his research on a sample size of one (himself), most laboratory experiments on learning and memory have employed special materials. These materials have included nonsense syllables (two consonants connected by a vowel to make a nonword syllable), meaningful words or phrases, simple perceptual configurations, and motor apparatus. The majority of the investigations have been concerned with remembering over several days or at least a few hours, but research in more recent years has focused on short-term memory.

## Short-Term Memory

Psychologists have been aware of short-term memory throughout this century, in part because many intelligence tests (yesteryear's "bread-and-butter of psychology") contain digit-span tasks or other subtests that measure immediate memory span for numbers or words. But systematic investigation of the characteristics of short-term memory and the factors affecting it began only about 30 years ago (e.g., Peterson & Peterson, 1959; Welford, 1958).

A typical experiment in short-term memory consists of showing the subject a very short list of letters, words, or numbers, and immediately thereafter requiring that he or she perform some unrelated activity to prevent rehearsal of the material. Then after a few minutes the subject is asked to recall the original list. The results of experiments of this sort have revealed how quickly people forget when insufficient time is provided for storage or encoding of the information into long-term memory. It has also been found that short-term memory behaves very similarly to long-term memory (e.g., the amount of material recalled decreases progressively with time since original learning).

Numerous investigations have been concerned with the relationship of short-term memory to age. In one of these (Inglis, Ankus, & Sykes, 1968), 240 people between the ages of 5 and 70 were tested on a rote learning task and a short-term auditory memory task. On both tasks, performance rose until adulthood and then fell in old age. The results of other investigations (e.g., Craik, 1968; Raymond, 1971), however, indicate that short-term memory remains fairly stable and efficient with aging. It does seem that, although short-term storage of material shows no appreciable decline, the rate at which such material can be retrieved from short-term memory does diminish with age (Anders, Fozard, & Lillyquist, 1972).

## Long-Term Memory

According to Bower's (1966) two-stage theory of memory, the first stage (short-term memory) involves a temporary memory-storage mechanism and the second stage (long-term memory) a more permanent storage mechanism. According to Bower, perceived information first goes into temporary storage and must then be coded in some way by means of a mnemonic (memory-facilitating) operation in order to be placed in permanent storage. With respect to the acquisition, encoding (storage), and retrieval processes involved in long-term memory, research has indicated that elderly people have problems both in storing and retrieving memories. In the storage or encoding stage, older people are less adept at organizing, associating, and integrating material in such as way that it gets into permanent storage (Hoyer & Plude, 1980). Not only do older people have greater difficulty sustaining attention to a new task, but they do not organize new information as quickly or as effectively as younger subjects; compared with the latter, the former have more problems in forming associations and using visual images in processing information into memory.

The difficulties that elderly people may experience in retrieving memories are due in part to the fact that the material was not processed adequately or deeply into memory storage in the first place. Thus, the gist of a text or other verbal/perceptual materials may be remembered, but details tend not to be recalled as well as they are by younger adults. Memory also waxes and wanes more as one gets older: one day the name or telephone number could not be remembered if your life depended on it, and the next day it "floats on the surface of your brain."

## Recognition and Recall

A distinction between types of memory at the retrieval stage is recognition versus recall. *Recognition memory* is used when one is required to select the correct response from a list or group of things, whereas *recall memory* is used when material must be learned "by heart" and the correct response given without using prompts. Schonfield (1965) was interested in determining whether the difficulty experienced by older people in learning new material is due to a problem of absorbing (storing) the material to be learned or of recalling it once it has been stored. His experiment consisted of presenting two lists of 24 words each on a screen at intervals of 4 seconds between words. Immediately after the last word was presented, memory was tested by the recall method for one list and by the recognition method for the other list. The participants were 134 people between the ages of 20 and 75, half of whom performed the recognition test first and half the recall test first. The results, which are illustrated in Fig. 4.3, revealed no deterioration in average recognition scores but a consistent drop in recall scores with age. It was concluded that older people do show a defect of memory, but it appears to be a loss of ability to retrieve memories rather than a deficiency in the storage system itself.

Schonfield's (1965) research findings led many other investigators to conclude that the difference between memory in older and younger adults is primarily a matter of retrieval rather than a lack of initial storage of the information in the brain. Not only is recall less accurate, but also slower than it was when the individual was younger (Cerella, 1985; Madden, 1985). Subsequent research has, for the most part, confirmed the notion that older people have more difficulty retrieving long-term memories than younger people. However, for whatever reasons—sensory deficits, inattentiveness, distractibility, insufficient time, or neurological deficits—elderly people also seem to have greater difficulty

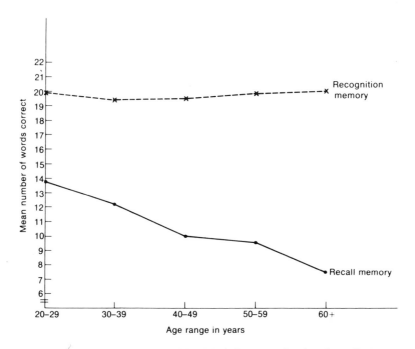

FIG. 4.3.    Mean scores on recognition and recall tests as a function of age. (Data from Schonfield, 1965 Copyright © 1965 Macmillan Magazines Ltd.)

storing memories initially. This is particularly true with more complex material (Adamowicz, 1976). Thus, one can reinterpret Schonfield's (1965) findings as demonstrating that the elderly do not acquire and store information as well as younger people, and consequently have incomplete knowledge of it. Incomplete knowledge is sufficient for them to recognize the material but not to recall it accurately.

## Interference and Arousal

Loss of memory in old age has traditionally been attributed to a decline in the number of brain neurons and to large accumulations of *plaque*—collections of altered dendrites and axons in the brain. Memory decrements cannot, however, be explained entirely in terms of structural changes in the nervous system. Motivation and other psychological factors play important roles in both learning and memory. For example, an older person is less likely than a younger one to attempt to learn something that is meaningless or seemingly useless to him or her—the kinds of tasks that psychologists frequently devise for their research. As the following two investigations demonstrate, interference, which causes attention to shift, and arousal may also be important in learning and memory.

Data collected by Kirchner (1958) indicate that an older person's problem with remembering is caused more by difficulty in retaining information in the presence of interference or shifting attention rather than a simple failure to recall. Older people appear to take longer to consolidate new information, and are more susceptible to the interfering effects of other stimuli. Kirchner's experimental task consisted of a row of 12 lights that went on and off at random; each light had a switch just below it. Older subjects did as well as younger ones when directed to press the switch below the light that had just gone off, but they did progressively worse than younger subjects when directed to press the switch below the next-to-the-last light to go off, the switch below the next-to-the-next-to-the-last light to go off, and so on. The poorer performance of older subjects was interpreted as a problem in retaining information in the face of interference or shifts in attention rather than a failure of recall.

Explanations of an age-related decrement in learning and memory must also take into account the fact that older people often fail to respond when a rapid response is called for. However, as noted previously, they tend to be generally slower than younger age groups, both in learning and performing. When elderly subjects are given more time in which to respond, their performance improves significantly.

Another finding is that older people show heightened, prolonged arousal of the autonomic nervous system during learning. Presumably, the heightened arousal causes them to commit more errors of omission when the learning situation is rapidly paced. Consequently, if autonomic arousal during learning could be controlled by an autonomic-blocking drug, perhaps elderly people would learn more quickly. Arguing in this vein, Eisdorfer, Nowlin, and Wilkie (1970) paid 28 male volunteers in the 60- to 78-year age range to have a drug (or placebo) administered to them and subsequently to learn a list of eight high-association words by the method of serial anticipation (recalling the next word in a sequence when the previous word is presented, etc.). Thirteen of the men (the experimental group) were chosen at random to receive an autonomic-blocking drug (propranolol hydrochloride); the remaining 15 men (the control group) received a saline solution. Heart rate, plasma-free fatty acid, and the galvanic skin response were monitored to measure autonomic activity during the learning task. As indicated by these physiological measures, the drug was as least partially effective in reducing arousal. In any event, the experimental group performed significantly better than the controls on the learning task. Unfortunately, these findings were not supported by those of Froehling (1974), whose older subjects did not appear to be anxious in the learning situation.

## Other Chemical Effects

Drugs may, of course, have an adverse effect as well as an ameliorating effect on memory, but the search for a "memory pill" or chemical has occasioned more scientific attention. Although many drugs have initially seemed to improve memory, the improvement is usually temporary or attributable to improvements in motivation and general health or to a "placebo effect." Some years ago interest was shown in a drug labeled Ribaminol, a compound based on the RNA molecule. This drug, which appeared to speed up protein synthesis in the brain, was tested on hospitalized senile patients and college students. Initial findings indicated that Ribaminol had some effect on short-term memory, but the results were not confirmed by further tests (Botwinick, 1967). Other drugs or substances reportedly associated with improvements in learning and memory are Gerovital, Dexedrine, glutamic acid, ascorbic acid, magnesium pemoline, vinpocetine, and sex hormones, as well as various dietary and vitamin supplements (see Maugh, 1986). Evidence to substantiate such claims is, however, at best inconclusive.

One physiological theory of age decrement in memory holds that hardening of the arteries starves brain cells of oxygen-bearing blood, causing the cells to stop receiving and processing information. For example, Jacobs, Winter, Alvis, and Small (1969) found that daily breathing of 100% oxygen at high atmospheric pressures (hyperbaric oxygen or *hyperoxygenation*) prevented a loss of memory in the older adults whom they studied. The benefits of hyperoxygenation reportedly lasted at least 2 weeks. The results were interpreted as being caused by improvement in the functioning of brain tissues that were deficient in oxygen rather than to a reversal of the degeneration process in neurons.

In a further investigation of hyperoxygenation and memory, Boyle ("Can Oxygen Fight. . . ", 1972) oxygenated patients at three atmospheres for 30 minutes—a higher pressure than Jacobs et al. (1969) had employed, but for a shorter period of time. As a result of these investigations and several others, many researchers became quite enthusiastic about the procedure, and especially its apparent ability to improve memory for recent events. Attempts to replicate the findings, however, have not been uniformly successful, and the earlier investigations have been severely criticized. It has been suggested, for example, that the care and attention received by older people while being hyperoxygenated may be sufficient in itself to stimulate their brains and motivate them to remember better (the *Hawthorne effect*). In any event, hyperoxygenation, or any other biochemical procedure for that matter, is not a technique that will cure memory disorders or empty all institutions for senile patients.

## LEARNING AND EDUCATION
## FOR THE ELDERLY

As indicated throughout this book, older people vary widely in motivation, experience, and test performance. Although the discussion of many topics deals with the hypothetical "average" older person, a specific elderly individual may be quite different from the average. For example, people who maintain an interest in their surroundings and those who are required to keep using their problem-solving skills decline less rapidly with age. Education is especially important, because highly educated people tend to show greater resistance to intellectual decline. Adults who read books and take courses, engaging in both sedentary and physical activities, experience less age-related decline in mental abilities (Jarvik & Bank, 1983; Schaie, 1983; Siegler, 1983). The limited time perspective to which Gergen and Back (1966) refer also seems less evident in those who have had more education. Nevertheless, as these investigators have noted, even those older people who have more education than average tend to prefer short-range solutions to problems over long-range ones.

### Older Learners

It is frequently alleged that elderly people are rigid or "set in their ways" and consequently have difficulty learning new things, not because of reduced learning capacity but because old knowledge and habits get in the way of new learning. Although there is some evidence in support of such "interference effects" in laboratory-type tasks (e.g., Kirchner, 1958), developmental psychologists now emphasize the modifiability or plasticity of behavior at any stage of life. It is recognized that continued learning and problem solving in later life can sustain and even improve intellectual abilities, attitudes, and interests—all of which interact to influence performance.[2] Even with people of limited abilities, special techniques, coupled with enthusiastic, patient instruction, can sometimes work wonders.

Among the differences between older and younger learners that teachers should be aware of are: In general, older learners prefer a slower pace, are more cautious (causing them to make more omission errors), are more disrupted by anxiety and arousal, show less capacity to pay attention, are less likely to use imagery and other kinds of memory schemes or mediators spontaneously, and are less willing than younger adults to exert themselves to learn meaningless laboratory-type tasks and other materials that they perceive as having no relevance to their everyday lives.

Some instructional techniques that take these differences into account and hence are recommended when teaching the elderly are to:[3]

1. Provide ample time for the learner to master the lesson or task.

2. Repeat the material to be learned several times if necessary; repetition can compensate for poor attention.

3. Teach the learners how to organize or encode the material to be learned, by the use of semantics, associative imagery (the ''method of loci''), and other mnemonic techniques.

4. Employ a generous amount of positive reinforcement, providing for success experiences if needed.

5. Set short-term goals that learners are capable of attaining within a reasonable period of time.

6. Because older adults are more easily fatigued, practice periods should be shorter than with younger adults.

7. When demonstrating a physical skill, verbalize what you are doing and have the learners do likewise.

8. Be aware of and make provisions for learners with visual or auditory defects: illumination should be brighter, and speech and tape recordings louder than normal; books should have larger print, etc.

---

[2]Bischof (1969) concluded that ''Old dogs can learn new tricks, but they may be reluctant to do so, particularly when they are not convinced that the new trick is any better than the old tricks which served them so well in the past. They may not learn new tricks as rapidly as they did in the past. But if they started out as clever young pups, they are very likely to end up as wise old hounds'' (p. 224).

[3]Adapted from ''Implications for Teaching,'' the third in the filmstrip series *Perspectives on Aging* (Concept Media, 1500 Adams Ave., Costa Mesa, CA 92626).

## Cognitive Training

Research by Baltes, Schaie, and their coworkers (Plemons, Willis, & Baltes, 1978; Schaie & Willis, 1986a; Willis, Blieszner, & Baltes, 1981) shows that people can continue to learn in old age and improve their performance on intelligence tests. Frequently, the interventions required to attain these improvements in intellectual functioning are fairly minor, often merely requiring that the learners be provided with materials that they can study and practice on their own. The effects of such learning are not restricted to a specifically learned task but transfer to other, similar tasks as well. Unfortunately, there are methodological problems with much of the research on cognitive training. Thus, in some instances it is not clear whether the procedures actually reverse cognitive declines or simply teach new skills to the learners. To make certain that the training really reverses losses resulting from disuse of abilities, the individual's ability level before the supposed decline must be determined.

In addition to teaching specific cognitive skills or approaches to learning, pretraining in anxiety reduction during learning may improve learning and remembering (Yeasavage & Rose, 1984). The older learner must also accept the fact that certain abilities have declined with age but that by restricting the areas in which one is active, optimizing participation in a particular domain (*selective optimization*) and depending more on other skills to compensate for the loss of abilities, he or she, like the pianist Artur Rubenstein, can continue to amaze the world with his or her performance during the ninth decade of life (Baltes & Kliegl, 1986). Abilities do not decline uniformly with age, and everyone has a great deal of reserve capacity, as well as a wealth of experience and perhaps wisdom that can be utilized despite a decline of quickness and potential.

## Education for the Elderly

As we have seen, older people are not necessarily impaired in intellectual abilities, and the majority are quite capable of new learning. As a group, the elderly have significantly less formal education and a higher illiteracy rate than the average adult, but their educational level has been increasing in recent years. Among noninstitutionalized Americans aged 65 and above the median level of education rose from 8.7 years in 1970 to 11.8 years in 1986 (11.7 years for males, 11.9 years for females, 12.1 years for Whites, 8.3 years for Blacks, and 7.2 years for Hispanics). The percentage of elderly Americans with a high school education rose from 28% in 1970 to 49% in 1986, and the percentage who were graduated from college also increased substantially during this 16-year period (American Association of Retired Persons, 1987). These numbers can be expected to continue rising during the remaining years of this century, as the difference between the educational levels of the young and old decrease. Thus, the advantage that younger people now have of being exposed to television and other media, as well as greater mobility and related intellectual stimulation, is being shared by all age groups.

Directed specifically toward helping elderly retirees who must live on a subsistence income to become more self-sufficient are job-training programs provided by organizations such as the Senior Skills Center at Santa Rosa, California. Enrollees at the Center can choose to be trained in office skills, home maintenance, small appliance and electronics repair, and offset printing. Classes in home health care, horticulture and gardening, arts and crafts, and English as a second language are also offered.

The stimulation provided by an educational atmosphere is an enriching experience for many elderly people, and thereby important to their physical and mental health. Recognition of this fact has been demonstrated by programs such Fordham University's College at Sixty and the Third Age College in Toulouse, France. For many years, New York City residents who are 65 or older have been enrolled "tuition free" in any undergraduate course at CUNY in which space is available. As one Columbia University dean observed, "Older people are good people to teach. We find them highly motivated, very thoughtful people and usually highly intelligent. Their life experience is rich."

Community colleges, such as Los Angeles City College and New York City Community College, both with several hundred students over age 60, have been especially forward looking in addressing the needs of the elderly. The Institute for Retired Professionals of The New School for Social Research has also developed a program of course work for retired persons. Every term, these institutions and many others throughout the United States register people in their 60s, 70s, 80s, and even 90s for courses dealing with such complex topics as "Illusions of Peace in the Middle East." It is anticipated that in the future more and more older adults will sign up for college courses and that a semester of art history or English literature will become an educational and recreational experience for increasing numbers. Older students are taking courses in self-help as well as academic subjects, including practical topics such as living on a fixed income, coping with illness, and adjusting emotionally to old age, as well as "Sex Over 65," "The Psychology of Dying," and "Film Time: Oldies But Goodies."

The most extensive effort to provide higher educational experiences for older Americans is Elderhostel (McCluskey, 1982), in which the college campus is the hostel and the elders are the hostelers. Begun in 1975 in a handful of New Hampshire colleges, Elderhostel now consists of a network of several hundred colleges and universities in all 50 states in America, 10 Canadian provinces, several European countries, and other parts of the world. It offers low-cost, 1-week summer residential academic programs for 60,000 or more participants aged 60 and over and their spouses in a wide range of liberal arts courses. Unlike regular college, there are no formal prerequisite courses, no required homework, no examinations, no grades, and (perhaps sadly) no credit. In addition to attending classes, students sleep in college dormitories, eat in college dining halls, and participate in a variety of extracurricular activities.[4]

Despite the success of Elderhostel, it would be misleading to paint an overly optimistic picture of education for the elderly. The fact remains that the vast majority of adult students in American educational institutions are young, and education for the elderly is a relatively modest enterprise. Furthermore, although the majority of older adults are alert and intellectually capable, they often discover on returning to school after a long absence that they must spend considerable time relearning how to learn or redeveloping the required study skills and routines. It is difficult to pick up the books again and to break through the nonscholarly habits of a lifetime.

Several professional organizations provide educational information and services to retired persons. The Institute for Retired Professionals of The New School for Social Research paved the way in the area of educational opportunities and activities for the elderly. But the largest organization in this category is The Institutes of Lifetime Learning, a combined effort of the National Retired Teachers Association and the American Association of Retired Persons. As the members of these organizations recognize, not only should opportunities be provided for retired persons to take course work and to receive training but that their services as teachers of the young should also be utilized to a greater extent. Much of our culture, which is often poorly communicated by courses in history and the social sciences, could probably be taught more effectively by knowledgeable elderly people. More generally, many qualified older persons could serve as professional aids, tutors, and advisors to the young.

## SUMMARY

The popular view of old age as a time of declining mental abilities is certainly not an accurate perception of all elderly people, and in any case it requires considerable qualification. Although the period of peak productivity among scholars, scientists, and artists is typically reached before later life, many people have continued their creative activities into the seventh, eighth, and even ninth decades of life.

Psychological testing of older adults poses particular problems of administration and interpretation that can affect the validity of the test results. The old age norms on standardized tests of intelligence are frequently not truly representative

---

[4]The national headquarters of Elderhostel is at 100 Boylston Street, Suite 200, Boston, MA 02116; telephone (617) 426-7788.

of that age group in the American population as a whole. Also older adults are typically not as motivated as younger adults to take psychological tests, which they often perceive as having no bearing on their lives.

The findings of developmental studies of general intelligence depend significantly on the research methodology employed. In general, the results of cross-sectional studies reveal a decline in overall mental ability after the late 20s or early 30s. Cross-sectional studies do not, however, adequately control for differences among age cohorts. The findings of longitudinal studies point to little or no decline in general mental ability after early adulthood, especially among people who have remained intellectually active. According to some researchers, cognitive abilities continue to develop, in a qualitative fashion, in adulthood. In any event, the question of age-related changes in mental abilities remains very much open and will require more careful definition and the application of a combination of methodological approaches to answer satisfactory.

Among the specific mental abilities that have been found to decline with age are both short- and long-term memory (especially the latter) and the ability to understand new ideas. The initial storage and subsequent retrieval of memories from storage appear to be affected bv age-related changes in the brain. Evidence also indicates that older people take longer to respond and have greater difficulty organizing and encoding new information, are more susceptible to interference and distraction, and manifest heightened and prolonged autonomic arousal during learning. Deficits in learning and memorizing new information are affected by sensory changes and practice and are more noticeable when the material is complex.

Some of the biological variables that are known to affect mental ability in old age are heredity, sex, nutrition, and health. Various chemicals and treatments (Ribaminol, magnesium pemoline, vinpocetine, hyperbaric oxygen, etc.) have been alleged to improve memory in the elderly, but research findings with these and other substances have been criticized because of inadequate controls and other methodological shortcomings.

Education and training programs for the elderly have received increased attention, and many educational institutions have designed specific courses of study and training for this age group. There is some evidence that cognitive training can improve the functioning of elderly people whose mental abilities have declined through disuse.

The elderly constitute a relatively small percentage of the American student population, but the success of educational programs for them indicates that many older people can and want to continue learning. This is especially true when the particular assets and limitations of older learners are taken into account in the instructional process. A number of organizations provide educational information and services to the elderly, who can perform in the role of students and also as teachers.

## SUGGESTED READING

Crossen, C. W., & Roberson-Tchabo, E. A. (1983). Age and preference for complexity among manifestly creative women. *Human Development, 26,* 149–155.

Denny, N. W. (1982). Aging and cognitive change. In B. B. Wolman (Ed.), *Handbook of developmental psychology.* Englewood Cliffs, NJ: Prentice-Hall.

Gribbin, K., Schaie, K. W., & Parham, I. A. (1980). Complexities of life style and maintenance of intellectual abilities. *Journal of Social Issues, 36,* 47–61.

Labouvie-Vief, G. (1985). Intelligence and cognition. In J. E. Birren & K. W. Schaie (Eds.), *Handbook of the psychology of aging* (2nd ed., pp. 500–530). New York: Van Nostrand Reinhold.

Lumsden, D. B. (Ed.). (1985). *The older adult as learner.* Washington, DC: Hemisphere.

Peterson, D. A., Thornton, J. E., & Birren, J. E. (Eds.). (1986). *Education and aging.* Englewood Cliffs, NJ: Prentice-Hall.

Robertson-Tchabo, E. A., & Arenberg, D. (1985). Mental functioning and aging. In R. Andres, E. L. Bierman, & W. R. Hazzard (Eds.), *Principles of geriatric medicine* (pp. 129–140). New York: McGraw-Hill.

Schaie, K. W. (1982). The Seattle longitudinal study: A twenty-one year exploration of psychometric intelligence in adulthood. In K. W. Schaie (Ed.), *Longitudinal studies of adult psychological development.* New York: Guilford Press.

Siegler, I. C., McCarty, S. M., & Logue, P. E. (1982). Wechsler Memory Scale scores, selective attribution and distance from death. *Journal of Gerontology, 37,* 176–181.

Willis, S. L. (1985). Towards an educational psychology of the adult learner. In J. E. Birren & K. W. Schaie (Eds.), *Handbook of the psychology of aging* (2nd ed., pp. 818–847). New York: Van Nostrand Reinhold.

# 5

# Personality and Problems of Adjustment

*Personality* is the unique organization of traits and behavior patterns that typify a person, making him or her psychologically different from other people. As with all human characteristics, personality is a product of the interaction between heredity and environment. Innate temperament and other predispositions combine with the influences of the physical and social environment to produce a continuously developing organism. Consequently, personality does not necessarily stop developing when physical growth ceases. As long as there are new experiences and challenges the individual must find new ways of adapting and adjusting to those changes. And just as infancy, childhood, adolescence, and early and middle adulthood pose developmental tasks that must be mastered, so, too, does the period of later maturity have its own challenges and crises.

## AGING AND ADJUSTMENT

Although growing old presents its own particular problems of adjustment, these problems are caused more by the changes accompanying the process of aging than by the fact that one has aged. Among the more stressful experiences affecting a person's outlook and expectations during later life are an altered physical appearance, chronic illness, retirement, and the deaths of loved ones. Physical changes in old age are especially difficult to cope with because the appearance and feelings of one's own body can have a pronounced effect on the self-concept.

Older and younger people alike tend to minimize their physical and mental limitations and disabilities, a response that is normal and self-protective. Most people do not like to think of themselves as aging or disabled, because such thoughts are likely to produce feelings of discomfort and anxiety. But everyone ages, and aging can affect personality adjustment—for better or worse. Furthermore, because the body and mind operate as a psychosomatic unit, the level of personality adjustment and mental health can influence the rate at which a person ages.

## Coping With Age-Related Changes

Some people are overwhelmed by the changes produced in their bodies by aging and literally grieve for the physical and psychological losses they have suffered. Others are able to transcend or overcome these physical changes and find satisfaction in spite of declining strength, appearance, and health. Having fulfilled their life goals or actively continuing to pursue them, they attain a sense of happiness and contentment despite declining health and abilities.

In order to compensate for a changing body and new social and occupational roles, older adults may adopt new diets, develop new skills, and find new ways of using their increased leisure time. Considerable readjustment to changing social values and mores is required, and experiencing a loss of status and self-satisfaction is common.

To the extent that it can be measured, reported overall satisfaction and happiness with life appear to decline gradually after the late 20s. For example, a Gallup poll was conducted in the late 1970s to determine how expressed happiness varies with chronological age and several other demographic variables. The poll question asked of 1,516 adults was "Generally speaking, how happy would you say you are—very happy, fairly happy, or not too happy?" From an analysis of replies to this question, the pollsters concluded that to be happy is to be young, married, and to have a college background (Gallup, 1977).

Young adulthood is also recalled by a large percentage of older adults as having been the happiest time of their lives. In two separate surveys conducted in New York (Morgan, 1937) and Iowa (Landis, 1942) some years ago, approximately 50% of the elderly respondents indicated that the years of young adulthood had been the happiest time for them. Subsequent research has shown, however, that the stage of life perceived as having been the "happiest" varies considerably with the individual and with socioeconomic status and ethnicity.

## THEORIES OF PERSONALITY DEVELOPMENT

Sigmund Freud and other early psychoanalysts maintained that personality is established during childhood and that little change occurs thereafter. These theorists considered biological variables, and sexual impulses in particular, to be especially important in the development of personality during the preschool years. Although modern psychoanalysts recognize the role of early experiences and sexuality in the growth of personality, they place greater emphasis than Freud on the role of learning and associated sociocultural variables. Childhood is admittedly a significant and perhaps crucial time in the formation of personality, but human beings are seen as having the capacity to grow and develop into adulthood and even later life.

## Erikson's Stage Theory

Illustrative of the importance given to social factors in personality development is Erik Erikson's descriptive taxonomy of the crises (conflicts) and goals in eight stages of life. According to Erikson (1963), the psychosocial development of a person can be characterized in terms of these progressive stages. During each stage a particular crisis or conflict comes into prominence and must be resolved if psychological development is to proceed normally. As indicated in Table 5.1, the crisis of trust versus mistrust in infancy must be resolved by acquiring a basic sense of trust. And the major crisis of the teenage years—identity versus role confusion—is resolved by achieving a sense of personal identify.

Erikson referred to the major crisis of middle age as one of generativity versus self-absorption. This is the time of life when people take an inventory of their lives and accomplishments. Realizing that one's personal future is limited, the middle-aged individual's time perspective begins to shorten. Perhaps spurred on by the awareness that death is imminent, people in their 40s and 50s may come to the conclusion that if a radical change in lifestyle or direction is to be made it had better be now.

According to Erikson, the major crisis of old age is integrity versus despair, and the primary goal is to become an integrated and self-accepting person. How the individual handles this crisis depends on personality characteristics that have been developing for years, as well as physical health, economic situation, and the meaningfulness of the social roles that can be played successfully. Thus, rather than resulting from aging per se, a sense of despair in old age stems more often from the health problems, financial insecurity, social isolation, and inactivity that so often accompany that stage of life.

Despairing people view life with a feeling of profound regret that they have not made better use of their assets, that potentialities have not been realized nor opportunities seized, and that the chances of achieving one's goals lessen with every passing day. Such individuals are keenly aware of old age as the *no-solution problem* referred to by gerontologists. Feeling that time is now too short to begin anew or to try to achieve success and contentment by a different approach, despairing individuals find it difficult to accept the inevitability of death. In such cases, life is ended with a whimper of despair, rather than a bang of joy or anger, demonstrating through this attitude the errors in one's personal philosophy.

TABLE 5.1
Erikson's Stages of Psychosocial Development*

| Stage | Crisis (Conflict) | Goal (Resolution) | Description |
|---|---|---|---|
| Infancy | Trust vs. mistrust | Acquire a basic sense of trust | Consistency, continuity, and sameness of experience lead to trust. Inadequate, inconsistent, or negative care may arouse mistrust. |
| Early childhood | Autonomy vs. doubt | Attain a sense of autonomy | Opportunities to try out skills at own pace and in own way lead to autonomy. Overprotection or lack of support may lead to doubt about ability to control self or environment. |
| Play age | Initiative vs. guilt | Develop a sense of initiative | Freedom to engage in activities and parents' patient answering of questions lead to intiative. Restrictions of activities and treating questions as a nuisance lead to guilt. |
| School age | Industry vs. inferiority | Become industrious and competent | Being permitted to make and do things and being praised for accomplishments lead to industry. Limitations on activities and criticism of what is done lead to inferiority. |
| Adolescence | Identity vs. role confusion | Achieve a personal identity | Recognition of continuity and sameness in one's personality, even when in different situations and when reacted to by different individuals, leads to identity. Inability to establish stability (particularly regarding sex roles and occupational choice) leads to role confusion. |
| Young adulthood | Intimacy vs. isolation | Become intimate with someone | Fusing of identity with another leads to intimacy. Competitive and combative relations with others may lead to isolation. |
| Middle age | Generativity vs. self-absorption | Develop an interest in future generations | Establishing and guiding next generation produces sense of generativity. Concern primarily with self leads to self-absorption. |
| Old age | Integrity vs. despair | Become an integrated and self-accepting person | Acceptance of one's life leads to a sense of integrity. Feeling that it is too late to make up for missed opportunities leads to despair. |

*After Erikson (1963), as adapted by Biehler (1981), pp. 122–123.

Although Erikson maintained that each of the eight crises described in Table 5.1 assumes central importance at a given time of life, all eight crises are actually of some importance throughout the life span. Furthermore, personality adjustment is usually not an "all or none" affair in which one pole of a given crisis overwhelms the other pole. For example, most people develop some degree of mistrust, but they are able to maintain a proper balance of trust and mistrust necessary for survival. Likewise, the great majority of older adults cannot be characterized as integrated on the one hand versus despairing on the other. Certainly, the "despairing person" described in the last paragraph is an accurate picture of only a small proportion of the elderly. But no matter how realistic they have been in their attitudes toward life, despair is no stranger in later life; almost everyone experiences a hopeless feeling at some time. A certain amount of despair is realistic, and the usual achievement of old age is not the total victory of integrity over despair but rather a favorable balance between the two extremes of the crisis continuum.

In contrast to a more despairing person, individuals who have developed effective solutions to the major tasks and crises of life during the preceding stages of development can look forward to old age as the capstone of a life well lived. Such a person has no overwhelming regrets and would be willing to go through it all again, but thinks less about the past and more about using the remaining time wisely. Having come to terms with personal goals and achievements, a well-adjusted older person is self-accepting and lives hopefully rather than helplessly. Old age is welcomed as an opportunity to take stock of and to clarify a lifetime of experience. Finding responses to these experiences satisfactory, such an individual is in a much better position to cope with the inevitable stresses and changes of later life.

With respect to Erikson's adolescent stage of identify versus identity confusion, it would be expected that persons over 65 would have a clear sense of identity. However, one must be cautious about viewing old age as merely a "summing up" period of no further development. Self-development and the search for identity may continue throughout one's lifetime. As Butler (1971, p. 51) said: "When identity is established or maintained, I find it an ominous sign rather than a favorable one. A continuing life-long identity crisis seems to be a sign of good health." A new identity in old age may come from finding novel uses for what has been learned during the preceding years and developing new ways of coming to terms with reality. That reality consists of weaknesses as well as strengths and a changing world that is not always to one's liking.

## Other Developmental Theories

Based on the results of clinical observations, case studies and interviews of older adults, Robert Peck (1968) extended Erikson's framework of the crises and conflicts of later life. According to Peck, old age is characterized by three subcrises or conflicts: (a) ego differentiation versus work-role preoccupation; (b) body transcendance versus preoccupation; and (c) ego transcendance versus preoccupation. The first of these subcrises is concerned with whether the individual views him or herself as a flexible, complex person who is able to perform several roles or as being limited to a single role activity. The second subcrisis centers on whether one is able to transcend the infirmities and unattractiveness of his or her own body and to come to value mental and social activities despite declining physical health. The third subcrisis is concerned with whether one can transcend his or her own ego or becomes constantly preoccupied with the self and unable to accept the fact of death.

In contrast to the stage theories of Erikson and Peck, transition theory assumes that psychological needs are not satisfied once and for all but must be continually renegotiated. According to Nancy Schlossberg (quoted by Tavris, 1987), such needs include control over one's life, enthusiasm for activities and commitments to other people and values, and the feeling that one matters to others. Transition theorists emphasize the individuality of development and that, as expressed by Orville Brim, "Unlike child development, which is powerfully governed by maturation and biological changes, adult development is more affected by psychology and experience" (Tavris, 1987, p. 92). Brim and Wheeler (1966) see personality change in terms of the changing demands and expectations of society as an individual passes through the age-graded social structure. Age-related changes in socially expected behaviors lead the aging individual to acquire new attitudes, roles, and beliefs (Reedy, 1983).

Daniel Levinson (1978), who is something of a combination stage and transition theorist, viewed the time between ages 60 and 65 as a transition period during which people realize that they can no longer occupy center stage. The heavy responsibilities of middle adulthood must be reduced as the aging individual learns to function in a changed relationship between him or herself and society. In the end, what matters is "one's view from the bridge"—the final sense of what life is all about and what it means. Such a perception typically takes place as a result of what Robert Butler (1971) termed a *life review,* a process of looking back over one's life. Although a life review may lead to preoccupation with the past, an accompanying nostalgia, regret, and even despair, depression and panic, Butler feels that it is a therapeutic process when it takes place in the presence of people who care.

## Continuity and Change in Personality

Both stage and transition theories emphasize the changes in personality and ways of adjusting to the environment over time. On the other hand, the results of a number of investigations (Costa & McCrae, 1980; Neugarten, 1977; Neugarten and Associates, 1964; Schaie & Parham, 1976) have revealed that although adult personality can change, most personality factors remain fairly stable into old age. According to Neugarten (1977), the typical thoughts, motives, and emotions of an individual tend to be much the same after age 50 as they were before. Consequently, if we know about an individual's personality in middle age and how events in his or her earlier life have been dealt with then we should be able to make broad predictions about how that person will react in old age.

Atchley (1972) described continuity theory in the following way:

> Continuity theory holds that in the process of becoming an adult, the individual develops habits, commitments, preferences, and a host of other dispositions that become a part of his personality. As the individual grows older, he is predisposed toward maintaining continuity in his habits, associations, preferences, and so on. (p. 36)

Adherents to this position realize that there are many possible adaptations to aging, but that more important than personality changes in determining how a person adapts in old age are changes in such things as health, finances, and marital status. According to continuity theorists, personality may change with aging, but the modifications are quantitative rather than qualitative. That is, the pattern of one's personality traits, established early in life, becomes more pronounced in response to the stresses of later life (Neugarten, 1971, 1973). But styles of coping, achieving life satisfaction, and goal-directed behavior remain consistent after mid-life (Botwinick, 1978; Neugarten and Associates, 1964; Ward, 1979).

Evidence from casual observation and research indicates that both positive and negative traits tend to persist throughout an individual's lifetime. From her talks with older people, Curtin (1972) concluded that those who were maladjusted had usually been uninvolved, passive, or unhappy when they were younger. They did not become radically different personalities on the day they turned 65; rather, they had much the same temperament as when they were 30, 40, or 50. Curtin also observed that aging does not solve one's personal problems, but instead compounds them. People who have difficulty coping with life at age 30 will most likely have similar problems at 65.

Evidence for the continuity of personality is impressive, but certain traits do change to some degree with age. Although research results suggesting that there is an age-related increase in "rigidity" are inconsistent, the finding of increased attention to the self, or introversion ("interiority"), with aging is well-documented (Botwinick, 1978; Neugarten, 1977). Furthermore, the degree of continuity or stability in personality varies with the antecedent characteristics of the individual. For example, Shanan (1985) found that two personality types ("active integrated copers" and "dependent passive copers") remained relatively stable during later life, but two other types ("failing overcopers" and "self-negating undercopers") were unstable. Among the personality changes observed in the last two ("unstable") types were attitudes toward work and family, shrinking time perspective, and increasing passivity.

Recent research and writings concerned with the question of the continuity of personality have emphasized the role of cognitive factors. For example, a certain amount of the observed continuity is attributable to the fact that people are attracted to environments that "fit" their personalities and hence do not require much change on their part (Ahammer, 1973). Thus, slow-paced, gentle people tend to prefer living in small towns, and shy people do not speak in public. In this way, individual decisions about preferred living environments and lifestyles result in greater stability of personality—a stability that is created more by the individual than by the environment (Lerner & Busch-Rossnagel, 1981).

According to one cognitive theory of personality, *script theory,* individuals attempt to maintain a sense of continuity or order (the "script") in the critical events, or *scenes,* of their lives:

> Personality development is best understood as the formation, growth or decline of (a) scenes that represent important features of an individual's life and (b) scripts that enable the person to anticipate, respond to, control, or create events in a meaningful fashion. An essential premise of script theory is that personality development is not plotted as a one-way progression from earlier to later constructions of experience. Instead, there is two-way traffic through time. Constructions of the past may be radically changed in the light of later experience; anticipations of the future may color the present and revise the past; old experiences may return to alter the present. (Carlson, 1981, p. 503)

As recognized by both continuity theory and script theory, there is no final stage of personality development. Although different lives follow different courses, with a large majority of individuals manifesting a great deal of stability and others changing substantially even in old age, all retain the potential for alteration and adaptation. Human personality is not completely static; it is modified to some extent by the very process of aging and the success of one's attempts to cope with the challenges and problems that aging presents (see Report 5.1).

## PERSONALITY CHARACTERISTICS
## OF OLDER ADULTS

### Self-Concept and Self-Acceptance

As we develop and become aware of the differences between our own aims and those of others, we usually come to behave in more realistic and socially appropriate ways. The reactions of other people to our appearance and behavior lead us to modify our actions (and, as best we can, our physical features) and our view of ourselves. These reflected evaluations from people who are significant in our lives, in addition to our successes and failures in dealing with other aspects of the environment, result in the acquisition of a *self-concept.* A person's self-concept includes the overall personal value placed on oneself as a personality, as well as self-evaluations of one's own body and behavior. Biological factors such as physical appearance, health, innate abilities, and certain aspects of temperament are important in determining the frequency and kinds of social experiences that a

---

**Report 5.1    AGING: WHAT WE'LL BE WE'LL BE\***

Ms. Adelson says age does not change people, but that, from my experience with dozens of elderly, including my own parents, simply is not true. In fact, through changes of circumstance, changes in physical well-being, many people as they grow older become quite different persons than they were in their earlier years.

It is easy for us, who still have most of our faculties, to eye these older people judgmentally and declare, "I'll never be that selfish-cantankerous-demanding-unappreciative-all-of-the-above when I am old."

But I've learned not to say "never." I've seen people change too often.

A man I once considered almost saintly in his charity, his even temper, is today so contentious, so prone to temper tantrums that friends of many years' standing can't believe the deviation. If we say it's a warm day, he's sure to shout, "Nothing of the sort! It's cold!"

I know a woman who in her middle years, as a hostess, demonstrated an unusual and exemplary thoughtfulness for each guest. Moreover, she never was too busy to help a friend. Today her demands on friends and relatives are endless and she complains her wishes are never carried out properly.

Another man, a relaxed, casual sort of person in his younger years, now insists the telephone be placed two inches from the edge of the table, turned at thus-and-such angle, and that his coffee cup be turned a certain way at the breakfast table. Any departure from his rules and he fumes, "No! No! No! Can't you understand?"

Now to suggest to the demanding woman that she be more considerate or to the contentious man that he be more docile is like telling a manic-depressive who is in the pits to cheer up! They can't help the way they are. Because they suffer deteriorating coordination, eyesight and hearing; hardening of the arteries, arthritis and other degenerative ills, and because they often are in pain, there is no way they can change back to the people they once were.

\*From Smith (1979). Originally printed in the *Los Angeles Times,* July 22, 1979. Courtesy Beverly Bush Smith.

---

person has and the degree of social acceptance that is attained. The social evaluations placed on the physical and behavioral characteristics of an individual who possesses a particular biological makeup—and consequently his or her self-evaluation—depend, of course, on the specific sociocultural group to which the person belongs.

Self-esteem increases with age, older adults tending to score higher than younger adults on measures of self-esteem (Cottrell & Atchley, 1969; Rosenberg, 1964). Self-esteem tends to decline somewhat in old age (Bloom, 1961), but the events occurring in later life rather than age per se are usually responsible for the decline. For example, a negative self-concept in old age has been found to be associated with having a lower standard of living than one had hoped for, and living alone or with relatives rather than as a couple (Kaplan & Pokorny, 1969).

The maintenance of high self-esteem in old age is important because it increases resistance to stress and contributes to physical and mental health (Antonovsky, 1981). How some individuals are able to maintain a stable self-concept and high self-esteem despite declining health and other difficulties in old age may seem puzzling, but even during early and middle adulthood, when the individual is no stranger to failure and other frustrations, self-esteem tends to be stable or to increase.

An explanation of how people are able to maintain a positive self-concept with aging must take into account the fact that not only does the individual learn how to protect his or her self-concept, but increasing successes and decreasing pretensions bring the real self (what a person views him or herself as being) and the ideal self (what a person would like to be) closer together. Furthermore, rather than remembering the outcomes of efforts and other personal experiences exactly as they occurred, people may fabricate their personal histories to guarantee positive self-evaluations; close family ties support these self-fabrications. Because a feeling of competence or being in control is important to a positive self-concept, the illusion of competence and control is created: Positive outcomes are attributed to one's own abilities and efforts, and outside circumstances or other people are blamed for negative outcomes. Although others may evaluate a person less positively than the person evaluates him or herself, people learn to defend themselves by assigning greater weight to what they think about themselves than to what others say about them. Negative evaluations made by others are defused by finding something negative about those people to explain the evaluations or by limiting one's interactions with them. In these ways, over time a great deal of personal credit and very little personal debt or blame are built up (Greenwald, 1980).

## Destiny Control and Interiority

People who feel weak and powerless—characteristics considered by many to be earmarks of old age—tend to resign themselves to a poor socioeconomic and physical condition. In fact, it has been shown that both the physical and mental health of older people are influenced by the feeling of having some control over the important events of their lives (Rodin & Langer, 1977). Those who feel that they have outlived their options and must submit blindly to whatever fate holds in store become easily depressed or angry. That this sense of "destiny control" changes with age was documented in a longitudinal study by Gutmann (1964). It was found that a typical 40-year-old man, who sees himself as having the energy and capacity to control his external environment, is willing to take risks and accept challenges. In contrast, a typical 60-year-old tends to see the world as more dangerous and complicated and no longer as likely to be within his control (Neugarten, 1968b). He becomes increasingly cautious and less impulsive (Botwinick, 1978; Riley & Foner, 1968), a tendency that reflects a greater need for certainty and a fear of failing. Cautiousness, passivity and lower self-confidence among elderly men is also seen in their tendency to conform more to group opinion in making judgments or decisions (Klein, 1972). This increased cautiousness with aging is understandably greater in older people with less education, who have less financial security, and perhaps less self-confidence than their better-educated peers (Botwinick, 1966).

Obviously, both the active, assertive orientation of the average middle-aged man and the more passive-conforming orientation of the older man represent reasonable attempts to adjust to the environment. As Gutmann's (1964, 1969, 1974) studies in the United States and other societies make clear, during the period between 40 and 60 years an individual's self-perception in relation to the environment gradually shifts from one of being generally strong and capable of overcoming obstacles to one of viewing the world as a complicated, dangerous place in which compliance and accommodation are the best policy. Thus, by age 60 or 70, a formerly bold, outer-directed orientation may have changed from involvement with people and things to an increasing preoccupation with the inner life (Ullmann, 1976). In contrast to men, who move from an active to a passive orientation as they become old, women tend to move from passive to active mastery (Neugarten, 1977).

As previously noted, during the sixth and seventh decades of life a man's interactions with people and other externals show a trend toward simplification or less active involvement. On the whole, the elderly man becomes more preoccupied with his inner experiences and the satisfaction of his own personal needs. This movement from active to passive mastery, or *interiority,* as it has been labeled by Neugarten (1968b), is an inner orientation beginning in middle age and continuing until death. Increased interiority in old age is a tendency that occurs among elderly men in most geographical regions, nations, ethnic groups, and cultures (Gutmann, 1977). One of its common manifestations across cultures is increased interest in the supernatural and religious devotion ("magical mastery") during later life.

A turning inward of the personality can have either a positive or a negative effect, leading to feelings of greater self-reliance on the one hand or to a sense of inadequacy and depression on the other. The positive side of interiority and associated egocentrism is illustrated by May Sarton's (1978) statement that "It is the privilege of the old to feel less guilt about the undone, and what a joy that can be!". What is positive for the elderly person, however, may not be perceived in the same way by younger people. Thus, a preoccupation with oneself and the resulting lack of attention to external matters may be viewed by others as a self-centered disregard of socially appropriate behavior.

## Rigidity and Flexibility

Older people sometimes appear to be easily annoyed with the ways of the younger generation. One study of men 70 years and older found, for example, that they were frequently annoyed by the behavior of teenagers, as well as by heavy drinking and intolerance in others. Their own inability to accomplish things, and feelings of helplessness and aloneness were other common sources of annoyance to these men (Barrett, 1972).

Younger adults might attribute such annoyances to inflexibility or contrariness, seeing older people as irritable, quarrelsome, and crotchety "fuddy-duddies" who "live in the past." The presumption that the elderly are rigid is not limited to teenagers. People of all ages view the aged as less adaptable, less willing or unable to change their ways of doing things, and more reluctant to try new approaches to personal and social problems.

Although the results of certain studies indicate that older people are more rigid and inflexible than their younger contemporaries (Riley & Foner, 1968; Schaie & Strother, 1968), Robert Butler (1974) referred to the so-called inflexibility of older people as a "myth." Butler admitted that the structure of a person's character is fairly well established by the time of old age, but unless a person is severely hampered by brain damage, low mentality, or lack of education, changes in behavior can and do occur right up to the time of death. He suggested that "cautious" is a better description of the elderly than "inflexible" or "rigid." Caution is realistic, because a lifetime of experience has taught elderly people not to expect miracles and to be suspicious about what can be accomplished by physicians, politicians, social planners, and others in positions of authority.

Elderly people are probably less likely to risk being wrong for the sake of being right or fast (Botwinick, 1967), but if the directions and structure of a task are clear, they will usually do their best. It is also true that old people are sometimes reluctant to make complex decisions in ambiguous situations, but the flexibility with which they respond depends on lifelong habits and behaviors. Some people, both young and old, can absorb new information more readily than others, and consequently they are less resistant to change. Those with higher intelligence and greater self-confidence are more willing to accept reasonable risks rather than adhering rigidly to what has worked in the past. In contrast, senile patients are more likely to be rigid and unadaptable in the face of environmental changes.

## Personality Types

The uniqueness of human personality is especially pronounced in old age: the aged manifesting an even wider range of personality characteristics than their younger contemporaries. Neugarten, Havighurst, and Tobin (1968) were more impressed by the differences than the similarities among the personalities represented in a group of 70-year-olds whom they studied. Such personality differences are quite apparent in the various patterns of coping and defensive behavior observed in older adults.

In a classic study of aging and personality, Reichard, Livson, and Petersen (1962) obtained 115 ratings of the personality characteristics of 40 well-adjusted and 30 poorly adjusted older men. The findings pointed to the presence of five personality types or clusters: mature (contructive), rocking chair (dependent), armored (defensive), angry (hostile), and self-hating. These five types represent fairly specific methods of coping with the problems of old age. The *mature* men, who were relatively free of neurotic conflicts, could accept themselves and grow old with few regrets. Also fairly well adjusted were the *rocking chair* types, who viewed old age in terms of freedom from responsibility and as an opportunity to indulge their passive needs. The *armored* type, who were somewhere in the middle in terms of adjustment, defended themselves against anxiety by keeping busy. The first of the poorly adjusted types, the *angry* men, expressed bitterness and blamed other people for their failures. Also maladjusted were the *self-haters,* who, depressed rather than angry, blamed themselves for their disappointments and misfortunes. These people, hating themselves and older people in general, viewed later life as a useless, uninteresting period of human existence.

Further evidence for the variety of individual differences in personality and adjustment in old age was obtained in the study by Neugarten et al. (1968) referred to earlier. The study was concerned with the relationships of long-standing personality characteristics and social activity to happiness in a sample of people aged 70 to 79. The four major personality traits, derived from an assessment of each person on 45 dimensions, were: integrated, armored-defended, passive-dependent, and unintegrated. The life satisfaction of each person was rated according to the extent to which the person appeared to take pleasure in daily activities, regarded life as meaningful, accepted responsibility for his or her past life, felt successful in having achieved major goals, had a positive self-image, and was generally optimistic about life. A measure of role activity consisted of observers' ratings of the extent and intensity of the social roles of parent, spouse, grandparent, kin-group member, and church member. A wide range of activity patterns and lifestyles, depending on the type of personality possessed by the individual, was noted.

Among the *integrated* personalities, who functioned well and had complex inner lives as well as intact intellective abilities and egos, were three patterns of role activity. The *reorganizers* engaged in a wide variety of activities, the *focused* types devoted most of their energies to a few important roles, and the *disengaged* people possessed high satisfaction with their lives but had voluntarily moved away from role commitments.[1]

---

[1]Lowenthal, Thurnher, and Chiriboga (1975) found that older people who had few social activities and involvements and few resources (''simplistic type'') reported higher life satisfaction than people who had many activities and resources (''complex type''). The lower life satisfaction of the second group was thought to be due to the fact that society does not provide enough opportunities for participation and self-expression in later life, activities that are essential to satisfaction for complex people.

The men and women who were labeled as *armored-defended* personalities were striving, achievement-oriented people who pushed themselves. The two patterns of aging observed in this group were the *holding-on* people who believed that they would be all right as long as they kept busy, and the *constricted* individuals, who reduced their involvement with other people and experiences and defended themselves against aging by concentrating on their losses and deficits.

Two patterns of aging were also found in the *passive-dependent* group: *succor-seeking* people with strong dependency needs who expressed medium satisfaction with life as long as they had at least one or two people to lean on, and *apathetic* people, who were passive individuals with few activities or social interactions and little interest in their surroundings. The fourth main type of personality observed in this investigation was the disorganized or *unintegrated,* who had serious psychological problems.

The overall results of the Neugarten et al. (1968) study support the common observation that whether one remains active or gradually disengages during later life, and what effects that choice has, depends on the individual. Well-integrated personalities tend to adjust well to old age, whereas people who are dissatisfied or unhappy with themselves and their previous experiences have difficulty adjusting to later life. Level of activity also appears to be a significant factor in life satisfaction: Those who keep a young, active, problem-solving attitude tend to be better adjusted. Furthermore, activity and motivation are interacting variables: motivation for living and orientation toward others is affected by whether or not a person is engaged in useful activities.

## Happiness and Survival

As the findings of the Reichard et al. (1962) and the Neugarten et al. (1968) studies indicate, different personalities have different ways of adjusting to the changes and stresses of old age. Elderly people do not have to be continually "on the go" in order to be happy, but neither do they have to be perfectly happy in order to survive. For example, in a study of residents of an old people's home in Chicago, Lieberman (1973) found that the best survivors were the "grouches." He concluded that combativeness or grouchiness may be highly adaptive and may contribute to longevity in later life, a conclusion supported by Gutmann's (1971) observation that combativeness is a primary characteristic of long-lived men in preliterate societies.

As Lieberman's findings suggest, personality characteristics and behaviors that may encounter disapproval in certain environments may have greater survival value than other characteristics in the same or other environmental contexts. In any event, the personality characteristics associated with successful adjustment vary with the external circumstances. Stephens (1976) found, for example, that older occupants of slum hotels who adjusted successfully to their circumstances did so by adopting a lifestyle characterized by suspiciousness, hustling, and rugged individualism.

Granted that there is a difference between happiness and survival and that people who are perfectly well adjusted in one situation can be maladjusted in another, several authorities (Butler, 1975; Hochschild, 1973; Medley, 1976; Neugarten, 1973) proposed a set of factors that seem to be important for effective adjustment in a wide variety of circumstances encountered by elderly people. Among these are: (a) some degree of independence, (b) a sense of accomplishment, (c) satisfaction in interpersonal relationships, (d) interest or involvement in some activity, and (e) flexibility or willingness to change. In general, people who are able to plan ahead without being overly rigid and who feel wanted and useful are more apt to be happy and survive longer.

## MENTAL DISORDERS

Despite the fact that the majority of elderly people are able to adjust well to the stresses and changes accompanying old age, mental disorders are more common in older than in younger adults. As indicated earlier in the chapter, maladjusted young adults tend to become maladjusted older adults. However, the same individual who at 30 or 40 was able to cope with pressures and frustrations at home and work can, when faced with the stresses of physical disability, retirement, or the loss of a loved one, experience a severe problem of adjustment.

It has been estimated that about 15% of older Americans, compared with 10% of the total U.S. population, suffer from at least moderate psychopathology (Reedy, 1983). Approximately 33% of these individuals are suffering from organic brain syndrome, which increases with age. Even these numbers are probably too low, because society is more tolerant of abnormal behavior in older people than in the young. The incidence of psychopathology is particularly high among the very old and those who are in poor physical health. And, as at all ages, being widowed, separated, or divorced is associated with a higher frequency of adjustment problems during later life. Women are more likely than men to be diagnosed as mentally disordered prior to age 65, but older men are more likely than older women to suffer from serious mental disorder (Bloom, White, & Asher, 1979).

The rate of milder as well as more serious adjustment problems varies with age. For example, it has been alleged that the loneliest people are teenagers and younger adults who are just starting out in new careers and relationships and are experiencing far more stress and are less effective in coping with it than the elderly (Tavris, 1987). Be that as it may, the results of a study by Meltzer and Ludwig (1971) of 143 industrial workers in five age groups (20–29, 30–39, 40–49, 50–59, 60–69) point to a pronounced decline in mental health during later adulthood (see Fig. 5.1). Caution should be exercised in interpreting these findings, however, because they are based on cross-sectional data and may be affected by cohort differences in mental health.

## Definitions of Abnormality

To a great extent, normality and abnormality of behavior are statistical concepts that vary in meaning with culture and time. Sociocultural factors, such as the attitudes and tolerance of other people, are important in determining what is normal or acceptable behavior. These factors are emphasized when an *abnormal* person is defined as one who has poor interpersonal relations, displays socially inappropriate behavior, and has no acceptable goals. According to this definition, people who repeatedly violate social norms are abnormal. But whether abnormal behavior is punished, ignored, treated, or even praised depends on society's interpretation of the value of the behavior and the extent to which other people are willing to tolerate it.

Most psychologists are not content with a purely cultural or statistical definition of abnormality. In determining whether or not a mental disorder is present, they look further into the personal experiences of the person, studying the satisfactions attained, the tension, anxiety, depression, and sense of isolation that are felt, and the effort expended. Thought processes, perceptions, and attitudes, which are not always apparent in behavior, are also important. Society may be willing to tolerate strange behavior or even be unaware of the problems experienced by a person, who may continue to function fairly effectively over a lifetime while enduring invisible anxieties and insecurities.

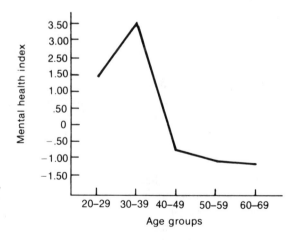

FIG. 5.1.   Changes in mental health with age. (Adapted from Meltzer & Ludwig, 1971.)

Normal personality changes that occur with age are exaggerated in people who become mentally disordered, with adjustment problems running the gamut from transient situational problems to severe psychotic reactions. The trend today is to avoid assigning nonuseful diagnostic labels to mental disorders whenever possible and to attempt to identify the causes of disordered behavior. Consequently, the psychiatric labels used in this chapter should in no way be viewed as either completely descriptive or explanatory of the behavior of a particular disordered person.

## Demographics of Mental Disorders

It is sometimes maintained that the ''stress of modern living'' is responsible for the high incidence of mental illness in the 20th century. Because diagnostic criteria and other factors affecting mental hospital admissions statistics vary with time and place, the question of whether people are more likely to become mentally ill in contemporary society than they were in the past is difficult to answer. The available data indicate, however, that the 20th century has not produced a greater proportion of most mental disorders (Goldhamer & Marshall, 1953). It is true that the number of first admissions to mental hospitals increased during the first half of the present century, but the admission rate did not change, and the average length of residence in the hospital decreased. In recent years there has been a drop in first admissions to mental hospitals for all patients— young and old. Unfortunately, this drop is not due to a decrease in the number of mentally disturbed people but rather to the fact that other facilities and institutions—nursing homes in particular—are handling larger numbers of mental patients.

Although the rate of serious psychotic disorders in men under 40 and women under 50 has not changed appreciably since 1885 (Goldhamer & Marshall, 1953), there has been an increase in mental disorders associated with old age. The increase is interpreted as being due largely to the fact that people are living longer and consequently are more likely to develop symptoms of mental disorder produced by changes in the brain accompanying old age (see chapter 3). The particular physical and interpersonal stresses to which the elderly are increasingly subjected as they grow older should also not be overlooked as causative factors.

Age differences interact with sex, location of residence, and socioeconomic status in affecting the incidence, severity, and type of mental disorder. The majority of elderly people admitted to mental hospitals are women, a statistic that is due to a combination of factors, including the greater number of elderly women than elderly men in the general population. Other contributing factors are the stresses of widowhood and the lower likelihood that older women have someone to take care of them at home. A larger percentage of mentally disturbed elderly people live in urban rather than in rural areas, probably because more older people—both normal and abnormal—reside in cites and not necessarily because cities are more stressful places in which to live. Having someone at home to care for them may also help explain why smaller numbers of rural-dwelling older people who are mentally disturbed come to the attention of authorities. Finally, severe mental disorders are more common among elderly people with lower than average incomes for their age group (see Busse & Blazer, 1980; Butler & Lewis, 1982).

## Defense Mechanisms

Many types of psychological reactions to stress, some adaptive and others maladaptive, occur in old age. Among the maladaptive responses are denial, anger, withdrawal, and dependency. In *denial,* the person simply denies the seriousness of a problem or that it even exists. Another reaction to stress is becoming angry at someone or something, perhaps someone other than the direct cause of frustration. This is the case in displaced aggression, in which the victim has nothing to do with the frustrating circumstance but is merely a convenient scapegoat.

Elderly people may also withdraw in potentially threatening situations, feeling that being close to others is risky and that self-isolation or retreat into fantasy is the best way to cope. Another type of reaction to frustration and conflict is to become helpless or overly dependent on other people. Older adults with strong dependency needs may also exaggerate and exploit a physical illness and associated depression. Such dependency is often fostered by well-meaning people who respond to older people as if they were unable to do anything for themselves and were in constant need of assistance.

All of these *defense mechanisms* are maladaptive because they are not permanent solutions to problems and usually create further difficulties for the person. Used to excess, many defense mechanisms can lead to more serious mental disturbances, for example, paranoia as a result of excessive anger or senile regression as a result of withdrawal (Verwoerdt, 1973).

## Psychophysiological Disorders and Hypochondriasis

Prolonged stress and anxiety can result in a variety of psychophysiological symptoms, including anxiety, depression, irritability, fatigue, loss of appetite, headache, and backache. Almost any organ or system of the body may show structural and functional changes under prolonged stress. Peptic ulcers and other gastrointestinal reactions are the most publicized psychophysiological disorders, but the course and severity of migraine headaches, skin conditions, chronic backache, and bronchial asthma are also affected by persisting emotional stress. In fact, it is generally acknowledged by medical scientists that all physical illnesses and their courses are influenced by the patient's emotional state.

A longitudinal study in which 204 men, who were students at Harvard University in the 1940s, were followed up for 30 years provided evidence linking personality adjustment to physical disorders (Valliant, 1979). Those men who had been diagnosed as "poorly adjusted" as students proved much more likely to become seriously ill and die in their middle years than those who had been diagnosed as "well adjusted." In contrast to the well adjusted, the group of poorly adjusted individuals had a greater incidence of cancer, coronary disorders, high blood pressure, emphysema, back disorders, and suicide. From these results, Valliant concluded that the personality adjustment or mental health status has a definite influence on a person's physical health in midlife. Good adjustment and positive mental health appear to retard the physical decline that begins in the middle years of life, whereas poor adjustment hastens it.

It does not require a traumatic experience to produce an adjustment problem. The process of change itself, whether unpleasant or pleasant, can create a disruption in daily living that places stress on the individual. Holmes and Rahe (1967) maintained that the stress of change, which requires a readjustment on the part of the individual, increases one's susceptibility to disease. The degree of increased susceptibility varies with the extent of readjustment necessitated by the change. These investigators constructed a "Social Readjustment Scale" on which events requiring changes in the pattern of daily living are scaled from 0 to 100, depending on the degree of readjustment ("points") required (see Table 5.2). The greater the degree of readjustment required in a given year, the greater the individual's chances of developing a stress-related physical illness.

## Neuroses

The psychodynamic explanation of the exaggerated use of avoidance behavior and defense mechanisms that characterize neuroses is that they serve to control the anxiety caused by the threatened breakthrough of unacceptable unconscious impulses. Although recognizing the fact that neurotic symptoms serve to control anxiety, behavior-oriented psychologists emphasize the learned nature and anxiety-reducing function of such symptoms rather than their unconscious origin. Anxiety during old age can be caused by a number of circumstances, chief among which are perceived helplessness or loss.

The neuroses, which are more common in young adults than in middle-aged or older adults, include conversion hysteria (sensory or motor disturbances of psychogenic origin), dissociative conditions (psychological amnesia, fugue, multiple personality), obsessive/compulsive conditions, phobias, hypochondriasis, and neurotic depression. Especially common are anxiety reactions, in which anxiety is not reduced or controlled by another neurotic symptom.

TABLE 5.2
Social Readjustment Rating Scale*

| Rank | Event (Change) | Readjustment Points |
|------|----------------|---------------------|
| 1 | Death of spouse | 100 |
| 2 | Divorce | 73 |
| 3 | Marital separation | 65 |
| 4 | Jail term | 63 |
| 5 | Death of close family member | 63 |
| 6 | Personal injury or illness | 53 |
| 7 | Marriage | 50 |
| 8 | Fired at work | 47 |
| 9 | Marital reconciliation | 45 |
| 10 | Retirement | 45 |
| 11 | Change in health of family member | 44 |
| 12 | Pregnancy | 40 |
| 13 | Sex difficulties | 39 |
| 14 | Gain of new family member | 39 |
| 15 | Business readjustment | 39 |
| 16 | Change in financial state | 38 |
| 17 | Death of close friend | 37 |
| 18 | Change to different line of work | 36 |
| 19 | Change in number of arguments with spouse | 35 |
| 20 | Mortgage over $10,000 | 31 |
| 21 | Foreclosure of mortagage or loan | 30 |
| 22 | Change in reponsibilities at work | 29 |
| 23 | Son or daughter leaving home | 29 |
| 24 | Trouble with in-laws | 29 |
| 25 | Outstanding personal achievement | 28 |
| 26 | Wife begin or stop work | 26 |
| 27 | Begin or end shcool | 26 |
| 28 | Change in living conditions | 25 |
| 29 | Revision of personal habits | 24 |
| 30 | Trouble with boss | 23 |
| 31 | Change in work hours or conditions | 20 |
| 32 | Change in residence | 20 |
| 33 | Change in schools | 20 |
| 34 | Change in recreation | 19 |
| 35 | Change in church activities | 19 |
| 36 | Change in social activities | 18 |
| 37 | Mortgage or loan less than $10,000 | 17 |
| 38 | Change in sleeping habits | 16 |
| 39 | Change in number of family get-togethers | 15 |
| 40 | Change in eating habits | 15 |
| 41 | Vacation | 13 |
| 42 | Christmas | 12 |
| 43 | Minor violations of the law | 11 |

*Adapted with permission from Holmes & Rahe (1967). Copyright 1967, Pergamon Press, plc.

One of the most common neurotic conditions in later life is *hypochondriasis,* an excessive preoccupation with one's health in the absence of significant physical pathology (Pfeiffer, 1977). Characterized by preoccupation with bodily processes and a fear of presumed disease, hypochondriasis has been interpreted as an escape from feelings of failure (Busse & Pfeiffer, 1977). To an elderly person who has been unable to achieve his or her ambitions or goals, becoming ill may be more acceptable than an admission of failure. The deception is not conscious, in which case it would be referred to as *malingering.* The patient is deceiving him or herself as well as the doctor, genuinely believing that he or she is physically ill with one or more disorders.

For the most part, neurotic behavior in old age is merely a continuation and intensification of personality characteristics that have been present since youth. The particular neurotic symptoms depend, however, on the existing personality structure as well as the social reinforcements that the individuals receive for the symptoms. For example, the greater frequency of hypochondriasis among elderly women is probably a reflection of the fact that the dependent, sick role is a more socially acceptable behavior pattern in women than in men.

## Depression and Suicide

Although depression is just as frequent during young adulthood as in later life, it is one of the most common of all reactions to stress and change in old age (Butler & Lewis, 1982). But unlike younger adults, in whom depression is based more on guilt, shame, and self-hate, depression in older adults is due more often to a loss of self-esteem occasioned by physical, financial, or social-role losses. Problems of health and disability are a common cause of depression among older adults, but retirement and relocation are apparently not as strong precipitating factors as one might suspect (Atchley, 1980). The symptoms of depression include feelings of intense sadness, hopelessness, pessimism, low self-regard, a loss of interest in people and things, problems in eating and sleeping, physical aches and pains, fatigue, and difficulty remembering. From this list of symptoms, it is understandable why psychological depression, like chronic alcoholism has often been misdiagnosed as senile brain disease (see chapter 3).

The intensity of depressive states varies from relatively mild reactions to specific situational factors (loss of a loved one, social isolation, physical problems, financial insecurity, institutionalization) to more serious depression that has no clear connection with external events. The former, which occurs in response to external sources of stress, is referred to as *neurotic depression,* and the latter as *psychotic depression.* The symptoms of psychotic depression include guilt, self-deprecation, and bodily complaints, whereas neurotic depression is characterized by "apathy, inertia, withdrawal into solitude, and quiet self-deprecation" (Epstein, 1976, p. 280).

Attempted suicide is an ever-present danger in cases of depression, with nearly one-fifth of the suicides being over age 65. Of the recorded 29,453 Americans who committed suicide in 1985, 5,795 were 65 or over (U.S. Department of Health and Human Services, 1987c). The relatively high incidence of suicide among the elderly is reflected in statistics from both the 19th and 20th centuries. As illustrated in Fig. 5.2, the increase in the overall suicide rate during old age is caused primarily by the very high rate for white males. The suicide rate for both White and nonWhite females actually declines after age 50. Also noteworthy in interpreting the age-related statistics on suicide is the fact that older adults are more likely than younger adults to be successful in their suicide attempts.

The cause of the sex difference in suicide rate among the elderly is not clear, but, in addition to differences in physical health, it is presumably affected by the different roles that men and women are expected to play in our culture and the resulting changes in those roles with aging. The assertive, achievement-oriented role of a typical middle-aged man is not so adaptable to later life as the more passive, nurturant role assumed by a typical middle-aged woman. Consequently, the greater change in behavior and self-esteem necessitated in the older man may

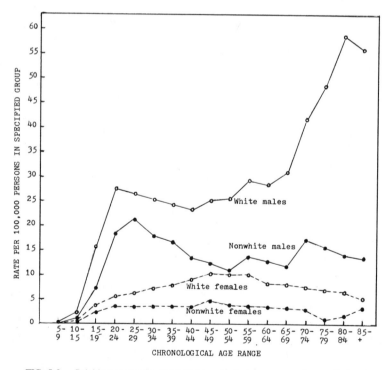

FIG. 5.2.  Suicide rate as a function of chronological age, sex, and race. (Adapted from U.S. Department of Health and Human Services, 1987.)

create more stress and resulting depression when he is unable to find satisfaction in his new role situation. It is noteworthy that men whose income from social security, pensions, and other sources is fairly high are less likely to take their own lives (Marshall, 1978).

One tends to think of a "suicide pact" as a phenomenon of romantic youth, but double suicide also occurs among elderly couples. Newspapers occasionally carry stories of older couples, who, because they have been the repeated victims of crime, or suffer from severe neglect or chronic illness, become despondent and decide to end their lives together.

## Character Disorders

Maladaptive personality patterns, or character disorders, may also persist into old age. Although these conditions are more common in younger age groups, there are elderly alcoholics, drug addicts, and sex deviates (see chapter 7). Many elderly alcoholics are simply continuing a lifelong habit, whereas others, in response to boredom, loneliness, or grief, take up drinking for the first time in old age. Unfortunately, chronic alcoholism, which affects some 2%–10% of older adults (Schuckit, 1977), is sometimes misdiagnosed as senility and consequently not treated properly.

Elderly antisocial ("psychopathic") personalities, individuals with little conscience or regard for the feelings or rights of other people, are less numerous than alcoholics. Most psychopaths appear to "burn out" by their 40s, their antisocial behavior having decreased markedly by the fifth decade of life. A related statistic, which is discussed in chapter 11, is the lower incidence of criminal behavior in later life.

## Psychotic Disorders

People who suffer from a psychophysiological disorder, a neurosis, or a character disorder can benefit from treatment and sometimes require hospitalization. Such patients, however, rarely manifest the severe distortion of reality, bizarre behavior, and extensive personality disorganization seen in institutionalized psychotics.

A substantial percentage of older Americans admitted to mental hospitals and nursing homes each year are diagnosed as psychotic. Their symptoms vary, but a diagnosis of psychosis implies the presence of a disorder in which the ability to recognize reality is severely affected. The distortion of reality is manifested by deficits in perception, language, and memory, as well as changes in mood. Approximately 50% of patients diagnosed as psychotic have a detectable brain disorder of the sort discussed in chapter 3. In the remaining 50% of the cases, who are referred to as *functional* psychotics, no brain damage or other organic cause for the disorder has been detected.

**Schizophrenia.** The three major types of functional psychoses—schizophrenia, delusional disorder, and mood disorders—all increase in frequency with aging. Schizophrenics, who comprise the largest category of functional psychotics, have severe disturbances in thinking and sometimes perception. They withdraw from contact with reality and lose empathy with other people. Disturbances in concept formation and regressive, bizarre behavior are characteristic of schizophrenics; hallucinations (false perceptions) and delusions (false beliefs) may also occur.

Some schizophrenics are in or in and out of mental hospitals for a large portion of their lives, growing old in institutions. Generally speaking, these long-term patients are meek and mild individuals who have adapted to institutional life and would probably be unable to cope with the decisions and stresses outside an institution. If they are not being treated for the disorder, a nursing home or some other less expensive facility is preferable to life in a mental hospital. Because of the law that people who are not being actively treated and are not considered dangerous to themselves or others cannot be retained indefinitely in a mental institution, many schizophrenics end up on city streets. There they manage to survive, but receive little assistance from the community and are perceived as an eyesore and an annoyance.

**Delusional (Paranoid) Disorder.** This category of psychosis includes a broad range of mental disorders of varying severity characterized by suspiciousness, projection, excessive feelings of self-importance and frequently complex delusions of grandeur, persecution, and ideas of references. The frequency of delusional disorder tends to increase with age, and is more common in elderly people who have sensory or cognitive defects. Pfeiffer (1977) maintained that, by reducing the ability to process information from the environment, such defects are more likely to make the individual a victim of his or her own fears. Delusional disorder, which is second only to depression of the frequency of mental disturbances among the elderly (Pfeiffer, 1977), are more common among elderly loners who have lived relatively isolated from other people for much of their lives (Berger & Zarit, 1978). On rare occasions, two or more people share the same delusional system, as in *folie a deux* ("madness of two") or, even less frequently, *folie a trois* ("madness of three") (see Report 5.2).

**Mood Disorders.** Also fairly common among the elderly are disorders involving disturbances in mood—either extreme elation (mania), profound depression, or periodic fluctuation between the two; in addition to extremes of mood, there is a loss of contact with reality. The major types of mood disorders are bipolar disorders and depressive disorders. The symptom picture in bipolar disor-

Report 5.2 FOLIE A TROIS*

Three elderly spinster sisters, aged 72, 68, and 65, were admitted to a psychiatric hospital after a neighbor called the police to report that one of them threatened to ''slit the throat'' of a 10 year old neighbor boy. These sisters had worked, eaten, and lived together for more than 40 years.

When interviewed in the hospital, each of the sisters told an almost identical story about how this 10 year old boy had been ''sent by them'' to remove the NO TRESPASSING sign from their front lawn. Close questioning revealed that many years earlier these women had posted such a sign on their lawn because both of their neighbors ''were spying'' on them by coming on their lawn and looking through the front window. It was also learned that these sisters had sued one of their neighbors with regard to a boundary dispute about their property lines. They lost the suit and attempted to find another lawyer to take up their case again, but no lawyer would do so. The boy they had threatened was the grandson of their neighbor, and they described him as ''rotten to the core from the day he was born.''

The two younger sisters also related that they and their sister had a good deal of trouble at vacation spots, usually rooming houses near resort areas, because other people were after their money and belongings. The oldest sister vehemently denied having had such difficulties and explained that her younger sisters occasionally ''told such lies,'' but that she would ''set them right'' as soon as she saw them on the ward.

When the younger sisters were again interviewed several days later, they both volunteered the information that their story about their rooming house troubles was untrue and that their neighbor had a way of influencing them to tell such stories. They then disclosed that they thought the doctor was conspiring with their neighbor against them and that he had better not ask them any more questions because he was being paid to keep the three in the hospital.

About three weeks after admission, the oldest sister had a massive cerebrovascular accident and died within hours of the attack. The two younger sisters at first became severely depressed, but then, as often happens with separation from the dominant person in such *folies*, several weeks after the death, they began talking about going back to their home and spoke of ''letting bygones be bygones.''

*From Kleinmuntz (1980). Copyright © 1980 by Benjamin Kleinmuntz. Reprinted by permission of Harper & Row, Publishers, Inc.

ders consists of severe mood swings from depression to elation, remission, and then recurrence. With aging, the manic and depressive phases of the cycle become more regular and hence predictable. During the manic state the patient is overtalkative, elated or irritable, and shows increased motor activity and bizarre ideation. During the depressive phase of the cycle the patient is deeply depressed in mood and activity, becoming agitated in some instances and stuporous in others.

Psychiatrists also differentiate between manic and depressed types of bipolar disorders. The symptoms of the manic type, which is less common than the depressed type, include overtalkativeness and the rapid production of bizarre ideas, undue elation or irritability, and increased motor activity (hyperactivity). Hostile, paranoid behavior of an accusatory nature may also occur in these patients. The depressed type is characterized by feelings of deep depression, guilt, self-deprecation, and bodily complaints, together with motor inhibition and either mental slowness or agitation.

**Depressive Disorders.**   The depressed type of bipolar disorders is distinguished from depressive disorders (psychotic depression), a mood disorder that was referred to earlier in the chapter. One type of psychotic depressive condition is the so-called "change of life" disorder, involutional melancholia. It is termed *involutional* because of its onset after age 40 and is more common in women than in men. The symptoms include extreme depression, agitation, self-deprecation, and feelings of guilt and failure. Involutional melancholia is relatively rare, and occurs during middle or late life in the absence of any prior history of depression. Because psychotic depression can occur at any stage of life and does not show a sudden rise in frequency after age 40, many authorities have questioned the need for such a diagnostic category (Winokur, 1973). Involutional melancholia is not listed as a separate category in the *Diagnostic and Statistical Manual of Mental Disorders* (American Psychiatric Association, 1987).

## SUMMARY

People vary extensively in their ability to cope with the tasks and problems of later life. Declining health and physical appearance, the loss of employment and loved ones, and an erosion of the sense of significance and meaningfulness of one's life can lead to depression and despair. On the other hand, more integrated persons who possess effective mechanisms for coping with the stresses of aging and are willing to search for a new identity in old age can find new challenges and sources of gratification at this stage of life.

Personality, the unique organization of abilities, traits, and behavior patterns characterizing an individual, manifests a substantial degree of consistency across the life span. People who are well adjusted in youth and middle adulthood tend to remain so in later life; people who are maladjusted in earlier life continue to have adjustment difficulties in old age. Developmental theories such as Erikson's conception of eight stages of human existence, Peck's descriptions of three conflicts of later life, transition theories such as Levinson's, and script theory recognize that personality can continue developing even in later life. Although the self-concept may decline in old age, rather than being a function of age per se the decline is related to health problems, decreased socioeconomic security, and other events associated with aging.

An age-related trend toward interiority or introspection, which is perhaps a normal coping response to the stresses of aging, has been observed. Increased rigidity or inflexibility has also been said to characterize the elderly, but a more accurate description of older adults is "realistically cautious" rather than "rigid."

Reichard and his colleagues found evidence for five types of adjustment patterns in older men—mature, rocking chair, armored, angry, and self-hating. Similarly, in a study of the relationships of personality and social activity to happiness in old age, Neugarten and her colleagues observed four personality types—integrated, armored-defended, passive-dependent, and unintegrated—with two or three subcategories under each of the first three types. A well-integrated personality and an active, problem-solving attitude were found by Neugarten to be associated with better adjustment in old age. Having socially meaningful roles to play is also important. Although the characteristics or factors associated with effective adjustment possess some cross-situational generality, there are situational differences in the effectiveness of personality traits. Depending on the environment, traits and behaviors that may be socially less acceptable and even lead to unhappiness may have greater survival value than more socially acceptable characteristics.

Owing to a combination of organic changes and psychological stress, the mental health of older adults tends to be poorer than that of younger and middle-aged adults. Although the young also have their share of adjustment problems, young adulthood is most often viewed by the elderly as the "happiest time of life." Mental disorders are more common in old age than at other times of life, but the incidence varies with sex, socioeconomic status, urban versus rural residence, and other demographic variables. The incidence of mental disorders does not seem to have changed greatly since the last century, despite the stresses and strains of living in the 20th century.

Psychophysicological disorders, neuroses, depression, and character disorders occur at all stages of life. Depression is the most serious mental disorder during later life, followed by delusional disorder and hypochondriasis. Suicide increases dramatically in old age, and is more common among older White men that in any other age, racial, or sex group.

Psychotic disorders, which are characterized by pronounced distortions of reality and may also involve disturbances in perception, language, memory, and mood, are less common and more serious than other functional disorders. The three main types of functional psychoses are schizophrenia, delusional disorder, and mood disorders. Mood disorders are further subdivided into bioplar disorders and depressive disorder.

## SUGGESTED READINGS

Berger, K. A., & Zarit, S. H. (1978). Late life paranoid states: Assessment and treatment. *American Journal of Orthopsychiatry, 48,* 628–637.

Costa, P. T., Jr., & McCrae, R. R. (1985). Personality as a lifelong determinant of well-being. In C. Malatesta & C. Izard (Eds.), *Affective processes in adult development and aging.* New York: Sage.

Costa, P. T., Jr., & McCrae, R. R. (1985). Hypochondriasis, neuroticism, and aging. *American Psychologist, 40,* 19–28.

LaRue, A., Dessonville, C., & Jarvik, L. F. (1985). Aging and mental disorders. In J. E. Birren & K. W. Schaie (Eds.), *Handbook of the psychology of aging* (2nd ed., pp. 664–702). New York: Van Nostrand Reinhold.

Neugarten, B. L. (1977). Personality and aging. In J. E. Birren & K. W. Schaie (Eds.), *Handbook of the psychology of aging.* New York: Van Nostrand Reinhold.

Pfeiffer, E. (1977). Psychopathology and social pathology. In J. E. Birren & K. W. Schaie (Eds.), *Handbook of the psychology of aging.* New York: Van Nostrand Reinhold.

Reedy, M. N. (1983). Personality and aging. In D. S. Woodruff & J. E. Birren (Eds.), *Aging: Scientific perspectives and social issues* (2nd ed., pp. 112–136). Monterey, CA: Brooks/Cole.

Weinberg, J. (1979). Psychopathology. In J. Hendricks & C. D. Hendricks (Eds.), *Dimensions of aging.* Cambridge, MA: Winthrop Publishers.

Zarit, S. H. (1980). *Aging and mental disorders.* New York: The Free Press.

# 6

# Treatment of Adjustment Problems and Mental Disorders

Although people experience difficulties during all phases of their existence, old age, perhaps more than any other stage of life, is a time of problems. Many of the problems encountered by older people are similar to those of younger adults: family and peer relationships, physical illness, financial affairs, and living conditions. Other problems, such as the stress of retirement or the death of a spouse, are more characteristic of later life. In any event, the depression, anxiety, grief, loneliness, dissatisfaction, and lack of self-esteem felt by many young and middle-aged individuals are also experienced by the elderly.

How the elderly handle or cope with their problems is as much a matter of subjective perception as it is objective reality. Thus, almost all older people experience anxiety, but by virtue of a better self-concept and a more optimistic outlook some are able to manage anxiety better than others. And all older people who have problems do not require the assistance of doctors or counselors. Most, by themselves or with the help of family members and friends, are quite successful in coping with the losses and changes of old age. However, others need medical and psychological help in dealing with life's vicissitudes and in finding satisfaction or contentment.

## TREATMENT RESOURCES

The elderly can avail themselves of a wide range of community, state, and federal facilities for the treatment of mental and behavioral problems. Unfortunately, these facilities, and community mental health clinics in particular, are frequented by a small percentage of older people who need help. Among the reasons for this state of affairs is the fact that older people are often proud individuals who view psychological problems as a sign of weakness or inadequacy. Consequently, they may be reluctant to construe their problems in psychological terms (Lawton, 1979) or to ask for help when they do. Related to this attitude is the fact that psychiatrists, psychologists, and other mental health professionals who treat such problems are sometimes viewed with suspicion and distrust by older people who grew up at a time when mental illness was more of a social stigma than it is today. In addition, the lack of interest and enthusiasm shown by many general practitioners, clergymen, and other referral sources concerning the effectiveness of psychological treatment of the elderly contribute to the infrequent use of mental health facilities by this age group. Other reasons why elderly people fail to make adequate use of psychiatric or psychological treatment facilities are inexperienced or poorly educated mental health workers, lack of knowledge of resources on the part of the elderly, and a scarcity of transportation to the clinic or other health facility.

## Voluntary and Involuntary Admission

Despite this somewhat negative picture, older people who realize that they need help and/or are encouraged by others to obtain it may seek assistance at a community mental health facility or request admission to a mental hospital for examination and treatment. A patient who is *voluntarily* admitted to a treatment facility can sign out at any time unless, in cases where the patient is considered dangerous to him or herself or others, the head of the facility is granted a legal postponement of release. *Involuntary admission,* or *commitment*[1], the laws and procedures for which vary from state to state, may be obtained after a petition is made by a family member or another person who is responsible for the patient. The petition is followed by a legal hearing at which it is determined whether the patient is harmful to himself (herself) or others; if so, a decision is then made as to where the patient should be admitted for treatment. The initial period of admission or hospitalization varies according to the judgment of institutional officials and other authorities; it is typically 30–60 days, but may be extended indefinitely by subsequent legal action.

Unfortunately, admission to a treatment facility is not always done for the best of reasons or necessarily accompanied by effective treatment. Many older people are left or abandoned in nursing homes, which in too many instances have replaced the state and county hospitals as "custodial warehouses" (Kahn, 1977). Like the French relatives described by de Beauvoir (1972), Americans may simply "deposit" their elderly parents in nursing or rest homes to die. A large

---

[1]Mental health professionals and legal experts object to the term *commitment,* with its implications of imprisonment, and have recommended that it be replaced with *hospitalization, admission,* or some other less offensive term.

percentage of such persons do die within the first year or so after being admitted, but to what extent the environmental change and loss of social support from relatives and friends contribute to this statistic is difficult to say.

## PHYSICAL TREATMENT METHODS

The prognosis with older patients who are seriously mentally ill is seldom good, and the goals of treatment may be more limited than with younger patients. Decreasing the patient's suffering so that his or her complaints and the complaints of others are minimized is important but not necessarily curative. A combination of physical, psychological, and environmental intervention procedures is usually necessary for the most effective results. Physical treatment methods, which depend on the symptom picture and other factors, include surgery, drugs, changes in diet, and electroshock therapy.

### Electroshock Therapy

Electroshock therapy (EST) consists of passing a 70–130 volt current through the patient's temples for approximately 1 second, inducing a convulsion similar to that of an epileptic seizure. The treatment is administered only a few times and, unlike most drug therapies, works immediately. It appears to be painless and has few serious side effects other than a loss of memory for events immediately preceding the shock. Although at one time it was a routine procedure in the treatment of both schizophrenia and psychotic depression, the manner in which EST acts to ameliorate these conditions is unclear. In any event, EST has been replaced in most cases by tranquilizing and antidepressant drugs.

### Drugs

A list of the most commonly prescribed psychotropic drugs for the treatment of mental disorders and stress-related problems of adjustment is given in Table 6.1. Commonly used with elderly depressed patients are the antidepressants, including tricyclic drugs (Elavil) and MAO inhibitors (Nardil). Lithium carbonate drugs are usually prescribed for manic conditions, and phenothiazine derivatives (Thorazine, Mellaril) for schizophrenia. Used with less serious, nonpsychotic personality problems or anxiety reactions are the minor tranquilizers (Equanil, Miltown). All of these drugs have side effects, some of them quite serious, and should be used for the shortest possible time.[2] In most cases they do not actually

---

[2]Because of the negative side effects that many of these drugs have on older patients, in recent years there has been something of a revival in the use of electroshock for certain mental disorders.

TABLE 6.1

Frequently Used Drugs for Treating Mental and Behavioral Disorders*

---

*Antipsychotic Drugs*. Phenothiazines (e.g., Thorazine, Mellaril), butyrophenones (Haldol), and thioxanthenes (Navane, Taractan). Used to treat psychotic symptoms such as extreme agitation, delusions, and hallucinations; aggressive or violent behavior. Side effects include dry mouth and, when used for a long term, motor disturbances such as Parkinsonism and tardive dyskinesia.

*Antidepressants*. Tricyclics (e.g., Tofranil, Elavil) and monoamine oxidase (MAO) inhibitors (e.g., Marplan, Nardil). Used to treat relatively severe depressive symptoms. Many side effects, some of which are dangerous. Use of MAO inhibitors requires dietary restrictions.

*Antimanic Drugs*. Generic name of drug is lithium carbonate (e.g., Eskalith, Lithane). Used to treat manic episodes and some severe depressions, particularly recurring ones or those alternating with mania. Multiple side effects occur unless carefully monitored; toxicity potential is high.

*Antianxiety Drugs* (minor tranquilizers). Propanediols (e.g., Equanil, Miltown) and benzodiazepines (e.g., Valium, Librium). Used to treat nonpsychotic personality problems in which anxiety and tension are prominent; also used as anticonvulsants and sleep inducers. Side effects include drowsiness and lethargy; dependence and toxicity are dangers.

*Stimulants*. Types include dextroamphetamine (Dexedrine), amphetamine (Benzedrine), and methylphenidate (Ritalin). Used to treat hyperactivity, distractability, specific learning disabilities, and, occasionally, extreme hypoactivity. Side effects often troublesome.

---

*Adapted from Carson, Butcher, and Coleman, 1988.

cure the patient but serve to contain or moderate the problem, making it possible for other treatment approaches (psychotherapy, environmental therapy, etc.) to be effective.

As Butler and Lewis (1982) pointed out, tranquilizers (antipsychotic and antianxiety drugs), antidepressants, and antimanic drugs perhaps serve to control the anxieties of the mental health staff and the family, who must deal with the patient on a day-to-day basis, as much as the emotional problems of the patient. Using psychotropic drugs more for patient management than for therapy can be criticized, but one can sympathize with caretakers who must deal with hyperactive, suicidal, or regressed patients on a daily basis. Certainly the families of severely psychotic or brain-damaged patients often face a harrowing future when they must provide in-home care for a prolonged period of time. It is difficult to control one's own feelings and maintain one's own health while providing almost constant care to a relative who progressively deteriorates over time.

## PSYCHOLOGICAL TREATMENT: BACKGROUND AND RESOURCES

It might seem that older people, by virture of the fact that they have lived until old age, have a proven track record of coping with the stresses of life. Old age, however, brings its own special crises—physical deterioration, retirement, widowhood—and a continuing need for helpful understanding and emotional assistance. Psychological methods of treatment are of great importance, not only with nonpsychotic disorders of adjustment but with psychotic disorders of both the functional and organic variety.

The distinction between *counseling* and *psychotherapy* is not clear-cut: Both involve discussing one's problems with another, usually professionally trained, individual. In counseling these discussions are usually of shorter duration; the techniques employed, somewhat more superficial; and the goals, more limited than those of psychotherapy. These discussions, which are encouraged by the development of a positive interpersonal relationship between the counselor (therapist) and counselee (client, patient), hopefully provide a psychological climate in which the counselee can examine his or her problems and can find solutions to them.

Counseling is not limited to any one profession; psychiatrists, psychologists, social workers, nurses, ministers, teachers, and many nonprofessional or paraprofessional persons provide counseling services. However, the practice of psychotherapy for the treatment of more serious disorders of personality and behavior is usually restricted to psychiatrists and clinical psychologists.

The efforts and procedures required in counseling vary with the individual and the situation. Serious mental health problems, especially depressions, may require in-depth personal counseling. On the other hand, patients with debilitating physical problems, which are aggravated by emotional reactions, require supportive counseling. Included in supportive counseling are techniques such as sensitive listening and reassurance, in addition to efforts to motivate the person, elevate his or her spirits, and reinforce the will to recover and to survive (Lombana, 1976). These approaches are especially necessary when the older person receives little or no emotional support from family and friends (see Report 6.1).

Counseling is also needed by elderly people residing in nursing homes or in similar institutions. Personal counseling and other psychological interventions can assist in the redevelopment of feelings of worth and independence to sustain patients in the institution and to help them cope with life outside. Another type of counseling, avocational counseling, can be combined with retraining to assist retirees in handling feelings of resentment and apathy accompanying forced retirement.

## Training of Counselors and Psychotherapists

The first old-age counseling center in the United States was established some years ago in San Francisco by Lillian Martin. The field of old-age counseling is, however, still not very popular, and only recently have concerted efforts been made to train counselors in problems of the aged. Many counselors and psychotherapists, because of the purported inflexibility or poorer learning and problem-solving abilities of the elderly, feel that psychological techniques are not very effective with this age group. In fact, Sigmund Freud, the father of psycho-

---

### Report 6.1    A SUCCESS FOR PSYCHOTHERAPY*

Anna was nearly 80 and living with a married daughter. For the past 5 years Anna had experienced a progressive loss of memory. At first, she just forgot a few insignificant things, such as where she had placed her reading glasses. Gradually, the problem got more serious until she sometimes could not maintain a conversation: she forgot what she had just been told and asked the same question again. At times she would get lost or would even lose her way inside her daughter's house. Anna became more and more of a burden. The advice of Anna's doctor was to have her placed in a home for the aged.

Anna's experience is all too common. Many older persons suffer from some sort of short-term memory impairment: they forget what just happened but can tell you the details of an incident that occurred half a century ago. All sorts of medical theories have been proposed to explain this phenomenon of senility. The one taught in most medical schools is that such mental deterioration is caused by physical changes in the brain . . . and is irreversible. Therefore, most physicians and medically trained psychiatrists tend to give up too easily on an older person with a failing memory.

Fortunately for Anna, her daughter did not take the advice of the first doctor. They saw another physician, who referred Anna to a psychotherapist specializing in geriatric practice. In less than two months, Anna's deteriorating mental condition was reversed. This psychotherapy was not cheap. However, it was less expensive than psychoanalysis and certainly a bargain compared to the cost of keeping Anna in a home for the aged.

*After Brink (1976), p. 24. Reprinted with permission from the National Mental Health Association, Inc.

---

analysis, did not advocate the use of psychotherapy with people over 40 years of age. Consequently, those counselors and therapists who subscribe to the stereotype of the aged as rigid, uncooperative, and mentally deteriorated have shown a reluctance to work with them. The fact that the elderly inadvertently remind counselors of their own mortality and relationships with their own parents may also play a role in this reluctance (Kastenbaum, 1964). In any case, these perceptions are unrealistic: There is little evidence that older people are any more difficult to treat or that they gain less from psychological treatment than younger persons.

Psychotherapists and counselors may be psychiatrists, psychologists, clergymen (pastoral counselors), social workers, and certain other "helpers." It is unfortunate, however, that in many states almost anyone can call him or herself a psychotherapist or counselor and "treat" people for a fee. Because of the danger of psychological quackery, elderly people who need psychological treatment should be aware of the credentials of the person to whom they are referred. A list of competent professional psychotherapists can usually be obtained from a family physician, clergyman, or public mental health agency. In addition, most mental health organizations publish directories of professionals who are qualified to offer psychological assistance to the elderly.

Considering the growth of counseling programs of various kinds, the need to establish criteria for counselors of the elderly and counseling training programs is apparent. Such training should not be restricted to professionals, because much of the counseling in family service agencies, Red Cross chapters, Senior Citizens and Golden Age clubs, departments of public welfare, recreation centers, nursing homes, and other organizations catering to the elderly is done by volunteers and other nonprofessional persons. In addition to being trained and experienced in the psychological aspects of counseling and geriatric problems in particular, counselors should be knowledgeable about appropriate agencies that can assist older people with housing, financial problems, health concerns, vocational and avocational activities, and other needs affecting mental health.

Particularly noteworthy among the many counselor training programs are the peer counselor (widow-to-widow, patient-to-patient, etc.) training programs of the University of Southern California and Oakland University (Michigan). The emphasis in these programs is on training counselors to assist the elderly without "taking over" or creating excessive dependency. As noted by Schwartz, Snyder, and Peterson (1984), efforts to help older people should not be made in a "take charge" or patronizing manner. Older people need to develop self-confidence in coping without relying entirely on someone else to solve all their problems or meet all their emotional needs.

## THEORIES OF PSYCHOLOGICAL COUNSELING AND THERAPY

Although counseling is possible without adhering to any elaborate theory of personality development and functioning, all counselors have some explicit or implicit framework for understanding other human beings. In fact, every layperson probably has some "theory" as to why people behave as they do. Such theories frequently consist of overgeneralizations or stereotypes but serve as rough guides to expectation and action. Realizing that every individual is different and that human behavior is very complex, professional counselors and psychotherapists have learned to be suspicious of the explanatory power of commonsense theories. It is generally maintained, however, that therapeutic interventions are more likely to be effective when guided by some explicit, professionally developed theory or set of principles concerning personality. Among the theories that have had the greatest impact on counseling and psychotherapy are psychoanalytic theory, phenomenological theory, and behavior theory.

### Psychoanalytic Theory

Sigmund Freud and other psychoanalysts have viewed human personality as a kind of battleground where three combatants—the id, ego, and superego—vie for supremacy. The *id*, a reservoir of instinctive drives of sex and aggression housed in the unconscious part of the mind, acts according to the pleasure principle. It runs into conflict with the *superego* (the "conscience"), which acts according to the moral principle. Although the id is inborn, the superego develops as the child internalizes the prohibitions and sanctions that the parents place on his or her behavior. Meanwhile the *ego* acts according to the reality principle, attempting to serve as a mediator between the relentless pressures of the id and superego for control. The id says "Now!," the superego says "Never!," and the ego says "Later" to the individual's basic desires. Although id impulses and the conflict of the id with the superego and ego usually take place in the unconscious mind, they are expressed in thoughts and behavior in various disguised forms.

Freud was perhaps the first personality theorist to stress the idea that "the child is father to the man," that the deprivations and dissatisfactions of childhood frequently have permanent effects on personality. His theory of psychosexual stages maintains that frustration and conflict at a particular stage of development affect an individual's personality structure in adulthood. Unresolved conflicts and frustrations may lead to *fixation,* a failure to progress psychosexually beyond a particular stage, or *regression,* a partial or complete return to behavior patterns typical of an earlier developmental stage, and the resultant imprint on adult personality.

From the psychoanalytic viewpoint, the basic goal of psychotherapy is to bring into conscious awareness repressed impulses that are causing anxiety. The primary techniques used to accomplish the goal of achieving insight into the bases of a psychological problem are free association (saying whatever comes into one's mind), analysis of transference (meaning of the relationship that develops between patient and analyst), analysis of resistance (reluctance of patient to discuss sensitive material), dream analysis, and interpretation of statements made by the patient during the course of therapy. Unfortunately, little research has been conducted on the treatment of elderly people by means of psychoanalysis (Blum & Tross, 1980). Although it is not the treatment of choice in dealing with most of the problems of the elderly, psychoanalysis has been helpful with certain intelligent, talkative older patients who suffered from milder mental disorders.

## Transactional Analysis

An offspring of classical psychoanalysis that has been somewhat more effective in treating problems of the elderly is *transactional analysis.* As described by Berne (1964), transactional analysis conceives of human personality as being composed of three ego states—adult, parent, and child. These three states are similar to the ego, superego, and id of classical psychoanalysis, but unlike the psychoanalytic emphasis on the unconscious, transactional analysis focuses on conscious, observable behavior. Similar to the Freudian notion of psychic conflict, the interactions, or *transactions,* among these three ego states lead to maladaptive personality development or emotional problems.

The goals of transactional analysis are to (Berne, 1966):

1. Help the client decontaminate any damaged ego state.
2. Develop in the client the capacity to use all ego states where appropriate.
3. Assist the client in developing the full use of his or her adult state.
4. Help the client rid himself or herself of an inappropriately chosen life position and life script, replacing them with an "I'm OK" position and a new, productive life script.

To accomplish these goals, the counselor tries to help the client understand the structures of his or her ego states ("structural analysis"), the transactions in which the client usually engages ("transactional analysis"), the payoffs that a client receives for playing certain games ("games analysis"), and the fact that the client's whole life script has been a mistake ("script analysis").

## Phenomenological (Self) Theory

Phenomenological, or "self," theorists maintain that attempting to analyze personality into a set of components such as id, ego, and superego or adult, parent, and child does an injustice to the integrated, dynamic nature of personality. In contrast to psychoanalysts, who emphasize sexual and aggressive drives, the unconscious, and the importance of psychosexual development, phenomenologists stress perceptions, meanings, attitudes, feelings, and the centrality of the self. According to phenomenological theory, people respond to the world in terms of their unique perceptions of it. The *phenomenal field* is that part of the physical environment perceived by and meaningful to a person, whereas the *self* is a portion of the phenomenal field that is related to the individual in a personal way. In the language of Abraham Maslow, Carl Rogers, and other phenomenologically oriented psychologists, the individual strives to attain a state of *self-actualization*—a congruence or harmony between the real and ideal selves.

Carl Rogers (1965) and other psychologists who have been greatly influenced by phenomenological and existential philosophers have emphasized an ahistorical, "here-and-now" (as opposed to "there-and-then") approach to counseling. Counselors subscribing to this point of view do a minimum of questioning, advising and interpreting. Rogers' client-centered counseling, for example, is based on the premise that people are free to control their own behavior and hence should assume responsibility for solving their own problems. The counselor simply acts as a facilitator, accepting what the client says, reflecting the feeling tone in the client's statements, or restating the content of a statement made by the client. By providing an accepting, nonjudgmental atmosphere (''unconditional positive regard'') in which clients can examine their own experiences freely and can be themselves, the counselor encourages clients to use their own resources to solve personal problems and to change their attitudes and behavior.

Rogers emphasized that people have the ability to grow and to fulfill their potentialities, that is, to ''become'' themselves. In successful counseling, clients initially express a rather low self-evaluation, but the evaluations become more positive as the counseling process proceeds. There is, however, no guarantee of success with client-centered counseling, especially when the counselee is highly dependent or has a severe emotional disorder. The client-centered approach tends to be more effective with mildly maladjusted but fairly self-sufficient people.

A number of variations and extensions of phenomenological (self) theory, some of which have implications for counseling the elderly, have been suggested. A noteworthy example is Carkhuff's (1969) model that is based on three counseling goals—self-exploration, self-understanding, and action. The counselor uses six conditions—empathy, respect, concreteness, genuineness, confrontation, and immediacy—to assist the client in attaining these goals. The first four conditions are most important during the initial or facilitation stage of counseling. This stage has as its primary objective the establishment of a working relationship such that the client will feel free to begin self-exploration, which will hopefully lead to self-understanding. During the second, or action, stage of counseling the last two conditions—confronting the client with discrepancies and getting the client to focus on the immediate situation in counseling—are most important.

The nine-step model advocated by Alpaugh and Haney (1978) for counseling older adults is based on the approaches of Rogers and Carkhuff (see Fig. 6.1). The objectives of the nine-step model are to (a) provide emotional support to the client and (b) clarify the client's problems and the issues contained in them. The first step in the model, understanding the client, consists of attending to the feelings expressed and the verbal and nonverbal content of the client's communications. The second step, establishing rapport, requires that the counselor be empathic, respectful, and concerned. The third step, defining the problem, is similar to reflecting the content of the client's communications. The counselor must listen carefully to what the client says and try to determine the central issue. When the problem has been defined, the fourth step—setting a goal—is easy. The goal of the counseling sessions becomes one of finding a solution to the problem. Step five is clarifying issues. The next two steps in the model, listening and exploring alternatives, are concerned with looking at possible solutions to the problem and their positive and negative features. Step eight, making a decision, does not usually occur without considerable soul searching, because most decisions have some negative consequences. The final step, providing closure, comes only after the client and counselor agree that the relationship should be

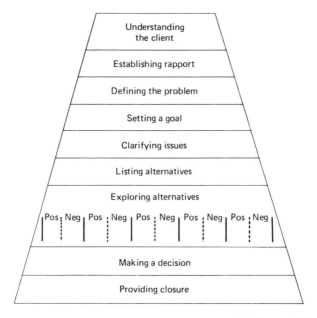

FIG. 6.1.    A nine-step counseling model. (After Alpaugh & Haney, 1978, p. 68.)

terminated. Closure is achieved by tying up loose ends but leaving the door open for further counseling sessions if the need should arise.

## Behavior Theory and Therapy

For many years almost all psychotherapists subscribed to the beliefs of psychoanalytic depth therapists that (a) simply removing symptoms rather than treating root causes does not produce permanent cures; (b) causes, and hence "cures," can only be found by studying the patient's life history in detail; (c) a transference relationship between patient and therapist must develop if therapy is to be successful; and (d) the patient can be cured only by gaining insight into his or her problems and personality. Although these beliefs are not held as tenaciously by phenomenological counselors, the latter still subscribe to the notion that clients must achieve some degree of self-understanding, or "insight," in order to solve their emotional problems. Since the 1950s, however, an increasing number of psychotherapists and counselors, particularly clinical psychologists who have been trained in learning theory, have questioned whether these beliefs are correct. Even some psychoanalysts have expressed doubt concerning the necessity of treating root causes, studying the life history, developing a strong transference relationship, and attaining insight (see Ellis, 1962).

Behavioral approaches to psychological treatment, referred to as *behavioral therapy* or *behavior modification,* are based on principles of learning and motivation formulated from the results of laboratory experiments on animals and humans. These principles involve shaping, discrimination, generalization, extinction, and mediating responses. Behavior theorists have argued that because many adjustment problems are the consequences of faulty learning, it should be possible to arrange conditions so that the maladjusted behavior is unlearned. For example, a behavior modification approach that has had some success with the elderly, particularly those in institutions, is *contingency management.* This approach makes positive reinforcement (pleasures or privileges of various kinds) contingent on socially approved behavior (keeping neat and clean, eating properly, interacting with other patients, etc.). As with all behavior modification procedures, the ultimate goal of contingency management is for the patient to learn to monitor and control his or her own behavior.

Other behavioral techniques have been devised for dealing with anxiety, which is considered to be at the core of many emotional disorders. In the technique of *systematic desensitization* the patient is exposed to an anxiety-arousing, or phobic, situation under contrived, "safe" conditions. Other, more normal responses can be conditioned to the situation by controlling anxiety responses. For example, the therapist may encourage the patient to become more relaxed, during which time increasingly more fearful stimuli are presented. The therapist begins with stimuli that normally produce a weak fear response and then presents more frightening stimuli as the patient becomes more and more relaxed. Besides relaxation, assertive behavior, sexual behavior, and eating responses have also been used to control anxiety.

## Cognitive Therapy

In recent years many behavioral therapists have become more cognitive in their orientation. Cognitive therapists emphasize the role of maladaptive thought patterns (specific attitudes, beliefs, expectations, etc.) in determining adjustment problems. Using self-monitoring, thought stopping, and other procedures, patients are taught how to identify and to gain control over their automatic, idiosyncratic mental reactions to disturbing stimuli. Cognitively oriented therapy has been particularly useful in the treatment of depression (see Beck, 1967). The patient keeps a diary of pleasant and unpleasant daily experiences and automatic negative thoughts and meets with the therapist for an hour each week to discuss and to analyze the material recorded in the diary. In this way the patient gradually becomes aware of how he or she is making him or herself miserable and learns how to cope with his or her negative thoughts and behaviors.

## Reality Therapy

Like behavior therapy, reality therapy did not stem from a complex theory of personality development and adjustment. Rather, this approach is based on a set of practical techniques devised by William Glasser (1965) from his personal experiences with emotionally disturbed individuals. Glasser conceptualized human personality in terms of how well people meet their needs, especially the needs to be loved and to feel worthwhile. The goal of reality therapy is to teach the client to meet his or her own needs by using the three R's of "Right, Responsibility, and Reality" as a guide. "Right" is an accepted standard or norm of behavior; "Responsibility" means satisfying one's own needs without interfering with those of others; "Reality" means understanding that there is a real world in which one's needs have to be satisfied.

The counselor uses the following techniques to teach the client to govern his or her life according to the three R's (Hansen, Stevic, & Warner, 1977):

1. Communicating to the client that he or she cares.
2. Getting the client to focus on present behavior rather than on feelings.
3. Helping the client to evaluate his or her own irresponsible behavior.
4. Getting the client to make a commitment to a specific plan to change his or her irresponsible behavior.
5. Refusing to accept excuses for failure to stick to a plan but not punishing the client for failing.

## TECHNIQUES OF COUNSELING
## THE ELDERLY

The focus of all counseling or psychotherapeutic approaches that have been applied to the elderly is to motivate the person to take an interest in things and to use his or her abilities in personally and socially acceptable ways. It is also important that the person be helped to feel wanted and valued by the family and community. The specific goals of counseling with the elderly are frequently more limited and involve fewer sessions and less in-depth analysis than with younger individuals. Although professional counselors of the elderly usually take a fairly directive role and make direct suggestions for change, they function primarily as facilitators and guides who encourage clients to review their experiences and behaviors. The counselor is typically quite supportive toward the client's ego defenses when they are effective but also toward the client's search for more effective coping techniques. The seriousness of the client's psychological and physical problems are not overemphasized, but are treated somewhat matter of factly. Clients may also be given "homework assignments," for exam-

TABLE 6.2
Suggestions for Giving Psychological Help to Older People*

---

1. Allow older people opportunities to talk about and resolve their problems and conflicts; pay attention to their reminiscences and try to understand them.
2. Do not be afraid to touch older people; a handshake, a friendly pat, or an arm about the shoulder can satisfy the desire for human contact and open up the discussion.
3. Assist older people to accept the fact that they are growing older, but emphasize the positive aspects of aging (e.g., reduced pressure to perform at high levels).
4. Help older people maintain human contacts and develop new relationships; encourage them to gain new friends to replace those that are lost.
5. Help older people cultivate pleasures of the mind and to find creative outlets in community activities, arts, and hobbies.
6. In counseling the elderly, it is as critical to identify and encourage areas of health as it is to clarify problems.
7. Persons caring for or counseling the ill or handicapped must assist them in finding ways to help themselves in a positive manner that brings at least a measure of the self-esteem necessary for human dignity.
8. Do not try to destroy the defenses of illusion and denial employed by older people. Rather than attacking these defenses directly, work toward understanding and encouraging a realistic lowering of them.
9. Always discuss the facts of death and loss and the problems of grief in the context of possibilities, restitution, and resolution.

---

*Adapted from University of California Cooperative Extension, (1978) and Butler & Lewis (1982).

ple, keeping a record of their own behaviors (self-monitoring) and trying out new approaches of dealing with their problems and other people.

Whether the counselor is a professional, a peer, or a relative, various techniques may be applied to achieve the goals of counseling. A list of practical suggestions, incorporating many of the specific techniques that have been used to provide psychological help for the elderly, is given in Table 6.2. Although these suggestions may be followed by anyone, trained or untrained, who has an interest in assisting older people, they are most effective when the counselor is trained in working with the elderly.

## Group Counseling and Psychotherapy

Butler and Lewis (1982) describe several individual and group-oriented techniques for use with the elderly, including telephone outreach therapy, group psychotherapy, life-review therapy, and life-cycle group therapy. All counseling and psychotherapy is concerned to some extent with interpersonal relationships, but the interpersonal aspect is emphasized in group methods. Older people who have feelings of alienation, loneliness, loss of self-esteem, and even despair can be helped greatly by group-oriented techniques. Although most group therapy with older people takes place in institutional settings, it is also helpful to noninstitutionalized individuals who are going through the stress of retirement, widowhood, or other potentially traumatic experiences.

Group counseling saves time over that required for individual counseling and is less expensive than the latter. The group also provides an opportunity for the counselee to communicate with someone other than the counselor, and thus be exposed to the kind of interpersonal stress that may have contributed to the problem with which the counselee must learn to cope. The members of a counseling group also obtain social support, the realization that their problems are not unique, and the advice and counsel of a number of other people who have experienced similar problems.

Butler and Lewis (1982) recommend that group therapeutic procedures be employed in all nursing homes, hospitals, and other institutions where the elderly are treated, and on an outpatient basis as well. Nurses are probably most often used as group counselors or therapists in such institutional groups, the usual goals of which are socialization, emotional catharsis, and behavior management. One method used to increase the sensitivity of nurses and technicians in nursing homes and other health facilities for the elderly is the Empathic Model described in chapter 2. In some instances health personnel who participate in the training sessions have been provided with an "Instant Aging Kit" containing a white wig, wire-rimmed spectacles, and theatrical makeup. Many who don these get-ups begin to see the world from an old-age viewpoint, thus acquiring greater empathy with the elderly residents.

A number of specialized techniques have been employed in counseling and therapy groups with the elderly, including "Here-and-Now" approaches, such as group discussion, relaxation, and role playing, and "There-and-Then" approaches such as reminiscence and life review. Reminiscing about personal experiences and other memories can serve as an effective form of therapy for older people who have a sensitive listener. Even elderly psychotic patients tend to feel comfortable with the familiar act of reminiscing (Lesser, Lazarus, Frankel, & Havasy, 1981). By associating their current problems with similar problems they have had in the past, patients learn to deal with them "here and now." Such reminiscences also form a part of *life-review therapy* and *life-cycle group therapy,* which Butler (1974) has advocated as being particularly helpful to older patients.

Life-review therapy begins by obtaining an extensive biography from the patient and from family members. Tape recordings, diaries, family albums, and other memorabilia can assist in the life-review process. Some of the goals of this type of psychotherapy are atonement for feelings of guilt, getting rid of childhood identifications that continue to cause trouble, and resolution of intrapersonal and interpersonal conflicts.

Life-review therapy can be either individual or group. Extended to a group setting consisting of 8 to 10 members of different ages, life review becomes life-cycle group therapy. Here the groups are oriented toward individuals who are experiencing life crises, ranging from adjustment difficulties in adolescence to fear of impending death. By interacting with people of different generations in a group setting (''age-integrated life-cycle group therapy''), the elderly person comes to see his or her problems in the perspective of the life cycle and continuing development.

Other therapeutic techniques that have been employed in group settings are role-playing therapy (psychodrama), scribotherapy, and self-image therapy. In *role playing,* group members act out situations related to their conflicts and problems. Other members of the group may play the roles of supporting characters to help a group member re-experience a situation pertaining to his or her most significant problem(s). In *scribotherapy,* group members write down their feelings about certain topics and then, after group discussion and individual interviews, develop them into a news format. Another ''literary'' technique is *self-image therapy,* in which a book selected by the group is read and discussed as a means of developing group cohesiveness and a sense of security among group members.

Many of the approaches employed in individual therapy, whether psychoanalytic, phenomenological, behavioral, or of whatever theoretical persuasion, have also been applied in group settings. Although encounter groups and other growth groups are not as popular with older as with younger adults, advocates of one humanistically oriented approach, Senior Actualization and Growth Experience (SAGE), claim some success in helping elderly with their psychological problems. The activities in SAGE groups, including exercises, massage, discussion, and training in meditation, are designed to assist older people in dealing with traumas such as death and dying and to gain greater vitality and purpose (Storandt, 1983).

*Family counseling,* a special type of age-integrated group counseling, involves an elderly counselee and one or more other member of the family interacting with a counselor and each other. Because family relationships are a common source of difficulty for older people, it is often important to include the family in the psychological counseling of the elderly. Herr and Weakland (1979) have provided some useful guidelines for counseling elders and their families.

The limited economic resources of the aged and the stigma of being referred to a psychological counselor frequently make it necessary to conduct family counseling under less than optimal conditions and to settle for limited goals. In any event, family counseling is as much a matter of not doing certain things as it is of doing others. Herr and Weakland (1979) point out that counselors should avoid arguments or overinvolvement with clients and their families and should not put words into their mouths. At the same time, family counselors should be genuine and empathic, express unconditional positive regard, and work toward improving their skills in communicating with older people and their families.

## Special Therapeutic Techniques

Additional techniques that have been employed in counseling and psychotherapy with the elderly include reality orientation, resocialization, remotivation, sensory retraining, biofeedback, art therapy, and pet-facilitated therapy. Each of these techniques, which may be used in combination with other procedures, is more effective with certain kinds of problems or patients. *Reality orientation,* the backbone of which is the repetition and learning of basic information (e.g., patient's name, place, day, date, time, etc.) is employed with confused patients. *Sensory retraining,* on the other hand, is most effective with withdrawn, regressed older patients who have difficulty interacting with the environment. In sensory retraining, various objects and activities are used to stimulate and to exercise the senses and hence to improve the patient's perception of the physical and social environment. Physical exercise may also be used to improve the cognitive functioning of other patients.

In *pet-facilitated therapy,* birds, dogs, or other pets are used to bring out depressed, withdrawn, love-hungry elderly patients. Well-trained wirehair fox terriers, which are resilient, playful, good humored, and aggressively friendly animals, have been found to be particularly effective for this purpose (see Galton, 1979). These "feeling heart" dogs are able to bring out patients emotionally so that they can interact more comfortably with other people and begin the process of psychotherapy.

## Milieu Therapy and Prevention

The counseling and psychotherapeutic techniques discussed thus far are remedial, but potentially even more contributory to good adjustment and mental health is preventive counseling. Preventive approaches include preretirement counseling and continued health education, as well as information and opportunities for avocational, educational, and recreational activities. For example, nursing homes usually provide a variety of avocational and recreational activities (arts, crafts, music therapy, exercise classes, field trips, etc.) to stimulate and interest the residents and emphasize the fact that they are still among the living.

Environmental arrangements or changes of the sort that play a role in prevention can also be used in remediation. Mental health professionals realize that physical and social surroundings are important in the course and treatment of psychological problems and disorders, a realization that is basic to the concepts of a *therapeutic community* and *milieu therapy.* It has been found, for example, that the introduction of simple changes—a record player, a decorated bulletin board, games, dressing patients in white skirts and ties, serving beer and crackers every day at 2 p.m.—can markedly alter the behavior of patients on a senile ward (Volpe & Kastenbaum, 1967). These changes resulted in decreased incontinence, a lessened need for restraint and medication, and marked improvement in the social functioning of patients. Such improvements may be interpreted as stemming from better patient attitudes, accompanied by an increase in the expectations of the institutional staff and the patients of what the latter are able to. Of course, this cuts both ways: Maladaptive behavior can be exacerbated in patients who are treated by the institutional staff as "sick inmates" who are incapable of making decisions or doing anything constructive for themselves. At least to an extent, mental patients—and people in general—become what they are viewed or labeled as being and do what others expect them to do.

A similar explanation can be applied to the findings of an experiment by Kahana and Kahana (1970a). Aged male psychiatric patients were assigned at random to one of two types of hospital wards, age-segregated and age-integrated. Patients on each of the age-segregated wards were all within a fairly narrow age range, whereas those on the age-integrated wards covered the entire adult age range. When re-examined after 3 weeks, older patients on the age-integrated wards manifested greater improvement in responsiveness and performance on mental status examinations than those on the age-segregated wards. Apparently, simply being around younger people, who may serve as more youthful behavior models, altered the negative attitudes of the older patients. In general, it has been found that an array of relationships, with people of different ages and circumstances, is important in coping with stressful situations.

Prevention of self-fulfilling prophecies concerning disability in the aged reaches beyond the institution. Negative images of older people as impaired and senile contribute to social treatment of the elderly as childish and incompetent. Consequently, an important preventive strategy involves the use of television and other media to change public attitudes toward the aged. When public expectations toward old age become more favorable, then perhaps the frequency of adjustment problems and mental disorders in later life will be reduced.

## SPECIFIC COUNSELING
## AND THERAPEUTIC PROBLEMS

The range and severity of psychological problems confronting the elderly are at least as great as in other age groups, but certain problem areas are more common. These include problems with marital and family relationships,[3] health, finances, living conditions, retirement, death, and bereavement. Counseling and psychotherapy for such problems are offered by a variety of public and private agencies, but in most instances elderly people must take the initiative themselves to come

---

[3]Counseling for sex problems is discussed in chapter 7.

in for counseling. Although in-depth counseling or psychotherapy usually requires many sessions, in certain cases one visit may suffice:

> A farmer's wife came and told a tragic story where nothing could be done, but her compassion and strength made it possible to continue. As usual with these cases, I asked if she would care to come again; she looked a little surprised, and said, "There is no need, I've told you everything." She had only wanted to confide in someone she respected, in case there was more she could do, and not to be so alone in her hard life. . . . One visit was enough for her. (Scott-Maxwell, 1968)

## Drugs, Death, and Bereavement

Certain types of counseling for the elderly, for example, drug counseling and bereavement counseling, have increased in recent years. The growing need for drug counseling of the elderly is not the result of older people taking illegal drugs, but rather the consequence of errors in prescribing or taking legal prescription and over-the-counter medicines. Drug-induced illness in the elderly is often overlooked because it produces many of the symptoms associated with old age—forgetfulness, weakness, confusion, tremor, and anorexia ("Senior Citizens . . . ," 1978).

With respect to counseling the bereaved and dying, there is no set prescription for dealing with the emotional needs of terminally ill patients and those who are close to them. What the physician, clergyman, or social worker tells the patient and the family must be adapted to the particular needs of the individuals being counseled (see Aiken, 1985, chapters 9 and 10). Many counseling methods have been employed with the dying, but the emphasis should be placed on helping the patient live each day for itself—as joyfully and peacefully as possible. This may best be achieved in an emotional and social environment with which the patient is familiar, usually at home. It is also recommended that counselors of terminally ill patients and their families be careful not to force their own moral or religious values on the counselees (Carey, 1976). In general, the counselor should try to understand and to share the feelings of those involved and to help them find their own ways of handling death, whether these be religious or secular.

Bereavement counseling is not greatly different from counseling for any other separation or loss. Counselors of the bereaved need to be supportive and empathic, but at the same time must encourage the counselee to take a realistic view of things. Often this can be accomplished most effectively by those who themselves have experienced the death of a loved one (Silverman, 1969). Much bereavement counseling is one-to-one, but group-oriented approaches are also fairly common. In these "Grief Groups" patients talk about mourning, their feelings concerning death, and how to survive the loss of a loved one. A professional counselor provides information and direction to the group, as well as individual counseling for those members who need it.

## Situational and Supportive Counseling

Situational or supportive counseling is frequently needed by elderly people, and specific counseling techniques and goals have been delineated for certain situations. For example, in training law enforcement officers to deal with elderly victims of crime, instructors recommend that officers (Symonds, 1978):

1. Tell the victim they're sorry it happened, they're glad he or she is all right, and that he or she did nothing wrong.
2. Describe to the victim the kinds of feelings that crime victims experience, so that the victim understands that his or her own emotions are actually very normal.
3. Confirm his or her belief that something terrible has happened to him or her, rather than arguing with a victim who does not want to be consoled.

Another common situation calling for counseling is impending retirement. Manion (1976) described a preretirement counseling program fashioned after the T-group model of the National Training Laboratory and a facilitator-learning model. In this small-group approach, preretirees review factual materials on retirement and also are encouraged to examine the needs, attitudes, values, and fears concerned with how they expect to cope with life after retirement. The objectives of this group-centered approach are to develop: skills in self-diagnosis, communication, interpersonal relations, and life planning; attitudes of independence, problem solving, decision making, and action taking; and an awareness of their retirement options. A group facilitator, who is assigned to each group of 10 to 12 persons, helps create an atmosphere of trust, openness, understanding, genuineness, and empathy in which retirement problems and potential solutions can be explored.

## SUMMARY

The treatment of milder mental disorders does not require institutionalization, but admission (commitment)—either voluntary or involuntary—is often necessary with more severe disorders. Treatment may involve a combination of physical (drugs, electroshock, surgery), psychological (psychotherapy, counseling), and environment (situational, milieu) methods. Mental health in old age is also affected by a person's attitude toward life and the perceived meaningfulness and value of his or her existence.

*Counseling* and *psychotherapy* are similar terms for psychological methods of treatment, individually or in a group context. Counseling is usually of shorter duration and does not deal with such deep-rooted problems as psychotherapy.

Various professional, paraprofessional, and nonprofessional persons provide counseling services for the elderly, but the practice of psychotherapy is restricted to psychiatirsts and clinical psychologists.

Elderly people can benefit from psychological treatment for different problems, but professional counselors and psychotherapists are often reluctant to work with them. It is frequently assumed that older people are too slow or too inflexible to profit from psychological methods of treatment. Professional and public educational efforts are needed to change this attitude.

Theories or models of personality development and functioning can serve as guides in counseling and psychotherapy. Psychoanalysis, with its emphasis on unconscious processes, psychosexual development, and the three-component structure of personality, has been the most influential theory. However, psychoanalysis has been less helpful in working with the elderly than transactional analysis, phenomenological (self) theory, behavior theory, and reality theory. Derivatives of Carl Rogers's self-theory of personality, when applied to counseling, have been especially popular among those who work with older people. An example is the nine-step model of Alpaugh and Haney (1978), which has as its objectives the provision of emotional support and the clarification of the problems of the elderly and the issues inherent in those problems. The progressive nine steps in this model are: understanding the client, establishing rapport, defining the problem, setting a goal, clarifying issues, listing alternatives, exploring alternatives, making a decision, and providing closure. Behavior therapy and behavior modification techniques (e.g., contingency management, systematic desensitization), as well as Glasser's reality therapy, have found some use in treating older people.

Dozens of special techniques have been applied in counseling and therapy with older people. Butler and Lewis (1982) report good success with life-review therapy and life-cycle group therapy in the treatment of guilt feelings, childhood identifications, and interpersonal conflicts in the aged. Other group-oriented approaches are role playing, scribotherapy, self-image therapy, and family counseling. Additional psychotherapeutic procedures applicable on an individual or group basis include reality orientation, remotivation, sensory retraining, biofeedback, and art therapy. Cognitive therapy, which involves discussing the contents of a daily diary with a therapist, and pet-facilitated therapy, in which pets are used to bring out withdrawn patients, have enjoyed some success in treating depression in the elderly.

Preventive counseling is considered to be even more essential than remedial counseling, and milieu (environmental) therapy is just as important as direct counseling. The effects of the living environment on the attitudes and functioning of older patients have been demonstrated in a number of research investigations, including those of Volpe and Kastenbaum (1967) and Kahana and Kahana (1970a). A particularly significant part of the environment of an institutionalized elderly person is the institutional staff. It is considered essential to train such workers to be sensitive to and competent in dealing with both the physical and psychological needs of elderly residents.

In recent years there has been an upsurge in the number of older people receiving counseling for drug and bereavement problems. Counseling of terminally ill patients—by physicians, nurses, clergymen, and others—has also become more acceptable. Although approaches to counseling differ to some extent with the specific problem, there are similarities across problem areas in the techniques employed. For example, bereavement counseling is not greatly different from counseling for any other kind of separation or loss.

Much of the counseling conducted with elderly people is situational or supportive in nature. Illustrative of situational counseling are the counseling of elderly crime victims and preretirees. Preretirement counseling has become an extensive, systematic process in many business and industrial organizations. Preretirement counseling programs are concerned both with presenting factual information pertaining to retirement and exploring the psychological needs and attitudes of participants.

## SUGGESTED READINGS

Alpaugh, P., & Haney, M. (1978). *Counseling the older adult*. Los Angeles: University of Southern California Press.

Blake, R. (1975). Counseling in gerontology. *Personnel and Guidance Journal, 53*, 733–737.

Gatz, M., VandenBos, G., Pino, C., & Popkin, S. (1985). Psychological intervention with older adults. In J. E. Birren & K. W. Schaie (Eds.), *Handbook of the psychology of aging* (2nd ed., pp. 755–785). New York: Van Nostrand Reinhold.

Herr, J. J., & Weakland, J. H. (1979). *Counseling elders and their families*. New York: Springer.

Keller, J., & Hughston, G. (1981). *Counseling the elderly: A systems approach*. New York: Harper & Row.

Landreth, G. L., & Berg, R. C. (1980). *Counseling the elderly*. Springfield, IL: Charles C. Thomas.

Myers, J. E. (1983). Gerontological counseling training. The state of the art. *Personnel and Guidance Journal, 61*, 398–401.

Nissenson, M. (1984, January). Therapy after sixty. *Psychology Today*, pp. 22–26.

Storandt, M. (1983). *Counseling and therapy with older adults*. Boston: Little, Brown.

Thompson, L. W., & Gallagher, D. (1985). Depression and its treatment in the elderly. *Aging, 348*, 14–18.

# 7

## Sex and Family Relations

Human beings are gregarious, mutually dependent creatures who thrive on being close and companionable. Expression of the social need to be with other people promotes security, species propagation, and other ends that protect and maintain humanity. This sociability of the human species is manifested most clearly in the desire to be touched, caressed, or held and by the verbal equivalents of these actions in a lullaby, a love song, or simply a comforting word. Nowhere is the need to be close to another person seen more clearly than in romantic love and sexual behavior.

### SEXUAL BEHAVIOR

Although the sexual urge is not lost with the decline of reproductive capacity in later life, in both men and women the ability to reproduce diminishes with age. There are, however, authenticated instances of men in their 10th decade of life siring children and women who gave birth when they were in their mid-50s. Even more startling is the feat purportedly accomplished by Rustam Mamedor and his wife, inhabitants of the Caucusus region of Russia, whose youngest son is said to have been born when the father was 107 and the mother 81 (Gots, 1977)! This was, of course, a very rare and questionable blessed event. Women normally lose the capacity to reproduce sometime between the ages of 45 and 50, the stage of life when ova are no longer regularly released from the ovaries and the corpus luteum fails to form.

It was formerly believed that aging of the reproductive system is caused directly by a decrease in the sex hormones testosterone and estrogens, which are

161

produced by the male and female gonads. Subsequent research, however, pointed to the importance of insufficient pituitary or hypothalamic sex hormones in reproductive aging. Now it is believed that reproductive aging is caused by defects in the production of chemicals (neurotransmitters) that assist in the release of sex hormones by the hypothalamus. Because the blueprint for production of these neurotransmitters presumably exists at the cellular level, we are back once again to an individual-cell explanation of aging—this time aging in the reproductive system (Arehart-Treichel, 1976).

## Incidence of Sexual Activity in Old Age

Reference to the "sexless older years" is a social stereotype contradicted by research findings. The results of investigations from the Kinsey studies (Kinsey, Pomeroy, & Martin, 1948) to the research of Masters and Johnson (1970) point to only a slight decline in sexual interest with age. [The frequency of coitus, which during late adulthood almost always takes place in a marital or marital-like relationship, declines.] Nevertheless, the results of various studies have indicated that approximately 70% of healthy elderly couples are sexually active (Sviland, 1975). The findings of a longitudinal study conducted at Duke University on 254 men and women aged 60–94 are instructive (Pfeiffer, Verwoerdt, & Wang, 1968, 1969) (see Fig. 7.1). Two-thirds of the elderly men who participated in this study stated that they were sexually active, and four-fifths of them admitted to a continuing interest in sex. The percentage of those interested in sex was the same 10 years later, but the number who were sexually active had fallen to 25% of the total. However, more than 20% of the men reported an *increase* in sexual activity as they grew older. This phenomenon, which was more common among unmarried men and due in large measure to meeting new partners, is dramatic evidence that sexual desire does not necessarily wane in old age.

The findings of surveys of sexual activity in elderly women are somewhat different from those of elderly men. At the beginning of the Duke University study, for example, one-third of the sample of women confessed to a continuing sexual interest and one-fifth reported that they still had sexual intercourse on a regular basis. Both these fractions were approximately the same 10 years later. In addition, whereas the median age for cessation of intercourse among elderly men was 68 years, it was only 60 years among women.

As indicated by the elderly men who were interviewed by Duke University researchers, being a widower or otherwise unmarried did not necessarily reduce their sexual activity. On the other hand, 90% of the older women interviewed in the study stated that they stopped having sexual intercourse when their husbands died or became ill and/or impotent (Pfeiffer, Verwoerdt, & Davis, 1972). Even when both partners were healthy, the decision to stop having sexual intercourse was almost always the husband's. Because most sexual activity in old age,

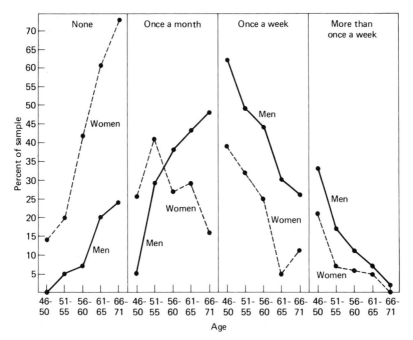

FIG. 7.1.  Frequency of sexual intercourse in middle and late life. (Data from Pfeiffer et al., 1972. Copyright 1972, the American Psychiatric Association. Reprinted by permission.)

especially for women, takes place within a marital relationship, the difference in the sexual behavior of elderly men and women is probably due more to reduced opportunity than to an absence of desire. The reduction in opportunity among older women comes about because of the many more unattached women than men in old age. Among those women who are widowed or unmarried, a lack of available men, a reluctance to engage in sex out of wedlock, concern over personal appearance and consequent self-image, and a belief that sex should cease after menopause all contribute to abstinence.

The investigations of Pfeiffer et al. (1969, 1972) and others (e.g., Newman & Nichols, 1960) also indicate that older people in lower socioeconomic groups are more sexually active than those in upper socioeconomic strata. Perhaps this is why certain studies have found that elderly Blacks, who are more likely than Whites to be of lower socioeconomic status, are more sexually active than elderly Whites. The overall results of studies of ethnic group differences in sexual behavior are, however, conflicting.

Whatever the gender, social class, or ethnicity of a person, research underscores the truism "Use it or you'll lose it." Continued sexual activity is most important for the ability to function sexually in old age. As documented by the fact that people who are more sexually active in their youth are also more active in old age (Shock et al., 1984), human sexual behavior is a lifelong habit pattern (Masters & Johnson, 1966; Newman & Nichols, 1960). Thus, given good general health and sufficient practice, men can remain sexually active into their 70s and 80s and women as long as they live.

> old folks stop having sex for the same reasons they stop riding a bicycle—general infirmity, thinking it looks ridiculous, no bicycle—and of these reasons the greatest is the social image of the dirty old man and the asexual, undesirable older woman. (Comfort, 1974, p. 440)

## Physiology of Sex

Whereas the Kinsey reports and the Duke University studies helped dispel the myth that sexual activity in old age is abnormal, precise information regarding the physiology of sex in the elderly was lacking prior to the investigations of Masters and Johnson (1970). In these studies, elderly people were interviewed and their physiological responses monitored during sexual intercourse. One of the findings concerning sexuality in older women, of which laypersons and health professionals alike should be cognizant, is that menopause does not eliminate sexual need or functioning—especially when hormone replacement therapy is applied—and sometimes even increases it. Because the clitoris remains intact and responsive to stimulation throughout old age, elderly women are physically capable of having just as many orgasms as younger women. Much of the older woman's sexual activity, however, does not result in orgasm.

The decrease in estrogen production after menopause is accompanied by both structural and functioning changes in women. The cervix and uterus become smaller, and the vaginal walls thinner. The degree of vasocongestion of the breasts, clitoris, and vagina is also affected, and vaginal lubrication is reduced. These changes in the vagina can result in discomfort and pain during intercourse and an aching, buring sensation afterward. The extent to which these symptoms are experienced, however, varies from person to person, and sex hormone replacement therapy can help to control them.

The effects of aging on male sexuality can be classified as primary and secondary. Among the secondary (superficial) changes signaling the so-called "male menopause" and produced by a decline in secretion of the male hormone testosterone are loss of hair, increased flabbiness, and elevated voice pitch. The primary changes include a slight shrinkage of the testes, production of fewer sperm, and a decrease in the volume of the ejaculate. In regard to sexual functioning, older men usually take longer to achieve an erection, which may be incomplete but sufficient for vaginal penetration. There are fewer genital spasms, and the force of the ejaculate is reduced, often seeping rather than spurting. The erection is lost more quickly after ejaculation, and it takes longer to have another erection. Finally, orgasm may occur only once every second or third time rather than every time that an elderly man has intercourse.

For both men and women, all four phases of sexual arousal and decline (excitement, plateau, orgasmic, resolution) are prolonged in old age. But none of the age-related physiological changes need detract from sexual appreciation, and the enjoyment of intercourse is usually retained by both sexes. Despite the physiological changes described here, the extent to which sexual intercourse is enjoyed by an elderly couple depends to a great extent on the psychological relationship between them. Following a hysterectomy or mastectomy, women, as with men who have had prostate surgery, may lose interest in sexual intercourse. The reasons, however, are almost always psychological rather than physiological.

## Attitudes Toward Sex

Defining *old age* as "the time when a man flirts with women but can't remember why," the description of the sex life of the elderly as "triweekly, try weekly, try weakly," and one-liners such as "What do you do with a dirty old man? Introduce him to a dirty old woman," suggest the mixture of humor and disapproval with which society views sex in the aged (Puner, 1974). Unfortunately, a disapproving attitude toward sexual activity in the elderly is held by many older people themselves. This is particularly true of older women, who, accepting the traditional stereotype, too often view sexual behavior on the part of older people as lecherous, dirty, and sick. As a consequence, older women patients may find it difficult to admit—even to an older woman physician—that they have sexual desires (Knopf, 1975). Because of negative attitudes and misconceptions regarding sex in later life, older people are cut off more than they need to be from one of the joys of life.

Many social organizations and institutions reinforce the notion that sex is only for the young and that elderly men and women who express an interest in the subject are "dirty old men" or "frustrated old women." The cultural emphasis on youthful beauty all too often causes older women to view themselves as physically unattractive and hence sex as no longer possible for them. And the overreactions of friends, relatives, and caretakers when an elderly person dares to become involved in a sexual affair leads to courtship in an atmosphere of secrecy and shame.

> An elderly woman in a nursing home pads quietly down the dimly lit corridor shortly after lights out for a rendezvous with her lover, a widower and fellow resident of the facility. Suddenly a staff member emerges from a doorway, scolds the woman and sends her back to her room, admonishing that sex is not permitted here. (Ingram, 1980)

A sexual relationship between two elderly people provides more than a means of releasing sexual tensions. The pleasures of companionship and sharing are an essential part of any enduring relationship. Furthermore, there is more to the physical aspect of sex than intercourse. As one 73-year-old man expressed it:

> I don't know if I'm oversexed, but I'm a lover. I like to pet, kiss, hug. I have more fun out of loving somebody I love than the ultimate end. You know, some people—and this is the failure of sex, too—some people want sex and forget the rest of it—the hugging and the petting and I think that's wrong. People say, "What will happen to me when I get older?" Well, I'm still alive! There's no thrill like that today. People try dope, they try smoking, they try drinking. This is the one thing that's good for the body. (Vinick, 1977, p. 12)

To counter the tendency of society—young, middle aged, and old—to label any older person who is interested in sex as a D.O.M. ("dirty old man") or an F.O.W. ("frustrated old woman"), one elderly Californian responded with a bumper sticker on his sports car that declared: "I'm not a dirty old man; I'm a sexy senior citizen" (Lobsenz, 1974). There are, of course, more effective measures than bumper stickers for helping older men and women satisfy their needs for sex and love without censure, embarrassment, of undue physical difficulties. Stereotypes concerning sex and the elderly on television programs, for example, can be reduced by advocacy of the guidelines recommended by the Gray Panthers. Several of the items in these guidelines are listed in Report 7.1.

Indications of the growing public acceptance of sexuality among the aged are also found in the mixed reactions to the recommendations of several gerontologists and laypersons that private rooms be provided in nursing homes so patients can have sex with each other and/or visitors. It has been suggested that the chronic anxieties of nursing home patients could be alleviated by sexual intercourse. Although most nursing homes do not publicly sanction conjugal visits and other sexual arrangements among patients, they have begun to show a greater tolerance toward sexual contacts.

## Sexual Problems and Deviations

It should be emphasized that sex in old age is not a preversion and that declines in sexual activity are due as much to social and emotional factors as to physiology. It is true that certain physical disorders and drugs (e.g., tranquilizers) can reduce sexual functioning, but equally important are the lack of privacy; insufficient practice; preoccupation with work; and emotions such as anger, anxiety, guilt, and depression (Masters & Johnson, 1970).

Older men are sometimes characterized as never-say-die impotents who will buy and try any potion or gadget that promises to improve their sex drive and functioning. In fact, most of these nostrums and devices are more likely to be

---

**Report 7.1    MEDIA GUIDELINES FOR SEXUALITY AND AGING***

While the range of age-related stereotypes used in the media is wide, elders are particularly denigrated about their sexuality. Sexuality—used here in its broadest meaning to include sensuality, physical desirability, vitality, physical enjoyment and relationships—is a fundamental human right/capacity. Therefore the portrayal of elders as nonsexual, the ridicule of their sexuality, or the omission of elders from sensual/sexual contexts, is a dehumanizing use of media. The inclusion of sex-positive and elder-centered images should be a vital part of all coverage.

We offer the following guidelines for non-agist portrayal of sexuality in the media:

- DO use words like elder, old, old age; and, in context, words such as experienced, wise, mature, and weathered.
- DON'T use words or expressions like balding, granny, hag, old bag, peppery, spry, old goat, old fogey, little old lady, dirty old man, sagging breasts or face, cranky, cantankerous, grouchy, or housewife (if not applicable).
- DO try to emphasize the positive aesthetic aspects of growing old: a face wrinkled with beauty; gray hair blowing in the wind.
- Be careful, in general, of age-related adjectives. DON'T use the word senile as a general adjective. Instead of saying "She's acting senile," be more specific: "She's acting confused and disoriented"; instead of saying, "Their love affair was almost adolescent in spite of their advanced age," say, "Their love affair was wild and fresh."
- DON'T assume that all elders are heterosexual; as with all ages, a significant proportion of elders are Lesbians, gay men, and bisexuals.
- AVOID portraying old men as needing young women for potent and vital sex. Include the portrayal of sexually active elders with contact with each other. Be careful in portraying old women in relationships with young men as "news"—you may be helping to generate yet another myth.
- All of the above apply to humorous depictions of elders. Avoid implying that sex for elders is absurd by snickering or being oblique about their sex lives or sensuality.

*From Davis (1980), pp. 83–84.

---

purchased by dirty old men of 27 rather than of 70 (Freiberg, 1987). Be that as it may, impotence is a serious concern for many elderly men. Because sexual prowess is a symbol of manliness, loss of ability to perform the sex act can lower the elderly man's feeling of competence and self-esteem. Although diabetes and removal of the prostate gland may cause impotence, when an elderly man is impotent it is usually a temporary condition produced by overeating, excessive drinking, medications, fatigue, boredom with the sexual partner, or emotional stress. Rather than taking constructive action, the impotent elderly man often perpetuates the condition by avoiding sex altogether and/or turning to alcohol.

As documented by Kinsey et al. (1948) and other researchers, masturbation is fairly common in both young and old, declining only slightly with age. There is, on the other hand, no evidence that voyeurism (peeping), exhibitionism (displaying one's sex organs), pedophilia (sexual relations with children, "child molesting"), or other sexual deviations are anything but rare exceptions in the elderly.

Although the 10% figure promoted by gay rights organizations is said to apply to older people as well, there are no adequate statistics on the incidence of homosexuality in old age. Since the gay rights movement began in 1960, the stereotype of the lonely, depressed, sexually frustrated aging homosexual has become less valid—if it ever was accurate (Kimmel, 1978, 1979–1980). In general, the lifestyles of aging homosexuals (gays, lesbians) in a predominantly heterosexual society create both problems and compensations. Certainly for lesbians there is no shortage of partners during later life (Raphael & Robinson, 1980).

## Sex Therapy

The frequency of sex problems in old age is indicated by the fact that in one community of 10,000 elderly people, therapists were consulted about sex problems twice as often as any other difficulty (Peterson, 1971). Many of these sexual problems would not occur or would be less serious if elderly people received good health care, adequate nutrition, and hormone replacement therapy. In any event, sound physical health and an adequate supply of hormones are seldom sufficient for coping with a problem having strong emotional components. Some form of psychotherapy or re-education is also required in the majority of cases.

Masters and Johnson (1970) pioneered in the rapid but effective treatment of sexual inadequacy. Many of their patients, and those of their students, have been elderly people who had stopped having sexual relations because of misunderstandings concerning the natural physiological changes accompanying aging. Report 7.2 describes one such case. It required approximately 1 week of therapy to restore the sexual functioning of this couple. They regained their confidence, and the sexual dysfunction disappeared when they came to realize that the symptoms they were experiencing—increased time to attain an erection and reduced seminal fluid in the man, decreased vaginal lubrication in the woman—were not abnormal in any way and that they could continue to enjoy sexual intercourse despite these problems.

The therapeutic procedures employed by Masters and Johnson produced improvement in 75% of the elderly men and 60% of the elderly women treated in one investigation. The 56 couples were, however, a select group of individuals whose sexual problems had persisted for a fairly short period of time. Other sex therapists have not always obtained such dramatic results.

A number of other therapeutic techniques, ranging from pornographic motion pictures and live strippers to self-stimulation and sex education programs, have been advocated by sex therapists. Butler and Lewis (1976) and Comfort (1980) are among those gerontologists who recommend masturbation and fantasy by

Report 7.2    SEXUAL INADEQUACY*

Mr. and Mrs. A were 66 and 62 years of age when referred to the foundation for sexual inadequacy. They had been married 39 years. . . .

They had maintained reasonably effective sexual interchange during their marriage. Mr. A had no difficulty with erection, reasonable ejaculatory control, and . . . had been fully committed to the marriage. Mrs. A, occasionally orgasmic during intercourse and regularly orgasmic during her occasional masturbatory experiences, had continued regularity of coital exposure with her husband until five years prior to referral for therapy. . . .

At age 61, . . . Mr. A noted for the first time slowed erective attainment. Regardless of his level of sexual interest or the depth of his wife's commitment to the specific sexual experience, it took him progressively longer to attain full erection. With each sexual exposure his concern for the delay in erective security increased until finally . . . he failed for the first time to achieve an erection quality sufficient for vaginal penetration.

When coital opportunity [next] developed . . . erection was attained, but again it was quite slow in development. The next two opportunities were only partially successful from an erective point of view, and thereafter he was secondarily impotent.

After several months they consulted their physician and were assured that this loss of erective power comes to all men as they age and that there was nothing to be done. Loathe to accept the verdict, they tried on several occasions to force an erection with no success. Mr. A was seriously depressed for several months but recovered without apparent incident. . . .

The marital unit . . . accepted their "fate." The impotence was acknowledged to be a natural result of the aging process. This resigned attitude lasted approximately four years.

Although initially the marital unit and their physician had fallen into the sociocultural trap of accepting the concept of sexual inadequacy as an aging phenomenon, the more Mr. and Mrs. A considered their dysfunction the less willing they were to accept the blanket concept that lack of erective security was purely the result of aging process. They reasoned that they were in good health, had no basic concerns as a marital unit, and took good care of themselves physically. . . . Each partner underwent a thorough medical checkup and sought several authoritative opinions (none of them encouraging), refusing to accept the concept of the irreversibility of their sexual distress. Finally, approximately five years after the onset of a full degree of secondary impotence, they were referred for treatment.

*From Masters & Johnson (1970), pp. 326–328. Used with permission.

elderly people who lack partners and wish to reduce their sexual tensions. When performed without guilt or other negative feelings, masturbation can help prevent the discomfort and impotence that often result from long abstinence from sexual intercourse. Given the social prohibitions against masturbation, however, supportive counseling and re-education may be required as well. Butler and Lewis (1976) have joined Masters and Johnson (1970) and other authorities in proposing a program of sex education for the aged. Such a program should include information on techniques of intercourse specific to the needs of the elderly, in addition to methods of coping with fears of sexual inadequacy, the reputed dangers of sex to health, and the disapproving attitudes of relatives and the larger society.

## MARRIAGE AND UNMARRIAGE

The majority of elderly men are married (77%), but the majority of elderly woman are unmarried (60%) (American Association of Retired Persons, 1987). These statistics would seem to be contradictory except for the fact that 60% of Americans aged 65 and over are women (U.S. Senate Special Committee on Aging, 1987). Men who lose a spouse through divorce or death are more likely to remarry, usually someone younger than they, than are women under the same circumstances. As shown in Fig. 7.2, although the percentages of elderly men and women who are divorced are the same, the percentage of older women who are widows (50%) is substantially greater than the percentage of older men who are widowers (14%).

The pattern of sex differences in the percentages of elderly married and widowed men and women is similar for all ethnic groups in the United States (see Fig. 7.3). Nearly twice as many elderly men as women are married, and over three times as many elderly women as men are widows. As might be expected, the percentages of married men and women in the 65- to 74-year age bracket is higher than the corresponding percentages in the 75+ age bracket. A complementary statistic is that the percentages of widows and widowers 75 years old and above are greater than those from 65 to 74 years old (U.S. Senate Special Committee on Aging, 1987–1988).

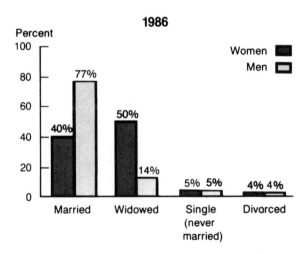

FIG. 7.2.    Marital status of Americans 65 years and older. (From *A Profile of Older Americans, 1987*. Copyright 1988 by the American Association of Retired Persons. Reprinted with permission.)

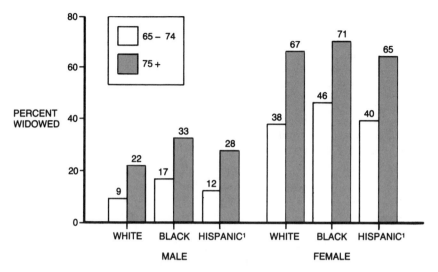

FIG. 7.3.    Percentages of widowed Americans by age, sex, and three ethnic groups. (U.S. Bureau of the Census, 1986a.)

## The Marital Relationship

In 1987, 78% of men and 41% of women aged 65 and over were married, the vast majority of whom were living with their spouses (U.S. Senate Special Committee on Aging, 1987). The percentage of elderly Americans who are married has increased during recent years and is predicted to continue increasing during the remainder of the century. Chief among the many reasons why marriage in old age appears to have become more popular are the improved health and economic status of older people. But whatever their reasons for remaining married, remarrying, or even marrying for the first time, for the majority of elderly people marriage is the most important of all interpersonal relationships.

It was noted in chapter 1 that married men tend to live longer than unmarried men. This finding has been attributed, at least in part, to the closer social ties and higher social status of married men (Kobrin & Hendershot, 1977). Other explanations for the greater average life span of married men have also been offered, but most authorities agree that psychological stress plays a role in longevity. A connection among marital status, psychological stress, and longevity is seen in the fact that the suicide rate is significantly higher for elderly men who are divorced or widowed than for those who are married.

Because of the physical and psychological changes accompanying aging, the relationship between a married couple undergoes modification in later life. In happy marriages, these changes produce greater equality among the marital partners. Equality is more likely because in some ways the sexes become more alike with aging. Both men and women become more eccentric and preoccupied with their own lives and personal needs, but the role relationships between the sexes may reverse after retirement. Women tend to become more aggressive or assertive and men more submissive and nurturant. Aging tends to make men more mellow, less ambitious, and more affiliative, whereas women become more assertive and controlling (Gutmann, 1972; McGee & Wells, 1982; Neugarten, 1968). According to Neugarten (1977), "older men seemed more receptive than younger men to their affiliative, nurturant, and sensual promptings; older women to their aggressive and egocentric impulses" (p. 637). This pattern is the opposite of typical sex-role behavior during the early adult years. Interestingly enough, the typical result of these changes is a reduction in emotional tension, easier communication, and a greater sharing of feelings.

Rather than developing suddenly in old age, the relatively greater aggressiveness manifested by elderly women may result from the release of aggressive urges that have been there all the time (Gutmann, 1964, 1967). During the years when she is rearing her children, a typical married woman suppresses her aggressive impulses, as is required by the nurturant, mothering role. But after her children have grown up and moved away, she feels free to release those impulses with impunity.

## Marital Happiness and Unhappiness

Elderly married couples often experience great pleasure in just being alone with each other. This idyllic picture is, however, far from universal. As with all married people, elderly couples have adjustment problems. Retirement, chronic illness, lack of money, and reduced sexual interaction are all potential sources of stress and marital friction in later life. Consequently, problems of marital friction in old age are particularly severe for elderly couples with insufficient income, physical disabilities, and low education (Duvall, 1977).

Being able to stay happily married into old age is attributable to a combination of affection, shared interests, habit, and a respect for the individuality of one's spouse. As concluded by Reedy, Birren, and Schaie (1981), "there is considerably more to love than sex and that at any age, emotional security—feelings of concern, caring, trust, comfort, and being able to depend on one another—is the most important dimension in the bond of love" (p. 62). Companionship, emotional security, and loyalty are more characteristic of love relationships in old age than sexual intimacy. Rollins and Feldman (1970) characterized the happily married older couple as similar to the young, newly married couple in their overall feeling of peacefulness and lack of stress.

Although marriage, in old age as at other times, does not guarantee happiness, older people who are married tend to be happier than those who remain unattached. Unmarried older people, especially older men, are more likely to be lonely and depressed (Tibbetts, 1977), to show more evidence of mental illness (Gove, 1973), and to have shorter lives (Civia, 1967) than those who are married.

As is true of social adjustment in general, marital happiness during old age is positively related to marital happiness during the earlier years. Happy marriages tend to remain happy, whereas unhappy marriages do not improve with age unless there are marked changes in the attitudes and actions of the marital partners. A marriage is, of course, not necessarily a happy one simply because the couple remain together. They may remain incompatible but unseparated for decades, living under an "armed truce" and finally "making the break" after their children grow up and move out.

Approximately 4% (1.1 million in 1986) of all individuals 65 and over are divorced. From 1976 to 1986, the divorce rate among the elderly increased almost four times as rapidly as the older population as a whole (American Association of Retired Persons, 1987). Despite the magnitudes of these numbers, the divorce rate among late middle-aged and older adults is significantly lower than the national average. In fact, many elderly people who might be better off divorced remain together because of the cultural stigma attached to divorce. But even in couples who have been married as long as 30–50 years, divorce is not as rare as it once was.

## Widowhood

According to U.S. Census figures, in 1986 over 50% of the women but less than 14% of the men in the 65-and-over age bracket were widowed. The ratio of widows to widowers varies somewhat with age, but the former outnumber the latter at every age level. The reasons for these sex differences in the incidence of widowhood are that men die at younger ages than women, tend to marry women younger than they are, and when widowed are more likely to terminate their widowhood status by remarrying fairly soon after bereavement. It is easier for widowers to remarry, which they usually do, and to marry younger women. This endorses the cultural stereotype, shared by elderly women themselves, that physical attractiveness is more important in women than in men and that aging women are less attractive than "distinguished" aging men. Consequently, widowhood in the United States is primarily a status of women, and the problems of widowhood are, by and large, women's problems.

A person who has just lost a spouse is likely to disengage somewhat from social activities. In cases where the widow's social entrees were provided in large measure by her husband's occupational contacts, the reduction in social activities may continue for some time (Glick, Weiss, & Parkes, 1974; Lopata, 1979). So where does an elderly widow seek companionship, and how does she live if she is unwilling to search for a new husband or unable to find one? The picture is not as bleak as one might imagine. Although elderly widows as a group experience frequent loneliness, especially at first (Lopata, 1973), the great majority are able to cope with the loss of a husband. It is not usually very difficult for a widow to establish friendships with other widows. Furthermore, churches, senior citizens centers, and various voluntary organizations provide opportunities to socialize. But widows are usually careful to avoid heterosexual situations in which they are apt to be perceived as "swinging singles" or "merry widows" who are making a play for someone else's date or mate. In any event, perhaps because the death of a spouse is more likely to be expected in old age, widowhood is usually less traumatic for older women than for younger ones.

The loss of a husband obviously creates problems for a woman: Her income, social life, and living accommodations may all decline. But even widows who were happily married, and who are admittedly lonely at times, usually become more competent and independent than they were when the husband was alive. They may miss their husband's companionship, but they now have time to devote to interests and to develop abilities that were suppressed or lay dormant during the years of service to the husband. This is less likely to occur if the widow was extremely dependent on her husband or identified too closely with him. And, strange as it may seem, widows who experienced the greatest amount of difficulty getting along with their husbands often find themselves least able to get along without him. Whatever the cause may be—a feeling of guilt, abandonment, or anger—adjustment is often quite difficult for widows whose marriages were unhappy.

Although the problems of adjusting to the loss of a spouse are often worse for a woman than for a man, any man who has lost his wife by death or divorce is faced with loneliness and a need for companionship. An elderly widow usually has more friends from whom she can seek sympathy and support, than an elderly widower. Pets, plants, and hobbies can also help to fill her time and to dull her grief. On the other hand, the elderly widower may discover that he was more dependent on his wife for physical and emotional support than he realized. Compared with women, men are typically not as close to other people and find it more difficult to make friends with other bereaved persons. Even when her husband is alive, a woman is more likely to have a confidante or other close friend of the same sex. Married men may also have close friendships with other men, but such is less often the case. And those men who failed to develop close relationships with other men while their wives were alive typically become even more socially isolated as widowers.

Sex differences in the effects of widowhood may be seen in both the incidence of mental illness and mortality. According to Stroebe and Stroebe (1983), "although women typically have higher rates of reactive depression, mental illness in general, and physical illness than men, when widowers' to married men's ratios are compared to widows' to married women's ratios to assess the deterioration associated with the partner loss, the men are worse off'' (p. 294). With respect to sex differences in mortality, Helsing and Szklo (1981) report that the mortality rate for elderly widowers is approximately 60% higher than it is for married men of the same chronological age.

## Remarriage

A few years ago a road sign at Sun City, near Tampa, Florida, cautioned motorists to "DRIVE SLOWLY. GRANDPARENTS PLAYING.'' For a number of reasons, one being the reduction in social security benefits that formerly occurred when retired people married, the elderly have sometimes engaged in what geriatric counselors refer to as "unmarriages of convenience." These are companionable, sexual relationships not formalized by a license or ceremony. The social security law was changed in 1977 so that newlyweds who are 60 or over lose none of their benefits. Nevertheless, certain older people, especially men, still confess to enjoying the secretive, "swinging singles" experience of living together without benefit of clergy. Most elderly couples, however, are not swingers, and they elect to marry rather than to face the censure of conventional society and their own consciences.

**Widowers.**    There are obvious compensations in being a widower, especially when one considers the large number of "casserole-carrying" widows who vie for the attentions of a few widowers. The competition among widows for their favors can be embarrassing to some widowers, but other widowers are undoubtedly pleased by all the fuss and the many social-sexual outlets provided by it. In any event, the relatively larger number of available women provides a better opportunity for elderly men to remarry. In 1984, the remarriage rate for widowers was eight times that for widows (National Center for Health Statistics, 1987a). The majority of widowers remarry within a year or 2 after their wife's death (Treas & VanHilst, 1976), having discovered that the companionship, sex, and physical and emotional support provided by a wife are things they would prefer not to do without. Quite often they marry someone whom they have known for years, long before they were widowed, and usually someone quite a few years younger.

**Widows.**    The ancient Hebrew custom of the *levirate,* according to which a widow married the brother of her deceased husband, was one way of coping with the fact that widows outnumber widowers. However, a contemporary American widow who wishes to remarry cannot count on her brother-in-law to espouse her. Finding herself in competition with a number of other women in similar circumstances, remarriage is not a highly probable event for an elderly widow. Even widows who eventually remarry tend to manifest greater loyalty to their departed spouse than widowers do, for when they remarry it is usually several years after their husband's death. As might be expected, younger widows are more likely than older widows to remarry. An older widow is supposed to respect and preserve the memory of her dead husband and not be interested in other men.

As difficult as remarriage in later life may seem, research suggests that it is easier for older men and women to remarry than one may think (Jacobs & Vinick, 1979). A typical couple meet through friends at a dinner party or other social occasion, begin seeing each other, and eventually marry. Elderly men usually show greater eagerness to get involved and remarry than elderly women, but sometimes traditional sex roles are reversed and the woman takes the initiative:

> He was sitting near me at the Golden Agers, and I didn't even know him. He was looking so depressed. You could see that the man needs something. The trouble is, when I see someone lonely, I want to know what's the matter. He was sitting just like a chicken without a head (sic). After that, he went his way, I went my way. So (the next meeting), he was sitting there again. So, my friend said, "Let's sit down

FIG. 7.4.   Social functions sponsored by Golden Age and Senior Citizens organizations provide opportunities for unmarried elderly people to become acquainted. (© Rollie McKenna/Photo Researchers, Inc.)

with him. It will warm him up a little." It was awfully windy. We sat down, and then we started to talk. You know the way it is. (Vinick, 1977, p. 6)

*Motives for Remarrying.*    Sex and romance are motives for marriage at any age, but apparently less so in later life. Newly married elderly people mention companionship, affection, regard, a desire to take care of someone, and intimacy more often than sex and romance as their reasons for remarrying. And when sex is mentioned, it is generally the warmth and feeling of togetherness rather than the physical pleasure that is stressed. As was true the first time around, remarriage does not guarantee happiness; however, people who remarry after the death of a spouse generally are happier than those who remain alone and unattached (Butler & Lewis, 1982). Older people who decide to remarry should consider such factors as how well acquainted they are, whether the proposed marriage meets with the approval of their children and friends, whether they will have sufficient income, how their estate(s) will be divided among their relatives, where they will live (preferably not in a home previously shared with the first spouse), and how they plan to spend the rest of their lives. Such considerations may seem to be unromantic, but a marriage's chances of surviving are greater when they are taken into account.

## Singlehood

In 1986, 5.1% of the elderly men and 5.2% of the elderly women in the United States had never been married (U.S. Senate Special Committee on Aging, 1987). Considering the fact that elderly singles do not live as long as elderly marrieds, one might expect to find the former group a lonely, dispirited lot. But this does not seem to be the case. For example, the results of interviews conducted by Gubrium (1975) of 22 never-married people aged 60–94 revealed that these singles were less lonely than the average elderly person. On the whole, they were more independent and competent than average. As a result of having lived alone for many years, they made use of other emotional resources and developed feelings of self-reliance in the face of the stresses and changes of aging. Despite having fewer social relationships, they felt happy and satisfied with their lives, expressed no need for intimate relationships, and remained single by choice rather than necessity.

Closeness can, of course, be attained in ways other than sexual and marital intimacy. Well-adjusted singles are also frequently close to their pets and non-relatives. Being free of the demands of a spouse and children, they have more time to devote to social interactions outside a family setting. Elderly singles also tend to have closer ties to their relatives, especially sisters with sisters, than elderly marrieds do (Shanas et al., 1968).

## FAMILY RELATIONSHIPS

Two-thirds of all noninstitutionalized older Americans live in family settings, and over 90% have living family members around whom their social lives are usually centered (U.S. Senate Special Committee on Aging, 1987). A large percentage of older Americans have living sisters and/or brothers, but an even greater number have children and grandchildren.

Elderly couples live together for 15 years or more on the average after the last adult child leaves home. During this time, which has been called the *postparental phase* of the family life cycle, the children have moved out but are not forgotten. As a result, some elderly women become depressed (the "empty nest" syndrome). Others, by way of contrast, discovering that they now have more time to devote to and achieve satisfaction from their marriages, gain a new enthusiasm for life.

### Elderly Parents and Adult Children

Exactly when the last child leaves home varies with ethnic group and social class. Middle-class and White Americans usually have fewer children than lower class and nonWhite Americans. Consequently, there are more children present and for a longer time in a typical lower class or nonWhite family. A similar pattern of more children in lower socioeconomic and minority group families prevails in other countries. White elderly Americans also live farther from their children, although in most cases it is less than an hour's drive away (Sussman, 1976). The parents continue to value contacts with their children, but the relationships are not always intimate or emotionally satisfying (Lee & Ellithorpe, 1982). In fact, childless older couples appear to be just as happy as those with children and grandchildren (Glenn & McLanahan, 1981).

The nostalgic multigenerational household of yesteryear was certainly more a matter of economic necessity than desire on the part of older and younger family members. Today only about 30% of elderly Americans live with their children. The great majority prefer to live independently, continuing to take part in the lives of their extended family from a somewhat "safe" distance (Troll, Miller, & Atchley, 1979; Yankelovich, Skelly, & White, 1977). For example, nearly all of the elderly people who were interviewed by Streib and Thompson (1965) stated that under no circumstances would they consent to move in with their children. Realizing that they would have trouble keeping quiet about mistakes and that their advice would seldom be welcome in their children's homes, most elderly people prefer the independence and freedom of living alone.

> Never try to live with your children. It's no good. I stayed there (at her daughter's house) a couple of months and I couldn't stand it. The kids, you know, have to do what they want to do. When I was listenin' to my TV, they were playin' games on the other side. . . . My daughter has a husband you can't take to, you know what I

mean? The minute he come home, I went upstairs and I stayed there. (Vinick, 1977, p. 3)

Although not desiring to live with them, most elderly parents continue to be interested in and concerned about their adult children. They expect them to visit often, an expectation with which the children generally concur, and to write frequently when they are too far away for frequent visits. The results of surveys (see Shanas et al., 1968) indicate that contact between elderly parents and their adult children is not merely a matter of expectation; a majority see each other every day.

Most elderly parents and children also continue to assist each other in various ways. The relationships, however, become more reciprocal or peerlike than they were in previous years. Older parents provide their children with money, household products (e.g., needlework and woodwork), and services (e.g., babysitting, household services, legal advice). Many adults assist their elderly parents by shopping for them, providing transportation to doctors' offices and elsewhere, and by helping them with governmental agencies and other organizations. Because mother–daughter relationships are usually closer than father–son relationships, the most frequent direction of help is from mother to daughter. It is a more common practice for elderly parents to assist their adult children than to receive help from them (Kivett, 1976). In some instances, however, old age may be a time of role reversal with respect to one's children—the aged parent now playing the role of the nurtured one and the son or daughter the role of caregiver. This is more likely to occur when the adult child feels that the parent is no longer competent to handle his or her own affairs.

## Grandparents and Grandchildren

Less closely related to them than their children, but still quite important members of an elderly person's family, are grandchildren. Grandchildren and great-grandchildren have multiple meanings for the elderly, including a source of biological renewal or continuity, the opportunity to succeed in new socioemotional and resource roles, and a potential source of pride and vicarious achievement (Neugarten & Weinstein, 1968). The new social role of grandparent brings with it the pleasure and excitement of a new personality that the grandparent has helped create, or, alternatively, a sense of growing old and a remoteness from the present and future.

The feeling of remoteness and insignificance that many elderly people feel in modern Western society[1] contrasts with the esteem in which they were held in

---

[1]An exception is Ireland, which, because of its primarily agricultural economy controlled by older people, continues to hold the elderly in high regard. Another country in which very old people are admired is the Soviet Union.

preindustrial cultures or are held in Asian countries such as Japan. The wisdom and practical knowledge of the elderly is valued less in the technically based industrialized societies of the United States and Western Europe than in societies with a traditional reverence for old age. Furthermore, the tendency of our society to segregate the generations has reduced the degree of social interaction and emotional interchange among different age groups, an important function of the extended family of yesteryear. This is unfortunate, because children need their grandparents as much as the latter need their grandchildren. Maintaining too much psychological distances between the young and old because of some irrational fear of old age is a disservice to both groups. Curtin (1972) expressed the fear of many adults that:

> mine will be the last generation to know old people as friends, to have a sense of what growing old means, to respect and understand man's mortality and his courage in the face of death. Mine may be the last generation to have a sense of living history, of stories passed from generation to generation, of identity established by family history. It is such an unholy waste. (p. 36)

Grandparents, who can add a sense of identity and stability to the family and society as a whole, vary extensively in their perceptions of the grandparenting role. On the one hand, there are those who see themselves as mere babysitters for someone else's children. On the other hand, are those who relate to their grandchildren with joy and love. The latter group often find that the role of grandparent is even more emotionally gratifying than that of parent. To these people the grandparent role involves its traditional elements of teacher and advisor to the young.

The age of grandparents has some relationship to the way in which they respond to their grandchildren. Younger grandparents are more likely to be somewhat fun seeking in their role, as if they were the child's playmate. Older grandparents tend to be more distant and formal in their behavior toward their grandchildren, becoming close only on special occasions (Christmas, birthdays, etc.) (Neugarten & Weinstein, 1968).

Most grandparents seem to enjoy the role of grandparent, but this varies with the age of the grandparent as well as with the grandparent's sex and the age and sex of the grandchild. Teenage grandchildren are appreciated least, and grandmothers usually enjoy interacting with their grandchildren more than grandfathers do. The relationship between grandmother and granddaughter is usually the strongest, probably because grandmothers have more pertinent knowledge and skills to communicate to their granddaughters than grandfathers do to grandchildren.

And how do grandchildren perceive their grandparents? To provide answers to this question, Kahana and Kahana (1970b) asked three groups of children (ages 4–5, 8–9, and 11–12) a number of questions about their grandparents and other elderly people. One finding was that all age groups of children felt closer to their mother's parents than to their father's parents and liked their maternal grandmother best of all. When asked what kind of grandparents they liked best, the 4- to 5-year-olds indicated that they preferred grandparents who gave them food, love, and presents; the 8- to 9-year-olds liked grandparents who did fun things with them; and the 11- to 12-year-olds preferred indulgent grandparents who let them do whatever they wished. Kahana and Kahana (1970b) concluded that the particular "style" of grandparenting that fits the child's needs varies with the age of the child. By early adolescence grandchildren are beginning to withdraw from their grandparents, and some adolescents become alienated from their grandparents. Many adolescents and young adults, however, remain close to their grandparents and view them as a special family resource (Hagestad, 1978; Robertson, 1976).

## Family Relationships of Widows

Widowhood has an effect on all of a person's family relationships. If there are children in the home, the widow or widower may have to play the roles of both mother and father. Although members of the extended family are usually in close contact with the widowed person for a while after the death of the spouse, interactions with them become less frequent as time passes.

Because of their lack of preparation for widowhood, the need to care for younger children, and assorted practical problems, younger widows usually have more difficulty adjusting than older widows (Glick et al., 1974; Lopata, 1973). Unlike the awkward status of a young widow, widowhood in older women is considered more "normal." Older widows tend to receive greater social support from family members and the wider community, making the transition from wife to widow less traumatic (Blau, 1961).

Regardless of age, a widow who was not congenial with her in-laws while her husband was alive may now experience even greater problems with them. In any event, social support is more likely to come from the widow's own family. Older widows, for example, tend to grow closer to their own children, and their daughters in particular. Sometimes they move in with their children, but the potential for intergenerational conflict makes this situation an undesirable one for most people (Adams, 1968; Lopata, 1973). Widows who liv with their adult sons or daughters are expected to help with the household chores and with the grandchildren. Unfortunately, the widow's position in her son's or daughter's household usually carries no real status or authority, and the fear of intruding makes her feel uncomfortable.

In addition to their relationships with living family members, widows may still "consult" or interact with their dead husbands. Uncertain about what to do—where and how to live, whether to buy or invest in this or that—a widow can become so desperate for advice and guidance that she even attempts to communicate with her deceased husband's spirit. Be that as it may, in most cases there are living relatives and close friends who are willing to act as confidants and advisors without pestering the dead.

## SUMMARY

The incidence of intercourse and other sexual outlets in old age varies extensively from person to person. As indicated by the findings of the Kinsey report and Duke University studies, elderly men are more sexually active and interested than elderly women, and the young–old are more active than the old–old. Interest in sex is greater than actual sexual intercourse and the frequency of intercourse is higher for healthy people and those of lower socioeconomic status. In elderly couples, the decision whether to stop having sexual intercourse is influenced more by the husband's condition and desire than those of the wife and is typically made by him.

The research of Masters and Johnson revealed that although marked changes in the structure and functioning of the sex organs takes place in later life, with proper medical and psychological treatment most couples can continue having intercourse into their 70s and 80s. The treatment of sexual problems in old age involves physical measures such as hormone replacement, sexual reeducation, and psychotherapy.

The degree of sexual activity in old age is as much a matter of attitude as it is of physiological change. Although public attitudes toward sex in the elderly, and the degree to which these attitudes are internalized by older people, are changing, too many people—both young and old—still regard elderly individuals who are interested in sex as dirty old men and frustrated old woman.

Masters and Johnson pioneered in rapid, effective treatment of sexual inadequacies at all stages of life. In one investigation, their therapeutic procedures resulted in improvements in 75% of the elderly men and 60% of the elderly women who were treated. Other techniques, including the viewing of pornographic films and live strippers, self-stimulation, and sex education, have also been used in the treatment of sexual disorders in the aged.

A majority of elderly men but a minority of elderly women are married, a difference due primarily to the substantially larger number of older women than older men. The percentages of married men and women decline with age, as more members of both sexes become widowed. The relationships between married men and women tend to change in later life, with wives becoming more assertive and controlling and husbands more submissive and nurturant.

The percentage of elderly people who get divorced is relatively small, but in 1985 over 8,600 Americans aged 65 and over obtained divorces. The divorce rate in both middle-aged and older groups has increased substantially during this century, but is still not nearly as high as the rate for younger adults.

Because there are more widows than widowers, the problems encountered by the widowed elderly are primarily those of widows. Included in these problems are reduced income, loneliness, and poorer living arrangements. Although widowhood can be painful, widows usually learn to cope with their problems and in the process become more competent, independent, and self-confident.

The greater availability of unattached women, added to the fact that men seem to need marriage more than women do, leads to a higher percentage of remarriages in elderly men. Both women and men who remarry or marry for the first time in later life do so more for companionship and closeness than for the physical act of sex.

Research findings indicate that married men are happier, healthier, and live longer than unmarried men. As a group, elderly women who remain single are neither chronically frustrated nor deeply unhappy. An adult lifetime of living alone and taking care of themselves appears to make single women more self-confident and capable, and consequently they do not seem to require intimate relationships with men.

The large majority of elderly parents desire to live in a separate residence from their adult children but to maintain frequent contact with them. Elderly parents continue to attain satisfaction from their children, assisting them in numerous ways. The role of grandparent also provides satisfaction to most older people, but the style in which that role is played varies with the age and sex of both grandparents and grandchildren. Grandmothers, and the mother's mother in particular, interact more with their grandchildren and are usually preferred by the latter to their grandfathers.

## SUGGESTED READINGS

Aizenberg, R., & Treas, J. (1985). The family in late life: Psychological and demographic considerations. In J. E. Birren & K. W. Schaie (Eds.), *Handbook of the psychology of aging* (2nd ed., pp. 169–189). New York: Van Nostrand Reinhold.

Brubaker, T. H. (Ed.). (1983). *Family relations in later life.* Beverly Hills, CA: Sage.

Bulcroft, K., & O'Conner-Roden, M. (1986). Never too late. *Psychology Today, 20*(6), 66–69.

Butler, R. N., & Lewis, M. I. (1976). *Love and sex after sixty: A guide for men and women in their later years.* New York: Harper & Row.

Cherlin, A. J., & Furstenberg, F. F. (1986). *The new American grandparent: A place in the family, a life apart.* New York: Basic Books.

Kimmel, D. C. (1978). Adult development and aging: A gay perspective. *Journal of Social Issues, 34,* 113–130.

Lopata, H. Z. (1979). *Women as widows: Support systems.* New York: Elsevier.

Solnick, R. E., & Corby, N. (1983). Human sexuality and aging. In D. S. Woodruff & J. E. Birren (Eds.), *Aging: Scientific perspectives and social issues* (2nd ed., pp. 202–224). Monterey, CA: Brooks/Cole.

Treas, J. (1983). Aging and the family. In D. S. Woodruff & J. E. Birren (Eds.), *Aging: Scientific perspectives and social issues* (2nd ed., pp. 94–109). Monterey, CA: Brooks/Cole.

Winslow, T. S. (1980). Grandma. In R. Lyell (Ed.), *Middle age, old age: Short stories, poems, plays, and essays on aging.* New York: Harcourt Brace Jovanovich.

# Social Status and Roles

**8**

It has been said that, next to dying, the realization that we are aging is the most traumatic event of our lives. This is certainly truer in a youth-oriented culture such as ours, where people spend considerable time and money trying to slow down or at least camouflage the effects of aging. They may dye their hair, invest in a host of skin preparations, get cosmetic surgery, dress like teenagers, and perhaps even become romantically involved with younger adults. By adopting a "not me, but that person over there" attitude, older people come to perceive themselves as exceptions to generalizations concerning the effects of aging and characteristics of the aged. Attempting to conceal their ages from others as well as from themselves, some people never come to use the word "old" as self-descriptive, even when they are in their 70s (Taves & Hansen, 1963). On the other hand, many older people give up the fight to stave off the ravages of time. Viewed by others as dull, forgetful, and incompetent, they come to accept these characterizations of themselves. The consequences of such a negative self-image is withdrawal—from social interactions, opportunities for new learning, and even efforts to assist them in coping with treatable disorders that they consider inevitable at their age (Rodin & Langer, 1980).

## STATUS AND ATTITUDES

Aside from its connotation that the termination of one's earthly existence is approaching, "old" in our society too often implies uselessness, rolelessness, and a consequent loss of status. The relatively low social status, or prestige, accorded the elderly is, however, not universal. Some primitive societies, in

185

particular, show great respect and even veneration for the aged. For example, the Jivaro Indians of the Andes believe that old people possess supernatural powers that increase with age. But in poorer tribal groups the elderly are viewed merely as a burden and are sometimes killed. Other primitive peoples, such as the Eskimos and certain Native American and African tribes, have respected the experience and wisdom of the elderly but left them to die when they could no longer take care of themselves. Older people in these societies have usually accepted the necessity of their demise and even assisted in it. Thus, an old man in a South Sea island native group, seeing himself as no longer useful or wanted, might voluntarily paddle out to sea and perish. Similarly, after deciding that he was ready to die, an older Native American warrior would tie himself to a stake in hostile territory and fight off braves and warriors of the hostile tribe until he was eventually killed.

The status, or position of value, honor, or prestige of elderly people throughout history has varied with the nature of the society. In nomadic, food-gathering and hunting societies, where strength, speed, and physical skill were critical for survival, the status of the aged—consistent with their contributions to the survival of the group—was typically quite low. In contrast, agricultural societies, depending more on the knowledge and advice of the elderly, have traditionally accorded them high status. In such societies elderly people have been able to amass considerable wealth and hence to demand respect and consideration. Subsistence systems based almost entirely on agriculture characterized Western societies until the 19th century, when the machine age and mass education intervened to diminish the high status of the elderly.

It is still true today that the elderly enjoy high status in those countries where the economy is based almost entirely on agricultural production. Besides economics, however, there are other important variables that affect the prestige of the elderly, such as the type of political system, religion, and cultural traditions. Older Japanese, for example, are accorded great respect, but Japan is a highly industrialized nation.

Despite the fact that their special knowledge and skills may be seen as less valuable in technically more advanced societies than in predominantly agricultural ones, it might be expected that the Western world's emphasis on humanism and mutual respect would produce more considerate treatment of the elderly. But old people in modern European and American society are not always treated humanely. Attitudes toward old age, of course, vary considerably from person to person in the same Western nation. Even the intellectual elite have expressed different viewpoints toward old age. For example, the English poet Robert Browning, in his 1864 poem "Rabbi Ben Ezra," extended an invitation to

> Grow old along with me!
> The best is yet to be,
> The last of life, for which the first was made.
> Our times are in His hand

Who saith "A whole I planned,
—Youth shows but half;
trust God;
see all nor be afraid.

The response of another 19th century English poet, Matthew Arnold, in his 1867 poem "Growing old," was

What is it to grow old?
Is it to lose the glory of form?
The lustre of the eye?
Is it for beauty to forgo her wreath?
—Yes, but not this alone.

Many Western Europeans and Americans do show concern and respect for the status of the elderly, but to Simone de Beauvoir (1972) it is Western society that truly degrades the old. She noted that sometimes an old man is a respected, venerated sage, but more often he is viewed as a ridiculous, doddering old fool and mocked by the young. Bernice Neugarten (1971) took a somewhat more optimistic point of view but still recognized the tendency of American society to stereotype the old as poor, isolated, sick, and unhappy, on the one hand, or as powerful, rigid, and reactionary on the other. Neugarten pointed out that these stereotypes influence our behavior and make the prospect of old age very unattractive.

## Stereotypes and Misconceptions

Stereotypes, or oversimplified, often caricatural descriptions of the aged, are found even in classical literature:

The sixth age shifts
Into the lean and slipid pantelone
With spectacles on nose and pouch on side;
His youthful hose, well-sewed, a world too wide
For his shrunk shank, and his big manly voice
Turning again to childish treble, pipes
And whistles in his sound. Last seen of all,
That ends this strange eventual history,
Is second childishness, and mere oblivion,
Sans teeth, sans eyes, sans taste, sans everything.
—William Shakespeare, *As You Like It*

Such overgeneralizations and caricatures have often been reinforced by scientific researchers who limited their study of the effects of old age to institutionalized samples of elderly people. Because no more than 5% of the elderly are in institutions, the residents of which are certainly not representative of the entire old-age population, the resulting unflattering descriptions lead to general misconceptions of what old people are like.

Robert Butler (1974, 1975), who coined the term *ageism* to refer to the social stereotyping of older people as well as to the social discrimination against them, cited many examples of negative attitudes toward the elderly. Future physicians, whose first encounter with an older person in medical school is in the form of a cadaver, may engage in gallows humor and refer to older patients as "crooks," "turkeys," and "dirt-balls." And Alex Comfort (1976) reported knowing licensed physicians who ridiculed and belittled older people whom they viewed as insulting to their medical skills.

All in all, health professionals are significantly more negative in their attitudes toward treating older patients than they are toward treating younger ones (Spence et al., 1968). It has been suggested that the stereotyping of the elderly by professional people may serve as a kind of justification for not attending to their needs. Personnel directors, for example, may use stereotypes as a rationalization for ignoring older workers (Pines, 1976).

To quote Butler (1974):

> Ageism can be seen as a process of systematic stereotyping of and discrimination against people because they are old—just as racism and sexism can accomplish this with skin color and gender. Old people are categorized as senile, rigid in thought and manner, old fashioned in morality and skills. Ageism allows the younger generation to see older people as different from themselves. Thus they subtly cease to identify with their elders as human beings. (p. 11)

This quotation refers to several stereotypes pertaining to the aged. Other stereotypes, myths, or misconceptions cited by Butler and others (e.g., Comfort, 1976; Perry, 1974; Verwoerdt, 1969) are that:

1. Most old people are ill or in poor health.
2. Most old people are senile or in their second childhood.
3. Most old people are rigid or inflexible.
4. Most old people can't do a good job and should retire.
5. Most old people have no sex life.
6. Most old people want to disengage or gradually withdraw from active participation.
7. Most old people live alone, abandoned by their families and other relatives.
8. Most old people do live or should live in institutions (nursing homes, hospitals, etc.).

There are other myths or misconceptions, for example, the myth that conceives of old age as a magic land where everyone is a happy, playful retiree, free from the worries of the world, and the myth that people automatically start going downhill when they are 65.

## Research on Attitudes Toward Aging and the Aged

Research investigations concerned with attitudes toward aging and old have employed a variety of techniques, ranging from the simple "Yes–No" poll questions of Gallup, Harris, and Roper to the more carefully constructed attitude questionnaires of Kogan (1961) and Palmore (1980) (see Table 8.1). Although the results of this research have varied with the way in which the questions are asked and other methodological factors, a general finding of studies with subjects from age 5 to adulthood point to a generally negative attitude toward old age. For example, Kogan and Shelton's (1962) sample of college students tended to downgrade the appearance of older people, felt that the old resent the young, and stated that they preferred to avoid direct personal contact with the aged. Kastenbaum and Durkee (1964) also found that adolescents usually have little regard for the elderly.

In an investigation of the attitudes of older children and adolescents toward adults of different ages, Hickey and Kalish (1968) asked groups of 8-, 12-, 15-, and 19-year-olds to evaluate adults at ages 25, 45, 65, and 85. The respondents showed a clear preference for younger adults over older adults, a perference that was not related to the age of the respondent. Ivester and King's (1977) study of students in Grades 9–12 also revealed no age differences in liking for older people, but in this study the respondents' attitudes toward the elderly were generally favorable.

The results of later investigations of the attitudes of children (e.g., Hickey, Hickey, & Kalish, 1968; Serock, Seefeldt, Jantz, & Galper, 1977; Seefeldt, Jantz, Galper, & Serock, 1977) substantiated earlier findings that children have a generally unpleasant image of growing old and old age. In a study conducted at the University of Maryland's Center on Aging, Serock et al. (1977) found that most of the 180 children (ages 3–11) who were questioned described the elderly in both negative and positive terms. The elderly were seen by these children as "wrinkled, short, and gray-haired" people who "chew funny," "don't go out much," "sit all day and watch TV in their rocking chairs," and "have heart attacks and die." The same children, however, described old people as wonderful and kind. Similar to the findings of Serock and his colleagues, Weinberger's (1979) study of 5- to 8-year-olds found that these children perceived the elderly as having few friends, less healthy and less attractive, and as being asked for help less often than people of other age groups when a person is lost. However, these children also viewed the elderly as people whom they would ask for help if they were hurt and whom they would want to help.

TABLE 8.1
Facts on Aging Quiz*

The reader is encouraged to test his/her knowledge and attitudes about aging by taking the following quiz. Specific items on the quiz are considered in the appropriate chapters of the text.

*Directions:* Mark "True" or "False"

1. The majority of old people are senile (i.e., defective memory, disoriented, or demented).
2. All five senses tend to decline in old age.
3. Most old people have no interest in, or capacity for, sexual relations.
4. Lung vital capacity tends to decline in old age.
5. The majority of old people feel miserable most of the time.
6. Physical strength tends to decline in old age.
7. At least one-tenth of the aged are living in long-stay institutions (i.e., nursing homes, mental hospitals, homes for the aged, etc.).
8. Aged drivers have fewer accidents per driver than drivers under age 65.
9. Most older workers cannot work as effectively as younger workers.
10. About 80% of the aged are healthy enough to carry out their normal activities.
11. Most old people are set in their ways and unable to change.
12. Old people usually take longer to learn something new.
13. It is almost impossible for most old people to learn something new.
14. The reaction time of most old people tends to be slower than reaction time of younger people.
15. In general, most old people are pretty much alike.
16. The majority of old people report that they are seldom bored.
17. The majority of old people are socially isolated and lonely.
18. Older workers have fewer accidents than younger workers.
19. Over 15% of the U.S. population are now age 65 or over.
20. Most medical practitioners tend to give low priority to the aged.
21. The majority of older people have incomes below the poverty level (as defined by the federal government).
22. The majority of old people are working or would like to have some kind of work to do (including housework and volunteer work).
23. Older people tend to become more religious as they age.
24. The majority of old people report that they are seldom irritated or angry.
25. The health and socioeconomic status of older people (compared to younger people) in the year 2000 will probably be worse or about the same as that of today's older people.

*After Palmore (1980) Reprinted by permission. The odd-numbered items are false, the even-numbered ones true.

When asked how they felt about growing old themselves, all but a few of the children questioned by Serock et al. (1977) said that they simply did not want to do it. The desire of these childen not to grow old is apparently shared by a sizable number of adults. For example, Kastenbaum (1971) estimated that 25% of all Americans have such a negative attitude toward old age that many would prefer to die before reaching it. And, as Butler (1975) pointed out, old people frequently look at themselves in a negative light, thereby perpetuating and reinforcing the social stereotypes of old age.

Indirect evidence of the negative image of old age in the elderly themselves was obtained by Kastenbaum and Durkee (1964), who found that people over 70 consistently classified themselves as middle-aged. These findings confirmed those of Phillips (1962) in a study of 346 people aged 60 and above. Sixty-one percent of Phillips' (1962) sample of older people thought that others viewed them as middle-aged, and 62% stated that they felt younger than most people their age.

To obtain more representative information on the attitudes and images of old age and the aged, the National Council on the Aging commissioned the Louis Harris and Associates (1981) public opinion agency to conduct an interview survey of a cross section of American adults. The results of 3,427 interviews make abundantly clear that adult Americans harbor many misconceptions about what old age is really like. Some of the results of the Harris survey, those comparing the expectations of a sample of adults aged 18–64 and a sample of adults 65 and over with the personal experiences reported by the elderly themselves of the "serious" problems of old age, are summarized in Table 8.2. Half or more of the 18- to 64-year age group expected fear of crime, not enough money to live on, inadequate transportation, loneliness, and not enough job opportunities to be very serious problems, but one-fourth or less of the elderly respondents actually reported these as problems. It is interesting that greater percentages of the older people who were interviewed considered the problems

TABLE 8.2
"Very Serious" Problems: Personal Experience of the Elderly vs. Public Expectation

| Problem | Percent of Public 65 and Over Experiencing as a "Very Serious Problem" | Percent of Public Expecting to be a "Very Serious Problem" | |
|---|---|---|---|
| | | 18–64 year olds | 65 years and over |
| High cost of energy (heating oil, gas, electricity) | 42 | 81 | 72 |
| Fear of crime | 25 | 74 | 58 |
| Poor health | 21 | 47 | 40 |
| Not having enough money to live on | 17 | 68 | 50 |
| Getting transportation (to stores, doctors, places of recreation, etc.) | 14 | 58 | 43 |
| Loneliness | 13 | 65 | 45 |
| Not enough medical care | 9 | 45 | 34 |
| Not enough job opportunities | 6 | 51 | 24 |
| Not enough education | 6 | 21 | 17 |
| Poor housing | 5 | 43 | 30 |

*Reprinted with permission from Harris & Associates, 1981.
Copyright © 1981 by the National Council on the Aging, Inc.

listed in Table 8.2 as more serious for other older people than for themselves.

The tendency to see themselves as better off than other people in their age group is also seen in the responses given by the elderly sample to the life-satisfaction questions in the Harris poll. Over four-fifths of the elderly respondents felt that, compared with other people of their age, they made a good appearance. And three-fifths felt that they had gotten more breaks in life than others. Somewhat reassuring to middle-aged Americans is the fact that over four-fifths of the elderly respondents were fairly well satisfied with their lives and had gotten pretty much what they expected to out of life. Over three-fifths indicated that their activities were as interesting to them as they had ever been, would not change their past life if they could, and expected some interesting and pleasant things to happen to them in the future.

It can be concluded from the results of the Harris survey that older Americans do experience problems, the top five being the high cost of energy, fear of crime, poor health, not having enough money to live on, and inadequate transportation. These problems, however, are not as pervasive as the general public—old or young—believes. In general the elderly are fairly happy with their lot, and perhaps their greatest problem is the perception of others of old age and the aged.

## Elderly Images in the Media

The fact that television has an impact on the attitudes and values of the entire population of viewers, which includes a large majority of the American population, is undeniable. Unfortunately, the images of the elderly depicted on American television have too often emphasized the traditional stereotype of older people as "ugly, toothless, sexless, incontinent, senile, confused, and helpless." ("New Image . . . ," 1977). Older adults are also depicted as narrow-minded, in poor health, floundering financially, sexually dissatisfied, and unable to make decisions (see Kubey, 1980). "When the entire country sees a cranky, out-of-touch, cane-wielding older woman (perhaps backing her Edsel into a tree) on a night-time TV show, what attitude will viewers demonstrate toward older women the next day?" (Gray Panthers, 1985)

Although a number of well-known actors and actresses in their 70s, 80s, and even 90s (George Burns, Bob Hope, etc.) are still quite active in their profession, until fairly recently elderly people have either been ignored or have served principally as objects of humor and ridicule for comedians (Johnny Carson's "Aunt Blabby," Jonathan Winters' "Maudie Pritchard," Red Foxx's "Fred Sanford"). Such characterizations may be amusing, but they reinforce the negative stereotype of the elderly as lazy, hypochondriacal, and oafish. Furthermore, it has been a rarity to see old people playing themselves; rather, a typical situation has been a young or middle-aged actor such as Vickie Lawrence playing an elderly role. When an elderly actor is seen on television, the role is more likely to be that of a pitchman for an arthritis remedy, a denture adhesive, or a laxative rather than a dramatic performance. There are, of course, exceptions, such as the "Golden Girls" series.

In general, research has shown that older people are usually underrepresented and assigned either uninteresting or unpleasant television roles that encourage stereotypes (Greenberg, Korzenny, & Atkin, 1979). Studies conducted by the Annenberg School of Communications (University of Pennsylvania) during the decade 1969–1979 revealed some of the disparities between television portrayals of the elderly and their real-life counterparts (see Signorielli & Gerbner, 1977). For example, although over 10% of the American population during the years of the study consisted of the over-65 group, less than 3% of fictional television characters in the 1,365 nighttime programs analyzed were elderly. Elderly people who did appear in television programs tended to be characterized as "stubborn, eccentric, ineffectual, sexually inactive, and downright silly." Furthermore, older women were given fewer romantic roles than older men of the same age, and elderly men were more likely to be cast as madmen or evildoers who ended up dead ("Warped View. . .," 1979).

Because elderly people watch more television than any other age group, it would appear that the treatment they receive by this medium is inconsistent with their influence. Television advertisers and executives realize, however, that it is young people rather than the aged who consume most of the products advertised on TV. With the possible exceptions of instant coffee, upset stomach remedies, soap flakes, and laxatives, older people consume less than the average and are also less likely to try new products or brands ("Elderly Demanding. . .," 1977). On the other hand, older people have more money to spend than ever before, and advertisers are becoming more conscious of them and making greater efforts to avoid offending them.

The results of a survey conducted some years ago (Harris & Associates, 1975) indicated that older people themselves are not critical of how the elderly are portrayed on television. A large majority felt that they were treated with respect. However, there has been no shortage of criticism from the Gray Panthers. The Media Watch Project of this organization has pointed to numerous age stereotypes (physical traits, attitude, clothes, activities, etc.) of the elderly, not only on television but in other media (women's magazines, children's literature, greeting cards) as well. Too often, witches and other demonic characters are old and frightening, grandparents are ill and dying, and in other ways older people are misrepresented as unpleasant. Television commercials may also reinforce old-age stereotypes by warning or joking about changes in appearance and personality with aging.

## Changing Attitudes and Images

The *self-concept,* or personally perceived value, of an individual is determined in large measure by the appraisals and attitudes communicated by other people. In old age a person's self-concept affects the very process of aging. Thus, people who are socially devalued and hence have negative self-concepts show the symptoms of biological aging sooner than those who are given more social status and acceptance. Consequently, one might expect that with the gradual erosion of the public's negative attitudes and stereotypes about aging, the elderly will begin to live more energetically and happily.

But how can attitudes and stereotypes pertaining to aging and the aged be changed? For example, does direct personal contact with older people help change attitudes toward them? Yes, to some extent, particularly when the contacts are spontaneous and the elderly people are not ill (Spence et al., 1968; Steinbaum, 1973). Although exposure to the aged and knowledge of the aging process do not necessarily have positive effects, courses in gerontology can help to change attitudes when classroom work and textbook readings are supplemented by positive contacts with older adults.

Certainly, improvements in the ways of depicting older people in the media and books can assist in changing attitudes. Television programs such as "Prime Time" and films such as *Peege* and *Portrait of Grandpa Doc* paint a better picture of old age than that seen on most evening television fare. In addition, children's fiction now portrays the elderly in less negative ways than in the children's books, nursery rhymes, cartoons, and stories of yesteryear (Ansello, 1977; Blue, 1978).

The Empathic Model, discussed in chapter 2, can also be applied to help younger people understand the elderly and hopefully improve their attitudes toward this age group. The frustrations, social roles, mourning, joblessness, sexual behavior, and political attitudes of the elderly have all been simulated by placing young people in a variety of contrived situations typical of those encountered by the elderly. This procedure serves to give participants greater insight into the situations faced by older people and why they respond as they do (Kastenbaum, 1971).

Many other interesting and often ingenious approaches to attitude change have been devised, but needless to say they are not always effective. After summarizing the findings of a number of studies on the topic, Bennett (1976) concluded that negative attitudes toward the elderly are very difficult to change. Consequently, she anticipated a continuation of the fear and even denial of one's own aging and a reluctance to work with old people. Denial of aging and the aged is, however, a two-edged sword, because in denying the aged we ultimately deny ourselves. As Butler (1975) expressed it, "We don't all grow Black or Chinese, but we do grow old."

Butler also recognized that overturning a deeply rooted prejudice is a slow process, requiring continuous effort. According to Anderson (1979) and Cottin (1979), much of this effort will have to be made by the elderly themselves. If society will not change its attitudes toward them, then the elderly will have to change society. This, in essence, is the argument of the Gray Panthers and other political lobbyists for the rights of the elderly.

Concerning the matter of elderly images on television, Gray Panthers (1985) wants to see the following changes in that medium: a proportionate representation of elders; portrayals of significant and influential characters by older actresses and actors; portrayals of a variety of meaningful relationships among people of all ages; the presence of older characters without reference to age; portrayal of aging as a natural process, not disguised and not ignored; fair and realistic representation of elders as diverse individuals; discussion of aging issues in media directed not exclusively to elders; acknowledgment of the realities of aging.[1]

## SOCIAL ROLES

*Social roles* are patterns of behavior that individuals are expected to display under certain conditions or in certain situations involving other people. People usually have many different roles that they are expected to play under different circumstances, for example, the roles of spouse, parent, grandparent, friend, employee, and churchgoer. Each role consists of an acquired set of behaviors that must be learned if the person is to be socially accepted in the position or status to which the role is appropriate.

Because roles are based on interactions with other people, it is not surprising that the most socially active people play the greatest number of roles. In addition, as is the case with personality traits in general, there is a continuity from youth to old age in the extensiveness of a person's social activities and hence in the number of roles played. Considering old age as a whole, however, a process of role reduction or gradual disengagement from social activities is quite common. Because the psychological needs and self-identity of a person are closely related to his or her social, occupational, and familial memberships, a loss of several of the roles prescribed by these memberships can produce feelings of alienation and marginality.

Some gerontologists have stressed the fact that role loss is a natural, perhaps even desirable, part of later life. On the other hand, Blau (1973) argued that, given the option, older people usually prefer to live their lives with the meaning and purpose that comes from having personally and socially significant roles to play. Eleanor Maxwell ("Aging . . .," 1976) noted that in certain primitive societies, old people keep young in spirit by "starring" in specific social re-ituals. For example, an elderly Eskimo woman in the Canadian Arctic may give her all in a tug-of-war contest, whereas elderly Apaches bless babies and senior members of the Bakongo tribe of Africa train youngsters for adult life. Although the setting up of rituals in which older people can play leading roles would not be

---

[1]A slide show, "Out of the Rocking Chair—Challenging Ageism in the Media," has been produced by Gray Panthers as part of the Media Watch Project.

easy in our society, Maxwell suggested that if the elderly are encouraged to participate in a variety of social groups they will find leading roles to play.

Some roles last from young adulthood through old age, but even these long-term roles undergo changes with aging. Furthermore old age brings with it the opportunity to establish new relationships, memberships, and roles. Among the types of social roles that give meaning to one's life in old age are those involving relationships with family and friends as well as the usually less intimate roles stemming from memberships in various organizations. Sex and family roles were described in chapter 7, and the roles of employee and retiree are considered in chapter 9. Other social roles—friendship, social organizational, religious, and political—are discussed in the remainder of this section.

## Friendships

In contrast to the formal support network (social agencies, health organizations, other official support services), family members, neighbors, and friends constitute what Kalish (1982) has termed an "informal support network" in old age. Because of their voluntary nature, friends may be valued even more than relatives. Friendships are typically closer than kin relationships (Dickens & Perlman, 1981), and life satisfaction in old age is more closely related to interactions with friends than with relatives (Wood & Robertson, 1978).

Almost all elderly people report having friends (Harris & Associates, 1975), who are similar to themselves in age, status, values, and interests. These friends usually live close by, but easily available transportation can extend the friendship circle beyond the immediate neighborhood. Elderly friends meet in their homes, at church, in community centers, and at many other locations within traveling distance.

Friends can be a source of emotional support as well as information and entertainment, and hence can contribute to the older person's sense of belongingness, meaningfulness, and social status. Therefore, it is understandable why close personal relationships with friends, which help to cushion the shock of physical deterioration, loss of loved ones, and other sources of stress in old age, are characteristic of physically healthier and personally happier elderly people. One friend is better than none, but because old friends die sooner than young ones, it is better to have several. This is particularly true in the case of older men.

The number and intensity of friendships in old age varies with a variety of factors. Women, who throughout the lives of a family tend to initiate the social interactions of the family with outsiders, usually have more friends and longer lasting friendships than men (Dickens & Perlman, 1981; Schonberg & Potter, 1976). Older men tend to have "associates," with whom they like to do things other than just talk. More so then in the case of women, the friendships of older men include members of the opposite sex. Women, on the other hand, being more "interdependent" (Gilligan, 1982) and receptive to self-disclosure, are more apt to express their feelings to friends and to rely on them in dealing with matters of concern or problems of living (Dickens & Perlman, 1981; Reisman, 1981).

Friendships also vary with social standing, people of higher socioeconomic status usually having more friends than those of lower socioeconomic status. In general, middle-class elderly people are more friend-oriented and working-class elderly more kin-oriented. Many of the friendships of middle-class people, however, are superficial, and older people in the lower social classes often have single friendships that last for a lifetime (Williamson, Evans, & Munley, 1980). Ethnic group differences in the number of friendships in old age have also been studied, with Whites reporting higher levels of contact with friends and neighbors than Blacks or Mexican Americans (Dowd & Bengtson, 1978). In this same study, however, Whites reported the lowest frequency of contact and Mexican-Americans the most frequent contacts with their children and grandchildren.

Also related to the number of friendships in old age are length of residence and the density of older people in the particular neighborhood. Being a long-term resident of a locality that has a high density of elderly people is associated with having a greater number of friendships. The size of the municipality is also related to friendships: Older residents of small towns tend to have more friends than those in larger cities (Riley & Foner, 1968).

Many of the demographic factors associated with a greater number of friendships in old age are brought together in retirement communities. It can be argued that the social identities and self-concepts of most elderly people are maintained more effectively by relationships within their own age group rather than by trying to emulate the behavior of young and middle-aged adults. By providing a better opportunity to develop friendships with one's own age group, retirement communities may be the best solution to loneliness and loss of status in old age. It is much easier to become socially isolated and the victim of negative attitudes toward the aged in an age-integrated situation than in an age-segregated setting such as a retirement community. Research has shown that the great majority of elderly people prefer living in environments restricted to older adults. Those who live in such age-segregated facilities have higher morale, are more satisfied with their housing, are more active, and get around more in the neighborhood (Teaff, Lawton, Nahemow, & Carlson, 1978).

## Organizational Memberships

Many adults obtain a great deal of personal satisfaction and a sense of identity and status from belonging to formal social organizations. Business clubs, trade unions, and other occupation-related organizations are of particular importance to young and middle-aged adults who are active in the work force. The influences of these organizations do not automatically cease when a member retires from formal employment, but they may become less important during the last years of life. Involvement in other social organizations, as with all social activities, declines in old age. The decline is, however, not universal, and many healthy, outgoing people remain actively involved well into their 70s, 80s, and even 90s. This is especially true of older people in the middle and upper social classes, who take a more active part in social organizations and have more friends outside the family than the working-class elderly (Cutler, 1977).[2] Of all organizations to which elderly people belong, memberships in churches (or synagogues or temples) are by far the most common. These are also the memberships that are most closely related to life satisfaction in the elderly (Cutler, 1976).

## Religion

Just as in younger age groups, there are religious fanatics, atheists, and moderates among the aged. Older adults, on the whole, are not doctrinaire, but they do attach more importance to religion than younger people. For example, a national poll (Harris & Associates, 1975) found that 49% of adults under 65 and 71% of those over 65 felt that religion was very important in their lives. A larger percentage of older than younger adults also believe in immortality, and more of them pray, read scriptures, and are involved in religious organizations (Blazer & Palmore, 1976; Moberg, 1971; Palmore, 1981). Older women show a greater religious interest than older men, and the middle and upper social classes are more active in religious organizations than the lower class.

Actual church attendance declines from ages 10 to 30–35 and then rises steadily until old age (Bahr, 1970; Harris & Associates, 1975). Church attendance begins to decline again in the last years of life, due undoubtedly to problems with health, transportation, and income. However, listening to or watching church services and other religious programs on the radio and television, praying, Bible reading, and meditating compensate for the decline in church attendance (Ainlay & Smith, 1984).

It is not clear whether the greater interest in religious matters among older people is a consequence of aging per se or generational differences. The findings are based on cross-sectional studies, and therefore it is impossible to separate age and cohort variables (see chapter 1). One can argue that the interest is a reflection of the fact that today's elderly grew up during a time when families stressed religion more strongly than later American families and that the effects of this training persisted throughout life. In any event, there is certainly no good evidence that the greater religious interest of the elderly is caused by the realization

---

[2]For some reason, a greater percentage of Blacks than Whites, or any other ethnic group for that matter, participate in voluntary social organizations (Cutler, 1977).

that they have little time left on this earth and should therefore begin thinking more seriously about the hereafter.

## Politics

Responding to the challenge to fight back against their public image and exploitation as well as to the need for companionship with a purpose, the elderly have become more organized during the past two decades than at any time since the Townsend movement of the 1930s. Many older individuals have shown great enthusiasm in demanding self-respect and protesting age discrimination in employment, housing, health care, and other areas.

Over 7 million older Americans, compared to approximately 250,000 less than 20 years ago, belong to local, state, and national organizations concerned with problems of the elderly. Chief among these organizations, which are not mere social clubs but political action groups, are the American Association of Retired Persons (AARP), the National Council of Senior Citizens (NCSC), the Gray Panthers, the National Alliance of Senior Citizens (NASC), and the National Caucus on the Black Aged (NCBA) (see Appendix A for a more detailed list, addresses, and descriptions). The two largest organizations, AARP and NCSC, boast memberships of several million adults of all ages. AARP's declaration of rights is a general inventory of the concerns of elderly Americans:

> To live with sufficient means for decency and self-respect; to move about freely, reasonably, and conveniently; to pursue a career or interest without penalty founded on age; to be heard on all matters of public interest; to maintain health and well-being through preventive care and education; to receive assistance in times of illness or need or other emergency; to peace and privacy as well as participation; to protection and safety amid the hazards of daily life; to act together to redress of grievances; to live life fully and with honor—not for their age but for their humanity.

Organizations such as AARP have been quite instrumental in lobbying for the establishment of the numerous social services and social programs for the elderly, including not only provisions for adequate income, health care, housing, nutrition, and transportation, but also for the opportunity to develop new interests and skills.

As a group, the elderly are admittedly more conservative in their attitudes toward domestic political matters (Cutler, 1974; Glenn, 1974) as well as more "militaristic" or "hard line" on foreign policy (Back & Gergen, 1963). Kastenbaum (1971) believed that the conservatism of older people is a reaction to what society has taken away from them in terms of status and opportunity. He suggested that they might feel less threatened and not so obsessed with clinging to what they possess if they were given more positive social roles to play and equality with younger adults in employment. In any event, older people may abandon their political conservatism when the issue pertains to the living conditions and rights of the elderly.

Older people as a group are concerned with self-maintenance, but this does not necessarily imply retaining the status quo. Members of the Gray Panthers, a grass-roots political movement of social activists founded by Margaret ("Maggie") Kuhn in the early 1970s, are quite "liberal" or "progressive" in their efforts to improve tax laws, health laws, bus service, and other rights and benefits for the elderly. Although small compared with many other organizations, Gray Panthers has been effective in raising the national consciousness about ageism. By emphasizing the interests and abilities of many older people to be active participants in society, this organization has been instrumental in ensuring that the civil rights and needs of the elderly are not overlooked by those in power (see Fig. 8.1).

That the elderly have the capacity to wield a great deal of political power when they are organized behind a common cause is shown by the fact that over 90% are registered to vote and that they vote quite regularly. Approximately 18% of those voting in the 1984 presidental election and 21% of those voting in the 1986 congressional election were 65 or over. As shown in Fig. 8.2, a higher percentage of people in the 55–64 and 65–74 year brackets voted than in any other age group (U.S. Senate Special Committee on Aging, 1987). Typical of voting patterns in old age are the facts that a greater percentage of older men than older women, a greater percentage of older Whites than older Blacks and Hispanics, and a greater percentage of those with more education voted in these elections. Polls conducted by the *Los Angeles Times* indicated that, similar to the pattern in the country as a whole, more elderly people voted Republican in the 1984 presidential election, in which participation was higher, and more voted Democratic in the 1986 congressional election.

Most politicians realize that the 1990s will be a time to focus on the rights of the aged and that the organized over-65 vote will carry considerable political clout. As shown in Fig. 8.2, more older people vote than any other age group. Consequently, they can wield considerable influence and power in matters of special concern to them. Political action by organized groups of older people has already been successful in shutting down inadequate nursing homes in certain states, stopping Medicaid cuts in New York, arranging for the placement of traffic lights at busy intersections in Michigan, and obtaining bus fare discounts in dozens of cities.

The hundreds of Golden Age, Senior Citizens, and Live Long and Like It clubs in several American cities are quite active politically. Some of their efforts are directed toward obtaining property and income tax reforms, more extensive health-care benefits, better housing, and better transportation for the elderly. Other issues are reforms in social security and private pensions. Considering the great diversity of interests and needs among the elderly, it is not always easy to

FIG. 8.1. Elderly demonstrators in Washington, DC (Reprinted by permission of Gray Panthers.)

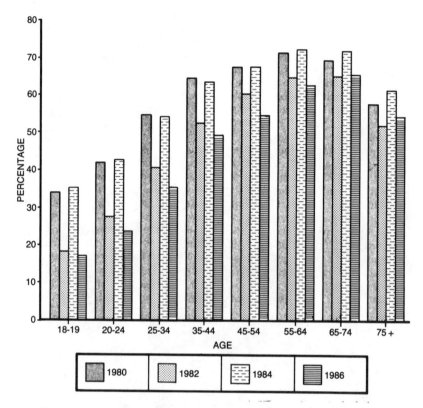

FIG. 8.2.   Percentages of people in eight age groups who reported voting in the 1980–1986 national elections. (U.S. Bureau of the Census, April 1982, November 1983, May 1986b, and unpublished data from the November 1986 Current Population Survey.

organize and motivate them to work for a common goal. Therefore, it is important for organizations concerned with the rights of the elderly to enlist the support of middle-aged and young adults—who will themselves be old before long and the direct beneficiaries of their own efforts.

## ELDERLY MINORITIES

It has been pointed out that the aged in America are similar to minority group members in terms of their status and the roles they are permitted to play. Furthermore, a large percentage of elderly Americans have been discriminated against because they are old and because they are members of ethnic minorities. The situation of these elderly minorities has been described as one of *double jeopardy*. In addition to being disadvantaged because of their ethnic-group status, they experience further loss of status because of their age (Dowd & Bengtson, 1978). Thus, the problems of low income, poor health, inadequate housing, and loss of status confronting all elderly Americans are particularly acute for elderly minorities.

Because so many elderly members of minority groups are "invisible," it is difficult to obtain an accurate census. An estimated 90% of Americans aged 65 and over in 1986 were White, 8% were Black, and 2% were other racial groups (American Indian, Eskimo, Aleut, Asian, and Pacific Islander). Individuals of Hispanic origin, who fall in various racial groups, constituted an estimated 3% of the U.S. population in 1986 (U.S. Bureau of the Census, 1987a). As shown in Fig. 8.3, the percentage of minorities in the American elderly population will increase from 13% in 1985 to an estimated 30% by the middle of the 21st century. As impressive as these numbers may be, lumping all the subgroups comprising the total number of ethnic elderly into a single category is misleading. Within each subgroup there may be wide diversities in language, customs, and expectations. For example, although they all speak Spanish there are important differences among elderly Americans of Cuban, Mexican, and Puerto Rican origins.

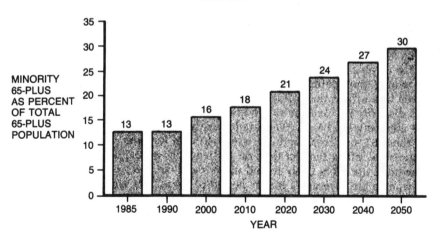

**GROWTH OF THE MINORITY ELDERLY POPULATION: 1985-2050**

FIG. 8.3.   Growth of the minority elderly population from 1985 to 2050. (U.S. Bureau of the Census, March 1986c.

## Common Characteristics of Elderly Ethnic Groups

Whatever the exact count of elderly minorities in the United States, and however extensive their differences may be, they have certain features in common (Federal Council on the Aging, 1979):

1. The large majority live in metropolitan areas. An exception are Native Americans (American Indians), but for this group there has also been a steady urban migration.
2. The average level of formal education is lower than that of their White counterparts.
3. The unemployment rate is higher, and average income is lower than for older White Americans.
4. A smaller percentage own their own homes, and they tend to live in less desirable neighborhoods.
5. Accurate data on the life expectancies of minorities other than Blacks are unavailable, but indications are that the average life span is shorter than that of Whites.[3] Of interest is the "crossover phenomenon," in which Blacks who live to be 75 have longer life expectancies than Whites.
6. The health status of elderly Blacks is poorer than that of elderly Whites, but the situation for other minorities is not clear.[4] Indications are that the health of elderly Hispanic-Americans and of Native Americans is substantially poorer than average.

Although there are differences among minority groups in life expectancy and other "life chances," when social class is controlled the needs of elderly minorities appear to be quite similar (Trela & Sokolovsky, 1979). A study conducted during the late 1970s on seven minority groups in San Diego—Black, Hispanic, Samoan, Japanese, Chinese, Philippino, and Guamanian—revealed that these groups were quite similar in their needs and attitudes toward federal, state, and local programs and services for older Americans (Center on Aging, 1978). What does vary from group to group are the ways in which the needs of the elderly are met, including the level of support from family and other nonpublic sources.

## Family Support

In the close-knit family structures of many ethnic minorities, care and respect for the elderly are often greater than in nonHispanic White families. Among Blacks

---

[3]The life expectancy of Native Americans is the shortest of any minority group (45–50 years); they also have a lower standard of living than other minorities (National Tribal Chairman's Association, 1976).

[4]Elderly Blacks, however, have better vision and hearing than elderly Whites (Dancy, 1977).

and Mexican-Americans, for example, multigenerational households in which elderly members make a valued contribution in child care and other domestic activities are more common. The custom in China and Japan of filial respect and caring for the elderly has also been transmitted to a large extent to Chinese- and Japanese-American families.

Coupled with a tradition of respect for the aged, the fact that older people are not a severe economic liability in minority families creates more positive attitudes toward them. But when westernization or acculturation of young minority group members is combined with poverty and low social status, negative attitudes toward the aged develop in these ethnic groups. As a consequence, feelings of being old and negative views of aging are also quite common among minorities in the United States (Bengtson, Kasschau, & Ragan, 1977). Like their Caucasian counterparts, minority group elderly deplore the lack of respect that younger people frequently demonstrate toward them and the fact that older people are no longer valued as models by the young. The result is that many minority elderly develop feelings of loneliness and alienation, from the wider American culture as well as from their children and grandchildren (Benitiz, 1976).

## Social Services for Elderly Minorities

Social service providers are aware of the special problems of minority elderly, but they also realize that efforts to solve these problems need to be made with an awareness of the cultural traditions and family dynamics of a particular person. Through research and careful observation, those who work with the minority elderly must attempt to learn more about them and to understand better whatever variations in the aging process exist within these groups. Attention should also be given by service providers to communicating in the native language of the elder person and to the ethnic and cultural differences of the group to which the older person belongs. Finally, one of the unique features of the lifestyles of many minority groups has been maintaining the elderly in the family unit. One alternative to providing services for the elderly is to work within this family unit as well as through subcultural organizations within the specific ethnic community.

Although elderly Blacks as a group appear to be even more aware than elderly Whites of the benefits and services to which they are entitled, many elderly minority group members are unaware of these benefits and services, unwilling to use them, or reside in areas where services are not readily available. This implies a program of providing information, transportation, and other measures that will bring the older person in closer contact with those social services to which he or she is entitled. In addition, because so many Blacks and other minority group members who pay social security taxes for a lifetime die before they can collect their benefits, it has been suggested that benefits be given earlier to older people in these subgroups. Such a suggestion is similar to the proposal that social security benefits should begin earlier for men because they don't live as long as women, and it is just as unlikely to be enacted into law.

The National Caucus and Center for the Black Aged, which sponsors employment and housing programs and monitors legislation and regulations affecting elderly Blacks, was the first national organization to focus on the needs and problems of American elderly minorities. Subsequently, other minority-based organizations—National Association for Spanish-Speaking Elderly, National Hispanic Council on Aging, National Indian Council on Aging, National Pacific/Asian Resource Center on Aging—concerned with the rights of other minorities have been established (see Appendix A for addresses and descriptions). From a political standpoint, these organizations are, however, less influential than the multimillion-member AARP or the more militant Gray Panthers.

## SUMMARY

Attitudes toward old age and the aged, as well as the status accorded elderly people, vary with the culture, subculture, and individual. Agricultural societies have traditionally held the elderly in higher regard than gathering/hunting societies or more technologically oriented societies. The elderly have also been accorded greater respect in Eastern than in Western cultures.

Modern society harbors many misconceptions and stereotypes pertaining to the aged, including the beliefs that most old people are in poor health, senile, inflexible, unemployable, sexless, inactive, and alone. The cultural stereotypes and negative attitudes toward aging expressed by adults and the media are transmitted to young children, many of whom also express negative feelings toward aging and the aged. Although the elderly themselves often share the general public's negative perceptions of old age, they do not necessarily agree with younger adults about what problems are most serious in later life. In fact, the results of a national poll indicate that a large majority of the older people who were questioned were pleasantly surprised to discover that old age was not as bad as they had expected it to be.

Stereotypes of older people portrayed on television are undergoing changes, as are images of the aged communicated by other sources of information and entertainment. Unfortunately, attitudes toward aging and the perceived status of older people are not easy to alter. Presentation of more positive images of the elderly in books, films, and the media, as well as exposure to "normal" older people, should help erode existing stereotypes. Experimental approaches for changing attitudes, such as the Empathic Model, also show promise. Nevertheless, politically active older people have come to the conclusion that they must work to change society, rather than waiting for society to change its attitudes and behavior toward the elderly.

Old age has been characterized as a period when the number of social roles played by a person declines. It would appear, however, that the majority of older people prefer to maintain rewarding friendships in addition to religious and other organizational ties. Positive interactions with other people, especially with those in their same age group, help older people retain a sense of belongingness, meaningfulness, and value. An advantage of retirement communities is that, by being age segregated, they increase the likelihood of friendships with other elderly people.

Interest and involvement in religion are greater among older than younger adults, but the difference is, at least in part, probably a generational rather than an age effect. Many older people are also quite active politically: The great majority are registered to vote, and a larger percentage than average vote in elections. Older people tend to be more conservative than younger people in their political views, but the former can be quite liberal on issues pertaining to the rights and privileges of the elderly. Many local and national organizations of and for the elderly are quite active politically. Of primary interest to those organizations are issues and problems concerning health care, nutrition, employment, social security, housing, transportation, and crime.

The situation of elderly minorities in the United States has been characterized as one of double jeopardy: They have lower status because they are both old and members of ethnic minorities. Although many minority elderly belong to close-knit family groups, the respect and consideration they have traditionally employed in such families often change with the acculturation of other family members into mainstream American society. In any case, social service providers need to be aware of the special needs and problems of elderly minorities and to seek alternative ways of making them aware of their rights and benefits and able to take advantage of them.

## SUGGESTED READINGS

Arluke, A., & Levin, J. (1984, June). Another stereotype: Old age as a second childhood. *Aging,* pp. 7–11.

Cottin, L. (1979). *Elders in rebellion.* New York: Doubleday/Anchor.

Cutler, N. E. (1983). Political behavior of the aged. In D. S. Woodruff & J. E. Birren (Eds.), *Aging: Scientific perspectives and social issues* (pp. 409–442). Monterey, CA: Brooks/Cole.

Davis, R., & Davis, J. (1985). *TV's image of the elderly.* Lexington, MA: Lexington Books.

Hudson, R. B., & Strate, J. (1985). Aging and political systems. In R. Binstock & E. Shanas (Eds.), *Handbook of aging and the social sciences* (pp. 554–585). New York: Van Nostrand. Reinhold.

Jackson, J. J. (1985). Race, national origin, ethnicity and aging. In R. Binstock & E.

Shanas (Eds.), *Handbook of aging and the social sciences* (pp. 264–303). New York: Van Nostrand Reinhold.

Moriwaki, S. Y., & Korbata, F. S. (1983). Ethnic minority aging. In D. S. Woodruff & J. E. Birren (Eds.), *Aging: Scientific perspectives and social issues* (pp. 409–442). Monterey, CA: Brooks/Cole.

McFadden, S. H. (1985). Attributes to religious maturity in aging people. *Journal of Religion and Aging, 1*(3), 39–48.

Powell, L. A., & Williamson, J. B. (1985, Summer). The mass media and the aged. *Social Policy,* pp. 38–49.

# 9

## Employment and Retirement

Sooner or later the decision whether to retire or to keep working at one's occupation faces those who have a choice. Some people look forward to retirement and the opportunity that it offers to pursue secondary interests and goals. Others, especially those who enjoy their work and who perceive it as more than simply a way of making a living, prefer to continue working even after they are eligible for retirement. Such people view the job as a central part of themselves, and becoming permanently separated from it has a marked effect on the self-concept. This is particularly ture of those who are higher on the occupational ladder and the self-employed, who view their work as more than mere drudgery to be abandoned as soon as possible. The contemporary viewpoint is that people should be permitted to continue working as long as they are capable and productive, but allowed and encouraged to retire when they need to.

### EMPLOYMENT IN LATER LIFE

Whether to retire or to continue working is a decision that historically has not been entirely up to most workers. Management, frequently after consultation with labor unions and an eye on government regulations, has made policies concerning retirement. Since the 1930s the marker retirement age has been in the 60s, typically 65. There are, however, wide differences in the rate of aging, and many people today can and want to keep working well beyond age 65. On the other hand, there are people who, because of chronic illness, injury, or other problems, are too disabled to work until their 65th birthday.

209

## Elderly Employment Statistics

With the exception of wartime, the percentage of elderly people in the work forces of industrialized nations has declined steadily throughout the current century. Nearly 70% of American men aged 65 and over were employed in 1900, a figure that had dropped to 46% by 1950, 19% by 1980, and 16% by 1986. In 1986, approximately 3 million Americans aged 65 and over were working or actively seeking work (U.S. Senate Special Committee on Aging, 1987). It is likely that the percentage of older Americans in the work force will be even lower by the year 2000. Among the causes of this decline are technological advances, less agricultural work, declines in self-employment, and more attractive retirement incentives. The increased educational and training requirements for most jobs have also favored younger workers over older ones.

Despite the decreases in labor force participation by elderly Americans, the percentages are still higher than those for any other developed country except Japan. In Japan, nearly one-half of the men and one-sixth of the women 65 years and above are employed. In developing countries, where retirement systems are not prevalent, participation rates of elderly in the work force are even higher than in Japan (Torrey et al., 1987).

In contrast to the pronounced decline in the percentage of employed elderly men, the proportion of employed elderly women has remained fairly constant during this century: it rose from 1 in 12 in 1900 to 1 in 10 during the 1950s, falling back to 1 in 12 in the 1970s and 1 in 13 in the 1980s. Although the percentage of elderly Black men in the labor force is smaller than that of elderly White men, the reverse is true for women (U.S. Senate Special Committee on Aging, 1987). That many of the nonworking elderly—both men and women, Black and White—prefer to be employed has been demonstrated by the results of nationwide opinion polls (Harris & Associates, 1975, 1981).

As shown in Fig. 9.1, the majority of older workers are employed in white-collar occupations and the smallest percentage are in farming and related occupations. Trade (wholesale and retail) and service industries employ the largest numbers of older people (U.S. Senate Special Committee on Aging, 1987). Many of these employees are managers and administrators, professionals and technical workers. Self-employment, which permits flexible scheduling and part-time work, is also common among the elderly (Schaie & Willis, 1986b).

## The Worker and the Job

Some time during middle age, at the height of their careers as well as their economic needs and responsibilities, most people begin to assess their accomplishments in terms of the time they have left. If their goals are found to be unrealistic, an adjustment may be in order (Neugarten, 1968a):

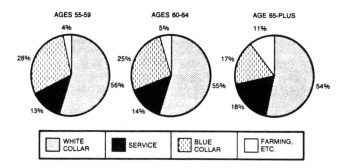

OCCUPATION OF OLDER WORKERS BY AGE: 1986

FIG. 9.1.    Percentages of older workers in four occupational groups by three age groups. (U.S. Dept. of Labor, Bureau of Labor Statistics. Unpublished data from 1986 Current Population Survey. NOTE: White collar occupations include managerial/professional and technical/sales/administrative support. Blue collar occupations include precision production/craft/repair, and operators/fabricators/laborers.

Men perceive a close relationship between life-line and career-line. Middle age is the time to take stock. Any disparity noted between career expectations and career achievements—that is, whether one is "on time" or "late" in reaching career goals—adds to the heightened awareness of age. One 47-year-old lawyer said, "I moved at age forty-five from a large corporation to a law firm. I got out at the last possible moment, because after forty-five it is too difficult to find the job you want. If you haven't made it by then, you had better make it fast, or you are stuck." (p. 96)

To many middle-agers, faced with Erikson's crisis of generativity versus self-absorption, the job is a central part of the self. Sexual, avocational, cultural, and even family interests may be perceived as less important than the job. People are often identified by the kind of work they do, and their status, social relationships, self-concept, and reason for living are all involved with their work. This is particularly true of men, who have traditionally been perceived as family bread-winners. But with the women's movement and the associated extension of the social identities of women beyond those of housewife and mother, it has also become true of more and more women during recent years.

Because the jobs of many people are such an important part of their life space, the satisfactions derived from work can affect and be affected by physical and mental health. For example, severe job stress, caused by heavy responsibilities and dissatisfaction with one's achievements, is related to heart attacks (Romo, Siltanen, Theorell, & Rahe, 1974). Job dissatisfaction is also associated with peptic ulcers, which affect blue-collar and white-collar workers alike (Kahn, 1969). The results of other research studies have shown that the suicide rate is higher among the unemployed than the employed (Rosenfeld, 1976b) and that

---

### Report 9.1    THE PSYCHOLOGICAL SIGNIFICANCE OF WORK*

Mr. Winter single-handedly ran an operation that nobody else in his company fully understood, nor in fact cared to understand. As Mr. Winter reached his 64th birthday, a bright and talented younger man was assigned as an apprentice to learn the complex set of activities so that at the end of the year, he could take over the operation and the old master could benefit from a well-deserved retirement. Mr. Winter objected, claiming that he did not want to retire, but the company had rules.

Not long after retirement a substantial change in Mr. Winter took place. He began to withdraw from people and to lose his zest for life. Within a year after his retirement this once lively and productive businessman was hospitalized, diagnosed as having a senile psychosis. Friends from work and even family soon stopped coming to visit, as they could evoke no response. Mr. Winter was a vegetable.

About two years after the apprentice had stepped up to his new position of responsibility he suddenly died. The company found itself in a serious predicament. The function that was vacated was essential to company operations but was one which no one else in the company could effectively perform. A decision was made to approach Mr. Winter and see if he could pull himself together enough to carry on the job and train somebody to take over. Four of his closest co-workers were sent to the hospital. After hours of trying, one of the men finally broke through. The idea of going back to work brought the first sparkle in Mr. Winter's eyes in two years. Within a few days, this "vegetable" was operating at full steam, interacting with people as he had years before.

*After Margolis and Kroes (1972). Copyright by the MIT Press.

---

work satisfaction is positively correlated with longevity (Palmore, 1969; Rose, 1964). Of course, whether job stress is the cause or the effect of physical and mental disorders is not clear from these studies. The direction of causation could be either way, and is most likely reciprocal and interactive. In any event, most people who live a long time continue to work at something throughout their lives (see Report 9.1).

## Characteristics of Older Workers

The results of a study conducted some years ago (Saleh & Otis, 1964) showed that job satisfaction reaches a peak in the mid-50s and then declines. Regardless of age, however, people who like their work and who see it as meaningful tend to want to keep their jobs as long as possible (Offir, 1974). This is especially true of older workers, who are usually more committed to their jobs and who experience greater job satisfaction than young adults. Reflective of these conclusions are the facts that older people are less likely to want to change their jobs, have less absenteeism, and express less job dissatisfaction than their younger coworkers (Doering, Rhodes, & Schuster, 1983).

Older workers also resent the assumption that they are incapable of doing a good day's work. Despite the fact that they often perform poorly on laboratory-type psychomotor tasks, under actual job conditions older men usually do as well or better than younger men (Riley & Foner, 1968). The volume of their work may be less than that of younger adults, but its quality is higher and it is accomplished with less wasted motion and fewer mistakes (Hurlock, 1980). Older workers are also quite capable of learning new job skills, especially when training methods take their capabilities into account. Whatever age-related declines in job performance are observed are usually minor and more likely to occur on tasks that are physically demanding or highly speeded. In most cases, the experience of the older worker compensates for any declines in speed or strength accompanying aging (Rhodes, 1983; Stagner, 1985).

The allegation that, because of personal problems, older people are hard to get along with on the job has also been contradicted by research. Compared with younger workers, older employees are less restless, less preoccupied with personal problems, and do not manifest any special difficulty in adjusting to other workers. Furthermore, older workers are less "accident-prone" and have fewer illnesses and injuries than one might suppose (Doering et al., 1983; Hurlock, 1980).

## The Unemployed Elderly

Although their job performance is not generally inferior to that of younger workers, the rate of unemployment tends to be higher for the elderly. Once out of work, older people remain unemployed on the average for a longer period of time than younger adults. Even the official unemployment figures for Americans age 65 and above (91,000 in 1986) are undoubtedly underestimates of the true situation (U.S. Senate Special Committee on Aging, 1987). One reason is that after a time, many older people simply give up and stop looking for a job, thereby no longer being counted among the unemployed. Those who are fortunate enough to find jobs are usually forced to take a cut in earnings and fringe benefits. Not only are the avilable jobs low paying, but they are often physically taxing and/or involve odd hours (e.g., cleaning woman, groundskeeper, handyman, night watchman).

During plant closings, mass layoffs, and company reorganizations, older workers, despite their level of education, experience, and technical "knowhow," are likely to be laid off first (Morrison, 1983). Although the Age Discrimination in Employment Act of 1967 (ADEA) promotes employment based on ability rather than on age, unemployed older workers still encounter age discrimination in applying for work.[1] In certain occupations requiring extraordinary degrees of speed, strength, agility, and alertness, a bona fide case may be made

---

[1]Charges of discrimination by employers against older persons are investigated by the Office of Fair Labor Standards of the U.S. Department of Labor.

for setting a maximum age for hiring. However, even in those occupations employers should be required to demonstrate that age makes a critical difference in performance.

Contributing to the relatively high unemployment rate among the elderly is the fact that the referral rate of older workers to jobs by the U.S. Employment Service is only about half that of younger workers (Quirk, 1976). The consequence of the lower referral rate is that the older would-be worker is often forced into early retirement, a retirement that should be based on individual needs and abilities rather than on chronological age.

The problem of obtaining employment may be even worse when the elderly job seeker is Black. It has been said that as far as employment is concerned, being young and Black is functionally equivalent to being old and White in our society (Kastenbaum, 1971). This does not mean that unemployment is necessarily psychologically harder on Blacks than on Whites. Psychological reactions to being unemployed depend, to some extent, on what a person is accustomed to or prepared for. Margaret Mead suggested, for example, that one reason why women live longer than men is that older men are cut off abruptly from their jobs, having a full life one day and nothing to do the next. The typical woman, on the other hand, does not retire from her housework but continues doing in old age what she has been doing throughout her married life (Hechinger, 1977).

## More Jobs for the Elderly

The results of surveys indicate that the majority of elderly Americans would like to see employment made available to those who need or desire to keep working past retirement age (see Harris & Associates, 1975). Changes in the system to make this possible have been proposed by many authorities and have been made in several developed countries. Faced with zero population growth and potentially fewer people in the work force, the governments of many industrialized nations perceive older workers as a valuable resource and attempt to delay their retirement by the use of various incentives. The effectiveness of these plans in countries such as Sweden, the Soviet Union, and Japan is seen in statistics that point to a large percentage of those eligible for retirement electing to remain on the job.

A particularly valuable resource in the United States are elderly doctors, lawyers, and businesspersons who possess professional knowledge and skills that have taken years to develop. For example, retired lawyers may offer legal services to the aged, retired teachers can give courses, and retired doctors and nurses can supply home medical care (Butler, 1975). A few business firms have started skill banks of retirees, which permit former employees of a firm to be hired for specific projects and programs on a full- or part-time basis.

An interesting new phenomenon on the employment scene are the "young–old" retirees aged 55 and over who, having retired from a first career but are still in good health, begin looking around for more varied life options (Neugarten, 1975). These well-educated, demanding individuals frequently begin second careers and find new avocations. Among the new work roles that might be considered in a second career trajectory are those involving artistic, technical, social, and political skills that were unexploited in the initial career. A number of venturesome retirees, having worked for others all their lives, decide to go into business for themselves. The best possibilities for such older entrepreneurs are retail stores (e.g., flower shops, auto supply stores), food businesses (restaurants, cafes, pizzerias, donut shops, etc.), handicraft businesses, consulting (marketing, engineering, or personal consultants), business services (secretarial services, instant printers, photocopy stores, income tax preparation firms), hospitality (hotels, motels, bed and breakfast inns, travel agencies), and franchises (candy shops, car washes, law-care outlets, etc.) (Brandt, 1987).[2] It has even been suggested that, with breakthroughs in prolongevity up to 100 years, people may someday engage in as many as three different careers in a single lifetime. Congressmen could be elected for as many as 40 consecutive terms, chief executives may continue working for several generations, and junior executives may have to wait as long as 50 years for their bosses to retire before they are promoted!

Whatever the future may hold in terms of prolongevity, the governments of most developed nations are faced with the immediate problem of using the abilities of older citizens who want to work. A number of federal employment programs benefiting older Americans are described in Table 9.1. Perhaps the most popular of these is the Foster Grandparent Program, which was designed primarily to give elderly people opportunities to provide love and care to institutionalized and handicapped children. Each of the 20,000 or so Foster Grandparents throughout the United States, Puerto Rico, and the Virgin Islands devotes 4 hours every weekday to the care of two children. Also noteworthy is the Senior Community Service Employment Program (SCSEP), or Senior Aides Program, one of three programs established under Title V of the Older Americans Act and controlled by the Department of Labor. The other two volunteer employment programs under this act are the Senior Community Service Aides and the Senior Community Aides.

Several other federally aided volunteer programs (e.g., RSVP, SCORE) make use of the time and talents of elderly volunteers (see Table 9.1). One of the largest of these programs is RSVP, whose participants, as in the other volunteer

---

[2]Information on how to start a business can be obtained from the Service Corps of Retired Executives (Small Business Administration, 1441 L St. N.W., Washington, DC 20416), New Career Opportunities, Inc. (P.O. Box 10226, Dept. P, Glendale, CA 91209), and the Institute for Success Over Sixty (Box 160, Dept. P, Aspen, CO 81612).

TABLE 9.1
Major Federal Employment and Training Programs for Older Americans*

| Program | Agency | Description |
|---|---|---|
| Family friends | National Council on the Aging | In-home care projects in which senior volunteers are paid $8–$12 per day for transportation, meals, etc. to work 20 hours or so per week in homes with seriously handicapped or chronically ill children. Also call-in service. |
| Foster Grandparent Program | ACTION | Federal grants to public and private nonprofit agencies for creating volunteer services opportunities for low-income persons age 60 and over to work in institutions with exceptional children having special needs. Volunteers receive at least federal minimum wage. |
| Retired Senior Volunteer Program (RSVP) | ACTION | Provides opportunities for people over 60 to use their talents and experience in volunteer service in hospitals, schools, libraries, day-care centers, nusing homes, courts, and other community organizations, according to their skills and interests. Compensation for out-of-pocket expenses (transportation, etc.) incidental to the services is provided. |

| Senior Community Service Employment Program (SCSEP) | Department of Labor & National Council of Senior Citizens (Senior Aides Program) | Provides funds for part-time community service work-training programs operated by national sponsoring organizations and state and territorial governments. SCSEP is aimed at economically disadvantaged persons ages 55 and over, who are paid at least federal minimum wage. |
| Senior Companion Program (SCP) | ACTION | Modeled after Foster Grandparent Program, SCP provides volunteer opportunities for low-income persons aged 60 and over to aid other adults, especially older adults, with special needs. |
| Senior Environmental Employment Program (SEE) | Environmental Protection Agency | Program in which the Environmental Protection Agency, in cooperation with AARP, provides senior workers with opportunities to support and augment EPA office efforts in meeting environmental mandates without displacing federal employees. |
| Service Corps of Retired Executives (SCORE) | Small Business Administration | Retired, semi-retired, and active business executives use their management knowledge to help small businesses and community organizations that have management problems. Volunteers not paid, but reimbursed for out-of-pocket expenses. |

*Adapted from *Washington Information Directory, Congressional Quarterly*, 1987–1988. Washington, DC: U.S. Government Printing Office.

programs, receive only travel and subsistence payments for their services. Also quite popular is SCORE, in which useful services to organizations needing the advice of retired executives are provided. Among the other governmental agencies for which older Americans can perform volunteer services are the Veterans' Administration and the Peace Corps. Unfortunately, elderly participants in many volunteer programs are assigned menial chores rather than meaningful, responsible tasks. The result is often a vicious circle in which, because of frustration and discouragement on the part of participants, the turnover rate is high and hence reinforces the reluctance of administrators to place volunteers on essential jobs (Atchley, 1987). As the population grows even larger, the service-providing sector will need to expand. Programs such as "Project Green Thumb," sponsored by the National Farmers Union in 24 states, pays older Americans for part-time work in beautification, conservation, and improvement projects in rural areas or existing community service agencies. Job opportunities for the elderly also exist in education, social services, and health areas. Older people can staff day-care centers and kindergartens, work on historical projects and crafts, and even become small-scale food producers by operating abandoned farms.

Another useful resource in providing jobs for older Americans are the employment referral services of a number of educational institutions. Employers who cooperate in these programs recognize that the primary qualification for employment should be the ability to perform the job rather than the applicant's age. Special arrangements, such as letting two older people or an older and a younger person share a position, with one working in the morning and the other in the afternoon, may also be made. Other possibilities for using the abilities of older people who want to work, and preserving their self-concepts as well, include part-time jobs, more flexible hours, and training programs to reduce skill obsolecence.

## RETIREMENT: EVENT, STATUS, AND PROCESS

The status of being retired does not mean that one is completely unemployed. It simply means that the retiree is less than fully employed for the entire year and that he or she is receiving a pension from governmental or private sources that was earned by previous years of labor. Rather than being a privilege accorded to only a fortunate few, retirement in contemporary society is viewed as a right earned by individuals in contributing to the growth and prosperity of that society. In addition to being a status and an event, retirement is a process involving the withdrawal from a job and assuming the role of a retiree.

The traditional retirement ages of 65 for men and 60 for women were selected by the U.S. government in the 1930s as a basis for paying Old Age and Survivors Insurance, otherwise known as social security. These ages were established in a political move to curb unemployment among younger, and therefore presumably more productive, workers by replacing older workers with them. Although the expected role for older Americans today involves retirement rather than work, many professions and organizations have no fixed retirement ages. For example, Bankers Life and Casualty Insurance Company of Chicago has never had a mandatory retirement age. On the other hand, employees of police departments and high-risk jobs in other organizations face early retirement. Still other organizations have policies of gradually reducing employee work load during the years just prior to retirement. In any event, age 65 has served for years as a kind of benchmark or point of passage between middle and old age and from the status of worker to that of retiree.

## Statistics Concerning Retirement

Owing to the relatively high growth rate of the older population, the number and proportion of retirees in the U.S. population had increased substantially by the 1980s. By 1985, nearly 27 million Americans aged 65 and above were classified as retired. Over four-fifths of these individuals were unemployed after retirement, but a sizable percentage continued to work at least part time (U.S. Senate Special Committee on Aging, 1987). Furthermore, because most people retire early the average retirement age of these individuals was closer to 62 than to 65.

Although there are indications that the trend toward early retirement has ended (Ekerdt & Bosse, 1985), it is estimated that the number of retirees in the United States will have increased to 33 million by the year 2000 (U.S. Bureau of the Census, 1985). Because life expectancy at age 65 is also increasing, the portion of life spent in retirement will undoubtedly be greater in the year 2000 than it was in the early 1980s (averages of 14 years for men and 18 years for women). Similar statistics have been reported by other developed countries.

Another way of looking at retirement statistics is in terms of the ratio of retirees to active workers. As this *dependency ratio* increases, the number of workers who must support one retiree decreases. It is estimated that the dependency ratio, which was approximately 1 : 4 in the mid-1980s will have increased to almost 1 : 3 by the year 2000. One important reason for the decline in the average retirement age and the increasing dependency ratio is that many people have been forced to retire before they need or desire to, although many others elect to retire as soon as they can afford to.

## Voluntary Retirement

A person may retire voluntarily at any age, depending on the particular company or other organization in which he or she is employed. Military and civil service personnel can retire any time after 20 years of service, the retirement benefits varying with the amount of time they have served. Federal regulations, and the policies of many organizations, allow for a variable retirement age depending on individual differences in health and abilities. Under such circumstances, increasing numbers of employees who will receive good pension benefits and lump sum payments from their employers are choosing to retire as soon as they can. Business organizations, especially those in France and Germany, encourage early retirement and view it as an opportunity for physical and mental regeneration (Cribier, 1981; Gibson, 1982).

In addition to their financial situation, individuals who retire early are influenced by factors such as poor health, social expectations, and long-held plans. Other factors influencing retirement are the relatively high rate of technological obsolescence of workers in their 50s and 60s, increasing relocation of major firms, cyclical employment, and stagnation of certain sectors of the economy. A large number of people who leave work before age 62 do so involuntarily and really cannot financially afford to retire on the small pension or disability benefits that they receive. Early retirement is especially difficult for Black workers and those in a lower socioeconomic stratum.

The decision to retire early or to keep on working is also related to demographic and personal variables. Streib and Schneider (1971) found that people with large incomes, more education, and occupations of higher social status preferred to continue working longer than those lower on the economic, educational and occupational scales. People who identify with their work and whose work is highly individualized tend to retire later than those with routine, impersonal jobs (Sheppard, 1979).

Streib and Schneider (1971) found that women were more reluctant to retire than men, but single and married women tended to retire earlier than divorced women and widows. Employed married women usually collaborate with their husbands in deciding when to retire, the adequacy of the husband's pension plan being a more important determinant of the woman's decision than her own retirement benefits (Gratton & Haug, 1983; O'Rand & Henretta, 1982).

At the upper end of the retirement age spectrum are individuals who retire at or after age 65. Over two-thirds of a sample of 65-and-over retirees surveyed in the late-1970s reported having left work by choice. Among the remaining one-third, two-thirds said that they retired because of poor health and one-fifth because they had reached the mandatory retirement age (Harris & Associates, 1979). Of course, the expressed reason for retiring is not necessarily the real reason. It is more socially acceptable, for example, to say that one retired for "health reasons" than simply because he or she was tired of the job and wanted to retire. In any event, the percentage of workers retiring for health reasons will probably decrease in the future as health care improves.

Whatever the reason for retiring may be, a sizable majority of retirees claim to be satisfied with retirement living (Streib & Schneider, 1971). Understandably, attitudes toward retirement are positively related to the retiree's financial situation. Some retirees miss their jobs, but what most of them report missing more than anything else is "the money." (Atchley, 1987; Shanas, 1972)

## Mandatory Retirement

Although not as crucial an issue today as it was in the 1970s, the pros and cons of a fixed reitrement age can still be debated. As was argued during the Great Depression of the 1930s, jobs vacated by retirees become available to younger workers and hence help combat unemployment. An argument against this point is that many new jobs become available every year, presumably enough to provide employment for younger workers without forcing older adults to retire. Another argument in favor of mandatory retirement is that it enables employers to get rid of incompetent workers by means of the natural attrition process of retirement without having to prove incompetence to perform the job.

When questioned, supervisors most often indicate that they prefer a variable retirement age that takes individual differences into account. For various reasons, however, supervisors are frequently reluctant to tell employees that they are incompetent, particularly when competence is not easy to judge. But when the retirement age is fixed, employees can be weeded out without engaging in the highly subjective task of evaluating work performance.

On the side against mandatory retirement is the fact that competent elderly workers can be kept on the job and can continue to pay in rather than withdrawing money from social security and other retirement plans. Such workers contribute their skills and productivity, and forced retirement pushes these experienced and talented workers aside. It can also be argued that simple justice and humanity demand that we recognize the value of older lives and their rights to determine their own futures and continue performing those activities that contribute to their sense of well-being.

Having concluded that the idea of a fixed rtirement age of 65 is not based on any scientific findings and is against the public interest, in 1978 the U.S. Congress amended the Age Discrimination in Employment Act to abolish mandatory retirement in the Federal Civil Service and to raise the mandatory retirement age in most occupations to 70. Even before the law was passed, many private companies had done away with mandatory retirement for employees as long as they could do their jobs and could pass annual physical examinations.

In 1986 Congress abolished age-based mandatory retirement for most workers in the private sector as well as state and local government employees. Exceptions are jobs in which the lives of other people are affected by the employee's efficiency (e.g., fire fighters, police, pilots); employees in these occupations may be required to retire as early as age 55. In all likelihood, however, the abolition of mandatory retirement will not have a significant effect on the number of older people in the labor force. Retirement is a status that most workers have come to accept and even to look forward to, and the majority will probably continue to retire as soon as it is financially feasible.

## Planning for Retirement

Many older employees look forward to retirement with optimism and eagerness for release from work and routine. Others, however, are concerned about money or anxious about how they will use their time. The anxiety felt by these people about retiring tends to increase as they reach retirement age, but their anxiety level decreases once they have retired and have become adjusted to a new way of life (Reichard, Livson, & Petersen, 1962). At least some of this anxiety and "postretirement shock" could be eased by planning and preparing for retirement; this is the goal of retirement planning programs.

> A person's retirement years are perhaps the most challenging and potentially devastating period of his or her life. It can be satisfying and rewarding, a culmination of a successful life. Or it can be a cruel, gradual, or sudden breakdown in the person's life style. "Retirement shock" is a common phenomenon. A combination of confusion and anxiety accompanying retirement is added to declining health and reduced income to produce not only general unhappiness but often physical symptoms as well.
>
> Planning for retirement can help workers make the transition from years of active employment to their leisure-time years. Our society is work oriented and youth oriented; retirement can produce a real identity crisis, and often a loss of interest in living. Yet, with adequate advance preparation, retirement from a job does not need to mean retirement from life. By learning to avoid the pitfalls of retirement, and how to get the most from the new opportunities being opened up, preretirement planning can facilitate the vital and necessary continuation of personal growth. (Mondale, 1975, p. S.19393)

Research has demonstrated that planning for retirement can go a long way toward relieving anxieties and improving attitudes toward the retirement process (Troll, 1982). Planning alone cannot eliminate all of the prospective retiree's uneasiness and concern, but combined with the reassurance and support of family and friends it can definitely help.

According to Porter (1977), at least 10 questions should be asked by anyone considering retirement:

1. When will I retire?
2. Will I lead a life of leisure or continue to work?
3. How much am I worth today?
4. Where will I retire?

5. What can I save by retiring?
6. How much money do I need in retirement?
7. When can I start drawing social security and my pension benefits?
8. What precisely is my benefit deal under my corporation's pension plan?
9. Will I have enough health insurance?
10. What kind of investments can help me obtain additional retirement income?

More than half of these questions are concerned with money matters, which is a realistic emphasis for workers who are wondering whether they can afford to retire. In addition to financial security, limited retirement planning should be concerned with health maintenance and activities during retirement.

Unfortunately, retirement planning, which should begin 5–10 years prior to retirement, is inadequate in the majority of cases (McPherson & Guppy, 1979). In a nationwide survey conducted a few years ago (Harris & Associates, 1975), a sample of older Americans was asked what they had done to prepare for retirement. Although many of the respondents reported having made some preparations, on the whole the plans of this group were inadequate in terms of such matters as savings, preparing a will, arranging for part- or full-time employment, and enrolling in retirement counseling programs. Furthermore, only 19% had taken a retirement planning course or had expected to do so. This was characteristic of the state of affairs in the early 1970s, but since then several events have transpired that have led to increased participation in retirement planning workshops.

The Employees Retirement Income Security Act (ERISA) of 1974, which required that employees be kept more fully informed of their pension benefits, was a stimulus for the development of retirement planning programs in many companies. A further impetus was provided by federal legislation in 1978 and 1986 that increased the mandatory retirement age in most organizations. The high cost of living, and the resulting concern of employees about whether they can afford to retire, also encouraged the development of retirement planning programs and increased the number of participants.

Depending on the objectives of the program designers, a retirement planning program may involve literature handouts; lectures on rights and benefits; media presentations; and in-depth seminars, workshops, and counseling sessions held after work hours. Retirement planning workshops cover such topics as providing for adequate retirement income, how to develop a realistic budget for the retirement years, social relationships, avocational and new vocational pursuits (e.g., voluntary services, part-time employment), as well as physical and mental health needs. Other topics include legal rights and procedures, sexual behavior, adjusting to changing morals and values, and even such mundane matters as planning and preparing meals. The use of leisure time for hobbies, entertainment, and further education is a sometimes neglected subject for discussion in these workshops. This subject would seem to be particularly important for those older people whose work-value systems have permitted little indulgence in leisure activities.

The majority of retirement programs are unsystematic and of limited scope, explaining only the company's pension plan and the retirement options to employees. A relatively small percentage of companies, perhaps 10%, have comprehensive programs that go beyond financial planning. Certain larger business and industrial firms have developed their own comprehensive programs, a good example being that of Philadelphia's Sun Company. A number of other companies have adopted the programs of the American Management Association, the American Association of Retired Persons, or the National Council on the Aging.

Even the most comprehensive retirement programs emphasize the practical aspects of retirement rather than more subtle psychosocial matters. Among the latter are stresses within the family and the loss of a sense of being important to others. Because these are events that preretirees may be unable to anticipate, there is a need for both pre- and postretirement counseling. Furthermore, the fact that reitrement affects not only the retiree but the entire family is a reason why retirees' spouses are also encouraged to participate in retirement planning and counseling sessions.

## Psychological Reactions to Retirement

A 65-year-old whose job gives him or her a sense of importance and meaning may view retirement as an insulting indication that society considers him or her as old and useless, ready to be put "on the shelf" or "out to pasture." The activity orientation and work ethic of Western culture do little to prepare such a person for the trauma of leaving the job. When people are almost religiously devoted to their work, the experience of suddenly being unemployed and presumably unproductive can be very damaging to the sense of self-esteem. In such cases, retirement is often accompanied by feelings of diminished usefulness, significance, and independence, and sometimes a sense that life is essentially over. The loss of meaning and significance that can occur in one's life after retirement may, like any prolonged stress, accelerate the processes of age-related decline:

> In retirement, otherwise perfectly healthy men and women may develop headaches, depression, gastrointestinal symptoms, and oversleeping. . . . Irritability, loss of interest, lack of energy, increased alcoholic intake, and reduced efficiency are all familiar and common reactions. (Butler & Lewis, 1982, pp. 128, 130)

Although this picture is undoubtedly true of some retirees, reactions to retirement vary widely from person to person. Physical and mental deterioration are far from being universal results of retirement. Health does, of course, usually decline in later life, but the effect is due more to aging than to retirement per se (Ekerdt, Bosse, & LoCastro, 1983). Furthermore, people who retire for health reasons tend to continue declining (Palmore, Burchett, Fillenbaum, George, & Wallman, 1985). On the other hand, the health of people whose jobs were quite stressful may actually improve after they retire (Troll, 1982).

With the exception of certain individuals who are strongly attached to their work, retirement is not generally debilitating (Gratton & Haug, 1983). In most cases it does not lead to decreases in life satisfaction, self-acceptance, or overall adjustment (Neugarten, 1971), mental illness (Lowenthal & Haven, 1968; Nadelson, 1969), or low morale (Streib & Schneider, 1971). Rather than suffering a pernicious decline in behavior and sense of well-being, people adjust to retirement similarly to the manner in which they adjusted to changes in their preretirement lives. Those who were able to cope effectively with changes in status and roles as preretirees are likely to do the same as retirees. However, those who were overstressed and found it difficult to adjust to changes as middle-agers experience similar reactions as retirees. This is true of both men and women, married and unmarried individuals (Fox, 1977). For example, if there were marital problems before retirement, they will not be resolved by retiring and may even get worse (Peterson & Payne, 1975).

Despite some adjustment problems, most older adults look upon retirement as providing an opportunity to satisfy previously neglected needs. When immediate postretirement anxiety and depression occur, they are usually mild and short-lived. And when severe depression occurs, it is usually attributable to physical disability or illness rather than retirement (Lowenthal, 1964; Spence & Robinson, 1966). Physical health is obviously a factor in one's enjoyment of retirement. Consequently, the results of studies that have found retirees to be more poorly adjusted than nonretirees may have been caused by inadequately controlling for the fact that less healthy workers retire earlier than healthy ones. Also, because mental attitude affects physical health, it is not surprising that the health of individuals who react negatively to retirement often deteriorates. In addition to physical health, economic status and social relationships are important factors in psychological reactions to retirement.

## Types and Phases of Adjustment to Retirement

Reactions to retirement depend to a great extent on the effectiveness of a person's adjustment mechanisms or coping behaviors. These mechanisms, which are not unique to later life, are behavioral patterns reflective of deep-seated personality characteristics that have persisted throughout a person's lifetime. In a classic investigation of the relationships between personality characteristics and adjustment to retirement, Reichard et al. (1968) identified three types of personalities associated with good adjustment and two with poor adjustment. The largest

category in the "well-adjusted" group consisted of "mature men," who accepted retirement easily without regrets about the past; these men were able to find
new tasks and to cultivate new relationships to occupy their time. A second
category of well-adjusted retirees, the "rocking chair men," welcomed retirement as a time to sit back, relax, and passively enjoy their old age. The final
category of well-adjusted retirees, who were labeled "armored men," developed
an active, highly organized lifestyle to defend themselves against the anxiety of
growing old. The two categories of poorly adjusted retirees were labeled "angry
men" and "self-haters." The former, unable to face the prospect of growing
old, bitterly blamed others for their failure to achieve their life goals. In contrast
to the "angry men," the "self-haters" blamed themselves for their misfortunes
and reacted with depression rather than anger.

Adjustment to retirement has also been characterized as a process involving a
series of stages (Atchley, 1977). As illustrated in Fig. 9.2, during the two
preretirement phases the individual changes his or her perception of retirement as
a *remote event* to that of a *near event* and develops realistic or unrealistic
fantasies about it. Realistic fantasies serve to ease the transition to retirement, but
unrealistic fantasies lead to false expectations and more severe disenchantment.
Retirement itself is divided into five phases. The first of these is the *honeymoon
phase,* in which a euphoric attitude of being able to do all the things one never
had time to do before prevails. This phase, which is more prolonged in people
who retire voluntarily and are relatively well off financially, typically gives way
to a retirement routine. But for some people, a *disenchantment phase,* characterized by a letdown, a feeling of emptiness, and even depression, ensues.
People who are disenchanted with retirement often go through a *reorientation
phase* in which they "take stock," "pull themselves together," and develop a
more realistic set of life alternatives. When they have developed stable criteria
for making choices, whether it be at the end of the honeymoon phase or the
reorientation phase, they enter a *stability phase.* For some people, retirement

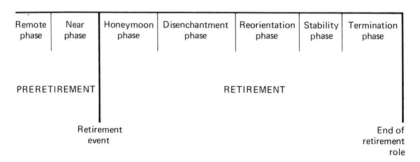

FIG. 9.2.    Phases of retirement. (From (2nd ed.) © 1977 by Wadsworth Publishing Company, Inc. Reprinted by permission of Wadsworth Publishing Company,
Belmont, CA 94002).

becomes irrelevant to their lives, and for psychological and/or financial reasons they go back to work. This *termination phase* can also be entered as a result of illness, disability, or loss of financial support, in which the retirement role is replaced by the sick role or the dependent role.

## Roles in Retirement

Viewed from a sociological perspective, retirement is a time when people exit from certain roles and seek other roles to replace those that have been terminated (Blau, 1973). Society's attitude toward the older person's social status as one of "role obsolescence" may also cause that person to withdraw into a feeling of outlived usefulness. This feeling appears to be especially pronounced in our century of rapidly changing lifestyles and the consequent isolation of generations. The segregation of old people from the rest of society is unfortunate, but those who have at least one or two close friends (confidants) are much better able to deal with the use of time and changing roles.

Because there are few formal roles for retirees in our society, they have to more or less work out their own social roles. This may be less troublesome for the older woman, especially the housewife, than for her retired husband who now finds himself spending almost all his time in his wife's domain. But the role of "mother-without-children" whose retired husband is always around represents a change that can create new marital tensions:

> I think it's harder on a wife when her husband retires. I mean, he was around underfoot all the time—and it meant three meals a day—you know—to get and prepare and clean up after and so on. (Mass & Kuypers, 1974, p. 140)

And another woman characterized retirement as "twice as much husband and half as much income."

On the whole, retirees adjust rather well to their changed occupational and social roles. Because new retirees are faced with long blocks of unstructured time, how to structure their time is one issue confronting them. Some find the sick role or eccentric role easier to tolerate than the role of failure, and so they become hypochondriacs or neurotics (Busse & Pfeiffer, 1977). But for most, and especially those who engaged in some preretirement planning of postretirement roles, activities, and interests, retirement itself is a challenge and an opportunity. In actuality, most people continue to do the same kinds of things that they did before retirement (Atchley, 1977).

Retirement may signal a decrease in interpersonal interactions and activities. Thus, most retirees engage in fewer social activities such as going to church, seeing friends, and participating in clubs or other organizations (Palmore, 1981). *Disengagement theory* characterizes old age as a time of declining involvement of the individual with society and society with the individual (Cumming, Dean,

Newell, & McCaffrey, 1960; Cumming & Henry, 1961). According to this theory, aging brings about a change in self-perceptions such that the individual is less interested in being actively involved in things but is content to reflect on his or her past life and accomplishments. To the disengaged person, adjustment comes through gradual withdrawal from responsibility and participation rather than continued activity.

Disengagement does occur, beginning as early as the 40s, but in many cases it is forced on older people as a consequence of society's failure to provide opportunities for them to continue being productive (Havighurst, Neugarten, & Tobin, 1973). Contrasting with the position that disengagement is voluntary is the *activity theory* that continued productivity and social interaction are essential to satisfaction and a sense of well-being (Maddox, 1968, 1970). An extreme form of this notion sees the individual as "dying with his boots on," but the usual form of the theory incorporates the facts of reduced activity and partial retirement due to decreased energy. Depending on their interests, temperament, health, and environmental circumstances, some retirees find satisfaction and happiness in a greater degree of activity than others. Approximately 80% of the retirees in Maddox's (1970) sample showed a high activity lifestyle pattern accompanied by high satisfaction, whereas only 14% showed the disengagement pattern and high satisfaction. The most active and involved retirees in Palmore's (1981) sample also reported the greatest life satisfaction. Nevertheless, a high level of activity in later life is not for everyone. Some research, in fact, has found that overall life satisfaction is negatively related to formal social activities (Longino & Kart, 1982).

## RETIREMENT PENSIONS

In most agrarian societies elderly people have traditionally been kept within the shelter of their own families, contributing whatever they could and being respected for their age and experience. Furthermore, the giving of alms and the construction of institutions for the elderly have been fostered by religious organizations for over a thousand years. It was not until the late 19th and early 20th centuries, however, that comprehensive pension prgrams for the elderly were mandated by law in Western nations. The first large-scale national pension program for retired workers was established in 1889 by Otto von Bismarck, Chancellor of Germany.[3] Similar programs were established during the same era or shortly thereafter in the Scandinavian countries and Great Britain.

---

[3]Rather than being based on humanitarian concern for the welfare of older Germans, Bismarck's reason for instituting such a program was to disarm the Socialist opposition to his government. Because few Germans in the late 19th century lived to be 65, the cost to the state of granting pensions to those who did was not great.

Among Western nations, the United States was rather late in enacting comprehensive federal pension legislation for the elderly. Proposals in this direction were made by the Social Democratic and Progressive political parties during the 1900 and 1912 presidential campaigns, respectively, but no legislation resulted from those proposals. A dozen individual states and Alaska enacted "old-age pension laws" during the period 1915–1935, but it was not until the mid-1930s that President Roosevelt was able to get a national pension program through both houses of Congress. At that time, the high unemployment rate of the Great Depression provided the stimulus and rationale for legislating support of old and disabled workers.

## Social Security

The major federal pension programs benefiting the elderly, their dependents, and survivors are listed in Table 9.2. The most extensive and costly of these programs is the Old Age and Survivors Insurance Program ("Social Security"), which, along with the Supplemental Security Income Program (SSI), is administered by the Social Security Administration.

The Social Security program, passed into law in 1945, provides for federally administered old-age, survivors', and disability insurance payments. The exact amount varying with the number of quarters worked, an insured person receives 80% of full payments when retiring at age 62, 86.8% of full payments when retiring at age 63, 93.4% of full payments when retiring at age 64, and full payments when retiring at age 65. The spouse of a retired person receives full benefits at age 62. Benefits are also paid to the wife or husband of a retired worker at any age if he or she is caring for a child who is disabled or under 16. Child benefits are paid to the retired worker's unmarried child under age 18 or from age 18–19 if he or she is a full-time student in elementary or secondary school. Monthly survivor benefits are paid to a widow or widower at age 60, or, if disabled, at age 50; to a widow or widower at any age if he or she is caring for a child, under age 16 or disabled, who is entitled to benefits on the earnings record of the worker. Finally, a lump sum death benefit of $255 is also payable on the death of an insured worker to the spouse or other beneficiary ("Social Security Programs . . . , 1987)

Supplemental security income (SSI) payments are also made to aged, blind, or disabled individuals whose financial needs cannot be completely met by social security. SSI was designed as a public assistance program for older Americans with insufficient income. Unlike Social Security, SSI is a welfare program funded through general federal and state revenues and has been becoming progressively smaller as the Social Security program expands (see Fig. 9.3).

An earnings test is applied to everyone who gets Social Security retirement or survivors benefits except persons 70 and over and disabled persons. For every $2

TABLE 9.2

Major Federal Pension Program Benefiting the Elderly*

| Program | Agency | Description |
|---------|--------|-------------|
| Civil Service Retirement | U.S. Civil Service Commission | Principal retirement system for federal civilian employees; financed by employee contributions matched by employing agency plus congressional appropriations. Provides monthly retirement benefits based on past earnings and length of service to eligible retirees and their survivors. |
| Old-Age, Survivors Insurance Program | Social Security Administration, HEW | Financed through the payroll tax on employees, employers, and self-employed persons. Social security pays monthly cash benefits to retired workers (their dependents or survivors). Entitlement and level of benefits is based in part on covered earnings. Eligibility at 65 or may opt for permanently reduced benefits at 62. |
| Railroad Retirement Program | Railroad Retirement Board | Financed through a payroll tax on employees and employers. Monthly benefits are paid to retired workers (their wives and survivors) after 10 years' employment. Coverage for individuals with less than 10 years' service is transferred to the Social Security system. |
| Supplemental Security Income Program | Social Security Administration, HEW | Aged, blind, and disabled persons, with no other income or with limited resources, are guaranteed monthly income. States may, and in some cases, must, supplement federal payments. |
| Veterans Pension Program | Veterans Administration | Provides monthly cash benefits to veterans aged 65 or older with at least 90 days military service, including 1 day wartime service, and who meet income limitation requirements. Benefits are also paid to designated survivor. Benefits vary according to veteran's annual income. |

*Adapted from Select Committee on Aging (1976)

earned above the annual exempt among ($8,400 for persons 65–69 and $6,120 for persons aged 65 in 1988), $1 is deducted from Social Security benefits. Approximate monthly retirement benefits for workers 65 and over who retired in 1988 after steady lifetime earnings ranged from $425 to $838, depending on the worker's earnings in 1987; a worker and spouse received $627–$1,257. Disabled workers and survivors of workers who worked in 1987 also received substantial benefits.

Since its inception the social security system has been supported by employee paycheck deductions matched with employer contributions, but has received no funds from general federal revenues. In 1937, when Social Security taxes were first levied, the rate paid by an employee was 1% of the first $3,000 of income. This tax remained unchanged until 1950, when it began to rise. As a consequence of inflation and a resulting increase in the cost of administering the program, it became necessary to tie social security payments to the consumer price index. Automatic annual cost-of-living adjustments (COLAs) in Social Security benefits went into effect in 1975, serving to keep retiree's real benefits from declining. However, COLAs are determined by the consumer price index, which underestimates the cost of certain items (food, fuel, health care) that are of particular concern to the elderly (Rosenblatt, 1987b). During 1988, 125 million Americans paid $248 billion in Social Security taxes. Approximately 38 million individuals, 3 million of whom were children, received Social Security benefits each month. A total of $232.1 billion, $210.7 billion for the old age and sur-

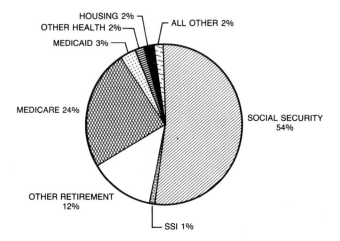

FIG. 9.3.   Percentages of federal outlays benefitting the elderly in eight categories. (Source: Executive Office of the President, Office of Management and Budget, February 1986.)

vivors program and $21.4 billion for the disability program, was disbursed in 1988 (U.S. Department of Health and Human Services, 1988).

Although the Social Security program was never designed to be the sole source of support for older Americans, approximately two-thirds of this age group have no other source of income. The Social Security system was designed to be self-supporting, but the ratio of wage earners to recipients had decreased from a comfortable margin of 35 to 1 in 1945 to approximately 3 to 1 by the end of the 1980s.

For many years, there was great concern that the Social Security system might become bankrupt and that little or no money would be available for future retirees. Current estimates, however, are that the system will remain solvent until at least the middle of the next century. Nevertheless, future generations of young and middle-aged Americans will undoubtedly find themselves contributing more and more to the economic welfare of their elders. The problem promises to be of even greater concern in countries such as Japan and West Germany, where the number of individuals receiving pensions is expected to grow to 40% by the year 2010 (Stephens, 1986). Whether this will result in a conflict of generations or whether young people will remain willing to shoulder the burden of providing adequate benefits to the elderly remains to be seen.

## Other Pension Plans

The first federal pensions in the United States were the military pensions granted in 1792 to veterans of the American Revolution. The present-day counterpart of these pensions is the Veterans Pension Program. Other federal pension programs are the Civil Service Retirement and the Railroad Retirement Program (see Table 9.2).

In addition to government pensions, many business, industrial, and professional organizations have their own retirement plans. These pension programs, unfortunately, cover less than one-third of retirees. Women in particular are less likely to qualify for private pensions, and those who qualify receive less in benefits because of their work histories. Private pension plans have also experienced some of the same financial problems as the Social Security system. The costs of all retirement programs have soared during recent years, and the ratio of the number of workers contributing to the plans to the number of retirees has declined dramatically.

Certain individuals, referred to somewhat disparagingly as "double dippers," draw two or more retirement pensions at the same time. For example, many military personnel and government employees are young enough after serving the requisite number of years for retirement to begin a new career and to take a second and even a third job. By working just long enough at each successive job to quality for a pension from the particular organization, they may eventually be eligible for pensions from several sources. Added to the Social Security payments to which they are entitled at age 65, the total sum that such individuals receive every month during later life can make their retirement years a time of relative affluence and leisure.

## SUMMARY

The percentage of elderly men in the U.S. labor force has declined steadily during this century, whereas the percentage of employed elderly women has remained fairly constant. The retirement rate among elderly men has been increased by those enticed by improvements in retirement benefits and also by those who have been forced by poor health or mandatory retirement policies to retire before they were ready to do so. A sizable portion of the latter group consists of men whose personal identity and self-respect are tied up with the job and who desire to keep working as long as possible.

Although the majority of retirees appear to be happy with retirement and do not miss their jobs, lack of satisfying work can affect both mental and physical health. In any event, older people who elect to continue working typically perform as well or better than younger adults. Despite this fact, both the rate and length of unemployment are greater for older than for younger workers. Unemployment is particularly high among Blacks and certain other minority groups.

In response to lower population growth and the increasing cost of retirement pensions, many countries have raised the retirement age. Special incentives and other moves can be used to increase the number of elderly people in the active work force. The developed country with the highest percentage of elderly people in the work force is Japan, followed by the United States. The percentage of elderly workers is even higher in underdeveloped nations.

The traditional retirement ages of 65 for men and 60 for women were established by Social Security legislation in 1935 and have no real medical or psychological foundation. Federal legislation in 1978 and 1986 first raised the mandatory retirement age to 70 and then did away with it entirely for most jobs in the public and private sectors. Mandatory retirement ages still prevail in high-risk jobs and certain other occupations where the speed, strength, agility, and sensory abilities of youth are required.

Retirement is a rite of passage from middle age to later life that may be anticipated with pleasure or foreboding. It is not necessarily a dreaded event, process, or status: Many people look forward to retiring and pursuing other goals. Even among those who do not relish the prospect of retiring, a large percentage discover that it is not as bad as they expected. In any event, when, where, how, and with what to retire are decisions that, insofar as possible, should be made by retirees themselves. Retirement planning programs can help workers consider retirement realistically and prepare for the changes in status and roles that accompany it. Clearly, not all the changes and stresses of retirement can be anticipated, but this fact can also be pointed out in preretirement counseling sessions.

Reactions to retirement vary with the personality and socioeconomic status of the retiree and whether he or she continues to have meaningful social roles to play. Reichard, Livson, and Peterson described five types of personalities in terms of their adjustments to retirement, whereas Atchley depicted adjustment to retirement in terms of five stages.

Blau emphasized the tendency of modern society to view the social status of retirees as one of role obsolescence. The lack of meaningful roles to play is perhaps less true of older women, who continue to take care of their homes, than of unemployed older men. Disengagement theory views old age as a time of reduced involvement with society, whereas activity theory emphasizes the importance of continuing productivity and social interaction after retirement.

The Social Security pension system is the most general basis of financial support for elderly Americans. The system has experienced some difficulties during recent years, but it now appears to be on an even keel for the foreseeable future. However, the cost of Social Security is rising, accounting for over half of the federal outlays for elderly Americans. Approximately 30% of retirees also receive private pensions, but because of increases in the cost and the dependency ratio, many of these plans have, like the Social Security system, been experiencing problems.

## SUGGESTED READINGS

Baugher, D. (1978, Fall). Is the older worker inherently incompetent? *Aging and Work,* pp. 243–250.

Birren, J. E., Robinson, P. K., & Livingston, J. E. (Eds.). (1986). *Age, health and employment.* Englewood Cliffs, NJ: Prentice-Hall.

Denis, H. (1984). *Retirement preparation: What retirement specialists need to know.* Lexington, MA: Heath.

Doering, M., Rhodes, S. R., & Schuster, M. (1983). *The aging worker: Research and recommendations.* Beverly Hills, CA: Sage.

Forman, B. I. (1984, June). Reconsidering retirement: Understanding emerging trends. *The Futurist,* pp. 43–47.

McCluskey, N. G., & Borgatta, E. F. (1981). *Aging and retirement: Prospects, planning and policy.* Beverly Hills, CA: Sage.

McConnell, S. R. (1983). Retirement and employment. In D. S. Woodruff & J. E. Birren (Eds.), *Aging: Scientific perspectives and social issues* (2nd ed., pp. 333–367). Monterey, CA: Brooks/Cole.

Morrison, M. H. (1982). *Economics of aging: The future of retirement.* New York: Van Nostrand Reinhold.

Sheppard, H. L. (1976). Work and retirement. In R. H. Binstock & E. Shanas (Eds.), *Handbook of aging and the social sciences* (pp. 286–309). New York: Van Nostrand Reinhold.

Stagner, R. (1985). Aging in industry. In J. E. Birren & K. W. Schaie (Eds.), *The handbook of the psychology of aging* (2nd ed., pp. 789–817). New York: Van · Nostrand Reinhold.

# 10

# Living Conditions and Activities

Whatever changes in attitudes and activities may occur with aging, they are, like the process of aging itself, usually gradual and predictable. Although serious illness, injury, or psychological trauma can result in abrupt deviations from previous behavior, by and large elderly people are creatures of habit. Most of them continue in much the same lifestyle, living in the same situation and pursuing similar pastimes as they did prior to old age. Those who were financially well off during middle age tend to be well off in old age, and those who were poor tend to remain at the lower end of the economic spectrum. Those who were active, sociable individuals in their 40s and 50s are likely to remain so in their 60s and 70s, and those who were maladjusted in their younger days will probably be maladjusted senior citizens.

Despite the wide range of individual difference in physical, psychological, and socioeconomic circumstances, old age is a fairly pleasant time of life for most people. There are, of course, sources of dissatisfaction and stress, including problems associated with income, health, housing, nutrition, transportation, and other life necessities. These problems are obviously not independent of one another. Health is affected by nutrition, housing, and transportation—all of which are affected by income. In fact, insufficient income is a contributing factor in a large proportion of the problems experienced by the elderly. Difficulties in later life are also caused by a loss of social roles, the use of leisure time, physical safety, and a host of other matters, ranging from filling out income tax forms to coping with theft and assaults against person and property (see chapter 11). But, at least to some extent, money can buy happiness—in old age as at other times of life.

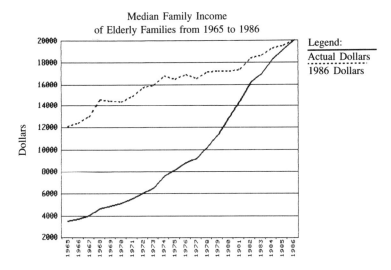

FIG. 10.1.    Median income of elderly families from 1965 to 1986. (Data from U.S. Bureau of the Census 1987b).

## ECONOMIC STATUS OF THE ELDERLY

As shown in Fig. 10.1, the median income of older Americans has increased considerably since 1965. Nevertheless, their median income remains significantly lower than that of younger adults. Variations in the annual income of elderly people are also quite large. In 1986, for example, 34% of families with heads 65 years and older had incomes of under $15,000, compared with only 18% of nonelderly families falling in that income bracket. On the other hand, 22% of elderly families had median incomes of $35,000 or more (U.S. Bureau of the Census, 1987b).

### Demographic Differences in Income

The average annual income of older Americans is related to a number of demographic variables, including age, sex, ethnicity, and location of residence. In 1985, families aged 65–74 had a median cash income of $20,354, but for families aged 85 and older the figure was $15,111. The median income for individuals was $8,160 for those in the 65–74 age bracket and $6,400 for those 85 years or over. This means that the median income of the oldest elderly people is close to the official poverty level (U.S. Bureau of the Census, 1986a).

With respect to the gender variable, the median income of women is substantially less than that of men (see Table 10.1). This is true of women in all ethnic

TABLE 10.1
Median Income and Percent Below Poverty Level of Americans
Age 65 and Over by Sex and Ethnicity

| Sex | Ethnicity | Median Income | Percent Below Poverty Level |
|-----|-----------|---------------|------------------------------|
| Male | White | $12,131 | 6.9 |
| Male | Black | 6,757 | 24.2 |
| Male | Hispanic | 7,369 | 18.8 |
| Male | All races | 11,544 | 8.5 |
| Female | White | 6,738 | 13.3 |
| Female | Black | 4,508 | 35.5 |
| Female | Hispanic | 4,583 | 25.2 |
| Female | All races | 6,425 | 15.2 |
| Both sexes | White | 8,544 | 10.7 |
| Both sexes | Black | 5,030 | 31.0 |
| Both sexes | Hispanic | 5,510 | 22.5 |
| Both sexes | All races | 8,154 | 12.4 |

*Source*: U.S. Bureau of the Census (1987b). Unpublished data from the March 1987 Current Population Survey.

groups and in various circumstances. Elderly widows, for example, have lower incomes than elderly widowers, one reason being that men are more likely than women to retain pensions or earned income after the death of a spouse. In addition, elderly women who live alone have lower incomes than married women, who share in the relatively larger income of the husband.

As shown in Table 10.1, the median income of elderly Hispanics is larger than that of elderly Blacks, but the income of both ethnic groups is substantially less than that of Whites. These ethnic group differences interact with sex, in that sex differences in income are greater for Whites than for other ethnic groups. The reason for this interaction is that elderly White men have relatively larger pensions and assets than other retirees.

Another demographic variable related to the income of elderly Americans is place of residence. Not only do larger numbers of the more affluent elderly retire in certain geographical areas (e.g., the Sunbelt), but older people can earn more extra income in certain localities than in other places. A good example of the relationship of economic status to locality is the fact that the annual income of elderly Americans who live in rural areas is less than that of the urban elderly (Youmans, 1977).

## Sources of Income

Social Security constitutes the major portion of the income of well over half of older Americans. Considering all sources of income and all older Americans,

Social Security makes up the largest percentage of the total (38%), with assets, earnings, and pensions in second, third, and fourth places, respectively (see Fig. 10.2). Most of the "other" category in Fig. 10.2 is comprised of a small amount of money received from sons, daughters, or other relatives (Grad, 1987). Included among the other economic benefits available to older Americans are: a one-time exclusion of up to $125,000 in capital gains on the sale of a home after age 55, tax credits for low-income individuals who receive few or no Social Security benefits, food stamps, energy assistance, public housing and rental assistance.

Next to Social Security, "assets" constitute the second largest source of income of older Americans. Many older people accumulate substantial material assets over a life-time of working and saving, which, when combined with Social Security and other income, enable them to live fairly comfortably in old age. For example, in 1984 the median net worth of households headed by an elderly person was $60,266. But, although their assets are usually greater than those of the nonelderly, with the exception of home equity elderly people typically have fewer assets (in savings, investments, etc.) than nonelderly adults (U.S. Bureau of the Census, 1986e).

## Expenditures

Despite the relative affluence of a small percentage, the average income of retired Americans is only about half that of what they earned when they were fully employed. It has been argued that the resulting 50% reduction in postretirement purchasing power is not as serious as it might seem, because less income is

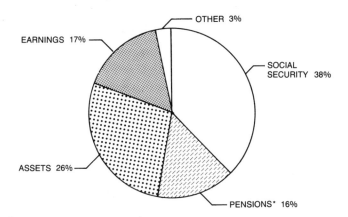

FIG. 10.2. Income sources of Americans aged 65 and older: 1986. (From Grad, 1987. Includes railroad retirement which accounts for about one percent of income for aged units. Railroad retirement has both pension and security components.)

required for job-related and social activities. It is true that, with the exception of the budget category of "health care," the elderly spend less than the nonelderly. But the percentage of income spent for different budget items varies considerably with age. Thus, compared with adults under age 65, those 65 and over spend a greater proportion of their income for food, utilities, and health care (items that the cost of living adjustment does not weight properly for the elderly) and a smaller proportion for transportation, clothing, pension and life insurance, and entertainment (U.S. Bureau of Labor Statistics, 1986). Because most of the last four items are job-related, it is understandable why the elderly spend a smaller amount of their income on them.

With respect to expenditures for taxes, almost half of elderly Americans pay no federal income taxes at all. But because the Social Security system is designed to discourage extra earnings, those elderly who do pay taxes tend to pay more than nonelderly taxpayers. The federal tax code excludes veterans pension income, railroad retirement benefits, Social Security benefits, and a certain amount of earned income. One might suppose that this would simplify the preparation of income tax forms, but the following steps show that even in old age calculating one's federal tax liability is not necessarily a simple matter:

1. Add your total income subject to tax, half your Social Security benefits, and your tax-exempt interest.
2. Subtract any adjustments claimed, such as employee business expenses, deductible IRA contributions, penalties for early withdrawal of savings, and alimony paid. The result is your "modified adjusted gross income."
3. From your modified adjusted gross income, subtract $32,000 for joint returns, $25,000 for single returns or married person not filing jointly who did not live with spouse at any time during the year, or zero for married person filing separately who lived with spouse at some time during the year.
4. Divide the difference by 2. Tax must be paid on this figure or your total Social Security Benefits, whichever is smaller. ("Additional Tips . . ., 1988)

## The Aged Poor

There is a great deal of truth in the saying that being sick but rich is better than being healthy but poor. Denials of the poets notwithstanding, money is related to happiness in old age. Income determines to some extent what people do with their time—whether they sit idly at home and brood or get out, interact with other people, and cultivate an interest in something other than themselves.

According to the official definition of the poverty level as $6,630 for an older couple household or $5,255 for an older individual living alone, 12.4% (3.5 million) of older Americans were below the poverty level in 1986. This percentage figure, which can be compared with 10.8% poverty among adults between 18 and 64, does not take into account an additional 2.3 million (8%) of elderly Americans who were classified as ''near-poor'' during that year. Thus, over one-fifth (21%) of the elderly populations was poor on near-poor in 1986 (American Association of Retired Persons, 1987).

Despite the sizable number of elderly individuals who still fall below the official poverty level, the drastic reduction in poverty among older Americans is one of the few clear success stories of the federal government's war on poverty. In actuality, during the 1970s and 1980s poverty rates declined for both elderly and nonelderly adults. Because of the cost of living adjustments (COLAs) in Social Security that went into effect in 1975, the real benefits of retired elderly people were kept from declining and the economic gap between elderly and nonelderly adults narrowed appreciably.

Table 10.1 indicates that two of the same demographic variables—sex and ethnicity—that are related to median income are also related to the percentage of the elderly population falling below the poverty level; education, marital status, and area of residence are also associated with poverty. Poverty is more common among elderly. women than men, Blacks and Hispanics than Whites, persons living alone than married persons, those with less education, and those living in certain geographical areas. The nine states having the highest elderly poverty rates in 1986 were all in the South: Mississippi, Alabama, Arkansas, Louisiana, Georgia, South Carolina, Tennessee, North Carolina, and Kentucky, in which poverty ranged from 23% to 34%.

Although the total number of elderly people who are destitute has declined appreciably since the 1960s, a substantial percentage remain poor. Those elderly couples whose annual incomes are less than $5,000, the majority of whom live in large cities, wage a daily battle against the rising costs of food, clothing, housing, and medical care. This group includes many people who have not been accustomed to poverty but whose savings have long since been depleted and who are now attempting to live on Social Security benefits. Unlike the traditional order of importance—food, clothing, shelter—the elderly poor spend the greatest amount of their income for rent and utilities, with clothing second and food in last place. The difficulty that the aged poor may encounter in attempting to live on fixed incomes was dramatically illustrated in the following excerpt from a story of an elderly New Yorker whose heating was cut off when he was unable to pay:

Last Thursday, on the day workers from a cleaning service arrived, along with a city social worker carrying a bag full of shirts, Joseph Stiletto was found frozen to death in his second-floor apartment at 160 Abingdon Square in Greenwich Village. He was 79 years old. (Barbanel, 1988, p. 1)

## LIVING ENVIRONMENTS

The living environment of a person includes the house, apartment, or room in which he or she lives, as well as the neighborhood or community in which the dwelling unit is located. Older people reside in a variety of living environments. The large majority (73% in 1986) live in metropolitan areas (32% in central cities and 41% in suburbs) (American Association of Retired Persons, 1987). The more well-to-do may live in retirement communities, and perhaps 5% live in nursing homes or other institutions. Most elderly people, and especially elderly men, live in family settings. The remainder, primarily older women, live alone or with a nonrelative (see Table 10.2). In general the elderly are less mobile than other age groups, typically spending 80%–90% of their time in their home environments. Thus, the home, neighborhood, and community are more critical to the elderly than to any other age group (Cox, 1987).

### Geographical Location

The residences of elderly people tend to be clustered in special buildings of large cities, in certain neighborhoods within suburbs, and even in specific regions of the nation. Over half of the 65+ population in the United States lives in eight states: California, New York, Florida, Pennsylvania, Texas, Illinois, Ohio, and Michigan. As might be expected, the percentage of Florida residents who are 65 or older is greater than that of any other state (17.7%). But the percentages of residents of Pennsylvania, Rhode Island, Iowa, and Arkansas in this age bracket are also substantial. Although large numbers of older people live in the large cities of the Northeastern and Midwestern sections of the United States, during the past few decades there has been a steady migration of retirees to Sunbelt

TABLE 10.2
Living Arrangements of Older Noninstitutionalized Persons: 1986

| Living Arrangement | Men (%) | Women (%) |
|---|---|---|
| With spouse | 75.3 | 38.3 |
| With other relatives | 7.2 | 18.2 |
| With nonrelatives | 2.5 | 2.1 |
| Alone | 14.9 | 41.3 |

*Source*: U.S. Bureau of the Census. Unpublished data from the March 1986 Current Population Survey.

Report 10.1    SOUTH, WEST FOUND BEST FOR RETIREMENT*

NEW YORK (UPI)—A survey of the best states in the United States to retire to, based on economy as well as climate and recreational facilities, concluded that 10 states in the South and West best fill retirees' needs.

The study by Chase Econometrics Associates, Inc., released in Money magazine, said the 10 states where the living is easiest and comparatively cheap are: Utah, Louisiana, South Carolina, Nevada, Texas, New Mexico, Alabama, Arizona, Flordia and Georgia.

All ranked high as areas where it is not only pleasant to live but which offer opportunities for part-time work, low living costs, low taxes, low fuel costs, availability of housing and proximity to medical services and shopping.

The survey also listed the worst retirement areas—New England, New York and New Jersey—because of high taxes, expensive utilities and unemployment. It said Massachusetts is the poorest bet in the nation for retired people.

Following is a state-by-state ranking:

—**Utah:** Moderate living costs and low utility rates. Exclusion of up to $6,000 a year pension income for people over 65 in computing state income tax. Recommended: around Salt Lake City and St. George.

—**Louisiana:** A cost-of-living 10% below the national average. A $400 tax exemption for people over 65. Incredibly low property taxes. Recommended: St. Tammany Parish.

—**South Carolina:** A special tax exemption of $800 and $12,000 deduction from property value assessments for 65 and over. Free hunting and fishing licenses. Recommended: coastal islands and Summerville.

—**Nevada:** No income or inheritance taxes, but high hospital costs. Recommended: Boulder City.

—**Texas:** A $15,000 exemption on the assessed value of houses for people over 65. Recommended: Austin and the Brownsville-McAllen area.

—**New Mexico:** A cost of living 10% below the national average, low taxes, low fuel costs. Recommended: Albuquerque and Roswell.

—**Alabama:** Low food costs. Recommended: Fairhope.

—**Arizona:** About the best medical care you can get anywhere. A personal income tax exemption of $1,000 for people over 65. Recommended: Tucson, Phoenix, Green Valley, Prescott.

—**Florida:** Many medical services geared to older people. A $5,000 deduction on property tax assessments for the over 65ers who are five-year residents. Recommended: away from the costly coastal areas.

—**Georgia:** Cost of living about 9% lower than the national average. Good medical services. Recommended: the Golden Isles area and Savannah.

*Reprinted with permission of United Press International. Copyright 1979.

states such as Florida, Arizona, California, and Texas. Report 10.1 summarizes the results of a survey conducted during the late 1970s of the economic, climatic, and recreational characteristics of the various states in terms of their appropriateness for retirement. According to the findings, the 10 states in which retirement living was considered easiest and cheapest with Utah, Louisiana, South Carolina, Nevada, Texas, New Mexico, Alabama, Arizona, Florida, and Georgia—almost all of which are in the Sunbelt. The worst retirement states, on the other hand, were the New England states, New York, and New Jersey. The situation has undoubtedly changed somewhat during the past decade, and now we are experiencing something of a countermigration from the Sunbelt states to the Northeastern and upper Midwestern states (U.S. Senate Special Committee on Aging, 1987). For example, Florida has recently lost significant numbers of elderly migrants to Michigan and New York, most of whom were originally Michiganians or New Yorkers, respectively.

The Sunbelt has its attractions, but most retirees remain in the same homes after retirement; only about 4%, usually the more affluent, move out of state. From 1980 to 1985, for example, only 16% of Americans aged 65 and older, compared with 45% under 65, changed residences. Of those who did move, the great majority (80%) moved to another home in the same state. Of those who moved out of state, 35% moved from Northeastern or Midwestern states to the South or West (American Association of Retired Persons, 1987).

Leaving one's lifelong friends, relatives, and familiar surroundings to move out of state (or even across town) can be a stressful experience. For this reason, as well as physical disability and economic problems, retirees tend to "stay put" in spite of deteriorating neighborhood conditions and frequent loneliness. Most retirees "like where they live," want to stay there as long as possible, and have no plans to move. This is particularly true of those who own their own homes, but even renters can develop a sense of belongingness and territoriality about a neighborhood (Willmann, 1987).

Whether or not they take it when offered, the opportunity to retire to another geographical location is usually reserved for those who are financially solvent. Thousands of older occupants of single rooms in old hotels located in the shabbiest sections of large cities are at the lower end of the economic scale. When they are not in these rooms, many urban elderly wander the streets or congregate in large outdoor parks, at bus terminals, and in other sheltered public places. Because of increasing rents, a large portion of the relatively small incomes of these inner-city residents goes for shelter. Consequently, malnutrition and other health problems are not uncommon. Because of somewhat lower rents and a different lifestyle, health problems and malnutrition are less characteristic of the elderly residents of publicly supported housing projects. Such housing projects have the advantages of improved living conditions and, particularly in age-segregated facilities, greater social interaction with one's age group.

## Elderly Homeowners

Although sizable numbers of elderly people live in low-cost public housing units and other rental accommodations, 75% own their own homes. Over 80% of these owner-occupied dwellings are owned free and clear, and over one-third are

occupied by older people living alone. In 1983, 81% of these elderly homeowners were men and 65% were women. Whites are more likely than Blacks and
other minorities to own their own homes, and elderly marrieds are more likely
than singles to be homeowners (U.S. Bureau of the Census, 1984).

Elderly homeowners spend 80%–90% of their lives in their homes (Hansen,
1975). A large number of these individuals, valuing their independence, prefer to
live alone rather than with family members. However, the spiraling costs of
home repairs, property taxes, and utilities in recent years have made it difficult
for persons on fixed incomes to maintain independent households. It is true that
nearly all states give a property tax break to senior citizens, and a few permit
them to defer their property taxes indefinitely, but housing and associated costs
are still more than many older people can manage on a retirement income.
Despite the expense and other problems, most single or married elderly people
choose not to move but continue to reside in quarters that may actually be too
roomy for them. Only a serious physical problem, loss of a spouse, or some other
severely stressful circumstance can induce them to move voluntarily. When they
reach a point at which they can no longer fend for themselves, elderly ''loners''
may reluctantly express a willingness to live with a family member. An alternative arrangement that may be acceptable to a widowed older person is to live
with another elderly individual of the same sex.

A variety of living options are currently being offered to elderly homeowners
who are cash poor but want to remain in their own homes. These include a
*reverse mortgage,* which is a loan based on the owner's equity in the home. The
homeowner receives regular monthly payments for 3–10 years or as long as he or
she lives in the home. The loan is not paid off until the home changes hands, so
the owner can remain there indefinitely and use the home as collateral for the
loan. A *sales leaseback,* in which the owner sells the home and simultaneously
leases it back from the buyer for an indefinite period is also available in some
states. Because the seller is now a renter, the responsibilities of home ownership
(taxes, repairs, maintenance, and property insurance) are eliminated. But because of the psychological factor of living in a home that one does not own, the
sales leaseback has not been very popular with older Americans. Another possibility for defraying home expenses, when local zoning laws permit, is to take in
boarders.

When elderly homeowners must move out of their own homes they still have a
variety of living options. For example, they might consider sh     l housing, in
which 5–15 unrelated people live together, sharing household expenses and
chores. In some localities these cooperative homes have become popular places
for people to move into in their later years (Freiberg, 1987).

An ECHO house, which is a small, temporary living unit in the yard of
another single-family dwelling, as well as accessory apartments built by middle-
aged adults within their homes for their aging parents are also fairly common
(Hare & Haske, 1984). Such living arrangements have the advantage of provid-

ing some privacy for the elderly, but there is the disadvantage of making the elderly parent or other resident feel like a boarder or renter rather than a home-owner.

Whether or not renting is desirable, 25% of older Americans are renters (U.S. Bureau of the Census, 1986). Unfortunately, many rental properties—walk-up flats, rooms in boarding houses or hotels, poorly heated trailers—are in poor condition. Rental housing subsidized by the federal government tends to be in better shape, but it is in short supply and concentrated in urban areas on the Atlantic, Pacific, and Gulf coasts (Freiberg, 1987). A limited amount of subsi-dized housing for elderly people of moderate means is also available through various religious and fraternal organizations.

## Services to Elderly Homemakers

Many community agencies and other organizations make a variety of homemaker services available to assist elderly people who, because of disability or illness, can no longer manage on their own. One-fourth or more of the elderly population need help in personal care activities (bathing, dressing, eating, getting in and out of bed and chairs, walking, going outside, using the toilet) and/or home manage-ment activities (preparing meals, shopping for personal items, managing money, using the telephone, doing light or heavy housework) (Dawson, Hendershot, & Fulton, 1987).

The Meals on Wheels program delivers meals to the home 5 days a week at a modest cost, and Aids to the Elderly provides trained personnel to help elderly people with bathing, personal grooming, cooking, and light housework. Handy-man services to help with yard work and motor home repairs, as well as major home repair services at reduced (subsidized) cost, are also available in many communities. Other services include telephone reassurance, in which someone calls every day to make certain that the resident is all right, and friendly visiting and escort services to help with feelings of loneliness and problems of safety and mobility.

Requiring a minimum of effort or intervention on the part of the helper is the service performed by the Gatekeepers program of Illinois Power and Light and similar programs in other localities. In this program, utility company workers are taught to recognize signs that an older person needs help, and to report the problem by making an anonymous telephone call to a local aging agency or to the State Department of Aging (Willmann, 1987).

## Retirement Communities

Other popular living arrangements for elderly Americans are mobile homes, retirement hotels, and, for those with fair-sized incomes, condominiums or smaller homes in retirement communities. Over three-quarters of a million retirees, who have been described as the "wealthiest, best-fed, best-housed, healthiest, and most self-reliant in our history" (Turpin, 1986, p. 1), live in retirement villages or adult communities. These retirement communities provide lifetime facilities for "woopies," well-off older people who are able to invest a sizable initial payment plus a maintenance charge in an apartment or house and who have a sizable annual income. Among the best-known of the "gerontopolises," which have blossomed throughout the nation but especially in the Southwest and Florida, are Sun City near Phoenix; Rossmoor Leisure Worlds in California (Laguna Hills, Seal Beach, Walnut Creek), and outside California in Arizona, Florida, Maryland, and New Jersey; Park West in Miami; and The Sequoias in San Francisco. Two of the major retirement community developers are Del E. Webb, who founded Sun City with the slogan "happiness equals activity plus friendliness," and Ross W. Cortese, the entrepreneur of Leisure Worlds. These retirement communities vary in luxuriousness and the restrictions that are imposed on residents and visitors. For example, no one under 50 can buy property in Sun City, and Park West bars dogs and has a time limit of 3 weeks for visits by children. Homes are usually purchased on a very long-term payment plan by older individuals who have a good income and desire to live in a community that offers a wide range of activities for older adults.

The cost of a condominium apartment in a large metropolitan area or a house in a retirement village is usually beyond the financial resources of most retirees. This is particularly true of the expensive facilities of a Leisure World, such as the cluster of Spanish-style dwellings at Laguna Hills, California for retirees aged 52 and up. Despite the cost, Leisure Worlds had no scarcity of applicants. The one in Laguna Hills features several heated swimming pools, tennis courts, a 27-hole golf course, bowling greens, restaurants, libraries, classrooms, a medical clinic, closed circuit TV, and free bus rides to Los Angeles. The residents, who are protected by 6-foot high walls and security guards who patrol around the clock, engage in a diversity of activities in physically safe surroundings. About the only activity not offered by Leisure Worlds is employment, but some of the residents hold full- or part-time jobs. Residents of retirement communities do admit to missing more frequent contacts with younger members of their families, but the increased social interactions with members of their own generation appears to result in greater life satisfaction (Rosow, 1967).

There are, of course, disadvantages to retirement communities, even in the plush atmosphere of a Leisure World, and such a lifestyle is not for everyone. One retiree declared that Leisure World is a "pain in the neck" if you don't play golf or pool. Living exclusively with one's own age and socioeconomic group can also be boring and, one might argue, unrealistic. Some of the most successful and talented people in our society, which badly needs their problem-solving "know-how," may become segregated from real life and stultified in a community dominated by play and relaxation.

## Better Housing for the Elderly

Specified flaws in plumbing, kitchen, maintenance of physical structure, public hall-common area, heating, electrical system, and sewage disposal have been found in 10% of households headed by elderly Americans (U.S. Dept. of Housing and Urban Development, 1983). These "inadequate" homes tell only part of the story. According to some estimates, as many as one-third of the living accommodations of elderly Americans are substandard, unsafe, and in disrepair; many lack private bathrooms, hot water, and other conveniences that Americans have come to expect (Butler & Lewis, 1982). In addition, many of these residences, rental housing in particular, lack telephones—a vital link to outside assistance for all people and especially elderly people who live alone (U.S. Dept. of Housing and Urban Development, 1983). Such facts, combined with the growth of the elderly population and the rising cost of repairs and rents, have created a priority for housing among public and private programs concerned with older Americans.

The major federal housing programs benefiting the elderly are described in Table 10.3. These programs are particularly concerned with subsidizing the construction and repair of housing for older people with low or moderate incomes. Another service, a directory of housing constructed especially for older

TABLE 10.3
Major Federal Housing Programs Benefiting the Elderly*

| Program | Executive Agency | Description |
|---------|------------------|-------------|
| Housing for the Elderly | Housing Production and Mortgage Credit of HUD | Federal loans for construction or rehabilitation of multifamily rental housing for elderly (aged 62 and over). Tenants may qualify for rent supplements under the Section B program. |
| Low- and Moderate-Income Housing | Housing Production and Mortgage Credit of HUD | Provides housing assistance payments for low-income persons and families who cannot afford "decent and sanitary housing in the private sector." Rent supplements cover the difference between the community's fair market rent down to 15% to 25% of the tenants' adjusted income. |
| Mortgage Insurance on Rental Housing for the Elderly | Housing Production and Mortgage Credit of HUD | Federal government insures against loss on mortages for the construction and rehabilitation of multifamily rental housing for the elderly (aged 62 and over) or disabled whose income is higher than the low- or moderate-income level. |

*(continued)*

TABLE 10.3    (*Continued*)

| Program | Executive Agency | Description |
| --- | --- | --- |
| Rural Rental Housing Program | Farmers Home Administration of Dept. of Agriculture | Federal government makes direct and guaranteed loans to construct, improve, or repair rental or cooperative housing in rural areas for low-income persons including senior citizens aged 62 or over. |
| Community Development | Community Planning and Development of HUD | Formula grants to urban communities, based on poverty population and other economic and population factors, for variety of community development activities, including construction of senior citizens centers. |
| Rental and Cooperative Housing for Lower and Moderate-Income Families | Housing Production and Mortagage Credit of HUD | Federal government subsidizes down to 1% of the interest on mortgages for private developers of multi-family housing for low- and moderate-income families, persons aged 62 and over, and handicapped individuals. |
| Low-Rent Public Housing | Housing Production and Mortgage Credit of HUD | Local housing authorities receive federal loans to aid in the purchase, rehabilitation, leasing or construction of multifamily housing for low-income families, individuals aged 62 and over, and handicapped individuals. Housing designed for the elderly may have congregate dining rooms and other special features. Rents may not be more than 25% of the family's income. |

*Adapted from Select Committee on Aging (1976).

people, is provided by the National Council on the Aging. Information on low- to moderate-income housing, tax relief, and grants for rent payments can also be obtained from local housing authorities, tax collection agencies, and Senior Citizens Centers in the community.

Social designers and managers have often failed to give enough attention to the physical and psychological needs of future residents in planning living enviornments for the elderly. Such engineers and architects may not be sufficiently aware of the profound effect that the intimate environment can have on the health and morale of older people. For example, apartments that are designed by architects who are insensitive to the activities and lifestyles of the elderly make it impossible for older people to retain their valued furnishings or to create a setting consistent with their lifestyles (Howell, 1980). More attention obviously needs to be given to the kinds of communities and housing that are adequate now and that will be appropriate for older people in the future. This requires the combined efforts of architects, home economists, builders, and developers in designing living spaces that are suitable during later life.

Regarding the design of the community or neighborhood itself, consideration should be given to factors such as nearness to medical and shopping facilities, availability and convenience of public transportation, air tempratures and pollution, degree of privacy and noise, safety and freedom from crime, and recreational facilities. In selecting a living enviornment, elderly people themselves will want to consider these factors and also factors such as closeness to relatives and friends of similar age. Finally, many of the structural features listed in Table 10.4 are important to elderly residents. Of course, not all physically hazardous conditions are within the residence itself. Such obstacles as high curbstones, high steps on buses, traffic lights of short duration, broken sidewalks, flagstone walkways, dim lighting and glare, and buildings with rooms of the same shape are also potentially dangerous when elderly people venture outside their homes (Kalish, 1982).

Housing units in the United States that are designed specifically for the aged include everything from apartments to intermediate and advanced medical care facilities. At one level is "congregate housing," consisting of rentals that provide limited or no services. At a second level is "continuum of care" housing, consisting mostly of rental housing in which services are usually paid on a user basis. At a third level is "life care," in which housing plus service and health care are provided on a "forever" basis for a sizable initial payment and a moderate monthly fee (Willmann, 1986). Housing may also be classified according to the age group for which it is intended as: (a) fully independent, including apartments for "go-go" people in the 65- to 75-year age range; (b) partially dependent, comprising something in between apartments and nursing homes for "slow-go" people in the 75- to 85-year range; (c) totally dependent, including nursing homes for the "no-go" people over age 85 ("Housing for the Aging," 1977).

Although rising construction costs and a shortage of funds have drastically limited the amount of federal subsidies for elderly housing, many of the adjustments required to make housing more suitable to the needs of this age group are neither difficult nor terribly expensive. Furthermore, lack of government funding should not interfere with proposing solutions to the housing problems of the aged. There are many questions that need to be considered more fully. For example, should there be more planned towns, one-level apartments, and single-person family dwellings, or are other alternatives more reasonable?

Even when considerable thought has gone into planning a retirement home, a geriatric clinic, or other living environment for the aged, mistakes are made. Thus, designers may emphasize the provision of more space for social interaction, only to have the increased space result in decreased interaction. Perhaps the most serious error in designing a living environment for older people is to assume

TABLE 10.4
Recommended Adjustments in Housing for the Elderly*

*Entrances*
_____

For persons with limited mobility, single-story or ground-floor residences are best. At least one unit should have a ramp, properly mounted handrails being placed on either side of the ramp. An open space adjacent to the door should be provided, and entrances should be well-lighted.

*General Structural Features*
_____

Doors should be designed for disabled persons lacking in strength, grasping power, coordination, or visual acuity; sliding rather than swinging doors are best. Doorways should be large enough to accommodate wheelchairs, but without risers that might trip people. If raised threshold cannot be eliminated, paint them with a constrasting color. Cover floors with nonslip but easy-to-maneuver surfaces. Make walls smooth, but mark boundaries with a constrasting paint.

*Kitchen*
_____

Storage facilities should allow for easy retrievability of items. Open storage shelves, revolving and pull-out shelves, pegboards, and magnetic catches are recommended. Kitchen counters should be low and have recesses. Dishwasher, washer, dryer, oven, and other large appliances should be front opening. Stoves should be designed so the user does not have to reach across them to reach the oven or things above it. Sinks and plumbing in kitchen and bathrooms should be built for use by someone in a wheelchair. Special kinds of kitchen equipment may be needed (e.g., a reacher for high cupboards).

*Bathrooms*
_____

Should be larger than customary in new homes to allow for wheelchair or walker. Bathroom doors should open outward. Install grab-bars near tub, shower, sink, and toilet. Have extra wide tubs, mount shower heads on flexible hoses, and install seat in tub or shower. Bathroom floors should be nonslip, with the shower floor flush with the outside floor and sloping slightly toward the drain. A wall-hung toilet that is higher than usual is an advantage in transferring from a wheelchair. Other fixtures should be low enough to permit easy use by those with limited mobility. Easily moved, nonscald handles and other controls rather than knobs or faucets, and wood handles rather than cold, slippery metal railings, are recommended. Help buttons, warm air dryers, counters on either side of the lavatory, and sinks positioned for ease of access are also good features.

*Bedrooms*
_____

Should be large enough to permit an elderly person to move around with ease. Mattresses should be level with wheelchair seat height. Closets should have sliding or swing-out doors and at least one rod. Light switches, telephone, and alarm units must be near the head of the bed. Windows should be constructed low enough so someone in a wheelchair or lying in bed can see outside. Couches in bedroom and living room should have rigid armrests and not soft cushions.

*Lighting*
_____

Light switches must be approximately 90 cm. (3 ft.) from the floor, and wall outlets 45 to 60 cm. (18–24 in.) high. Lights must be placed near bed, bath, and medicine cabinet.

*Other Considerations*
_____

Large elevators should be provided in multiple family dwellings. Easy accessibility to public transportation, parking spaces, adjacent to units if single story, and patios or balconies for entertaining friends are suggested. Emergency buzzers or bells in several locations and an alarm system connected directly to police headquarters would be helpful and reassuring in some units. Climate, air quality, and noise control are also recommended.

*Data from Agan, Casto, Day, and Schwab (1977), Ryan (1978), and Kalish (1982). Portions of this table were reprinted by permission of the American Home Economics Assn., publishers of the *Journal of Home Economics.*

that, because of their age, all older people have the same requirements. Nothing could be further from the truth. Individual differences in needs and preferences are, if anything, greater among older than younger adults. Special age-segregated environments, for example, may help some old people maintain social interactions and a sense of dignity in the face of advancing years, whereas for others they produce only feelings of detachment and loneliness. It is noteworthy that, despite the seeming social advantages of age-segregated environments, two-thirds of the elderly people who were questioned in one survey preferred to live among people of various ages (Lawton, 1975).

## Nursing Homes and Other Institutions

Although a relatively small percentage (approximately 5%) of elderly Americans reside in nursing homes or other extended health-care facilities at any one time, at least 20% of the 65+ population spend some time in these institutions. The 1.3 million residents of nursing homes, who have doubled in number since Medicare and Medicaid were introduced in 1966, tend to be very old, White, and female (Hing, 1987). It is estimated that the nursing home population will increase to 2 million by the year 2000 and to 4.6 million by 2040 (U.S. Senate Special Committee on Aging, 1987).

The majority of residents in nursing homes, who suffer from various chronic illnesses, are unmarried and have no children. Thus, an important factor in determining whether an elderly person is placed in a nursing home is whether there is a family member who is willing and able to provide health support and maintenance at home.

As pointed out in chapter 3, nursing homes are viewed negatively by most older adults. They prefer to remain with their families in familiar surroundings and may feel that placement in a nursing home is a sign that death is near. A psychological state labeled by Butler and Lewis (1982) as *institutionalism* is a frequent response to being placed in such an institution. The symptoms of institutionalism are automatic behaviors, expressionless face, general apathy, disinterest in personal appearance, and deteriorated morale.

Not all institutional health care requires admission to a skilled nursing facility. At a second level are intermediate care facilities that emphasize personal care service rather than intensive nursing care. Patients in an intermediate care facility need help with daily routines (eating, bathing, dressing, walking, etc.), but are not in medical distress. A third type of institutional care is the residential care facility, which caters to functionally independent people who need a clean, safe, sheltered living environment in which housekeeping, laundering, and meal services are provided. Last, there is the adult day-care facility, where people receive daily nursing, nutritional, and medical monitoring, while continuing to live in their own homes (Barrow & Smith, 1983).

## ACTIVITIES OF THE AGED

The problem of how to use one's time in old age is probably not as serious for people who continue to work full- or part-time after age 65. Whether they work for pay or volunteer, these individuals are not usually at a loss for something to do. In addition, workers who view their occupations as dull or taxing and those who have become accustomed to long vacations (e.g., teachers) are less likely to experience problems in occupying themselves after retirement. Many other retirees, however, have to learn by themselves or be taught how to cope with their newly found leisure time. Retired urban office workers who have failed to plan for postretirement activities and whose circumstances do not permit part-time work may find themselves with nothing but time on their hands. In contrast, retired farmers or mechanics can continue to till or tinker within the limits of their strength and ability.

People who are facing retirement often worry about how they will use their time, and, to be sure, the complaint of "too much time on my hands" is often heard from the recently retired. Those who fail to develop hobbies or other interests can easily become worried and anxious when faced with a succession of empty days. For this reason, retirement counselors stress that it is just as important for the retiree to develop a program of activities as it is to make financial plans.

Planning for the use of leisure time should certainly not be confined to later life. As people put in fewer and fewer hours each day on the job and retire earlier, the question of how the increased leisure hours can be used to help them grow and fulfill their potentialities becomes crucial for all age groups. Just as people are taught to have the traditional, culturally prescribed "right" attitude toward work, so too they must learn a newer "right" attitude toward leisure.

## Transportation

The ability to extend one's environment and to participate in the wider community greatly depends on communication and transportation facilities. Transportation is often a problem for the elderly in rural areas that have little public transportation as well as in many suburban and urban communities. Whenever food stores, doctors' offices, banks, and other shops and facilities are not near their residences, problems of transportation can arise for older people. Those who are impaired by disease or disability have special difficulties in getting from place to place, particularly when they do not drive and public transportation is scarce and costly. Even when public buses and trains are available, the high steps, sudden stops and starts, and rapidly closing doors are often nerve rattling and unsafe for the elderly. Buses are also inconvenient and potentially dangerous modes of travel for an older person who has to wait on a cold street corner in a high-crime area. Because of the greater expense, one would expect taxi service to be a more efficient means of traveling than riding a bus. But waiting for a cab can also be a problem for older people when cab drivers, viewing the elderly as passengers who take more time and tip less, simply pass them by.

Having to depend on other people to take them from place to place restricts the life space and lifestyle of many elderly individuals. This is particularly true in the case of the poor, who, because of lack of money for transportation or the unavailability of public transportation in their area, become isolated and lonely. Transportation is less of a problem in places where transit companies offer reduced fares to senior citizens and in those states that provide free statewide public transportation to the elderly. "Medicabs" or special vans for persons who are confined to wheelchairs, and Dial-a-Ride or Dial-a-Bus programs, in which elderly passengers can obtain reduced-fare rides, are other examples of special transportation services for the elderly at the community level. Illustrative of elderly fare reductions at the national level is Amtrak's policy of offering a 25% fare discount to senior citizens and handicapped people.

The U.S. Department of Transportation, through its Urban Mass Transportation Administration, makes grants available to public and nonprofit groups to support mass transit and reduced-fare programs for the elderly and handicapped. In addition, grants are awarded by the Federal Highway Administration for projects aimed at developing and improving the use of public mass transportation in rural areas, where many aged Americans live. These federal programs, and those at the state and local levels, have not taken care of the transportation needs of older Americans, but they have made important contributions. The regular public transportation system in many communities also offers reduced fares to riders who show Medicare cards or other proof of age.

## Using Leisure Time

The ways in which older people fill their time are greatly influenced by the leisure activities in which they engaged during middle age. The activities and avocations developed in early and middle adulthood provide a greater number of role options and hence increase the likelihood of successful adjustment in later life. These activities need not be limited to the traditional retirement pastimes of fishing, gardening, shuffleboard, pool, and golf. Only a minority of noninstitutionalized elderly are seriously restricted in their activities, and many take up tennis, jogging, and other vigorous sports. It is true that only a few exceptional individuals are able to approach the feat of 98-year-old Dimitri Iordanidis, who, by rigorous training and cessation of sex at age 85, was able to run a 42-mile marathon in 7 hours and 40 minutes.[1] For most elderly individuals, daily walks

---

[1]From the *Albuquerque Journal,* August 27, 1977, p. B-12.

rather than marathon running constitute the best kind of physical exercise.[2]

Sun City's slogan that "happiness equals activity plus friendliness" is sub-scribed to by a number of organizations for the elderly. There is merit in the slogan, because people who continue to interact with others and who pursue outside activities seem to adjust better in old age than those who become isolated and idle after retirement. Unfortunately, retirees are not always able to do what they desire. Many cannot afford to pursue crafts and hobbies or intellectual and artistic pursuits that interest them. Arbitrary age limits may also inhibit the minority who try to become proficient in a new craft or vocation. A case in point is that of a retired furniture salesman who finally had the time to become what he had always wanted to be—a carpenter. Offering to work free as an apprentice in order to learn the trade, he was told that unions would object or that insurance would not cover the risk. Because he was too old to enroll in a trade school carpentry class, he was directed to a hobby shop where he was forced to settle for wood burning rather than the furniture making that he had always wanted to learn (Curtin, 1972).

Surveys of leisure activities in later life have found that the types or range of activities participated in by older people are more restricted and narrower than those in which young and middle-aged adults engage (Gordon, Gaitz, & Scott, 1976; Robinson, 1969). Dancing, drinking, attending movies, participating in sports or physical exercise, using guns, performing outdoor activities, traveling, reading, and doing cultural productions are all reportedly less frequent in older than younger adults. On the other hand, the frequencies of television viewing, discussion, spectator sports, cultural consumption, entertaining, participating in organizations, and home embellishment are about the same in older as in younger adults. The fact that activities are more sedentary and restricted to the home in later life is indicated by the greater incidence of solitary pursuits and cooking (by men) (Gordon et al., 1976).

Care must be taken in interpreting the findings of the preceding survey, because the effects of age are confounded with cohort (generational) differences. In addition, the average results do not indicate the wide range of differences in the leisure-time activities of elderly individuals. Thus, the survey results suggest that interest in reading declines in old age, but any public librarian knows that many older people read a great deal. Acknowledgment of this fact is seen in the publication of magazines directed especially at older Americans (*Active Aging, 50-Plus, Golden Years, Modern Maturity, Prime Time, Seniority*). In addition, various newspapers throughout the nation have columns or entire pages devoted exclusively to matters of interest to senior citizens.

---

[2]Lovers of golf, tennis, or bowling may obtain membership in the National Sports Association by writing to Dept. P, 317 Cameron St., Alexandria, VA 22314, and ski buffs may wish to contact The Over the Hill Gang, International at P.O. Box 6777, Denver, CO 80206) or the 70+ Ski Club by writing to Lloyd T. Lambert, Dept. P, Ballston Lake, NY 12019.

Library facilities are used extensively by the aged for recreational purposes and for obtaining information on health, financial, and vocational matters. Special book lists, books with large print, and places where older people can meet for discussions are also made available by libraries. At the national level, the Library of Congress offers free library services (e.g., Braille, cassette, and diskette books and magazines) to persons with visual or physical handicaps. The Older Reader Services program of the Department of Education also makes grants available to public libraries for the purchase of special materials and the development of other programs and services for the aged. Combining education with socialization is Elderhostel, which sponsors low-cost academic programs for people over 60 at more than 850 colleges throughout the United States and abroad. Many colleges also offer reductions in tuition and other fees to seniors.[3]

Many organizations that sponsor activities for the elderly (e.g., Senior Citizens Centers and Golden Age clubs) provide discount tickets to entertainment programs, travel, and other forms of recreation and services. The National Park Service offers Golden Age passports to permanent U.S. residents aged 62 and over. These passes enable the holder to pay a reduced fee for use of the facilities at any national park, monument, or recreational area.

As noted earlier, older people also use their leisure time to engage in volunteer work and club and lodge activities and for visiting friends and relatives. The Older American Volunteer Programs sponsored by the federal ACTION agency, for example, enable the elderly to perform volunteer services for day-care centers, hospitals, schools, and other public service agencies. Additional activities of the aged include going to church and other meeting places, shopping, listening to the radio, and watching "60 Minutes," "Over Easy," "The Golden Girls," and the nightly news. Closed-circuit programs designed especially for the elderly, whether in households or institutions, are also broadcast in many cities.

Visitors to Atlantic City and Las Vegas casinos, and especially players of slot machines, can attest to the popularity of these places among senior citizens. Although many such leisure-time activities tend to become more solitary in old age, the role that certain activities play in socialization should not be overlooked. Daniel Rubinstein, a social researcher who wondered what attraction racetracks, bus depots, bingo parlors, and jai alai frontons could have in common for elderly people, spent years studying the lifestyles and "lovestyles" of men and women over 60 who congregate at these establishments. He concluded that rather than simply providing gambling or amusement, the places represent social organizations for older people (McCormack, 1979).

Outlets for the social and political needs of older people can also be found by serving on town councils and planning commissions. Those who become in-

---

[3]For more information on educational opportunities in later life, write to Elderhostel, 80 Bylston St., Dept. P, Boston, MA 02119 and The Institute of Lifetime Learning, AARP, Dept. P, 1909 K St., N.W., Washington, DC 20049.

volved in such community service activities may make important contributions to traffic control, regulation of land use, setting priorities for health and social services, and other matters of concern to the elderly and to the community at large.

An obvious conclusion that can be drawn from personal observation as well as research findings is that the leisure activities of the older generation differ in many respects from those of younger people. However, the differences are undoubtedly due as much to upbringing and to cultural contrasts between generations as to chronological age. Because the prior experiences of tomorrow's elderly will have been different from those of today's, we should expect their behavior to be different too. Rather than playing checkers or shuffleboard and doing gardening, the next generation of older adults may spend more of their leisure time swimming, playing musical instruments, visiting museums, and in other ways continuing to engage in the interests of today's young and middle-aged adults.

## The Elderly Consumer

Although inflation has eroded the value of the dollar during the past quarter of a century, the steady expansion of Social Security and pension programs has made the purchasing power of America's elderly citizens greater than ever before. Increasing numbers of older Americans are becoming freer spenders, no longer feeling as concerned with the traditional practice of saving everything for their heirs.

Older people are not nearly as homogeneous in their purchasing behavior as teenagers, but the disproportionate growth of the elderly population and the likelihood that the trend will continue in the foreseeable future has been affecting the plans of manufacturers and adventurers of consumer products. Manufacturers and advertisers continue to view this "maturity" market with some caution, but they have begun to tailor their products and messages to the changing structure of the population ("Rich New Market. . .," 1979).

It is now recognized that vitamins, laxatives, moisturizers, and other health and beauty aids are not the only items purchased by the elderly. Sales of clothing, books, games, art supplies, and vacation trips also thrive in the 65-and-over group. Adult toys and games such as backgammon and mah-jongg, as well as electronic games of all kinds, have become popular at senior citizen centers and in the homes of older people. Luxury cars, motor homes, and campers are also doing better than might be expected in the elderly market.

The large number of readers of magazines such as *Modern Maturity, 50 Plus,* and *Prime Time,* which are aimed specifically at older Americans, have attracted ads by travel firms, restaurants, clothing stores, banks, and many other business organizations. Awareness of the over-65 market is also indicated by discounts offered to senior citizens by tour companies, motion picture theaters, hotels, airline and bus companies, and even MacDonald's and Fred Astaire Dance Studios. Cosmetic and clothing companies are designing products especially for the over-50 set, which are being demonstrated by older models. To entice the older homemaker, General Electric offers Braille-style (feeler) knobs on many of its ranges and home laundry appliances at no extra charge. Free bus rides are also being offered as an allurement for seniors to shop at discount grocery stores, and banks offer free travelers checks to elderly customers. The fact that these methods are effective points to a new generation of older people—one not so willing to sit back, let the world go by, and remain "brand loyal."

Because elderly people do not enjoy being reminded that they are old, marketers have been reluctant to position products specifically for the elderly market. For example, Proctor and Gamble had problems with its product Attends, a type of diaper for incontinent adults. And Heinz's strained "senior foods" did poorly with elderly people, who bought baby food instead, ostensibly for their grandchildren (Mowen, 1987). During the past decade, however, companies such as Ford Motors, Campbell Soups, Bulova, and American Home Products have shown a greater willingness to direct products toward older consumers (Assael, 1987). Sears, De Beers, AT&T, and Smith-Barney are among the companies that have used older people in their advertisements. So has Wendy's Hamburgers, whose Clara Peller made "Where's the beef?" a household expression. However, seniors probably responded more positively to McDonald's "new kid" commercial, which depicts an older man during his first day on the job, than they did to the demanding, cranky old lady image of the Wendy's advertisement (Randall, 1988).

## SUMMARY

The relatively low income of the majority of older people has an effect on many of the other problems that they experience—problems with housing, health, nutrition, transportation, and the use of leisure time. The income of retired elderly people is, on the average, about half that of the actively employed. The median income of elderly men is higher than that of elderly women, and the median for older Whites is greater than that for Blacks and other minority elderly.

Social Security is the major income source for most older people, but private pensions, assets, earnings, and gifts contribute to the income of some. In spite of the low average, the income range of older Americans is actually quite large. The percentage of older Americans whose incomes fall below the official poverty level has declined substantially during the past two decades, and the number of those who are destitute is quite small. Of those who continue to live in poverty, a disproportionate number are members of minority groups. Unlike the traditional order of food, clothing, and shelter, the elderly poor must spend the greatest amount of their income for rent and utilities, with clothing in second place and food third.

Older people live in a variety of shelters—houses, mobile homes, apartments, single rooms, and so on. These residences are also in various locations, although they tend to be clustered in certain suburban neighborhoods, in special buildings of large cities, and in rural areas. There has been a growing migration of retirees to the Sunbelt states, but the majority remain in their home communities. Certain states, depending on their cost of living index, climate, and recreational facilities, are considered better than others as places to retire.

Approximately 75% of the elderly own their own homes, but most of these homes are quite old and in need of repairs. The deteriorating or substandard condition of much of the housing for the elderly makes it unsafe and unhealthful. Consequently, improved housing has a high priority among the many federal programs benefiting older Americans.

Great concern about the living environments of older people has been expressed by the general public and professionals. The living environment of a person includes the neighborhood or community of residence as well as the dwelling unit itself. The expertise of architects, engineers, home economists, and social psychologists has been applied to the design of safe and comfortable living environments for the elderly. Many of the recommended changes in current housing are not particularly expensive, but entire communities designed for older people run into millions of dollars.

Less serious than income and housing, but also a problem for elderly people is the lack of adequate transportation. Federal, state, and local programs have made buses, trains, and taxis less expensive, more convenient, and safer modes of transportation for elderly passengers, but difficulties still exist.

Individuals who have not engaged in any preretirement planning of how they will use their leisure time often find themselves restless and dissatisfied after retirement. On the other hand, those who have developed hobbies during early or middle adulthood and are accustomed to long vacations are less likely to be at a loss for something to do. In addition to the traditional activities of fishing, gardening, and the like, many take up jogging, tennis, and other vigorous activities. They also enjoy arts and crafts, reading, and travel, none of which is necessarily very costly.

Research has shown that the leisure-time activities of older adults tend to be more solitary and restricted than those of younger adults. Although a certain amount of disengagement is to be expected in old age, the slogan that "happiness equals activity plus friendliness" is as good a prescription as any for effective adjustment in later life. Thus, appropriate amounts of physical and mental exercise, combined with pleasant and mutually rewarding social interaction with one's peers, appear to contribute to a long and interesting life.

The growth of the elderly population, the amount of money that many older people have, and their increasing willingness to spend it have stimulated manufacturers and marketers to pay closer attention to the needs and desires of this age group. Some of the effort that in the past has gone into capturing the teenage "Pepsi-generation" market is now being expended on the "Geritol generation"—the fastest growing segment of the population. Special incentives to purchase products and services are being provided for older consumers, among which are discounts, free rides, product adaptations, and sales for elderly shoppers.

## SUGGESTED READINGS

Davis, R., & Davis, J. (1985). *TV's image of the elderly*. Lexington, MA: Lexington Books.

French, W. A., & Fox, R. (1985). Segmenting the senior citizen market. *Journal of Consumer Marketing, 2*, 61–74.

Gerbner, G., Signarielli, N., & Morgan, M. (1980). Aging with television: Images on televison drama and conceptions of social reality. *Journal of Communication, 30*, 37–47.

Lawton, M. P. (1980). *Environment and aging*. Belmont, CA: Brooks/Cole.

Moos, R. H., & Lemke, S. (1985). Specialized living environments for older people. In J. E. Birren & K. W. Schaie (Eds.), *Handbook of the psychology of aging* (2nd ed., pp. 864–869). New York: Van Nostrand Reinhold.

Myles, J. (1984). *Old age in the welfare state: The political economy of public pensions*. Boston: Little, Brown.

Regnier, V. (1983). Housing and environment. In D. S. Woodruff & J. E. Birren (Eds.), *Aging: Scientific perspectives and social issues* (pp. 351–369). Belmont, CA: Brooks/Cole.

Schultz, J. H. (1985). *The economics of aging* (3rd ed.). Belmont, CA: Wadsworth.

Strieb, G. F., Folts, W. E., & Hilder, M. (1984). *Old homes new families: Shared living for the elderly*. New York: Columbia University Press.

Walther, R. J. (1983). Economics of aging. In D. S. Woodruff & J. E. Birren (Eds.), *Aging: Scientific perspectives and social issues* (pp. 370–390). Belmont, CA: Brooks/Cole.

# 11

# Crime and Justice

The problem of crime in the United States, as publicized continuously in the media, is a topic of great concern to law enforcement officials, politicians, and particularly the victimized public. Daily newspapers and television news programs are replete with reports of robberies, rapes, murders, and kidnappings at all levels of society. To document the crime problem, each year the FBI issues its *Uniform Crime Reports,* consisting primarily of detailed tables of statistics on arrests in the various categories of criminal offenses committed during the preceding calendar year. Considering the publicity given to crime, it is not surprising when a public opinion poll reveals that a sizable percentage of respondents sampled from the general population consider crime to be the nation's number one problem.

## ELDERLY CRIMINALS

Although crime against the elderly has received more public and professional attention than crime by the elderly, approximately 1% of those arrested each year in the United States are people who have reached their 65th birthday. As indicated in Table 11.1, however, considering the fact that 12% of the American population is 65 years and older, 1% of all those arrested is a disproportionately small number. Compared with the 74% of those arrested in 1986 who were 15–34 years old, the incidence of criminal activity by elderly people is unimpressive. As shown in Table 11.1, the elderly have the lowest crime rate of any group. The overall age trend is an increase in the relative frequency of arrests

TABLE 11.1
Percentage Distributions of Persons Arrested
and Total U.S. Population in 1986

| Age Group | Percent of Total Population | Percent of Arrests |
|---|---|---|
| Under 15 | 21.6% | 5.2% |
| 15–24 | 16.2 | 43.7 |
| 25–34 | 17.7 | 30.3 |
| 35–44 | 13.7 | 12.7 |
| 45–54 | 9.5 | 4.9 |
| 55–59 | 4.7 | 1.4 |
| 60–64 | 4.5 | .9 |
| 65 and over | 12.1 | .9 |

Sources: U.S. Department of Justice (1987), National Center for Health Statistics (1987b).

until young adulthood, and then a gradual decline through middle and late adulthood.[1]

One percent is clearly a small portion of the total number of people who are arrested each year, but in 1986 it translated into 92,488 arrests of older Americans. For what crimes were these people arrested and why did they commit them? The "why" question is difficult to answer, but some insight into the "what" question can be obtained by examining Table 11.2. As shown in this table, the total number of arrests of elderly people increased from 1969 to 1979 but decreased slightly from 1979 to 1986. Considered collectively, the largest numbers of arrests in these years were for drunkenness, disorderly conduct, driving under the influence, and larceny–theft.

Despite the fact that older women substantially outnumber older men, over four-fifths of the older people arrested are men. The ratio of women to men arrested is even less in old age than it is in the general population. But women have a proportionally higher share of arrests for major crimes than for minor ones, a statistic that holds more for older than for younger women. Also, women's share of major property offense arrests is greater than for major violent offense arrests (Shichor, 1985). As shown in Table 11.3, by far the most common type of offense for which older women are arrested is larceny–theft.

Although difficult to interpret, the changes in the number of arrests of older people for specific crimes from 1969 to 1986 are interesting. Table 11.2 shows, for example, that during the 17-year period from 1969 to 1986 the number of arrests for all the major offenses increased. The exceptions were arrests for drunkenness, disorderly conduct, gambling, and vagrancy, all of which de-

---

[1]A possible exception to the age decline in crime is suicide, which, especially among White males, increases with age (see chapter 5). Many authorities, however, question the classification of suicide as a crime. In the seriously ill it may well be viewed as self-euthanasia rather than a criminal action.

creased. Interpretation of these differences should take into account the changing material conditions and social roles of the elderly and the population as a whole, as well as changes in arrest procedures and the reporting of crime statistics. For example, it has been alleged that law enforcement officers are more likely to overlook less serious crimes such as drunkenness and disturbing the peace when they are committed by older persons than when the perpetrator is a young adult. Only in the case of more serious crimes (e.g., larceny, assault, narcotics law violations) are the elderly likely to be treated in the same manner as younger offenders. It could well be that the increases in the number of arrests for these crimes from 1969 to 1986 were due more to a tightening up of law enforcement than to changing patterns of criminal behavior among older Americans. Obviously, crime statistics become difficult to interpret when the strictness of law enforcement varies with time and with the age of the offender.

Some authorities maintain that criminal behavior in older people is associated with mental deterioration and personality disorders (Shichor & Kebrin, 1978).

TABLE 11.2
Arrests of Persons 65 and Older in 1969, 1979, and 1986*

| Offense Charged | 1969 | 1979 | 1986 |
|---|---|---|---|
| Drunkenness | 56,099 | 28,400 | 15,271 |
| Disorderly conduct | 7,795 | 6,421 | 5,818 |
| Driving under the influence | 6,178 | 19,130 | 18,115 |
| Gambling | 4,406 | 2,418 | 1,035 |
| Larceny–theft | 3,634 | 12,223 | 15,078 |
| Vagrancy | 2,615 | 365 | 422 |
| Liquor law violations | 1,566 | 1,914 | 2,177 |
| Aggravated assaults | 1,129 | 2,389 | 2,500 |
| Weapons: carrying, possessing, etc. | 847 | 1,374 | 1,322 |
| Sex offenses (except forcible rape and prostitution) | 712 | 908 | 1,665 |
| Fraud | 311 | 1,207 | 1,841 |
| Murder and nonnegligent manslaughter | 259 | 304 | 233 |
| Burglary | 223 | 460 | 542 |
| Drug abuse violations | 198 | 574 | 1,542 |
| Prostitution and commercialized vice | 188 | 336 | 457 |
| Offenses against family and children | 182 | 190 | 260 |
| Vandalism | 120 | 547 | 615 |
| Motor vehicle theft | 56 | 147 | 164 |
| Forgery and counterfeiting | 37 | 110 | 202 |
| Forcible rape | 37 | 130 | 203 |
| Total Offenses Charge | 86,624 | 94,264 | 92,488 |

Source: U.S. Dept. of Justice, Uniform crime reports for the United States. Washington, DC: U.S. Government Printing Office, 1970, 1980, 1987.

*A few offenses are not included, so the numbers listed in a column may not add up to the total.

TABLE 11.3

The 12 Most Common Crimes with Which Elderly Men and
Women Were Charged in 1986

| Rank and Offense Charged | Men | Women |
|---|---|---|
| 1. Driving under the influence | 16,752 | 1,363 |
| 2. Drunkenness | 14,556 | 715 |
| 3. Larceny–theft | 8,713 | 6,365 |
| 4. Vagrancy | 5,023 | 795 |
| 5. Other assaults | 3,498 | 567 |
| 6. Aggravated assault | 2,261 | 239 |
| 7. Liquor laws | 1,964 | 213 |
| 8. Fraud | 1,190 | 651 |
| 9. Sex offenses (except forcible rape and prostitution) | 1,651 | 14 |
| 10. Drug abuse violations | 1,363 | 179 |
| 11. Weapons (carrying, possessing, etc.) | 1,259 | 63 |
| 12. Gambling | 968 | 67 |
| Total Offense Charged* | 78,010 | 14,478 |

Source: U.S. Department of Justice (1987).

*This includes all offenses charged, not just those listed in the table.

This would seem to be a more likely explanation in the case of crimes against persons, in which brain-damaged or psychotic individuals may lose control and commit impulsive acts of violence. Vagrancy, drunkenness, and certain other crimes may also be indicative of a loss of control due to senility. Nevertheless, there are perfectly sane elderly people who, for various reasons, commit misdemeanors and felonies. In addition to economic needs, criminal activities may serve social motives. Barrett (1972) referred to certain crimes committed by older people—for example drunkenness, disorderly conduct, gambling—as "companionship delinquencies," because he considered these crimes as stemming prmiarily from a search for companionship.

A crime that has reportedly increased in frequency among the elderly during the past two decades is larceny–theft, and shoplifting in particular. One elderly woman devised an effective technique for shoplifting in department stores. Pretending to be senile, she would "accidentally and awkwardly" knock piles of items off the shelves and slip them under her clothes during the ensuing confusion. We may smile at the ingenuity of this woman, but shoplifting by an older person is frequently a desperate act with heart-rending consequences. Consider the case of a 91-year-old white-haired widow who, having been caught shoplifting in a supermarket, was forced to spend 24 hours in jail. On being released, she stated that she had not slept all night and that the experience of being locked up was terrible. Then she sighed deeply and added: "I wish God would close my eyes, I'm so tired of living." The feelings of shame and guilt experienced by this woman are not uncommon among elderly people who have committed petty theft, and they can persist over many years in a person who has had a strong moral upbringing (see Report 11.1).

## VICTIMIZATION AND EXPLOITATION OF THE ELDERLY

"Widow, 87—Mugged— Home Set Afire"

"Elderly Woman Clubbed, Robbed by Intruder"

---

Report 11.1    WAS IT ALL FOR NAUGHT?
46 YEARS LATER, OLDSTER TRIES TO PAY $1.50
BILL*

DORIS A. BYRON, *Times Staff Writer*

SANTA ANA—Somewhere among the 20,000 inhabitants of the Missouri boot-heel town of Poplar Bluff, there is at least one very honest old soul.

How else can one explain the one-page unsigned letter containing $10 that arrived recently in the Orange County recorder's office bearing a Poplar Bluff, Mo., postmark and an April 1 date?

The letter was addressed to the recorder's office at the "Court House Annex"—an extension of the old county courthouse that was vacated by the recorder and his staff nearly 10 years ago.

"In what used to be Santa Ana Gardens, at the corner of Edinger and Sullivan St., was a filling station owned by a Mr. Forbes—I think," the handwritten letter read.

"Anyway I or we left there owing $1.50 for gas which was forgotten. I do not know how to settle this unless someone there will look up records and forward half of $10 enclosed to heirs and keep the other half for yourself.

"Thanks."

There was no signature, but there was a postscript.

"PS," the leter closed, "this was in 1934."

Assistant Recorder Ella M. Smith said the letter apparently came from someone whose conscience was troubled by the depression-era debt that was never paid.

Though the missive was dated on April Fool's Day, the $10 was real, and only someone who knew his or her way around Santa Ana could have known about Santa Ana Gardens, Edinger Avenue and Sullivan Street and the old courthouse annex.

But if the sender is the honest soul he or she appears to be, there's at least one not-so-honest soul walking the corridors of Orange County government.

Smith said the recorder didn't know what to do with the $10 bill when it arrived—there's no provision for accepting unpaid gasoline bills in the county law—so he tucked it back into its envelope and left it on his desk.

And when he arrived at work Thursday morning and opened the envelope, one person's good deed had been undone by another's bad one: The $10 bill was gone.

*From Byron (1980). Copyright, 1980, Los Angeles Times. Reprinted by permission.

"Elderly Frequently Abused by Children"

"How Con Artists Rob Elderly"

These are just a sample of headlines from newspaper stories describing incidents in which elderly people have been victimized and exploited. Typically, such stories give a few details without adequately describing the anxiety and pain of defenseless elderly people who are the repeated victims of crimes against themselves and their property, or who have been exploited by con artists.

## Incidence and Type of Victimization

Older people are not usually victimized by crime, especially violent crime, more than the rest of the population. According to unpublished data from the National Crime Survey, the elderly are victimized less often than younger adults by rape, robbery, assault, and larceny. Only about 1% of known rape victims are women over 50 years of age, and a very small percentage of these are over 65 (U.S. Dept. of Justice, 1979).

Because many crimes go unreported, accurate statistics on victims are difficult to obtain. The FBI reports statistics on the age, sex, race, and ethnicity of murder victims, but does not collect data on the victims of other crimes. Table 11.4, which is adapted from the *Uniform Crime Reports for the United States-1986* lists the

TABLE 11.4

Number of Murder Victims in U.S. in 1986 by Age, Sex, Race, and Ethnic Group

| Category | Age | | | |
|---|---|---|---|---|
| | Under 18 | 18–64 | Over 65 | Unknown |
| Sex | | | | |
| Male | 999 | 12,449 | 666 | 341 |
| Female | 599 | 3,603 | 484 | 88 |
| Unknown | 1 | 2 | 0 | 25 |
| Race | | | | |
| White | 830 | 8,338 | 771 | 260 |
| Black | 721 | 7,293 | 362 | 133 |
| Other | 41 | 389 | 15 | 7 |
| Unknown | 7 | 34 | 2 | 54 |
| Ethnic Group | | | | |
| Hispanic* | 208 | 2,501 | 41 | 91 |
| Non-Hispanic | 1,097 | 10,716 | 855 | 200 |
| Unknown | 294 | 2,837 | 254 | 163 |

*Source*: U.S. Department of Justice (1987).

*Hispanic may be of any race.

number of murder victims by four demographic variables. As shown by these numbers, about 6% of the 19,257 people who were murdered in the United States during 1986 were 65 or older. Older men were more likely to be murdered than older women, and both men and women were more likely to murder men than women (U.S. Dept. of Justice, 1987). In the 65-and-over age group, as in all age groups, the majority of murder victims were male, White, and nonHispanic.

Despite the fact that rape, murder, and other violent crimes are the ones occurring the least often, they are the very crimes that older people fear the most. This is especially true of elderly women and Blacks, who, to a significantly greater extent than elderly men and Whites, confess to being afraid of crime. The fears of these people are, of course, not totally unrealistic. Inner-city residents express greater fear than suburbanites, a fact correlated with the reported incidence of crime in the two locales. The magnitudes of the relationships of crime to sex, race, and location of residence are not entirely clear, because, through fear of retaliation or whatever reasons, the great majority of crimes probably go unreported.

More common than crimes of violence are property crimes, which are much more likely to occur when the property is unoccupied. In the case of the elderly, however, personal larceny with contact, in which a purse, wallet, or cash is taken directly from the victim's person by snatching or pocket picking, has the highest rate (Antunes, Cook, Cook, & Skogan, 1977).

## Why Designate Elderly Victims for Special Attention?

Elderly people may be more afraid of crime than victimization statistics seem to warrant, but there are reasons for their fears and for singling out the elderly for special attention. One reason is that the effects of any economic loss on the elderly are, because of their lower average income, greater than for any age group over 30 (Cook, Skogan, Cook, & Antunes, 1978). Associated with diminished income is residence in high-crime, inner-city neighborhoods rather than more affluent suburbs. Low-income elderly of all ethnic groups who live in neighborhoods that may once have been safe but now have high crime rates are often trapped because of their reluctance to move to new, unfamiliar surroundings. By remaining in these neighborhoods, a large percentage of older people become victims because of their physical proximity to their most frequent victimizers—school dropouts and other unemployed teenagers and young adults. The proximity, and hence the probability of being victimized, is greater for those older people who live in age-integrated rather than age-segregated housing (Lawton & Yaffe, 1980).

Although the results of studies indicate that the elderly are no more likely than juveniles to be victimized by younger people, it has been found that fear of teenagers keeps many older people at home (see Report 11.2). The main crime

---

**Report 11.2    FEAR OF TEEN-AGERS KEEPS ELDERLY HOME, STUDY SHOWS\***

UNIVERSITY PARK, PA (UPI)—Elderly persons living in cities are so afraid of teen-agers many of them remain indoors after 3 P.M., a new study reports.

The study of Geoffrey C. Godbey, Pennsylvania State University professor of recreation and parks, also found that fear of crime keeps many of the elderly away from senior citizen centers, parks and other places where they would normally go.

Godbey found that 66% of about 2,000 people in his study said fear of crime affected the use of such facilities.

"Everyone knows that many older people are afraid to leave home after dark, but we were surprised to find that 3 P.M. is a cutoff hour, too." Godbey said, "About one-fifth of the elderly in our study wanted to be home by the time school let out."

The fear of teen-agers is so great, the study found, that 888 of those surveyed said that many times they cross the street or change directions to avoid them.

Funding for the study came from the Andrus Foundation of the American Association of Retired Persons. It was conducted in several cities, including Pittsburgh, Philadelphia, Boston, Baltimore, and Newark, N.J.

Nine percent of the elderly in the study had been crime victims within the 12 months before the survey. Most had been robbed or had their homes burglarized.

"There is a tendency to think old people are unreasonable in their fear, that they curtail activities when there is no need to do so," Godbey said. "But we found a high correlation between fear and victimization."

A total of 33 robberies, 22 assaults, and 5 other crimes had been committed against the elderly en route to senior citizen centers in a 12-month period, the researcher was told.

\*Reprinted with permission of United Press International. Copyright 1980.

---

against the elderly is robbery on the street by armed Black youths who are acting alone or who are strangers to the older person. Consequently, for older people living in high crime areas any strange Black youth on the street is seen as a potential threat (Antunes et al., 1977). In recent years, many of the assailants in burglaries, robberies, rapes, and murders of the elderly (and others) have been involved with drugs, mostly crack cocaine. Knowing the habits of elderly people and their vulnerability makes them easy targets for those looking for drug money.

Another reason why the elderly are more afraid of crime and deserve special consideration is their poor physical strength and health. Older people are less able to defend themselves and otherwise escape from threatening situations. They are also more easily hurt and have greater difficulty recuperating once they have been injured. Sensorimotor problems and various chronic disorders make the elderly more vulnerable to attack, and it takes longer for their torn flesh to heal and for their broken bones to knit. An elderly victim of a purse snatching can easily sustain a broken arm, a broken hip, or serious internal injuries that can cause permanent disability. Furthermore, the cost of medical care for physical injuries to the elderly represents the highest proportion of income in any age group (Cook et al., 1978).

Awareness of the more fragile physical condition of the elderly causes potential criminals to view them as easy targets. Perhaps the fact that they are less able to defend themselves, and therefore not as likely as younger adults to resist and be confronted with weapons, explains why older people are less apt to be injured during a criminal act. The chances of injury and even death are increased when a crime victim attempts to resist. But even when they are not physically injured, a larger proportion of older victims are emotionally debilitated by an attack against their person or property. The emotional stress provoked by an attack tends to be greater in an elderly victim, who usually takes longer to recuperate psychologically.

Poorer physical strength and skill, coupled with the tendency to live alone, increases the vulnerability of the elderly to crime and the likelihood of being victimized repeatedly—often by the same thieves or attackers. This likelihood is especially high for the large number of elderly people who, not having access to a private automobile, must rely on public transportation. Being alone, defenseless, and having a small lifetime accumulation of keepsakes and cash makes them tempting prey to potential thieves. Knowing the dates of receipt of monthly pension and benefit checks, and consequently when older people are more likely to have cash, young hoodlums may lie in wait for the vulnerable elderly at these times. Quite often the victimizer does not even wait for the check to be cashed. Thousands of social security and relief checks are stolen each year in purse snatchings, muggings, and burglaries of homes and mailboxes.

Because of their inability to resist, aged widows and others who live alone are the favorite targets of teenage and young adult hoodlums. Unable to sleep at night through fear of being robbed or mugged, elderly people residing in large cities may be forced to sleep during the day. Some are so afraid that in spite of the need to get out and enjoy exercising and interacting socially, they literally become prisoners in their own homes. Such fears are greatest among those who live in areas having high crime rates, in large communities, and in age-integrated facilities. One 82-year-old woman who, after finally overcoming her fear of going outside, was robbed of her groceries and money as she re-entered her apartment, and then raped. Adding insult to injury, she contracted a venereal disease from the incident (Loether, 1975). Occasionally, an elderly victim of continued muggings and thefts is murdered or, simply giving up out of weariness and despair, decides to die by his or her own hand. Others, perhaps manifesting more spunk, refuse to give in to their attackers or to let them destroy their self-esteem and sense of purpose (see Report 11.3):

> Houston, April 6—Novella Davis spends her days tending her rose bushes, snapdragons and chrysanthemums, and her nights guarding her fortress-like brick house. "I've got a .30-06 rifle and a Remington automatic," said Mrs. Davis, a

---

**Report 11.3    VICTIM, 85, HAS SURPRISE FOR MUGGERS\***

OAKLAND (UPI)—Mary Fuller, 85, the most mugged senior citizen in Oakland, now has lost her hearing aid to two young toughs, but she remains undaunted and vows to strike back.

"The hell with them—I'm still going out," said the plucky grandmother, who packs a can of tear gas spary up her sleeve.

On Monday night, two young men followed her as she walked to a store near her apartment. "Oh, oh, here we go again," she thought.

They accosted her and "told me I had no use for that hearing aid, and I told them they had even less use for it," she recalled.

But they forced her to take it off and hand it over, she said. "Then they told me I had no use for that ring, either."

She was referring to her gold wedding band. She said it had been given to her by her husband, "the most wonderful man who ever lived." He died 51 years ago.

The attempt to take the ring was the last straw. "I just whipped it (the tear gas spray) out and gave the boy a whiff," she said. "I told the police that a person had the right to protect herself."

The muggers? They ran off—with the $300 hearing aid but without the ring.

Police said Mary has been mugged so many times on the street that she doesn't carry a purse anymore. Her grocery bags have been yanked from her arms, outside stores, her 5-foot, 90-pound body stripped by thugs of objects valuable only to her. And her small apartment has been invaded by robbers.

Mary said one young man who snatched her groceries told her, "We need this food more than you."

If this really was the case, she said, "then I really don't mind. Nobody should go hungry."

Mary said that from now on she is going to be more careful, "but I'm not afraid of them. What's left for them to take, my life? I'm 85 years old. I hate to be afraid."

"If necessary, I'll walk in the middle of the street. A person has to get out once in a while—some fresh air, sunshine."

And to show her spunk she has pinned this sign on her apartment door:

"You bastard thieves.

"I know who you are. If you take one more article from this place, I'm going to police, and you're going to jail."

\*Reprinted with permission of United Press International. Copyright 1980.

---

79-year-old widow . . . "If one doesn't get them, the other will." (Applebome, 1988, p. A-16)

## Elder Abuse

Unfortunately, strangers are not the only ones who abuse the elderly. It has been estimated that each year 1 million elderly Americans are physically, psychologically, sexually, or financially abused by relatives (Pillemer & Finkelhor, 1988). This figure is undoubtedly an underestimate because the victims themselves, because of their reluctance to cause trouble for abusive family members, seldom report incidents of elder abuse to authorities. More than 70% of the cases of elder abuse are reported by third parties. Examples of the "battered elderly syndrome," in which an older parent or other relative is physically abused, are plentiful (McCormack, 1980, p. 2):

> A woman, 70, is placed in a tub of cold water by her daughter and left there for several hours.

> A woman, 19, confesses to torturing her father for 7 days by chaining him to a toilet and hitting him with a hammer when he is asleep.

> A son, 22, fights with his parents over money late at night. He hits his mother with a frying pan and clubs his father.

Congressional hearings on elder abuse have revealed many such incidents, including both physical and psychological (threats, "beating with words") mistreatment. The reasons for such abuse are varied (e.g., financial gain, revenge, hatred of the aged and old age), but it is generally agreed that the problem has grown in recent years.

The most common and least serious type of elderly abuse is leaving an older person alone, isolated, or forgotten. Next most common is verbal or emotional abuse, in which an elderly person is frightened, humiliated, insulted, threatened, or treated like a child. Less common is active neglect, by confining, isolating the person, or withholding food or medication. Even less common is hitting, slapping, restraining, and other kinds of physical mistreatment (Hickey & Douglass, 1981).

Although it is widely believed that elder abuse is related to impairment or dependency on the part of the victim, there is no evidence for this supposition (Pedrick-Cornell & Gelles, 1982). The picture of an overstressed son or daughter who is pushed to the breaking point by having to shoulder the burden of caring for a frail, bedridden, incontinent parent is true in some cases but is simply not the characteristic secnario of elder abuse. In fact, research has shown that in the majority of cases the abuser is the spouse (59%) rather than the children (24%) of the abused person. And rather than the abused being dependent on the abuser, in most cases the abused person describes the abuser as depending on him or her for finances, housing, transportation, cooking, cleaning, or other services (Pillemer & Finkelhor, 1988).

The fact that elder abuse occurs most often in a shared living situation, more frequently with a spouse than with children, suggests that retired people need better preparation for the difficulties of living together 24 hours of the day. Preretirement counseling of older workers should help them prepare for the stresses of constant companionship. In addition, shelters for abused elderly people should be provided.[2]

---

[2]Project Focus (Dept. P, FAS, Room 9438, 600 Hudson St., New York, NY 10013) provides information concerning services for older adults who may need protection from abuse.

## Exploitation of the Elderly

Assaults on elderly people walking or traveling by bus to the supermarket or bank, or robbery in their homes, are not the only ways in which they are fleeced. Most of the victims of bunco and confidence games are elderly (Younger, 1976). Con men, door-to-door salesmen, and medical quacks also exploit them by falsely promising renewed health, physical attractiveness, a comfortable estate in the Sunbelt, or a way to get rich quick by making a small monetary investment. Loneliness, pain, and fear, combined with a desire to improve their economic, physical, and social status, make many elderly Americans the gullible victims of smooth, fast-talking promoters or newspaper ad "come-ons."

Defrauding elderly people is a lucrative business in California, where they are the victims of 90% of the swindles. The amount of money that older people lose from con games in Los Angeles alone in a given year is estimated as greater than the total amount netted in bank robberies in that city ("Step-up in Fight. . .," 1977). And on the national level, the annual "take" from swindling operations is estimated to be several billion dollars.

Ranking high on the list of swindles are hearing aid and insurance ripoffs, medical quackery, and work-at-home rackets (Lipman, 1979). A common type of fraud is the retirement land deal in which an elderly person, slight unseen, purchases a distant property that sounds attractive. All too often the property is a swamp in Florida or a lizard patch in Arizona that is miles from the nearest roads and facilities. And sometimes it turns out that the "seller" of a piece of property does not even own it:

> Typical is the story of one old man who lost $3,400 in a housing swindle. The $3,400 was a 10 percent down-payment on a house that was soon to be built. It turned out that the developer—who netted $100,000 in the operation—had no intention of ever building. How could he? He didn't even own the land he was selling.
>
> "I couldn't believe it," the victim said sadly. "He was such a nice, pleasant fellow—well-dressed, with a fancy office and a Lincoln Continental. Why, I talked to him just four days before he disappeared, and he was as cheerful as could be." (Lipman, 1979, p. 23)

In another scheme, an older person is sold a water softener or new driveway surface for a very low price, only to find, after the contract is signed, that he or she is legally obligated to pay a much higher price. Elderly people who are unable to pay for the contracted product or service may lose their homes to the schemer. In addition, the social security, disability, and welfare payments of thousands of elderly Americans are expropriated by dishonest operators of boarding homes and other living and treatment facilities for the elderly.

Certain kinds of swindles are so common that they have been christened with special names. Two of these bunco schemes are the "pigeon drop" and the "bank examiner swindle":

*The Pigeon Drop.*   The victim is approached by one of the swindlers and engaged in a conversation on any sympathetic subject. Let's say the victim is an older man. When the swindler has gained his confidence, she mentions a large sum of money found by a second swindler who, at the moment, "happens" to pass by. The victim is led to believe that whoever lost the money probably came by it unlawfully. The swindlers discuss with the victim what to do with the money. One of the swindlers says that she works in the vicinity, and decides to contact her "employer" for advice. She returns in a few minutes and states that her boss has counted the money and verified the amount, and that he agrees that as the money undoubtedly was stolen or belonged to a gambler (or some such variation on a theme), they should keep and divide the money three ways but that each should show evidence of financial responsibility and good faith before collecting a share. The victim is then induced to draw his "good faith" money from his bank. After he has done this, either alone or in the company of one of the swindlers, the money is taken by the swindler to her "employer." Upon the swindler's return, the victim is given the name and address of the employer and told he is waiting with his share of the money. The victim leaves and, of course, cannot find the employer or sometimes even the address. When he returns to where he left the swindlers they, of course, are gone.

*The Bank Examiner Swindle.*   A phony bank or savings and loan "investigator" calls you or comes to your home. He is very serious, and may have brought along deposit slips from your bank and other official-looking papers. He tells you that the bank is checking up on a dishonest employee and explains how you can help. He says he wants to make a test to see what the suspected employee does when a customer draws money out of his account. He suggests that you go to your bank, draw out a specified amount of money, then let him use it for the test. Either he or a "bonded messenger" or some other official will pick up the money at some nearby point. You withdraw the money. Advised of the need for "absolute secrecy" and that the money must be in cash "in order to check serial numbers," you ignore the bank teller's concern that you are drawing out such a large sum of cash. You give the money to the "examiner," who hands you a receipt, thanks you for your "cooperation," and may tell you how he plans to use it to trap the suspected employee. Once he is gone, you'll never see him again, or your money. The bank, of course, has never heard of him.

Senior citizen centers and other organizations concerned with the needs and activities of the elderly distribute materials designed to help elderly Americans reduce their chances of being exploited by con men and bunco artists. In addition, these materials suggest ways of minimizing the financial loss and physical damage resulting from being victimized.

## PREVENTING AND COPING WITH CRIME

A generally accepted principle of crime prevention is that potential victims should be informed of the dangers, how to take precautions against them, and how to respond when danger becomes imminent. In recent years, workshops, seminars, and training programs in crime prevention and self-defense for people of all ages have blossomed throughout the United States and particularly in large cities. Although training in self-defense may not be very effective with older people, they can be educated to take precautions both inside and outside their places of residence. They can also be taught how to respond after being victimized.

## Crime Prevention Tips for Elderly Residents

When one lives in an apartment or house, the following precautions can help prevent crime against person and property in the place of residence (California Dept of Justice, 1979; Gross, 1979):

1. Have deadbolt locks rather than chain locks installed on outside doors, and always lock doors and windows when leaving.
2. Change door locks if keys are lost, which clearly identify the location of the residence or automobile ownership, or if your place of residence was previously occupied.
3. Separate house keys from car keys when leaving an automobile in a public garage or a service station.
4. Be wary of unsolicited telephone calls and "wrong numbers." Do not give information to strangers over the telephone; hang up and report nuisance callers.
5. Do not keep large amounts of money and valuables in predictable or accessible places; use a bank safety deposit box. Have social security and/or pension checks deposited directly to your bank account.
6. Leave a light and maybe a radio on when away for short periods of time. Discontinue mail, dairy, newspaper, and other deliveries when away for long periods of time. If you have a lawn, have it tended while you are away.
7. Notify the police immediately when you see suspicious-looking persons loitering about your place of residence, going from door to door and trying doors, sitting in parked cars or repeatedly cruising by. The description of the person(s); color, make, and license number of car; time and location should be noted and reported.
8. Set up a neighborhood security watch or mutual protection system. Neighbors can watch out for each other, go shopping together, and the like.
9. Consider keeping a pet—even a small dog—if the rules permit animals.
10. Ring your doorbell just before entering your place of residence to give burglars ample time to escape. This will prevent a confrontation. Never

rush into dark rooms without reasonable caution. Before closing and securing the door, take a quick look around to determine if there is an intruder hiding somewhere inside. Should this be the case, leave the door open for a hasty retreat.

In addition to the preceding precautions, apartment residents would do well to follow these recommendations:

1. Do not ride in an elevator with a person who looks suspicious.
2. List your name at the entrance and in the telephone directory as ''M. Smith'' rather than as ''Mary Smith.''
3. Never use the laundromat in your apartment complex by yourself; team up with a neighbor.

## Precautions When Walking or Traveling

The New York City Police Department and the New York Department of Aging (1978) recommend a number of precautions that elderly people are advised to consider when walking or traveling. First, *be alert:* Do not be afraid, but look around occasionally to see who is standing near you or walking toward you. Second, *be determined:* If you are on an unfamiliar or lonely street, quicken your pace and act as if you are going to meet someone who is waiting for you. Third, *walk carefully:* Walk where it is well lighted, staying away from darkened building entrances, doorways, alleyways, and high shrubbery. Fourth, *walk or travel together:* Travel and shop with companions whenever possible during the daytime and especially at night, remembering that there is greater safety in numbers. Fifth, *plan ahead:* Know where you are walking, know the general day and evening conditions of the streets you use, and know which stores are open late at night. If an emergency situation arises, walk to these stores rather than down your own quieter residential street.

When going out, elderly people should carry as little money as possible and even that in an inconspicuous place. It is best not to carry a purse, but if one is needed for shopping purposes it should not be left unattended at any time. And when returning home, an elderly shopper or traveler should not spend time at the door searching through a purse or pocket for the key; it should be in hand on arrival at the door.

## Rules for Self-Protection Against Fraud

The increasing susceptibility of the general public, and the elderly in particular, to fraud has prompted responsible public agencies to expand their efforts to inform potential victims how to protect themselves. One of the first rules for self-protection against fraud is never expect to get something for nothing. "Unbeliev-able bargains" are usually just that—unbelievable, especially when the seller or promoter is a stranger. When doing business, it is always advisable to know the person(s) with whom one is dealing and to refuse to discuss personal finances with strangers. An example of a potential pitfall of failing to investigate before giving cash to a stranger is the "bank examiner swindle" described previously in the chapter. The rule is: Investigate before investing. Never sign anything hast-ily, and don't give money to strangers.

One type of exploitation of the elderly that may be blatant embezzlement or may simply tread the fine line between the legal and illegal is tax fraud. An example of the former is the situation in which a bogus "IRS collector" tele-phones a newly bereaved widow or widower to arrange for an audit or payment of back taxes owed by the deceased. The would-be extortionist in this case can be stopped dead in his tracks by a widow(er) who is smart enough to examine his identification carefully and to call the local office of the Internal Revenue Service for verification. Potential victims of this racket should also know that before making personal contact with a taxpayer the Internal Revenue Services sends a written notice of intent to audit and that the IRS does business from 9 to 5 weekdays and not at odd hours.

The complexity of federal and state income tax laws also leads many elderly taxpayers to consult a tax preparer for assistance in preparing their returns. Whenever this is done, it is advisable to ask in advance how much the preparer's fee will be and whether it includes both federal and state forms. Forms contain-ing blank spaces that could be filled in later should never be signed, and copies of all prepared documents should be obtained by the taxpayer. Finally, because many tax preparers rent office space between January and April, it is wise to obtain a year-round address for a tax preparer (California Dept. of Justice, 1979).

## Crime Prevention Programs

Top priority is being given in many American cities to the prevention of crimes against the elderly and to assisting elderly victims of crime. Representative of these efforts are specially trained police units that perform surveillance and escort services for the elderly at times when the latter are most vulnerable—at night, while shopping, going to the bank, and the like. The officers in these special teams are also charged with the mission of dealing with older victims. Their duties consist of providing older people with information on crime preven-tion, referral sources, and emergency services. Instructional programs include such precautions as how to carry purses to avoid injury, how to trim shrubbery around places of residence to eliminate hiding places for robbers, how to make breaking and entering more difficult, and how to organize neighborhood sur-veillance systems. Police officers may also counsel and advise elderly on how to prepare for court appearances (Goldsmith & Goldsmith, 1976; Kalish, 1982).

The activities of a special police group in the Bronx, the Senior Citizens Robbery Unit, include informing the elderly about recent trends in crime, how to detect criminal behavior, and how to serve as witnesses in criminal cases. The officers in this unit are also trained in preventing crimes against the elderly as well as in helping older victims cope with the shock and loss resulting from a crime and in being of assistance in apprehending and prosecuting the criminal(s).

Another program that has been instituted in many cities is "Neighborhood Watch," which teaches people how to spot ongoing crimes and to protect themselves against burglaries and other felonies. Special monitoring equipment in high crime areas, special buses and drivers (especially on "check day"), "ride-along" escorts and security aids to walk the streets in high crime areas, and encouragement of direct depositing of checks are other features of crime-prevention programs in certain cities. Furthermore, not all the programs cost the taxpayers money. New York City's service of 1,000 teenage escorts for the elderly, for example, is completely voluntary. The use of teenagers for this purpose is particularly helpful, because it serves to persuade older people that those teenagers who victimize them are not representative of teenagers in general. Another volunteer program is RSVP, which has made progress in organizing the elderly themselves to fight crime in such cities as Baltimore, Las Vegas, and Okalhoma City.

Anticrime programs having the purpose of providing help to the elderly have also been established at the state level, for example, in California, Connecticut, Florida, Michigan, New York, and Pennsylvania. But much of the support for state and national efforts in combating crime against the elderly comes from the federal government. The Administration on Aging, for example, has sponsored projects designed to reduce the effects of crime on elderly victims and potential victims in several cities throughout the nation. Information and assistance is also provided by each state's Criminal Justice Planning Agency, which receives funds from the Law Enforcement Assistance Administration. Activities pertaining to security against residential theft are funded by the Department of Housing and Urban Development, the Federal Housing Administration and the Farmers Home Administration. In the private sector, the American Association of Retired Persons has prepared complete courses or workshops, including audiovisual materials, concerned with understanding, preventing, and in general, coping with crimes against the elderly.

## Elderly Victims

Victim compensation laws, according to which restitution to the victim of a crime is made by the offender or the state, are in existence in many states. Under these laws, victims of buglary and assault are entitled to a variety of compensations, for example, money and medical care. Such compensation is particularly needed by those who are so often victims—the elderly poor.

Other legal measures that have been advocated to cope with crime against the elderly are stronger laws against misrepresentation and fraud and more effective enforcement of those laws. Of course, stronger laws and stricter law enforcement alone will not protect the elderly from medical quackery and other forms of exploitation. Improvements in legitimate medical care and public education campaigns directed against fraud are also essential. Special orientation services for elderly victims/witnesses and mandatory penalties for crimes involving body injury of the elderly and handicapped have also been proposed (National Retired Teachers Association-American Association of Retired Persons, 1978).

## Reporting, Testifying, and Assisting

Although elderly people are no less likely than others to report crimes (Dussich & Eickman, 1976), they are often reluctant—due to embarrassment or fear of retaliation—to report a crime or serve as a witness in a criminal trial. Because it is impossible to apprehend and sentence criminals unless people are willing to report crimes and serve as witnesses, it is important for older people who have been victimized to contact the police. When an individual suspects that he or she has been swindled or otherwise exploited in some way by a businessperson or organization, a report should also be made to the Better Business Bureau.

Programs for training the elderly in the identification and reporting of suspicious activities and crimes have been established by a number of police departments. When a criminal is caught and brought to trial, efforts are also made to convince the elderly victim that his or her testimony will help curtail further illegal activities on the part of the culprit. Unfortunately, elderly people do not always make good witnesses in court trials. Because of transportation problems and physical difficulties in walking, they may fail to arrive at court on time. Poorer memory for details and overreaction to the stress of cross examination may also lead them to become more easily confused and flustered under the relentless probing of a defense attorney.

Despite the shortcomings of many elderly people in reporting and testifying, certain police departments have made effective use of elderly volunteers in crime prevention. Many of these older aides already possess skills in human relations and other aspects of police work, and some can be easily trained to provide services that release officers for many demanding tasks. Most older volunteers are viewed as conscientious, dependable, and ethical in their performance of the community relations tasks or other activities assigned to them by law enforcement officials (U.S. Dept. of Justice, 1979).

## LEGAL SERVICES AND ELDER ADVOCACY

Crime is a serious matter, but the elderly also need assistance with a host of other legal affairs. These problems include social security, old-age assistance, pension rights, Medicare, special housing, probate matters, workmen's compensation, consumer fraud, property tax exemptions and assessments, guardianships, involuntary commitment to an institution, nursing homes, and probate matters (U.S. Senate Special Committee on Aging, 1985). The need for legal counsel and advocacy is greater in the case of poor elderly people, many of whom do not know their rights and are unable to find their way through the bureaucratic maze of red tape involved in social security, SSI, Medicaid, and Medicare.

Efforts to develop legal services for the elderly in all states and territories of the United States have been fairly extensive. Under Title III of the Older Americans Act of 1965, each state and more than 550 city and county governmental agencies on aging are designated to serve as advocates for older persons, coordinate activities on their behalf, and provide information to them about services and opportunites (U.S. Dept. of Health, Education, & Welfare, 1977). The Legal Services Corporation was established during the Nixon administration as an independent, nonprofit corporation insulated from political pressures. It has never been properly funded, due in large measure to budget reductions during the Reagan administration accompanied by a call for more pro bono work by attorneys and private participation in the delivery of services. A federally funded National Senior Citizens Law School has also been established as a legal services clearinghouse. Legal service centers for the aged have also been established at many American universities (e.g., Syracuse University's Legal Center on Aging) to help older people cope with the bureaucracies in both the governmental and private sectors.

An example of what can be done at the local level is Elderline, a legal referral service in Los Angeles. Established to help people aged 60 and over find legal assistance, Elderline tries to connect senior citizens' legal needs and their abilities to pay with the right lawyers. The kinds of problems with which a lawyer can help a senior citizen range from the routine (faulty automobile repairs, bothersome door-to-door salesmen, writing a simple will) to the catastrophic (missing Social Security benefits, evictions or home foreclosures, etc.).

### Attorneys as Elder Advocates

The various area agencies on aging are required by law to cooperate with local bar associations in arranging legal services for the elderly. The American Bar Association has responded by encouraging lawyers to launch outreach programs. Workers in outreach programs in states such as Florida, Georgia, New Hampshire, and Ohio identify elderly people who have legal problems requiring the assistance of an attorney. Participating attorneys then offer low-cost legal services to these persons. Alternatively, lawyers may go to senior homes or other centers on certain days to consult with elderly people who need legal assistance. The initial consultation for clients 60 years and older is usually free, and subsequent services are paid for at a reduced rate.[3]

Basically, the lawyers in these programs, and all lawyers with elderly clients, provide three types of services to older people: (a) information and referral, (b) routine litigation, and (c) law reform activity. In the first type of service, lawyers provide older people with informational and educational materials concerning their rights and benefits under the Social Security and Older Americans acts. In routine litigation, lawyers contest on behalf of older clients or defend them against evictions, involuntary commitments, and the like; they also prepare suits for clients to establish their eligibility for benefits or to protect them against repossessions and unfair contracts (Nathanson, 1977).

Routine litigation may also be referred to as *case advocacy,* in that the attorney functions in the interest of an older client so that the kind of treatment to which the client is legally entitled can be obtained. The concept of *elder advocacy,* however, is broader than that of case advocacy. The term *advocate,* which as traditionally referred to a person who pleads another's case before a tribunal or judicial court, has been broadened in this context to mean concern for and action on behalf of a particular group of people—namely, the elderly. Elder advocacy includes the third type of service provided by lawyers—law reform activity, or *monitoring.* Attorneys concerned with the monitoring function keep watch to make certain that laws and programs pertaining to the elderly are carried out as intended by the legislators who drafted them. In cases where a law is being incorrectly applied, a *class action suit* on behalf of an entire group of elderly people may be necessary. Such a procedure, for example, might be used to improve conditions in nursing homes or in the treatment of elderly customers by utility companies.

Two other types of advocacy that are important in ensuring the legal rights of the elderly are legislative advocacy and administrative advocacy. Efforts to make certain that the Older Americans Act, the Social Security Act, and other laws pertaining to the elderly are approrpiate to their needs is known as *legislative advocacy.* Legislative advocates for the elderly apply pressure, usually by lobbying, on state and federal lawmakers to draft and vote for legislation that better meets the needs of older people. Finally, the notion of *administrative advocacy* is a recognition of the fact that the administrators of governmental agencies are often in positions to take action in support of older Americans (Suran & Rizzo, 1979).

---

[3]Further information on these programs may be obtained from: Commission on Legal Problems of the Elderly, American Bar Association, 1800 M Street, N.W., Washington, DC 30036.

## Commitment

The "routine litigation" issue of commitment versus release has been hotly debated in recent years and has led to laws requiring that more attention be given to the rights of elderly and younger patients. Because these laws state that a patient must be either treated or released, mental hospitals and other long-term care institutions can no longer be used as "dumping grounds" for older people who are unwanted by their families. In every case, however, an attempt must be made to balance the rights of the patient against the welfare of the larger society. Although some people argue that the practice of involuntary commitment should be completely abolished, others maintain that society has a right to protect itself against potentially dangerous mental patients, both young and old. Most experts now agree that, with sufficient legal safeguards of a patient's civil rights and periodic reviews of his or her therapeutic progress, families need not feel guilty about having an older relative admitted to an institution having good treatment facilities.

## Competency, Capacity, and Conservatorship

The question of *competency* to handle one's life and property arises when a plaintiff makes a legal declaration that, because of physical or mental infirmity, an elderly relative is unable to take care of his or her property and other affairs, and formally requests that the court appoint someone to handle these matters. Obviously, legal action of this sort should be considered only after other possibilities have been examined carefully. Being forced to become entirely dependent on someone else—even a relative—may be the last straw for an elderly person who is barely managing to hold on. For this reason, Butler (1975) suggested that a legal concept of "partial competency" is needed. Such a concept would preserve the civil rights of a person and yet would protect the person against exploitation and victimization when his or her judgment becomes poor.

*Testamentary capacity* is, in a sense, a kind of partial competency, in that it refers specifically to competency to make a will. Testamentary capacity is possessed by a person who knows (a) the nature of his or her property, (b) that he or she is making a will, and (c) who his or her natural beneficiaries are. Testamentary capacity is not the same as competency to handle one's life and property. A person's competency, if questioned by relatives or heirs, must be determined by a separate legal hearing from that required to establish testamentary capacity.

When an elderly person is judged to be incompetent, his or her estate is turned over to a court-appointed guardian to be managed—a process known as *legal conservatorship*. In effect, the person forfeits his or her legal and personal autonomy, and the guardian makes decisions regarding the older individual's property. The transfer of authority in legal conservatorship, and the circumstances under which it occurs, are matters of some dispute in the legal community.

## Wills[4]

Drawing up wills is a big business in the United States: At any one time an estimated 70% of the elderly population and 25% of all adults in this country have made wills (American Bar Foundation, 1976). Although most states have a common procedure for implementing a written, attested will, there is actually no standard legal form on which a will must be prepared and no universally required procedure for making a will. In fact, certain states accept an unwitnessed will prepared in the testator's own handwriting (holographic will) or even an oral will (nuncupative will). A nuncupative will, however, is acceptable only under the most limited circumstances and can only be used by a person in fear of imminent death from an injury sustained on the same day.

Included in a will are the name, address, and age of the person making the will (the testator), followed by a statement of his or her capacity to make a will (testamentary capacity) and voluntariness of the action. Next comes a listing of the disposition of specific items in the estate and the names of the heirs (distributees, legatees). The name of the appointed executor of the will or estate should also be given, followed by the dated signature of the testator and the signatures and addresses of two witnesses. The will may be altered, added to by means of a codicil, or destroyed by the testator at any time.

Laws concerning inheritances and wills vary from country to country and, within the United States, state to state. Most states, however, require that either a will be filed or the nonexistence of a will be disclosed to a probate court within 10 days of a death. Certain procedural matters pertaining to the legality of a will are usually resolved fairly easily. If a person names an executor of the estate, that executor serves under the jurisdiction of a local probate court. But if no executor is named by the testator or if a person dies *interstate* (no valid will having been located) the court appoints an administrator to handle the distribution of the decedent's property. Probate courts also become involved in disputations about whether a will is valid or which of several wills takes precedence (usually the most recent).

One of the most common disputes regarding bequests and wills has to do with the question of legal heirs or beneficiaries. British law historically subscribed to the rule of *primogeniture,* in which the male was preferred over the female line and the eldest over the youngest in the distribution of real property. A decedent's personal property, however, went to the next of kin. Furthermore, illegitimate

---

[4]The material in this section was critically reviewed by Professor Charles I. Nelson, J.D., of the O'Dell McConnell School of Law (Pepperdine University).

children had no rights of inheritance under English common law (Arenson, 1982). Such distinctions have largely disappeared in modern inheritance laws, and, depending on the particular state, anyone—relative or not—can be a legal heir to an estate.

## SUMMARY

The problem of crime in the United States is a topic of great concern to Americans, but only a small percentage of criminals are elderly people. Because a fraction of the crimes committed lead to arrests, the number of arrests is not a precise indicator of criminal activity. For whatever reasons, only about 1% of those arrested in the United States each year are 65 years old or over. The crime for which elderly men were arrested most frequently in 1986 was driving under the influence, whereas elderly women were most frequently arrested for larceny–theft; the next most common cause of arrest in that year were drunkenness (men) and driving under the influence (women). In general, there has been a substantial increase in the number of arrests of older Americans for larceny–theft during the past two decades.

Elderly people are apparently not victimized any more frequently than other age groups, but the economic, physical, and psychological effects of crime tend to be more serious in the case of older victims. A variety of crimes are committed against the elderly—theft, mugging, and fraud in particular, but more serious crimes of violence such as murder and rape are less common. Many of the victimizers of older people, and especially older poor people living in high crime areas of large cities, are teenagers. In any event, the elderly are swindled and abused by people of all ages—including their own age group and their own relatives. Guillible, lonely, and perhaps somewhat greedy older people are easy targets for exploiters and con artists. Among the most common types of fraud are those involving health cures and real estate. Confidence games such as the pigeon drop and the bank examiner swindle are also widely practiced.

An estimated 1 million Americans are victims of elder abuse, which may be either physical or psychological ("beating with words"). Elderly people are more likely to be abused by their spouses than their children, and the abuser is more likely to be dependent on the abused person than vice versa.

The key to crime control is crime prevention, and there are many precautions that elderly residents, walkers, and travelers can take to prevent crime against themselves and their property. Education in crime prevention also involves learning the rules for self-protection against fraud and exploitation. Law enforcement agencies in many large cities have special programs designed to inform the elderly about crime and how to protect themselves against it. Victim compensation laws, under which restitution is made to crime victims by the state or offender, exist in many states.

Elderly people are no less likely than others to report crimes, but because of fear of embarrassment or retaliation they are often reluctant to testify in court. Many elderly people, however, cooperate fully with law enforcement officials in reporting and testifying with regard to crimes committed against themselves or others and also by acting as volunteer workers in criminal justice activities.

Older people require legal assistance for a variety of reasons, but many do not know their civil rights and the appropriate legal procedures and are too poor to afford the services of an attorney. As a result of the Older Americans Act, all states and territories now have agencies that provide information and coordinate legal activities on the part of the elderly. Through local outreach programs, older people who need legal help are identified and attorneys are able to provide consultation and other legal services to them on a pro bono or discount basis. Attorneys also serve as elder advocates in several ways: by providing information and referrals, routine litigation services (case advocacy), and law reform activity (monitoring and class action suits). Two other types of elder advocacy are legislative advocacy—applying pressure on legislators to draft and vote for certain measures, and administrative advocacy—action on behalf of a group (the elderly) by agency administrators.

The questions of commitment, competency, conservatorship, and testamentary capacity are serious matters to older individuals who may experience difficulties in handling their own affairs. Commitment refers to legal admission (voluntary or involuntary) to an institution for purposes of treatment for a mental disorder. Diagnosis of a mental disorder and commitment do not automatically imply incompetency, which must be determined at a separate legal hearing. The purpose of a competency hearing is to determine whether an individual is able to handle his or her life and property. Legal conservatorship consists of turning over to a guardian for management the estate of a person who has been found incompetent. The question of testamentary capacity is more narrow than that of competency. The determination of testamentary capacity involves a legal hearing to decide whether a person knows what property he or she has, who the natural beneficiaries are, and that he or she is making a will. Procedures for preparing wills are discussed in some detail.

## SUGGESTED READINGS

Chaneles, S. (1987). Growing old behind bars. *Psychology Today, 21*(10), 47–51.

Cook, F. L., Skogan, W. G., Cook, T. D., & Antunes, G. E. (1978). Criminal victimization of the elderly. *The Gerontologist, 18,* 338–349.

Fulmer, T., & Wetle, T. (1986). Elder abuse screening and intervention. *Nurse Practitioner, 11*(5), 33–38.

Hickey, T., & Douglass, R. S. (1981). Nelgect and abuse of older family members: Professionals' perspectives and case experiences. *The Gerontologist, 21,* 171–176.

Malinchak, A. A. (1978). *Crime and gerontology: The venerable (vulnerable) Americans.* Englewood Cliffs, NJ: Prentice-Hall.

Pedrick-Cornell, C., & Gelles, R. J. (1982). Elderly abuse: The status of current knowledge. *Family Relations, 31,* 457–465.

Quinn, M. J., & Tomila, S. K. (1986). *Elder abuse and neglect: Causes, diagnosis, and intervention strategies.* New York: Springer.

Robinson, D. (1985, Feb. 17). How can we protect our elderly? *Parade Magazine,* pp. 4–7.

Shichor, D. (1985). Male–female differences in elderly arrests: An exploratory analysis. *Justice Quarterly, 2,* 399–414.

# 12

## Dying and Bereavement

The realization that humans are mortal and the fear of death begin early in life, but it is often difficult to contemplate and to accept the inevitability of one's own demise. People in modern societies, which keep the dying and deceased from public view, usually go through life without thinking much about death. Unless they become chronically ill or are seriously injured, young people in particular give little thought to death. Death is perceived impersonally as something that happens to other people, or at the very least is far off in the future and not worth worrying about. Consequently, they are surprised when someone whom they know—particularly someone in their own age group—dies.

As one grows older, the physical changes accompanying aging, coupled with the aging and dying of family members and friends, force a person to face the event in life that is looked forward to the least. Erikson (1968) maintained that the realization that time is short and death is imminent precipitates the integrity versus despair crisis of the terminal period of life. Attempting to cope with death, however, is not something that waits for the final developmental period of life. Conquest of the fear of death usually begins in young adulthood or middle age, and by the time one reaches old age the process of dying is feared more than death itself.

Whether or not they fear it, preparations for death must be made, including practical matters such as getting insurance, dealing with medical care needs, and making arrangements for a funeral and other matters following death. Kalish and Reynolds (1981) found, however, that although 66% of their sample of people over 60 had taken out life insurance, 44% had paid for a burial plot and made arrangements for someone to handle their affairs after death, only 33% had made out a will and 24% had made funeral arrangements.

TABLE 12.1
Death Rates for 10 Leading Causes of Death
Among Older Americans by Age: 1986*

| | Age | | |
| Cause of Death | 65–74 | 75–84 | 85+ |
| --- | --- | --- | --- |
| Diseases of the heart | 1,020 | 2,556 | 7,122 |
| Malignant neoplasms | 846 | 1,283 | 1,632 |
| Cerebrovascular diseases | 153 | 563 | 1,734 |
| Chronic obstructive pulmonary diseases | 146 | 306 | 363 |
| Pneumonia and influenza | 57 | 235 | 1,029 |
| Diabetes mellitus | 60 | 122 | 207 |
| Accidents and adverse effects | 50 | 103 | 259 |
| Atherosclerosis | 16 | 76 | 426 |
| Nephritis, nephrotic syndrome, nephrosis | 28 | 80 | 231 |
| Septicemia | 25 | 66 | 187 |
| All causes | 2,764 | 6,266 | 15,406 |

Source: National Center for Health Statistics (1988b).
*Based on a 10% sample of deaths. Rates per 100,000 population in specified group.

## STATISTICAL AND BIOLOGICAL ASPECTS OF DEATH

The *death rate,* defined as the number of deaths per 100,000 resident population in a specified group, is at its lowest point from 5–14 years and increases gradually with age after then. Except for the period of infancy, the death rate remains below 1,000 until age 60. The high death rate among the elderly is evidenced by the fact that over 70% of the more than 2 million Americans who died in 1987 were 65 or older (National Center for Health Statistics, 1988b). As shown in Table 12.1, the death rate is particularly high after age 85. Nearly half the deaths after that age are caused by diseases of the heart, followed by cerebrovascular diseases and cancer. For all three age groups shown in Table 12.2, the death rate

TABLE 12.2
Death Rates for Older Americans, by Age, Sex, and Race: 1986*

| Age Range | Male | | | Female | | | Both Sexes | | |
| | White | Black | All Races | White | Black | All Races | White | Black | All Races |
| --- | --- | --- | --- | --- | --- | --- | --- | --- | --- |
| 65–74 | 3,586 | 4,592 | 3,636 | 2,012 | 2,879 | 2,070 | 2,711 | 3,609 | 2,764 |
| 75–84 | 8,200 | 9,239 | 8,206 | 5,076 | 5,980 | 5,102 | 6,244 | 7,210 | 6,266 |
| 85+ | 18,456 | 14,957 | 18,037 | 14,642 | 11,921 | 14,377 | 15,699 | 12,869 | 15,406 |

Source: National Center for Health Statistics (1988b).
*Rates are deaths per 100,000 resident population in specified group.

is higher for men than for women. For the first two age groups (65–74 and 75–84), the rate is higher for Blacks than for Whites, but the reverse is true for the 85+ age group.

## Medical and Legal Definitions of Death

The traditional definition of death as the cessation of heartbeat has been a topic of controversy and debate in medical and legal circles for many years. The usually accepted medical definition of death is cessation of all electrical activity of the brain for a certain period of time. When a person is "dying," the cells of the higher brain centers, which are very susceptible to oxygen deprivation, die first—within 5 to 10 minutes after their oxygen supply is cut off. Next, cells in the lower brain centers die, including those in the medulla oblongata, which regulates respiration, heartbeat, and other vital reflexes. Thus, "brain death," indicated by a flat or no-response pattern on the electroencephalogram (EEG), leads to death in other body organs.

According to the laws of most states, a person is alive as long as a heartbeat and respiratory movements, no matter how they are maintained, can be detected. In states that have not passed legislation defining death, the definition is based on hospital policy. But because different hospitals may follow different definitions, it is conceivable that a resident of one of these states could be pronounced dead in one hospital and not in another.

Until the past two decades or so, failure to detect a heartbeat and cessation of breathing were the definitive signs of death in most hospitals throughout the United States. Since then, the criteria recommended by an Ad Hoc Committee of the Harvard Medical School (1968) have been widely considered and adopted in some states. These criteria of death include: (a) unreceptivity and unresponsiveness to external stimuli; (b) absence of movements, especially spontaneous breathing; and (c) absence of reflexes. A flat EEG pattern is also used as confirmatory evidence of death defined by these three criteria, but the criteria are not trustworthy in cases of severe hypothermia or barbiturate overdose. The Harvard criteria are met in cases of irreversible coma, and the Ad Hoc Committee did indeed recommend that irreversible coma patients be certified as medically dead.

Some states have adopted the concept of brain death—flat EEG for at least 10 minutes—as the legal definition of death and a condition for the removal of donated organs for transplant purposes. Most states, however, still use the traditional definition of death as the cessation of all vital functions. In an attempt to provide some legal uniformity throughout the 50 states, the President's Commission for the Study of the Ethical Problems in Medical and Biomedical and Behavioral Research recommend in 1981 that the states adopt the following legal definition of death: A person is to be considered dead if there is an irreversible cessation of circulation and breathing or irreversible cessation of all functions of the entire brain, including the brain stem (Rossiter, 1981). Meanwhile, the problem of how to determine exactly when a patient has died and when all heroic measures should be suspended has not been solved. The central recommendation of a 1988 report published by the Hastings Center (''Guidelines on the Termination of Life-Sustaining Treatment and the Care of the Dying'') recommended that the patient, or the patient's representative, has the right to refuse or to halt life-sustaining treatment (feeding tubes, blood transfusions, antibiotics, dialysis machines, ventilators, etc.) that simply postpones death. Even so, the individual physician continues to bear a heavy responsibility for the final decision. To protect themselves, most physicians are advised to consult with the family of the dying person and to obtain legal counsel before deciding to suspend treatment.

## Other Biological Aspects of Death

The death of a human being does not occur in a single instant. Certain body structures, such as the thymus gland, deteriorate before a person is fully mature. In fact, body cells are constantly dying and being replaced by new cells even before an individual is born. The building up and breaking down of body cells and structures (anabolism and catabolism) are complementary metabolic processes. As a person ages, the rate of breakdown begins to exceed the rate of building up, a point reached earlier in some body structures than others.

Cessation of a heartbeat is a natural consequence of brain death, but the brain is not always dead when the heart stops. The heart can stop, and its pumping action can be restored before the vital centers of the brain are affected. Restoration of the heartbeat by use of electric shock (''countershock'') is a common procedure in hospitals today. Unfortunately, if the heart has stopped for too long, or for other reasons the blood supply to the brain is interrupted, the higher brain cells will be deprived of oxygen and their functioning affected. In this case, the sensorimotor and mental skills of the person may undergo some deterioration.

The cells of certain glands and muscles die only after the medulla has stopped functioning, but skin and bone cells can live for several hours longer. The hair is still growing some hours after death, and the growth of fingernails has often been observed even after interment. The liver continues to convert glycogen to glucose, and other intestinal tissues also keep functioning for some time after a person is pronounced clinically dead. In fact, such tissue has been kept ''alive'' for years when placed in a special physiological solution.

In a dying person, loss of sensorimotor functions begins in the legs and spreads gradually to the arms. The sense of pressure remains, but pain and other cutaneous sensations diminish. The decline in peripheral circulation frequently produces a ''drenching sweat,'' followed by a cooling of the body surface. Characteristically, a dying person, who may be conscious until the very end, turns his or her head toward the light (Gray, 1984). *Rigor mortis,* a general contraction of the muscles, sets in about 2 hours after death and continues for approximately 30 hours.

There are, of course, many cases in which a patient has been pronounced clinically dead but "comes back to life" before he or she is buried. Furthermore, even when a deceased person is not immediately restored to life there are those who believe that a resurrection of the body at some future time is possible. For example, one occasionally reads a newspaper story about a dead person whose body was deep-frozen in liquid nitrogen at the time of death and is being kept in a special aluminum capsule. It is an article of faith of the Cryonics Society that a body preserved in this manner can be thawed and restored to life at some time in the future when a cure for the disease from which the person died has been discovered. Whether those few bodies that are being preserved in this way can be restored to life with any semblance of the former self is debatable, but most authorities are dubious.

## FEAR OF DEATH AND HOPE OF AFTERLIFE

A young man who has had a serious accident or a young pregnant woman may experience some anxiety about dying, but the fear of death does not intrude upon the consciousness of most people until middle age. Cross-sectional surveys of adults are fairly consistent in showing that fear of death is more common and more intense during middle age than in later life (Bengston, Cuellar, & Ragan, 1977; Kalish & Reynolds, 1976). This fear, which has been identified as part of the "midlife crisis," is precipitated by the individual's awareness of his or her declining health and appearance, coupled with unfulfilled dreams and unattained goals. An inventory of one's assets and liabilities, combined with a reasonable assessment of the time remaining in life, often serves as a stimulus to anxiety, sometimes hastening the very event that the individual dreads the most. Fear of death can be particularly intense in middle-aged people who are living enjoyable, personally meaningful lives.

Compared with the middle aged, older adults are more likely to see themselves as having had their day and view death in old age as only fair. Realizing that time is shorter than in earlier years, older people do not plan as far ahead and are more inner directed or private in their activities (Kalish, 1976). The deaths of friends and relatives, a lack of satisfying social roles, health and financial problems, and increased dependency on others all contribute to the feeling of having outlived one's usefulness and becoming resigned to one's fate. Whatever the reasons may be, most older adults do not express much fear of death (Wass, 1979). This does not mean that the elderly never fear their own demise. Butler and Lewis (1982) reported, for example, that although 55% of the elderly people whom they surveyed had realistically resolved their fears of death, 30% were overtly afraid of it, and the remaining 15% used defensive denial to cope with their fears of dying.

Chronological age is not the only factor related to fears and attitudes toward death. For example, such fears may be quite strong in elderly people who are in poor physical or mental health, or who have a disabled spouse, dependent children, or important goals that they still expect to attain.

Attitudes toward death in later life are related to emotional adjustment, socioeconomic status, and achievement. People who are emotionally and financially stable and have attained most of their life goals are typically more accepting of death. But those who have many unresolved frustrations or are extremely self-centered are more likely to view death from a negative perspective or as an escape from an unrewarding life (Hinton, 1972). Attitudes toward death also vary with sex. Back (1971) found, for example, that in comparison with older men, elderly women tended to be more accepting and benevolent in their attitudes toward death, likening it to a compassionate mother or an understanding doctor rather than an opponent. Men, on the other hand, are more likely to see death as an evil antagonist, a grinning butcher or hangman with bloody hands, who must be combated.

The event of death can obviously be seen in a number of ways—as the final insult to humanity, as the last developmental task, or as a rite of passage to another plane of existence. However it may be perceived, the fact remains that death comes to all and must be dealt with by everyone. Whether acceptance of the fact that one is going to die produces motivational paralysis on the one hand or a beneficial or destructive change in personality on the other depends on the individual's past experiences and present social supports. The effects of increased awareness of death also depend on the person's philosophy of life, a philosophy that is shaped by the multiplicity of social interactions taking place from childhood to senescence. A part of that continually developing philosophy is concerned with a sense of purpose in life, a purpose that serves as a mainstay in coping with the problems and emotions precipitated by the inevitability of life's ending.

## Meaning and Religion

Fear of death has both positive and negative aspects. On the one hand, it may result in despair and a sense of meaninglessness. On the other hand, the realization that life will end may inspire one into making his or her life more meaningful. The philosopher Jean-Paul Sartre (1957) maintained that the awareness of our own mortality creates a condition of anxiety and concern over whether we are living meaningful lives. As a result, he concluded that the true meaning of one's life comes from an awareness that it will end. By facing the inevitability of a personal ending, the individual is spurred into action to live a life that will have some significance. Fearing not death so much as an absurd, valueless life, Sartre and other existential philosophers have viewed death as losing much of its terror for the person whose life has been filled with meaning. The very fact of death energizes the drive toward a meaningful existence, the attainment of which overcomes the fear of death and nothingness.

## Religious Beliefs

Belief in the meaningfulness of existence and an acceptance of death can also come through religious beliefs. The great majority of humankind, since time immemorial, has found a purpose in life through religious beliefs. A strong belief in conventional religious principles is not essential to a calm acceptance of death, however, and certainly does not guarantee fearlessness in the face of it. Erikson (1976) maintained, for example, that an identification with the human race is the best defense against death anxiety.

Simply professing a belief in God and an afterlife and attending church regularly are not likely to protect people from fears of death and dying. Nevertheless, studies have shown that strong religious and philosophical beliefs are frequently a comfort to dying people (Becker, 1973; Mathieu, 1972). Those who believe in some form of God and have truly integrated religion into their lives are usually better able to face death without overwhelming fears than are those who are uncertain about religion (Kübler-Ross, 1974; Nelson & Nelson, 1973). Also of interest is the fact that affirmed atheists usually profess few fears of death. Greater apprehension concerning death is found among sporadically religious people whose beliefs are uncertain or inconsistent.

Characteristics of religions that give comfort to dying people vary widely with time and culture, but all religions try to provide a purpose and meaning for human existence. Although most religious people believe in some form of personal afterlife, such a belief is not essential to facing death calmly (Kalish & Reynolds, 1976). In fact, elderly people are usually more concerned about death per se and their own demise than they are with life after death (Hurlock, 1980). It is understandable, however, that feelings of personal transcendence and belief in an afterlife often provide comfort and reassurance to dying people. Such beliefs may be interpreted as wishful thinking or defensive denial, and those mechanisms do operate in many cases. The threat of total extinction and nothingness is a fearsome prospect, and it is natural for the human ego to defend itself against such a threat.

Conceptions of immortality and afterlife, heaven, and hell form a part of most religions. Christians are frequently unclear about the nature of the life to come, but a large percentage believe that something of human personality survives the death of the body. Hindus, Buddhists, and members of certain other religious groups believe in reincarnation or metempsychosis, in which the soul of the deceased passes into another living body. The particular form in which the deceased is reincarnated is determined by his or her *karma,* or actions in previous lives (Long, 1975).

The United States prides itself on being a religious nation, and belief in a hereafter is held quite strongly by many Americans. In a Gallup poll conducted a few years ago, 67% of those surveyed stated that they believed in life after death. However, the percentage professing such a belief varied significantly with geographical region, size of community, ethnicity, religion, and other demographic variables. Greater percentages of southerners and midwesterners than easterners and westerners, and a greater percentage of small-city dwellers than large-city dwellers, reported believing in an afterlife. Greater percentages of Whites than Blacks and of Protestants than Catholics also stated that they believed in an afterlife. Although a majority of those polled said that they believed in an afterlife, only 20% felt that life after death would ever be scientifically proven (Gallup & Proctor, 1982).

Most elderly Americans believe in an afterlife, but as they approach the end of their lives few people emphasize the religious side of death—heaven, hell, and the last judgment. Furthermore, it is the quality of the affiliation that is related to a person's attitude toward dying (Carey, 1976), rather than merely the affiliation with some religious organization. Experiences with the deaths of others and strong interpersonal ties to family and friends, which help provide the strength to face the inevitable and a sense of the continuity of life, are also associated with more accepting attitudes toward death.

## Near-Death or Out-of-Body Experiences

Despite the conclusion of the philosopher Blaise Pascal that it is wise to bet on the existence of an afterlife, little if any direct information on the outcome of the wager has been forthcoming. A wealth of anecdotal data on ''out-of-body'' experiences has been obtained, however, from people who almost died and were actually pronounced medically dead in some instances. Particularly influential in stimulating both popular and scientific interest in such transcendent experiences has been the work of Raymond Moody (1975). Moody's research methodology, which has also been employed by Sabom (1983) and others, consists of interviewing people who have been resuscitated after having been pronounced clinically dead. Although the 150 or so individuals whom Moody interviewed had difficulty describing their experiences, there were some common features. Most people referred to a feeling of peace and quiet, a sense of floating out of and above one's own body, traveling through a dark tunnel and toward a distant white light. On approaching the light, the person had a powerful sense of love and an impression of being interrogated about his or her life and degree of satisfaction with it. At this time the person experienced a colorful, panoramic review of his or her life, which was totally accepted by the "being of light." Many of those who reported having these experiences confessed that they were reluctant to return to their physical bodies, but the need to complete unfinished earthly tasks made them do so.

According to Sabom (1983), the experiences of Moody's patients are not rare; millions of people, of all ages, cultures, religions, and educational levels, have had them. The question is not whether the experiences are genuine, but rather how to explain and interpret them. Siegel (1980) admitted that Moody's findings can be interpreted as demonstrating that people survive death, but he said there is a more parsimonious explanation. Noting the similarity of these afterlife visions to hallucinations produced by drugs related to PCP ("angel dust"), Siegel preferred to regard them as dissociated hallucinations caused by normal brain activity. Consistent with Siegel's (1980) viewpoint, Thomas (1975) suggested that these experiences are caused by the release of opiates produced by the body at the time of death. In describing what he labeled "the Lazarus syndrome," Simpson (1979) interpreted near-death or out-of-body experiences as delirious states, romantic wish fulfillment, or psychological attempts to survive death.

Whatever their ultimate explanation may be, the occurrence of near-death or out-of-body phenomena has served as a consolation to many people—both those who have had such experiences and those who are mourning a loved one or who are anticipating death. These experiences also demonstrate that the moment of death need not be feared; the pain goes away, and the feeling can be calm and peaceful. Unfortunately, it is not always so. Although reported visits to the "other side" are generally pleasant, they have in some cases been terrifying. One physician (Rawlings, 1978) found that half the 30 resusitated patients whom he interviewed had unpleasant visions of hell when they were near death.

## TREATMENT OF THE DYING

Unlike preindustrial societies, in which personal contacts with the dying and dead were fairly commonplace, modern society keeps the terminally ill and deceased away from public view. Approximately 70% of all deaths today take place outside the home—in large, anonymous intensive care units or wards of hospitals, or in long-term care institutions ("A Better Way . . . ," 1978). Yet most dying people would rather spend their last days at home, in familiar surroundings and among those whom they know and love (Garrett, 1978). Dying at home, however, may impose a heavy burden on the family. Although most family members would rather have their loved ones die at home (Cartwright, Hockey, & Anderson, 1973), attending to a dying relative can place severe physical and emotional strains on the family. Furthermore, private homes are usually poorly equipped to handle medical emergencies and other special procedures that may be required to sustain life and to make dying patients comfortable.

## A Conspiracy of Silence

Although they may accept death in the abstract, the reactions of most people to the actual facts of dying and death are sufficiently negative to make them uncomfortable and inadequate in dealing with the concerns of terminally ill patients. Even medical personnel, who are trained primarily to save lives and hence to consider death as an enemy, are often uncomfortable with the topic and do not like being present when their patients die. The physically oriented training of physicians typically fails to prepare them to handle the emotional needs of patients. Carrying out one's medical duties in a technically proficient but fairly impersonal manner is viewed as safer than becoming emotionally involved with patients and trying to answer their questions about death. But many dying patients, as well as their families and friends, benefit from discussing their feelings with doctors and nurses.

Sometimes it seems as if family, friends, and medical personnel are participants in a *conspiracy of silence,* a conspiracy that the patient may also tacitly understand and agree to. Unfortunately, the consequence is that the patient is left to face death psychologically alone or with impersonal nursing care—a frightened, machine-like object attached to life-sustaining equipment, rather than a valuable human being. This conspiracy of silence was described by the Russian writer Leo Tolstoy in "The Death of Ivan Ilych" (Tolstoy, 1960):

> What tormented Ivan Ilych most was the deception, the lie, which for some reason they all accepted, that he was not dying but was simply ill, and that he only need keep quiet and undergo a treatment and then something very good would result. He, however, knew that do what they would nothing would come of it, only still more agonizing suffering and death. This deception tortured him—their not wishing to admit what they all knew and what he knew, but wanting to lie to him concerning his terrible condition, and wishing and forcing him to participate in that lie. Those lies—lies enacted over him on the eve of his death and destined to degrade this awful, solemn act to the level of their visitings, their curtains, their sturgeon for dinner—were a terrible agony for Ivan Ilych. And strangely enough, many times when they were going through their antics over him he had been within a hair-breadth of calling out to them: "Stop lying! You know and I know that I am dying. Then at least stop lying about it!" But he had never had the spirit to do it. The awful, terrible act of his dying was, he could see, reduced by those about him to the level of a casual, unpleasant, and almost indecorous incident (as if someone entered a drawing-room diffusing an unpleasant odor) and this was done by the very decorum which he had served all his life long. He saw that no one felt for him, because no one even wished to grasp his position. Only Gerasim recognized it and pitied him. And so Ivan Ilych felt at ease only with him. (pp. 137–138)

## Communicating and Counseling with the Dying

It is unfortunate that relatives and medical professionals find it difficult to discuss death, because most dying persons are eager to share thoughts with others. Medical judgment is obviously important in determining whether or not to tell a patient that death is imminent, because not all patients can or want to deal with this information. The personality, emotional state, and stress tolerance of the patient must be taken into account in deciding how much to reveal (DeSpelder & Strickland, 1983; Veatch & Tai, 1980).

Even when they are not told directly by a family member, friend, doctor, or nurse, a large majority of terminally ill patients realize that they are going to die in the very near future. They sense it in the changes in their bodies and the attitudes of other people. Consequently, honesty on the part of others frequently comes as no surprise but simply confirms what the patient suspected all along (Kübler-Ross, 1969). Being told, whether outright or by intimation, however, opens the door for the ventilation of feelings and constructive discussion. Thus, a consequence of openness toward death is meaningful communication with others. It also gives patients a chance to take care of financial matters, items pertaining to bequests, and other business or family affairs.

Communication and companionship go hand in hand. Dying people need to know, but that knowledge can be dealt with more effectively in the presence of loving care and companionship. Fears can be expressed, confessions made, and emotional support and forgiveness found only with someone who cares. The need of a dying person for a warm, supportive, caring listener, however, cannot be met by just anyone. As Kübler-Ross (1969) pointed out, to listen to a dying person in a warm and supportive manner requires acceptance of one's own mortality and a comfortableness in the presence of death. Such companionship is usually provided by a relative or perhaps a caring professional.

Counseling and psychotherapy with the dying involve no fixed prescription and are not restricted at this time to practitioners possessing specific professional credentials. Family members, medical staff members, clergymen, and social workers all perform counseling services at one time or another. Professional counselors, such as clinical psychologists and psychiatrists, are also available to work with terminally ill persons whose dying trajectories permit more prolonged psychological treatment efforts. Whoever the counselor may be, he or she should be a compassionate individual who shares a feeling of mutual trust with the patient and can help deal with fears of the unknown.

In addition to helping dying people concentrate on taking life one day at a time and living each day as joyfully and peacefully as possible, professional counselors employ a variety of techniques. These techniques include uncritical acceptance, attentive listening, reflection of feelings, life review, group-oriented therapy, and even consciousness-altering drugs (Kalish, 1977). The specific objectives of counseling with the dying vary with both the patient and the situation, but some overall goals are to help patients overcome their feelings of sadness and despair, to resolve interpersonal (especially intrafamilial) conflicts, and to obtain insight into the meaning and value of their lives. Counselors must be careful not to force their own values—religious or secular—on dying patients. Rather, they should attempt to understand and share the fears, hopes, and other feelings of dying persons and assist them in finding their own ways of meeting death.

One phenomenon that frequently occurs when a patient becomes aware that he or she is dying is a *life review*. According to Butler (1975), mentally reviewing one's life is a universal process ranging in duration from a split-second overview to a lengthy reminiscence. Whenever a life review occurs, in later life (which is more likely) or earlier, it provides an opportunity to relive old pleasures and sufferings and to work through persisting problems. Consequently, reviewing one's life can be a healing process, and is recommended by Butler and Lewis (1982) and others as a counseling technique for use with dying patients. Butler maintained that surveying, observing, and reflecting on one's past experiences leads to insight and understanding, a sense of continuity, a strengthening of one's identity, and a feeling of inner peace.

## Hospice Treatment

The first hospice, St. Christopher's Hospice in London, was started in 1967 by Cicely Saunders to provide an atmosphere that would foster positive attitudes toward death in terminally ill cancer patients by helping them die with comfort and dignity (Saunders, 1980). Following its initiation in England, the hospice movement spread to the United States in the mid-1970s and subsequently throughout the world. The first U.S. hospices, including the pioneering efforts at St. Luke's Hospice in New York and the New Haven Hospice in Connecticut, were modeled after St. Christopher's Hospice. By the early 1980s, an estimated 300 hospices were either already operating or in the process of being established. These hospices were designed to provide an alternative for terminally ill people and their families, not only an alternative between impersonal hospital care and personalized but exhausting home care but also an alternative to euthanasia.

Although active euthanasia (using active measures to end a suffering person's life) has been proposed in both England and the United States as a means of avoiding death in a dehumanized hospital environment, Saunders has been an outspoken opponent of attempts to legalize it. To her and other hospice advocates, the pain experienced by dying people—not only physical but also psychological and spiritual pain—does not require a speeding up of death but can be controlled in a specially designed hospice environment.

The major features of hospice care are control of the patient's pain and discomfort, personal caring contact and discussions of death and dying between patients and medical staff, and death with dignity and a sense of self-worth rather than feelings of isolation or aloneness. As these goals imply, hospice care is centered not only on meeting the medical needs of the terminally ill but also their socioemotional and spiritual needs. The focus of this kind of treatment is on coping with pain and depression, which are frequent companions of fatal illness, without making an extraordinary effort to prolong life.

A special pain-relieving concoction known as *Brompton mix,* which is a mixture of morphine, cocaine, ethyl alcohol, and a sweetener, has been used in hospice treatment to provide maximum relief from pain with minimal sedative effects. Morphine by itself is also employed with similar results. Regular periodic doses of the pain killer are used initially, but by keeping a "control chart," patients can learn to manage their own medication.

Hospice treatment pays a great deal of attention to pain control, but patients are not so sedated that communication is hindered. To do so would ignore the important goal of bringing patients and family members together. By providing a warm, homey atmosphere in which pain is controlled, patients can remain alert, active, and productive until they die. The efforts of the entire staff in a hospice center are directed toward helping patients feel accepted and significant and to use their remaining time wisely. Patients are urged to communicate with counselors, family, and others, showing their feelings and exploring the meaning of death. Through such procedures the terminally ill are helped to die with dignity and grace, and to believe that their lives have meaning even if they are about to die. Home care is an important part of most hospice treatment programs. With good home care, patients can remain in their own homes as long as they desire— even dying there if they wish. A typical treatment program allows the patient to be cared for at home until transfer to a medical facility is deemed advisable. In both the home and medical settings, an interdisciplinary, nurse-coordinated team of health professionals and volunteers is available to provide round-the-clock medical care for the patient and counseling for both the patient and the family. The professional members of the team include physicians, nurses, a social worker, and a chaplain. In addition, a psychologist and other health professionals are on call as needed.

Hospice is actually a concept rather than a place or building, but one model of a hospice is that of a house where people go for visits and counseling. A second model of hospice care is a segregated or separated hospital ward where patients are cared for by a roving hospice team. A third model, which is more in line with the primary thrust of the hospice movement toward home care, is home-care service only. The original British model emphasizes the coordination of home care with a central hospice administration.

The existence of various models, ranging from free-standing buildings to hospitals and home care, has led to a certain amount of confusion about what *hospice* really means. In some instances, the term has been used so loosely that it is difficult to differentiate between what is called a hospice and a back ward or terminal-care unit of a general hospital. Such confusion has created problems of identity and quality control for the hospice movement.

Associated with the problem of quality control is the attitude of the medical and nursing professions. Doctors and nurses, who are traditionally trained in curative therapy and rehabilitation, are not always prepared to accept the hospice approach of helping patients cope with death. Many health-care professionals view the hospice concept as an overly romantic notion of dying and death. Supporters of the hospice movement have argued, however, that health professionals have a responsibility for dealing with society's denial and fears of death and other negative attitudes that are perpetuated when death is hidden away in back wards of hospitals. To its advocates, the hospice approach provides one way of bringing death back into the community, so to speak, and getting the entire health-care system back on the right track (Kimmel, 1980).

## TIME AND SEQUENCE IN DYING

People die at different rates. The rate of decline in functioning from health to death can be fast or slow, with many starts and stops. This *dying trajectory* depends on the nature of the disorder, the patient's age and lifestyle, the kinds of medical treatment received, and various psychosocial factors. The effects of a specific disorder are seen in the "staircase" trajectory of multiple sclerosis, in which there are rapid declines followed by periods of remission (Glaser & Strauss, 1968). A long dying trajectory, although it provides the deceased a better chance to put his or her affairs in order and is perhaps less stressful to the survivors, is not always desired by the dying person. Given a choice, many people would rather die quickly and avoid much pain and psychological stress for themselves and, presumably, their loved ones (Feifel, 1959).

Whether the dying trajectory is long or short, and especially when it is short, people of all ages are expected to deal with impending death in a reasonable manner. What is socially accepted as "reasonable," however, varies with the age of the person. It is generally expected that young people will actively and antagonistically fight against death and attempt to take care of unfinished tasks. Older adults who are dying, on the other hand, are expected to be more passive than the young and to express less anger and frustration toward death (Sudnow, 1967).

### Awareness and Control of Death

Many individuals realize when they are about to die, a realization that affects different people in different ways (Kalish & Reynolds, 1976). Some who no longer wish to live may give up without a struggle and die rather quickly. Having

## *My Living Will*
## *To My Family, My Physician, My Lawyer and All Others Whom It May Concern*

Death is as much a reality as birth, growth, maturity and old age—it is the one certainty of life. If the time comes when I can no longer take part in decisions for my own future, let this statement stand as an expression of my wishes and directions, while I am still of sound mind.

If at such a time the situation should arise in which there is no reasonable expectation of my recovery from extreme physical or mental disability, I direct that I be allowed to die and not be kept alive by medications, artificial means or "heroic measures". I do, however, ask that medication be mercifully administered to me to alleviate suffering even though this may shorten my remaining life.

This statement is made after careful consideration and is in accordance with my strong convictions and beliefs. I want the wishes and directions here expressed carried out to the extent permitted by law. Insofar as they are not legally enforceable, I hope that those to whom this Will is addressed will regard themselves as morally bound by these provisions.

*(Optional specific provisions to be made in this space — see other side)*

DURABLE POWER OF ATTORNEY (optional)

I hereby designate ______________________ to serve as my attorney-in-fact for the purpose of making medical treatment decisions. This power of attorney shall remain effective in the event that I become incompetent or otherwise unable to make such decisions for myself.

*Optional Notarization:*

"Sworn and subscribed to

before me this ______ day

of ________, 19_____."

______________________
Notary Public
(seal)

Signed______________________

Date ______________________

Witness ______________________

______________________
Address

Witness ______________________

______________________
Address

Copies of this request have been given to ______________________

______________________ ______________________

*(Optional)* My Living Will is registered with Concern for Dying (No. ________)

**Distributed by Concern for Dying, 250 West 57th Street, Room 831, New York, NY 10107 (212) 246-6962**

FIG. 12.1. "My Living Will." Prepared by Concern for Dying, it expresses the signer's wish to avoid the use of "heroic measures" to preserve his or her life in the event of irreversible disease or injury (reprinted with permission from Concern for Dying, 250 West 57th Street, New York, NY 10107) lost the will to live, they embrace death as a solution to their personal problems. For example, Kastenbaum (1981) found that over 25% of a group of terminally ill patients whom he interviewed wished to die soon.

Another group of terminally ill people, those who find themselves unable to cope with the pain and frustration of prolonged illness but are also afraid of death, continually vacillate between a desire to live and a wish to die. The conflict between living and dying is aggravated when the person has one or more dependents but is afraid of becoming a burden on them. Some individuals, concerned with the physical and financial cost to themselves and to their loved ones of a long illness, assert their "right to die" in the form of a "living will" (Fig. 12.1). Although such a document is not legally binding, it does represent an attempt to permit the dying individual some choice, even during the last days or months of life.

## Personal Control Over Death

Whether they wish to die sooner or later, it is generally acknowledged that people can, through their own attitudes and efforts, either hasten or delay their own death. Evidence for this point was obtained by Kastenbaum and Aisenberg (1972), who found that cancer patients who had strong motivation to survive—as indicated by resentment against the illness and positive attitudes toward treatment—survived longer than patients whose will to live was weaker. Also associated with longer survival times is the maintenance of cooperative, happy social relationships, as opposed to the depressive reactions and destructive social relations that are associated with shorter survival times (Weisman & Worden, 1975).

Both John Adams and Thomas Jefferson died on July 4 of the same year, and Mark Twain died on the eve of the second arrival of Halley's comet—the date on which he had predicted that he would die. Observations such as these suggest that individuals can exert some control over the time when they die. For example, a priest who worked with Indians in the interior of Alaska observed that these people could to some extent, control the time, place, and manner in which they died; the majority died shortly after they had received the last sacrament (Trelease, 1975). More systematically obtained data also point to a relationship that time of death and important events (birthday, holidays, etc.) in a dying person's life. Research by Phillips (1975; Phillips & Feldman, 1973) found evidence of fewer deaths than expected before three ceremonial occasions—presidential elections, the Jewish Day of Atonement, and the person's birthday. These findings suggest that people may have the ability to postpone dying until after occasions of great personal significance to them. The reasons for these findings are far from clear, however, and they have been criticized on methodological grounds (Schultz & Bazerman, 1980). A patient's attitude or state of mind is unquestionably an important factor in the progress of an illness, but whether or not dying people can actually delay their day of death by attitude or will power has not been demonstrated conclusively.

## Psychological Stages in Dying

Elisabeth Kübler-Ross, as a result of her writings, talks, and workshops, has probably done more than any other person during the past two decades to stimulate both popular and professional interest in death and dying. Information obtained from her interviews with over 200 dying patients led her to postulate five psychological states through which people presumably pass as they become aware of their impending death (Fig. 12.2). She maintained that most people, whether they die slowly or quickly, pass through these successive stages in their attempts to deal with death. Throughout the five stages the patient continues to hope for recovery or a cure, a hope that Kübler-Ross believes should be supported by reassuring patients that everything that is humanly possible will be done to help them.

During the first stage, *denial,* the patient refuses to accept the doctor's diagnosis and consults other medical and nonmedical people. It is always important for a seriously ill patient to ask for a second opinion on medical matters, but in attempting to defend him or herself against the realization that he or she is dying, the patient may spend a great deal of time and money on faith healers and medical quacks. According to psychoanalysts, at an unconscious level most people do not really believe they are going to die. By refusing to accept the fact of personal death they protect themselves against anxiety resulting from the realization that their time is short.

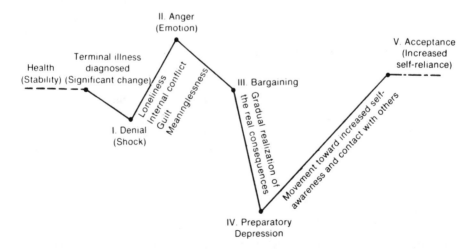

FIG. 12.2.   Psychological stages in the dying process (from Kübler-Ross, 1975)

As the patient's health continues to deteriorate, it becomes increasingly difficult to deny the imminence of death. Thus, denial gradually fades into a partial acceptance of the inevitable. During this second stage, *anger,* the patient feels angry and even enraged at the unfairness of having to die before his or her work has been completed and while others go on living. It is important for the family and hospital staff to be alert to this stage, because they may be the apparent targets of the patient's anger. The anger, however, is actually directed not so much toward them but toward the unfairness of death.

Patience and understanding on the part of the hospital staff and family are very important during the second stage. In any event, the anger slowly abates, to be replaced by desperate efforts on the part of the patient to buy time by *bargaining*—with fate, God, the doctors, or anyone or anything that offers hope. The patient promises to take his or her medicine and to go to church regularly. Prayers for forgiveness and even rituals or magical acts designed to ward off the demon Death are common. The bargaining stage is not obvious in all patients, but when it occurs it appears to represent a healthier, more controlled approach than denial or anger.

During the fourth stage, *depression,* the patient now fully accepts his or her impending death, but becomes depressed by all that has been suffered and all that will have to be given up by dying. Depression, at least to some degree, is a necessary part of the acceptance of death and the final peace that comes with acceptance. Consequently, the patient should be allowed to feel depressed for a while, and not be continually pestered by denying, "sweet lemon" Pollyannas. The patient should be permitted to share his or her grief with others, and then cheered up and reassured after he or she has been sad for a time.

The last psychological stage of dying, *acceptance,* is characterized by "quiet expectation." Now very weak and tired, the patient accepts the inevitability of death and desires only freedom from pain. This is a time to be alone with one or two loved ones, erasing old hurts and saying last goodbyes. The calm acceptance of death has been expressed poetically by William Cullen Bryant ("Thanatopsis"), Robert Louis Stevenson ("Requiem"), and other writers. Just before he died, the noted journalist Stewart Alsop (1973) wrote: "A dying man needs to die as a sleepy man needs to sleep, and there comes a time when it is wrong, as well as useless, to resist" (p. 299).

Kübler-Ross has made important contributions to attitudes toward dying and an understanding of the dying process, but her theory of stages has not gone unchallenged. Shneidman (1976, 1983) concluded from his observations that there is no inevitable progression of stages in the dying process, but rather a continual alternation between denial and acceptance. He noted that dying patients display a wide range of emotions, needs, psychological defenses, maneuvers, and themes that appear, disappear, and reappear in the process of attempting to deal with death. Both Shneidman (1983) and Kalish (1985) maintained that the dying process is highly individualized and personalized and need not follow a fixed sequence of stages. Perhaps an even more serious criticism of Kübler-Ross's theory is the way in which it is sometimes applied in working with the dying. Thus, medical personnel, subscribing to the theory of a fixed sequence of stages in dying, have been known to chide terminally ill patients for not going through the stages in the proper order and for failing to complete the required emotional tasks on time (Kalish, 1985).

Alternative ways of viewing the dying process have been proposed by Weisman and Kastenbaum (1968), Shneidman (1980, 1983), and Pattison (1977). Weisman and Kastenbaum (1968) observed two broad patterns of response in dying persons whom they studied. One group of individuals either seemed unaware of the fact that they were dying or accepted it; both subgroups became less and less active as the time of death approached. A second, contrasting group of individuals remained active in hospital life up until the very day on which they died.

Shneidman (1976), referring to the dying person's task as "death work," maintained that the person first deals with his or her impending death at a psychological level and prepares to meet the end. Next is the task of readying oneself for death in a way that assists loved ones in preparing to be survivors. As recognized by Schneidman (1980), however, there is a great deal of individuality in how people face death. As in any life crisis, the manner in which a person approaches death is a reflection of the total personality. Consequently, reactions to impending death reveal something about the individual's personality and the kind of life that has been lived. One person may see death as a punishment for wrong doing, another is afraid of the separation resulting from death, and still another perceives death as an opportunity to be reunited with departed loved ones.

Various emotions and concerns are expressed by dying people, including fear of the unknown, loneliness and sorrow, pain and suffering, loss of body, loss of self-control, and loss of identity. Pattison (1977) proposed a three-phase descriptive model including these reactions and other psychological responses of persons during the *living–dying interval*—the interval between the initial death crisis and the actual time of death. In the *acute phase,* which corresponds to Kübler-Ross's denial, anger, and bargaining stages, anxiety and fear are at a peak. The high level of anxiety experienced during the acute phase is reduced by defense mechanisms and other resources of the person. During the *chronic living–dying phase,* anxiety is reduced and questions about the unknown are asked: What will happen to my body, my "self," and my family and friends while I am dying and afterward? Considering my present situation, what realistic future plans can I make? It is also during the chronic living–dying phase that the person begins to accept death gracefully. In the third and final phase, the *terminal phase,* the person still desires to live but now accepts the fact that death will not go away. Functioning at a low level of energy and wanting mainly comfort and caring, the person begins a final social and emotional withdrawal from the living.

## BEREAVEMENT AND MOURNING

Death during old age is usually considered a normal occurrence rather than a tragedy. The elderly are seen as having had their chance to attain happiness and to make whatever contributions they desire, and so death in later life is viewed as only fair. Dying is considered more of a tragedy when it occurs in a young person, who has not had sufficient opportunity to experience life and to achieve his or her goals. It would seem, then, that death in old age, especially if the dying trajectory of the deceased has been long, would not be the cause of so much grief and mourning in the survivors. Even when expected, however, the death of an elderly loved one can be a very stressful experience for the family and friends of the deceased.

### Funeral Rituals

Historically, the purpose of funeral rituals were to honor the dead, to supply them with the necessities for surviving in the next world, and to gain favor with the gods. The term *funeral* comes from the Sanskrit world for "smoke," presumably stemming from the early practice in northern India of burning the dead. In the ancient custom of *suttee* the widow of the deceased was burned alive on the funeral pyre of her husband, a practice that was fairly common in India until outlawed by the British in the 19th century. The custom among newly bereaved Egyptian widows, on the other hand, was to run through the streets, beating their breasts and tearing their hair.

With respect to treatment of the corpse, both cremation and earth burial were practiced by the ancient Greeks and Romans. Anointing and decorating the dead in preparation for the afterlife were also practiced in ancient times, as they are today. Many of our own funeral customs—wearing black, walking in procession, raising a mound over the grave—were introduced into Britain by the Romans and subsequently transported by the British to North America (Hambly, 1974). The origins of other rituals—the wake, shibah, wearing armbands, the eulogy, bringing food and condolences to the survivors, and so on, are also ancient. Many customs, however, have changed. Mourners are no longer summoned to the wake by bidders or to the funeral service by bell ringers, as they were in earlier times. Rather, a notice is usually placed in the obituary column of a newspaper, and relatives and close friends are informed by telephone, telegram, or in person. Honoring the dead still forms a part of funeral rituals today, but the emphasis has shifted somewhat from the deceased to the survivors. A primary function of the modern funeral is to provide a mechanism for those who were close to and/or admired the deceased to work through their own feelings connected with the death. By providing specific roles for bereaved persons and their family and friends to play, the rituals help ease their grief and may also provide a sense of transcendent meaning to the death of the deceased. Honoring the deceased and grieving for him or her at the funeral and during the subsequent mourning period serve both to affirm the value of the deceased and to achieve emotional closure with respect to the life and death of the departed. However, there is no evidence that placing the corpse on display (open casket) during the wake or funeral service hastens the resolution of grief. In addition, expensive caskets, embalming, cosmetology, and other embellishments offered by funeral homes add little or anything to the occasion other than expense.

Wherever the funeral is held—in a funeral home, a church, a chapel, or elsewhere, the trend during this century has been to tone down the more emotion-arousing features of the service. Another trend has been away from larger church funerals and toward simpler funerals or memorial services. Neither the funeral service nor the procession from the place where the service is held to the final resting place is as dramatic or flamboyant as it once was. The de-emphasis on funeral rituals in recent years has been interpreted as a manifestation of the denial of death that has come to characterize Western culture during the 20th century (Aries, 1974).

The final resting place of the deceased is usually a private cemetery maintained by a religious order or other nonprofit organization, or by a commercial enterprise. When the body has been cremated, the remains, which are actually a few pounds of calcified material rather than ashes, may be sprinkled over a mountain or ocean or saved in an urn or vault.

## The Stress of Bereavement

Mourning for the deceased and grief at his or her departure do not automatically cease when the funeral is over. The death of a loved one, and a spouse in particular, is often an extremely stressful experience from which the bereaved has difficulty recovering. Preoccupied with loss and grief, the bereaved may ignore other people and let things go, having little or no energy to cope with the external world.

Various household and business duties must now be performed without the help and guidance of the deceased. Medical bills and funeral expenses need to be taken care of, a difficult chore even when life insurance and/or savings cover the costs and a severe burden when they do not. Payment of taxes (income, inheritance, and gift) and the implementation of conditions stated in the will are other duties of the survivors.

Survivors are usually eligible for some kind of death benefit or burial payment from Social Security, typically a lump sum for burial expenses and a burial plot. They may also be entitled to veterans' benefits when the deceased had a service-connected disability and to funds from a labor union or fraternal organization. Whatever the benefits may be, when there has been a terminal illness a good portion of the total usually goes for hospital bills. The cost of a casket, a hearse, a cemetery plot or use of a crematory, and music for the funeral service must also be taken into account in the overall bill.

Whether the survivor is a man or a woman, the death of a loved one deprives the survivor of various kinds of satisfaction. The deceased served as a satisfier of the physical needs of the bereaved as well as a source of emotional gratification. As a consequence, over the years the bereaved's sense of identity and the meaning of his or her life may have become intertwined with the personality of the deceased. Somehow he or she must now learn to cope with the loss and the resulting stress.

The period of greatest stress for the bereaved is usually immediately after the death of the deceased. This is the time when the reactions of the bereaved are most intense. Among the behaviors observed during the first month of mourning are periodic crying, difficulty sleeping, loss of appetite, and problems in concentrating or remembering (Fig. 12.3). The emotional disturbances and insomnia associated with bereavement can also lead to dependence on tranquilizers, sleeping pills, and/or alcohol. In some cases, the symptoms of bereavement stress are so severe as to be considered pathological (see Report 12.1).

The emotional reactions of a surviving spouse, who in 75% of the cases is the wife, may be so intense that severe physical illness, a serious accident, or even death—occasionally from suicide—occurs. Not only does bereavement stress exacerbate existing illness, it can also contribute to new disorders. For example, a study of 4,500 British widowers aged 55 and over found that 213 died during the first 6 months of their bereavement (Parkes, Benjamin, & Fitzgerald, 1969). The rate of death, most instances of which apparently resulted from heart problems, was 50% higher than expected in this age group (see also Helsing & Szklo, 1981). Concluding from a series of related investigations that grief and consequent feelings of helplessness make people more vulnerable to pathogens, Seligman (1975) suggested that individuals who have recently lost a spouse should be very careful about their health and should have monthly medical checkups during the first year after the loss.

Although anxiety and depression are the most common reactions to bereavement, anger, guilt, and even psychotic symptoms (hallucinations, feelings of depersonalization, etc.) have been observed. Depression is a normal response to any severe loss, but it is augmented by feelings of guilt in cases where interpersonal hostilities and conflicts with the deceased have not been resolved. Anger may be expressed—toward nurses, physicians, friends, and family members whom the bereaved believes to have been negligent in their treatment of the

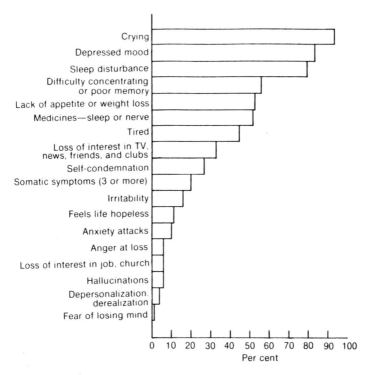

FIG. 12.3. Percentages of recently widowed persons expressing various psycho-physiological symptoms (adapted from Clayton, Hallikes, & Maurice (1971), Table 1. Courtesy of Physicians Postgraduate Press, Inc.)

deceased. For various reasons, survivors may also experience anger toward the deceased or relief at his or her death—both of which can lead to feelings of guilt.

## Stages of Mourning

The notion that grieving or mourning takes place in a series of stages, similar to Kübler-Ross's (1969) psychological stages in the dying process, has been considered by a number of researchers. Three-stage (Glick, Weiss, & Parkes, 1974; Gorer, 1967), four-stage (Parkes, 1972), five-stage (Bowlby, 1960), and even seven-stage (Kavanaugh, 1974) theories have been proposed. The first stage in almost all of these theoretical formulations is described as a period of shock, numbness, or disbelief, lasting a few days or at most a few weeks. Loss of self-control, reduced energy, lack of motivation, bewilderment, disorientation, and a loss of perspective characterize this initial period in the mourning process. Following the first stage is a long period of grief and related emotions (pining, depression guilt, anger), in which the bereaved tries to find some meaning in the catastrophic loss. In a large percentage of cases, the bereavement process runs its course after approximately 1 year following the death. By that time, the bereaved individual has given up any hope of recovering the deceased and is ready to reorganize his or her life and to focus on new objects of interest.

As with any theory of developmental stages or periods, there is a danger that "stages of mourning" will be construed as a fixed sequence through which bereaved people must pass. As most theorists undoubtedly recognize, the different stages of mourning blend together and overlap, are not necessarily successive, vary in intensity and duration, and are not experienced by every bereaved person. Consequently, it can be argued that all stage theories of the mourning process are only descriptive accounts of various emotional states experienced by bereaved people (Bugen, 1977).

---

### Report 12.1   PATHOLOGICAL GRIEF REACTION*

Nadine, a 66-year-old former high school teacher, lived with Charles, age 67, her husband of 40 years (also a retired teacher). The couple had been nearly inseparable since they met—they even taught at the same schools during most of their teaching careers. They lived in a semirural community where they had taught and had raised their three children, all of whom had married and moved to a large metropolitan area about 100 miles away. For years, they had planned their retirement and had hoped to be able to travel around the country visiting friends. A week before their 40th anniversary, Charles had a heart attack and, after 5 days in the intensive care unit, had a second heart attack and died.

Nadine took Charles's death quite hard. Even though she had a great deal of emotional support from her many friends and her children, she had great difficulty adjusting. Elaine, one of her daughters, came and stayed a few days and encouraged her to come to the city for a while. Nadine declined the persistent invitation even though she had little to do at home. Friends called on her frequently, but she seemed almost to resent their presence. In the months following the funeral, Nadine's reclusive behavior persisted. Several well-wishers reported to Elaine that her mother was not doing well and was not even leaving the house to go shopping. They reported that Nadine sat alone in a darkened house—not answering the phone and showing reluctance to come to the door. She lost interest in activities she once enjoyed.

Greatly worried about her mother's welfare, Elaine organized a campaign to get her mother out of the house and back to doing the things she had formerly done. Each of the children and their families took turns at visiting, spending time with her, and taking her places until she finally began to show interest in living again. In time, Nadine agreed to come to each of their homes for visits. This proved to be a very therapeutic step because Nadine had always been very fond of children and took pleasure in the time spent with her eight grandchildren. (She actually extended the visits longer than she had planned.)

*After Carson, Butcher, & Coleman, 1988, p. 155. Copyright © 1988, 1984 by Scott, Foresman and Company. Reprinted by permission.

## Readjustment and Renewal

For a variety of reasons, survivors often find it difficult to let go of the dead and many purify or idealize the deceased in their memory. The result can be a persistence of grief beyond a reasonable period of time. Nevertheless, the old cliché that time heals all things is to a large extent true. Some people never completely get over the death of a loved one, but in most cases the emotional effects of death do not persist more than 2 years. In one study, 48% of the widows who were interviewed a year after their husbands had died reported that they had gotten over their husband's death. Only 20% said they had not recovered and did not expect to do so (Lopata, 1973).

The support of others is crucial after the death of a loved one. Warm, supportive family members and friends who appreciate the situation of the bereaved and continue to visit during the weeks and months after the funeral can have a definite therapeutic influence (see Report 12.1). Physicians, funeral directors, lawyers, clergymen, and other professional persons with whom the bereaved person comes into contact with can also be helpful. Reviewing the circumstances and effects of the death with a sympathetic, understanding listener can do more than all the tranquilizers, sleeping pills, and other medicines combined to assist bereaved people in coping with loss and grief.

In many communities, social and psychological assistance for bereaved people is available from a number of public and private organizations. Churches, mental health clinics, community bereavement centers, and mutual-aid societies such as various widow-to-widow programs, Compassionate Friends, Parents Without Partners, and Big Brothers/Big Sisters of America offer assistance to bereaved persons and their families.

In widow-to-widow counseling programs, newly bereaved widows are counseled by trained individuals who have themselves lost a spouse and have completed their grief work. In addition to providing understanding and sympathy, these volunteer counselors make referrals to other sources when assistance and information beyond their training are needed. Social support for bereaved individuals is also provided by *grief groups* consisting of a small number of persons who share the common trauma of having lost a loved one. Under the direction of a professional counselor, the members of a grief group talk about their feelings and how to survive bereavement. The counselor–director provides both information and a focus for group discussion.

The ability of the bereaved to go on living and to develop new social relationships depends on the kind of gratification gained from the relationship with the deceased. It is difficult to begin anew when there are persisting interpersonal problems and negative emotions. But when the relationship has been built on mutual trust and fulfillment and there are no serious unresolved conflicts, the bereaved can more easily begin the process of readjustment and self-renewal.

## SUMMARY

There is no universally agreed upon legal definition of death, but the medical definition of death as being the cessation of circulation, respiration, and brain activity is generally accepted. Not all parts of the body die at the same time: Certain tissues can live for hours and even days after the heart and brain have stopped functioning. By using countershock, it is also possible to "resurrect" a person whose heart has stopped beating.

Fear of death is usually greater during middle age than old age. Even among elderly people, there are extensive differences in fears and attitudes toward death. Older women are more likely to view death in a benevolent way, whereas older men are more likely to perceive it as an enemy. More positive attitudes toward death and dying are also found in more emotionally adjusted individuals and those higher on the socioeconomic scale than among the maladjusted and the poor.

Philosophical and religious beliefs, as well as music, literature, and the visual arts, can be a comfort in the face of death. Existential philosophers have stressed the fact that the true meaning of one's life comes from an awareness that it will end. Western culture, with its emphasis on individualism and self-determination, has tended to characterize death as man's worst enemy or as outside of life. Oriental philosophers, on the other hand, view life and death as complementary phenomena.

Deeply religious individuals and atheists tend to be less afraid of death than those who are inconsistent in their religious beliefs. Religion, by providing a meaning for human existence and a hope for an afterlife, can give comfort to the dying. Transcendent, "out-of-body" experiences in patients who are near death may be interpreted as either bona fide visits to the "other side" or as hallucinatory phenomena with a biochemical or psychological basis. Because such experiences are usually pleasant, they may provide hope and comfort to survivors.

Perceiving themselves as trained to save lives, even physicians are sometimes uncomfortable in the presence of death and dying. Traditionally, health personnel have favored not telling patients when death is imminent, but medicine has changed in recent years and so have the attitudes of doctors and nurses. The "conspiracy of silence," in which death is not discussed with dying patients, is reportedly less common than it once was. Open communication between patients, medical staff members, and families is now more of a rule than an exception. Most dying patients want to discuss their fears and feelings and be permitted to make decisions concerning their lives. In general, it is felt that honesty concerning their condition, when combined with open communication, companionship, and caring, is therapeutic for dying patients.

Counseling terminally ill patients, whether done by professional counselors, family members, or friends, involves attentive listening and uncritical acceptance. The counselors should be gently available, quiet, and compassionately realistic, encouraging the patient to engage in a life review and other activities that may be deemed appropriate.

A primary goal of hospice care is to control physical, psychological, and spiritual pain. Additional goals include personal, caring contact between dying patients and their families and health personnel, and facing death with dignity. Introduced by Cicely Saunders during the late 1960s, hospice care concentrates on making dying as pleasant as possible but uses no heroic measures to keep dying patients alive. The traditional hospice model, in which the patient is kept in the home environment as long as possible, is an individualized, team-oriented effort involving patient, medical staff, volunteers, and family members. The introduction of a variety of other models of hospice care has led to some confusion about what hospice is. The hospice movement has been criticized as advocating an overly romantic attitude toward death and as inefficient health care, but at the very least the movement has prompted a more humane approach to care of the terminally ill.

Elisabeth Kübler-Ross maintained that patients pass through five psychological stages—denial, anger, bargaining, depression, and acceptance—in the process of dying. This theory has been criticized as implying an invariant, uniform sequence that seldom occurs in dying patients. Rather than a stepwise progression from denial to acceptance of death, dying patients are more likely to fluctuate between two or more emotional states. The alternative formulations of Shneidman, Pattison, and others, however, have not found as much favor among doctors and nurses as Kübler-Ross's theory.

The rituals of modern funerals stem from several historical practices and serve a number of therapeutic functions. The traditional emphasis on the funeral as a rite for honoring the dead has changed somewhat in the modern era to a concern with the feelings of the survivors. Funerals have become simpler and less emotional, but their elaborateness and character vary with cultural background and other demographic variables.

The death of a relative or close friend is a stressful experience that can have wide-ranging psychological and physical consequences for the survivors. The reactions of the bereaved include anxiety, depression, guilt, and anger. Other reactions include disorientation; an inability to concentrate or remember; crying; insomnia; and a loss of appetite, energy, and weight. In addition to psychological reactions, the loss of a loved one can result in pronounced physical changes and can even contribute to serious illness in the bereaved.

Various stage theories conceptualize mourning as beginning with a period of shock or numbness, followed by a long period of grief and related emotions, and ending in recovery and reorganization. Such theories are little more than descriptions of the feelings and behaviors of grieving people, rather than an unvarying sequence followed by all mourners. The quality and intensity of reactions to bereavement vary greatly with the age, sex, social class, and personality of the bereaved. The quality and intensity of the psychological and physical changes of mourning, and whether or not the bereaved is able to readjust, depend on the kinds of gratification gained from the relationship with the deceased and the resolution of any interpersonal problems or negative emotions regarding the latter. Grief groups and other bereavement counseling procedures can assist in recovering from the loss of a loved one. Widow-to-widow counseling has been found to be especially helpful when a spouse has died.

## SUGGESTED READINGS

Aiken, L. R. (1985). *Dying, death, and bereavement*. Boston: Allyn & Bacon.

Greer, D. S. (1983). Hospice: Lessons for geriatrics. *Journal of the American Geriatrics Society, 31*, 67–70.

Kalish, R. A. (1985). *Death, grief, and caring relationships* (2nd ed.). Monterey, CA: Brooks/Cole.

Kastenbaum, R. (1985). Dying and death: A life-span approach. In J. E. Birren & K. W. Schaie (Eds.), *Handbook of the psychology of aging* (2nd ed., pp. 619–643). New York: Van Nostrand Reinhold.

Leming, M. R., & Dickinson, G. E. (1985). *Understanding dying, death, and bereavement*. New York: Holt, Rinehart & Winston.

Meiner, D. E., & Cassel, C. K. (1983). Euthanasia in old age: A case study and ethical analysis. *Journal of the American Geriatrics Society, 31*, 294–298.

Monley, A. (1985). *The hospice alternative*. New York: Basic Books.

Raphael, B. (1983). *The anatomy of bereavement*. New York: Basic Books.

Shneidman, E. S. (1983). *Deaths of man*. New York: Jason Aronson.

Old age has yet his honor and his toil.
Death closes all; but something ere the end,
Some work of noble note, may yet be done,
Not unbecoming men that strove with Gods.
                    —Tennyson, *Ulysses*

# Appendix A:
# Agencies, Organizations, and Programs for the Elderly

*ACTION*, 806 Connecticut Ave. N.W., Washington, DC 20525. (Programs: Foster Grandparent Program, Retired Senior Volunteer Program, Senior Companion Program.)

*Administration on Aging*, Health and Human Services Dept., 330 Independence Ave. S.W., Washington, DC 20201. (Implements programs under Older Americans Act.)

*Alzheimer's Disease and Related Disorders Assn.*, 7979 Old Georgetown Rd., Bethesda, MD 20814. (Provides research funding and family support for Alzheimer's disease.)

*American Assn. of Homes for the Aging*, 1129 20th St. N.W., Washington, DC 20036. (Organization of nonprofit homes for the elderly; conducts National Certification Program for Retirement Housing Professionals.)

*American Assn. of Retired Persons*, 1909 K St. N.W., Washington, DC 20049. (Health Care Campaign, Senior Community Service Employment Program, information and consultation on housing for older Americans.)

American College of Health Care Administrators, 8120 Woodmont Ave., Suite 200, Bethesda, MD 20814. (Conducts research and educational programs designed to improve skills of people who deliver long-term care.)

*American Geriatrics Society (The)*, 770 Lexington Ave., Suite 400, New York, NY 10021. (Organization of physicians and other health-care professionals specializing in health care for the elderly.)

*American Health Care Assn.*, 1200 15th St. N.W., Washington, DC 20005. (Organization of owners and administrators of private proprietary and nonprofit nursing homes, and long-term care homes.)

*Bureau of Indian Affairs*, Department of the Interior, 1951 Constitution Ave. N.W., Washington, DC 28245. (Concerned with rights and privileges of Native Americans, including elderly.)

*Employment and Training Administration* (Labor Dept.), Older Worker Programs, 200 Constitution Ave. N.W., Washington, DC 20210. (Administers Senior Community Service Employment Program, which provides funds for government-based part-time, community service, and work-training programs for economically disadvantaged persons 55 and over.)

*Federal Council on the Aging,* Health and Human Services Dept., 330 Independence Ave. S.W., Washington, DC 20201. (Reviews, evaluates, and makes recommendations concerning federal policies on the aging.)

*Gerontological Society of America (The),* 1411 K St. N.W., Washington, DC 20005. (Professional and scientific organization of researchers and practitioners in the field of gerontology.)

*Gray Panthers,* 311 S. Juniper St., Suite 601, Philadelphia, PA 19107. (Political organization whose aim is to provide a better life for older Americans.)

*Health Care Financing Administration* (Health and Human Services Dept.), Institutional Ambulatory Services, 6325 Security Blvd., Baltimore, MD 21207. (Oversees compliance of hospitals, psychiatric hospitals, clinical labs, home health agencies, nursing homes, and long-term care facilities with federal standards.)

*House Select Committee on Aging,* 714 HOB Annex #1 (300 New Jersey Ave. S.E.), Washington, DC 20515. (Subcommittees: Subcommittee on Retirement Income and Employment; Subcommittee on Health and Long-Term Care.)

*International Association of Gerontology,* Duke University Medical Center, Box 2948, Durham, NC 27710. (Member organizations consist of professional societies and associations of geriatrics and/or gerontology; dedicated to research on care and well-being of elderly throughout the world.)

*International Federation on Aging,* 1909 K St. N.W., Washington, DC 20049. (Federation of organizations serving as advocates for the elderly in 43 countries.)

*Japanese American Citizens League,* 176 Sutter St., San Francisco, CA 94115. (Concerned with rights and other matters pertaining to Japanese Americans, including the elderly.)

*Leadership Council of Aging Organizations,* 1909 K. St. N.W., Washington, DC 20049. (Federation of organizations of older persons and professional groups serving them. Promotes issues, acts as an information clearinghouse, and cooperates with Congress and private agencies in improving programs affecting the elderly.)

*National Alliance of Senior Citizens,* 2525 Wilson Blvd., Arlington, VA 22201. (Organization of persons 50 and older concerned with Social Security, Medicare, crime against older Americans, and other matters pertaining to senior citizens.)

*National Assn. for Home Care,* 519 C St. N.E., Washington, DC 20002. (Organization of professionals and nonprofessionals in home care; advocates rights of infirm and terminally ill aged to remain independent in their own homes as long as possible, and monitors laws and regulations concerning home care.)

*National Assn. for Human Development,* 1620 I St. N.W., Washington, DC 20006. (Promotes social, physical, and intellectual fitness; produces educational materials on health and nutrition, and sponsors health education and physical fitness programs for older Americans.)

*National Assn. of Area Agencies on Aging,* 600 Maryland Ave. S.W., Washington, DC 20024. (Provides information, training, and technical assistance to local agencies on aging; monitors laws and regulations affecting older Americans.)

*National Assn. of Retired Federal Employees,* 1433 New Hampshire Ave. N.W., Washington, DC 20016.

*National Assn. of State Units on Aging,* 600 Maryland Ave. S.W., Washington, DC 20024. (Provides information and assistance on the problems and concerns of older Americans to state and territorial agencies dealing with the aging and to the general public.)

*National Caucus and Center on Black Aged,* 1424 K St. N.W., Washington, DC 20005. (Sponsors employment and housing programs for elderly blacks and educational and training programs in the field of gerontology.)

*National Citizens' Coalition for Nursing Home Reform,* 1424 16th St. N.W., Washington, DC 20036. (Seeks to improve the system of long-term care and the quality of life for residents in nursing homes and other facilities for the elderly.)

*National Council of Senior Citizens,* 925 15th St. N.W., Washington, DC 20005. (Federation of senior citizen clubs, associations, councils, and other groups concerned with problems of the elderly. Concerns include Social Security, employment, education and health programs, housing, nursing home standards, group travel, and other matters pertaining to the elderly. Through its Senior AIDES Programs, operates the Labor Department's Senior Community Service Employment Program.)

*National Council on the Aging,* 600 Maryland Ave. S.W., Washington, DC 20024. (Operates National Institute on Adult Daycare; National Institute on Community-Based Long-Term Care; National Center on Health Promotion for the Aging; National Institute of Senior Housing; National Voluntary Organization for Independent Living for the Aging; National Institute on Age, Work and Retirement; and Senior Community Service Project.)

*National Hispanic Council on Aging,* 2713 Ontario Rd. N.W., Washington, DC 20009. (Organizations of senior citizens, health-care workers, psychologists, and other individuals in the United States and Puerto Rico interested in topics related to Hispanics and aging.)

*National Hospice Organization,* 1901 N. Fort Myer Drive, Suite 902, Arlington, VA 22209. (Association concerned with all matters related to hospice care.)

*National Indian Council on Aging,* P.O. Box 2088, Albuquerque, NM 87103. (Concerned with the rights and other matters pertaining to elderly Native Americans.)

*National Institute on Aging* (National Institutes of Health, Health and Human Services Dept.), 9000 Rockville Pike, Bethesda, MD 20892. (Conducts and funds research on the biological, medical, and behavioral aspects of aging.)

*National Pacific/Asian Resource Center on Aging,* Colman Bldg., Suite 210, 811 First Ave., Seattle, WA 98104. (Concerned with the rights and other matters pertaining to elderly Americans of Pacific/Asian descent.)

*National Senior Sports Assn.,* 317 Cameron St., Alexandria, VA 22314. (Sponsors sports programs and trips for persons 50 years of age or older who want to maintain or improve their physical fitness and health through participation in sports.)

*Pension Rights Center,* Women's Pension Project, 1701 K St. N.W., Washington, DC 20006. (Provides information, conducts workshops and seminars, and monitors legislation and regulations concerning pensions for women.)

*Retired Officers Assn.,* 1625 I St. N.W., Washington, DC 20006.

*Senate Special Committee on Aging,* SH-628, Washington, DC 20510. (Studies and makes recommendations on legislation and federal programs in the areas of age discrimination, compensation, and unemployment; health problems of the aged, including quality and cost of long-term care and access of minority elderly to quality health care. Oversees Medicare, Medicaid, and other federally funded programs for the elderly.)

*Social Security Administration* (Health and Human Services Dept.), Central Operations, 6401 Security Blvd., Baltimore, MD 21235. (Maintains records concerning social security payments, claims, and benefits for retirement, disability insurance and beneficiaries.)

# Appendix B:
# Glossary

*Ability:* The extent to which a person is capable of performing a certain task, such capability being the joint product of hereditary endowment and experience.

*Acceptance:* According to Kübler-Ross, the final stage in a person's reactions to impending death. This phase is characterized by "quiet expectation" and acceptance of the inevitability of death. The dying person wants to be alone with one or two loved ones and desires only freedom from pain.

*Accommodation:* The automatic change in the shape of the lens of the eye so that an image can be brought into sharper focus on the retina.

*Activity theory:* The theory that active, productive people are happiest at any age.

*Acute brain syndrome:* Reversible, but frequently severe, brain disorder resulting from disease, injury, malnutrition, alcoholism, and other conditions.

*Adjustment:* The ability to get along with people and to satisfy most of one's needs.

*Administrative advocacy:* Activities by administrators of governmental agencies on behalf of a person or group.

*Affective psychoses:* Functional psychoses characterized by extremes of emotion (elation or depression).

*Ageism:* Social stereotyping of and/or discrimination against older people.

*Age norm:* The average or expected characteristics or behaviors of a person of a particular chronological age.

*Aging:* The continuous process (biological, psychological, social), beginning with conception and ending with death, by which organisms mature and decline.

*Alienation:* A state of indifference to or withdrawal from the world of other people.

*Alzheimer's disease:* A chronic brain syndrome, usually occurring in later life, characterized by gradual deterioration of memory, disorientation, and other features of dementia.

*Anger:* According to Kübler-Ross, the second stage in a person's reactions to impending death. During this stage the person partially accepts the knowledge that he or she is going

319

to die but becomes angry at the unfairness of having to die while others go on living.

*Angor anima:* A fear of impending death, often accompanying a heart attack.

*Angry type:* A maladjusted personality pattern persisting into old age. The person is bitter and blames other people for his or her failures (Reichard).

*Anxiety neurosis:* A type of neurotic disorder in which persistent anxiety is the major symptom.

*Apoplexy:* See *Cerebrovascular accident.*

*Aptitude:* The ability to profit from training and experience in an occupation or skill.

*Arcus senilis:* A cloudy ring that forms around the cornea of the eye in old age.

*Armored-defended personality:* A personality pattern, persisting into old age, in which the person defends him or herself against anxiety by keeping busy (Reichard).

*Arteriosclerosis:* Abnormal hardening and thickening of the walls of the arteries in old age.

*Arthritis:* Degeneration and/or inflammation of the joints.

*Atherosclerosis:* A type of arteriosclerosis resulting from an accumulation of fat deposits on the walls of arteries.

*Attitude:* A tendency to react positively or negatively to some person, object, situation, or event.

*Audiometer:* A frequency generator for measuring a person's sensitivity to various frequencies in the audible range of human hearing; used to determine the degree of deafness.

*Autoimmunity theory:* Theory that the immunological defenses of a person decrease with age, causing the body to "turn on itself," and consequently increasing the likelihood of autoimmune diseases such as arthritis.

*Autointoxication:* A state of being poisoned by toxic substances produced within the body.

*Bargaining:* According to Kübler-Ross, the third stage in a person's reactions to impending death. This stage is characterized by the patient's attempts to buy time by bargaining with the doctors, God, or with anyone or anything that the patient believes can protect him or her from death.

*Behavior modification:* A group of counseling or psychotherapeutic techniques based on principles of conditioning and other kinds of learning.

*Behavior therapy:* Psychological methods of treatment employing the principles of learning theory. Specific techniques include reinforcement, desensitization, counterconditioning, aversion, extinction, and modeling.

*Bereavement:* The loss of a loved one by death.

*Biological age:* The anatomical or physiological age of a person, as determined by changes in organismic structure and function; takes into account such features as posture, skin texture, hair color and thickness, strength, speed, and sensory acuity.

*Case advocacy:* Routine litigation in which lawyers contest on behalf of clients.

*Centenarian:* A person who is at least 100 years old.

*Cerebral arteriosclerosis:* Chronic hardening and thickening of the arteries of the brain in old age.

*Cerebrovascular accident (CVA):* A sudden rupture (hemorrhage) or blockage (thrombosis) of a large cerebral blood vessel, leading to impairment of brain functioning (stroke, apoplexy).

*Cherry angiomas:* Small red spots on the skin in the trunk area of the body.

*Chronic brain syndrome:* Mental disorder caused by long-standing injury to the brain; gradual, insidious changes in personality occur.

*Class action suit:* Litigation on behalf of an entire group of people.

*Climacterium:* Changes in the ovaries, and associated processes, including menopause, in middle-aged women.

*Cockayne's syndrome:* A childhood form of progeria (premature aging).

*Cohort:* A group of people of the same age, class membership, or culture (e.g., all people born in 1900).

*Cohort differences:* Physical and psychological differences between individuals born in different time periods and hence belonging to different generations.

*Cohort sequential design:* Developmental research design in which successive cohorts are compared over the same age ranges. For example, changes in attitude or ability from age 60 to 70 in a group born in 1910 are compared with changes in attitude from age 60 to 70 in a group born in 1920.

*Collagen:* Fibrous protein material found in the connective tissue, bones, and skin of vertebrates; becomes gelatinous when heated.

*Competency:* Legal determination that a person's judgment is sound and that he or she is able to manage his or her own property, enter into contracts, and so on.

*Conduction deafness:* Deafness resulting from failure of the mechanical vibrations corresponding to sound waves to be transmitted adequately through the three small bones in the middle ear into the cochlea of the inner ear.

*Confabulation:* Filling in memory gaps with plausible guesses or untruths.

*Confounding:* Situation in which two measures or characteristics vary in such a way that the independent effect of each cannot be determined. Age and cohort differences are confounded in cross-sectional research, and age and time of measurement in longitudinal research.

*Contingency management:* Control of instutionalized persons by differentially reinforcing them for socially approved and socially disapproved behavior; makes certain kinds of pleasures or privileges contingent upon keeping neat and clean, eating properly, interacting with other patients, or engaging in other socially acceptable behaviors. Also known as *token economy* when the reinforcers are tokens that can be exchanged for something that the patient desires.

*Continuity theory:* Persistence of personality characteristics and typical behaviors throughout the individual's lifetime.

*Coronary:* A heart attack, resulting from obstruction of a coronary artery and usually destroying heart muscle.

*Correlation:* The degree of relationship between two variables, signified by an index (a "correlation coefficient") ranging from $-1.00$ to $+1.00$.

*Counseling:* A general term for giving advice and guidance to individuals who need assistance with vocational, academic, or personal problems.

*Creatine:* A white crystalline substance found in the muscles of vertebrates.

*Cross-linkage:* Inadvertent coupling of large intracellular and extracellular molecules, causing connective tissue to stiffen.

*Cross-sectional study:* Comparisons of the physical and psychological characteristics of different age groups of people.

*Cross-sequential design:* Developmental research design in which two or more successive cohorts are studied longitudinally. For example, the change in attitude or ability from 1970 to 1980 in a groups of individuals born in 1910, 1930, and 1950 are compared.

*Crystallized intelligence:* R. B. Cattell's term for mental ability (knowledge, skills) acquired through experience and education. Specific to certain fields, such as school learning, and applied in tasks where habits have become fixed (see *fluid intelligence*).

*CVA:* See *Cerebrovascular accident*.

*Death rattle:* A rattling or gurgling sound produced by air passing through mucus in the lungs and air passages of a dying person.

*Defense mechanisms:* In psychodynamic theory, psychological techniques that defend the ego against anxiety, guilt, and loss of self-esteem resulting from awareness of certain impulses or realities.

*Delusion:* A false belief, characteristic of paranoid disorders. Delusions of grandeur, persecution, and reference are common in these psychotic conditions.

*Dementia:* Severe mental disorder involving impairment of mental ability.

*Denial:* According to Kübler-Ross, the first stage in a person's reactions to impending death. During this stage the person refuses to accept the fact of death and seeks reassurance from other medical and nonmedical people.

*Dependency ratio:* The ratio of the number of dependent (retired) persons to the number of active wage earners in a population.

*Dependent variable:* The variable in an experiment that changes as a function of changes in the independent variable. Variations in magnitude of the dependent variable, plotted on the Y axis of a graph, can be viewed as the experimental effect.

*Depression:* According to Kübler-Ross, the fourth stage in a person's reactions to impending death. The patient fully accepts the fact of death but becomes depressed by all that has been suffered and all that will have to be given up.

*Densensitization:* The extinction of anxiety evoked by a stimulus or situation, resulting from repeated exposure of the individual to that situation under "safe" conditions.

*Disenchantment phase:* The second of Atchley's five phases of retirement, characterized by a let-down, a feeling of emptiness, and even depression.

*Disengagement theory:* Cumming's theory that aging brings about a change in self-perception, and adjustment occurs through withdrawal from responsibility and participation.

*Dying trajectory:* The rate of decline in functioning from health to death; can be fast or slow, with many starts and stops, depending on the nature of the disorder, the patient's age and life-style, the kinds of medical treatment received, and various psychosocial factors.

*Ego:* Loosely speaking, the "I" or "self" of personality. In psychoanalytic theory, the executive, reality-oriented aspect of personality, which acts as a mediator between id and superego.

*Elder advocacy:* Concern for and legal action on behalf of the elderly.

*Electroshock therapy (EST):* A form of treatment for severe depression and certain other mental disorders; electrical current is passed briefly through the head, producing unconsciousness and convulsions.

*Embolism.* Obstruction of a blood vessel by an air bubble or other abnormal particle (thrombosis).

*Empathic Model:* Use of special devices (earplugs, special glasses, etc.) to simulate the sensorimotor disturbances of older people, and especially handicapped older people. The methods used enable younger people to experience the world from the perspective of an elderly person, and hence to understand the sensorimotor limitations of old age.

*Euthanasia:* Either active or passive contribution to the death of a human being or animal suffering from a terminal illness or injury.

*Excitement phase:* The first phase in the sexual response cycle. In the male, the penis becomes erect, the scrotal sac is flattened and elevated, and the testes are partially elevated; vaginal lubrication and enlargement and vasocongestion of the clitoris occur in the female. Muscle tension, blood pressure, and heart rate increase in both sexes.

*Extended care facility:* As originally designated by Medicare legislation, a health facility that provides more extensive professional care than a nursing home.

*Family Counseling:* Simultaneous counseling of two or more people who are members of the same family.

*Fertility rate:* Average number of children per woman of childbearing age in a given population.

*Fixation:* Any stereotyped form of behavior resulting from frustration and resistance to change.

*Fluid intelligence:* R. B. Cattell's term for inherent, genetically determined mental ability, as seen in problem-solving or novel responses.

*Fraternal twins:* Twins resulting from coincident pregnancies in the same person. Originating from two separately fertilized eggs, fraternal twins are genetically no more alike than nontwin siblings.

*Free radicals:* Highly reactive molecules or parts of molecules, which may connect and damage other molecules; thought to play a role in the process of aging.

*Functional psychosis:* A psychotic disorder having no clearly defined structural (organic) basis.

*Geriatrics:* Branch of medicine dealing with the prevention and treatment of health problems of the elderly.

*Geronto:* An old person (Greek *geron* = old man).

*Gerontocracy:* Government by the aged; a social organization in which a group or council of old people govern.

*Gerontology:* A branch of knowledge (science) concerned with the characteristics and problems of the aged.

*Gerontophobia:* Unreasonable fear and/or hatred of old people.

*Gingivitis:* Inflammation of the gums.

*Glomerulus* (*i*): A compact cluster of capillaries, especially in the kidneys.

*Gradual reawakening of interest:* The last stage of Gorer's three-stage conception of mourning, during which the mourner finally accepts the reality of the loved one's death and all that it means.

*Gray Panthers:* A politically active group concerned with legislation and programs for the aged.

*Hallucination:* Perception of an object or situation in the absence of an external stimulus.

*Hemorrhage:* Heavy discharge of blood from a blood vessel; uncontrollable bleeding (see also *Cerebrovascular accident*).

*Honeymoon phase:* The first of Atchley's five phases of retirement, during which a euphoric attitude of being able to do things that one has never had time to do prevails.

*Hospice:* An organization that provides services to dying persons and their families.

*Huntington's chorea:* A progressive disorder of the central nervous system, presumably hereditary, characterized by jerking movements and mental deterioration.

*Hutchinson–Gilford syndrome:* See *Progeria.*

*Hyperoxygenation:* Breathing pure oxygen under high atmospheric pressure, a process that in certain investigations has improved learning and retention of information by the elderly.

*Id:* In the psychoanalytic three-part theory of personality, the reservoir of instinctive impulses and strivngs. The id, or "animal nature" of man, is concerned only with immediate gratification of the pleasures and destructive impulses.

*Identical twins:* Twins produced by a single fertilized egg. Because they are genetically identical, they are often used in studies of the effects of heredity on structure and behavior. Also called *monozygotic twins.*

*Identity:* Term used to describe the individual's gradually emerging, and continually changing, sense of self.

*Incompetency:* Legal decision that a person is suffering from a mental disorder, causing a defect of judgment so that the person is unable to manage his or her own property, enter into contracts, and take care of other affairs.

*Independent variable:* The variable whose effects (on the *dependent variable*) are attempting to be determined in an experiment.

*Infant mortality:* Death before the age of 1 year.

*Initial shock:* The first stage of Gorer's three-stage conception of mourning. It lasts only a few days, and is characterized by a loss of self-control, reduced energy, lack of motivation, bewilderment, disorientation, and a loss of perspective by the mourner.

*Insanity:* An imprecise legal term for severe mental disorders involving lack of responsibility for one's actions. According to the M'Naghten Rule, an insane person is one who cannot distinguish right from wrong. However, other precedents such as the Durham decision are used in some states to determine insanity.

*Intelligence:* Many definitions of this term have been offered, such as the "ability to judge well, understand well, and reason well" (Binet) and the "capacity for abstract thinking" (Terman). In general, what is measured by conventional intelligence tests is the ability to succeed in school work and similar academic tasks.

*Intense grief:* The second stage of Gorer's three-stage conception of mourning. It often lasts for several months and is characterized by periodic crying and confusion about what has happened.

*Interiority:* A turning inward of the personality, or movement from active to passive mastery, observed in many people during old age.

*Involuntary commitment:* Legal process by which a person is committed to a mental institution against his or her will.

*Involutional period:* Decline in body energy during middle age or early old age, signaled by the menopause in women.

*Involutional psychosis (melancholia):* A term, now rarely used, for a disorder characterized by deep depression or paranoia, presumably precipitated by the "change of life" in middle-aged women and somewhat older men.

*Korsakoff's syndrome:* Chronic brain disorder associated with alcoholism.

*Legislative advocacy:* Applying pressure, usually by lobbying, on lawmakers to draft and vote for specific legislation.

*Levirate:* Custom of marriage between a man and his brother's widow, required in Biblical times under certain circumstances.

*Life-cycle group therapy:* Life-review therapy extended to a group of 8–10 members of different chronological ages.

*Life expectancy:* The average life span of people born in a certain year; probable length of life of an individual.

*Life review:* Reminiscence, or a split-second review of one's life just prior to impending death.

*Life-review therapy:* Form of psychotherapy in which patients reminisce about their personal experiences.

*Life span:* Theoretical maximum number of years of life that are biologically possible for a given species.

*Lifestyle:* Relatively permanent organization of activities, including work, leisure, and associated social activities, characterizing an individual.

*Lipofuscin ("age pigment"):* A pigmented granule containing lipis, carboydrates, and protein. The number of these granules in various body cells increases with aging.

*Longevity:* Length of life, long duration of life.

*Longitudinal investigation:* Studying the development of the same individual(s) at different ages over a period of years.

*Long-term memory (LTM, or secondary memory):* Memory that lasts at least 10–20 minutes, involving more permanent storage mechanisms of the brain.

*Major stroke:* Heart failure resulting from blockage of a large cerebral blood vessel (see also *Cerebrovascular accident*).

*Manic-depressive psychosis:* An affective disorder characterized by severe mood swings and excitability.

*Manic disorder:* Excessive agitation and excitability, which may or may not alternate with depression (see also *Manic-depressive psychosis*).

*Mature type:* According to Reichard, a personality pattern persisting into old age in which the person is relatively free of neurotic conflicts and can accept him or herself and grow old with few regrets for the past.

*Maximum breathing rate:* Amount of air moved through the lungs in 15 secs while breathing as rapidly as possible.

*Medicaid:* Comprehensive health-care program, in which funds for emergency and long-term care are made available for the poor.

*Medicare:* National health insurance program, primarily for acute care, for persons 65 and above who are covered by Social Security.

*Menopause:* Cessation of menstruation, usually occurring sometime between ages 45 and 50.

*Mercy killing:* See *Euthanasia.*

*Monitoring:* Law reform activity in which steps are taken to make certain that laws and programs are carried out as intended by the legislators who drafted them.

*Multi-infarct dementia:* Severe mental disorder due to significant cerebrovascular disease, resulting in destruction of regions of the brain and consequent deterioration of intellectual functions.

*Near event:* The second phase of preretirement, during which individuals orient themselves toward a specific retirement date (Atchley).

*Nerve deafness:* A form of deafness caused by damage to the inner ear or auditory nerve; usually involves a loss of sensitivity to sounds of high frequency. Also called *presbycusis.*

*Norms:* Average scores of people in a given demographic (age, sex, race, geographical region, etc.) on a psychological test or other assessment device.

*Octogenarian:* A person who is 80 to 90 years old.

*Older Americans Act:* Federal legislative act that provides for a national network of services and programs for older Americans, in addition to funds for research, training, and model projects concerned with the aged.

*Organic brain damage:* Damage to brain tissue caused by disease or injury; may result in mental disorder.

*Organic psychosis:* Severe mental disorder caused by organic brain damage resulting from alcoholism, encephalitis, cerebral arteriosclerosis, and other diseases, drugs, and injuries.

*Orgasmic phase:* The third phase in the sexual response cycle. Breathing rate, blood pressure, and heart rate reach a maximum, resulting in a release of muscular tension and vasoconstriction built up during the first two phases. The orgasmic phase ends with ejaculation by the male and contractions of the orgasmic platform in the female.

*Osteoarthritis:* Chronic degenerative disease process creating changes in the bones of the joints associated with the wear and tear of aging.

*Osteoporosis:* A gradual, long-term loss of bone mass in old age, especially in elderly women; the bones become less dense, more porous, and fracture more easily.

*Paranoid disorder:* A general term for a broad class of mental disorders of varying severity characterized by suspiciousness, projection, excessive feelings of self-importance, and frequently complex delusions of grandeur, persecution, and ideas of reference.

*Parkinsonism:* A progressive brain disorder resulting from damage to the basal ganglia and occurring most often in later life. The symptoms are muscular tremors; spastic, rigid movements; propulsive gait; and a masklike, expressionless face. Also called *Parkinson's disease.*

*Personality:* The sum total of all those qualities, traits, and behaviors that characterize a person's individuality and by which, together with his or her physical attributes, the person is recognized as a unique human being.

*Phenomenal field:* That part of a person's physical environment that is perceived by and has meaning for him or her.

*Placebo effect:* Change in behavior resulting from the administration of a chemically inert substance to people who believe they are receiving an active drug.

*Plaque:* Accumulation of fatty tissue and calcified material in the cerebral blood vessels of old people, resulting in clogged arteries and interference with blood circulation.

*Plateau phase:* The second stage of the sexual response cycle; muscle tension, blood pressure, and heart-rate changes become intensified, terminating in the production of an orgasmic platform in the female and rapid breathing in both sexes.

*Presbycusis:* See *Nerve deafness.*

*Presbyopia:* Literally, "old-sightedness," a condition of far-sightedness resulting from a loss of elasticity of the lens of the eye due to aging.

*Progeria:* A very rare disorder that mimics premature aging. A progeric child typically begins to look old as early as age 4. Also known as *Hutchinson–Gilford Syndrome.*

*Psychodrama:* A method of psychotherapy, devised by J. L. Moreno, in which the problems and experiences of a person are acted out in a stage setting by the person him or herself and other "actors."

*Psychological age:* The age of a person as determined by his or her feelings, attitudes, and life perspective.

*Psychological autopsy:* Postmortem analysis of the psychosocial aspects of a person's death.

*Psychosis:* Severe mental disorder characterized by faulty perception of reality, deficits of language and memory, disturbances in the emotional sphere, and other bizarre symptoms. Psychoses are classified as organic or functional, depending on whether they are associated with a known organic change.

*Psychotherapy:* Psychological methods of treating mental disorders, involving communications between patient(s) and therapist and other special techniques.

*Reciprocal inhibition:* A behavioral therapy technique involving presentation of the conditioned stimuli for an anxiety response while the individual is making responses incompatible with anxiety.

*Refractory period:* A period of time, after orgasm, during which sexual arousal cannot recur.

*Regression:* Return or reinstatement of an early stage of development; a common response to frustration (e.g., thumbsucking in an older child or adult).

*Reliability:* The extent to which a psychological test or other assessment instrument measures whatever it measures consistently.

*Remote event:* The first phase of the preretirement period, during which the individual views retirement as a vague, positive thing that will occur someday (Atchley).

*Reorientation phase:* The third of Atchley's five phases of retirement, during which retirees take stock, pull themselves together, and develop more realistic life alternatives.

*Resolution phase:* The final phase of the sexual response cycle; there is a gradual return to the physiological state that prevailed prior to the excitement phase.

*Retirement:* Withdrawal from one's occupation or from active work.

*Rigidity:* Inflexibility or unwillingness to change one's way of thinking or behavior; allegedly a characteristic of older people.

*Rocking chair type:* According to Reichard, a personality pattern persisting into old age, in which the person views old age in terms of freedom from responsibility and as an opportunity to indulge passive needs.

*Role:* A social behavior pattern that an individual is expected to display under certain conditions or in certain situations.

*Role exit theory.* Blau's sociological theory of old age as a time for abandoning certain roles and assuming other roles.

*Schizophrenia:* A broad category of psychotic disorders characterized by distortions of reality and disturbances of thought, behavior, and emotional expression.

*Scribotherapy:* Form of psychotherapy in which group members write out their feelings about certain topics and then, after group discussion and individual interviews, develop them into a news format.

*Self:* That part of an individual's phenomenal field (or "awareness") that he or she perceives as his or her own personality.

*Self-actualization:* Fulfillment of one's potentialities; to attain a state of congruence or harmony between one's real and ideal selves.

*Self-concept:* Fairly consistent cluster of feelings, ideas, and attitudes toward oneself.

*Self-hating type:* According to Reichard, a maladjusted personality pattern persisting into old age, in which the person is depressed and blames him or herself for his or her disappointments and misfortunes.

*Senescence:* The state of being old or the process of growing old.

*Senile keratoses:* Brown spots dotting sun-exposed areas of the skin.

*Senile purpura:* Purplish skin spots caused by cutaneous bleeding.

*Senility:* An imprecise term used to refer to deterioration in the brain and behavior observed in some elderly individuals; disability caused by illness or injury as a person ages.

*Senium praecox:* Premature senility (see also *Progeria* and *Werner's Syndrome*).

*Septuagenarian:* A person who is 70–79 years old.

*Serial anticipation* (*method of*): Method for studying memory or learning, in which the learner is exposed to a list of items and then attempts to anticipate successive items in the list over a series of trials until they are anticipated perfectly.

*Sex roles:* An aggregation of traits and behaviors that males and females in a given culture are expected to display.

*Short-term memory* (*STM*): Retaining items of information in memory from 1 second to several minutes at most; also known as *primary memory*.

*Small stroke:* Blockage of a small blood vessel in the brain.

*Social age:* Age of a person as determined by the social roles and activities in which he or she is expected to participate or which are considered appropriate for an individual at a particular age or stage of maturity.

*Social gerontology:* Subfield of gerontology dealing with social factors in aging, elderly group behavior, and the causes and effects of growth in the elderly segment of the population.

*SSI:* Supplemental Security Income; federal program of financial assistance to elderly poor people.

*Stability phase:* The fourth of Atchley's five phases of retirement. It may succeed either the honeymoon phase or the reorientation phase.

*Stimulus persistence theory:* Theory that aging causes recovery from the short-term effects of stimulation to be slowed down.

*Superannuation:* Retirement and pensioning because of age or infirmity.

*Superego:* In psychoanalytic theory, that aspect of personality representing the internalization of parental prohibitions and sanctions—the moral aspect of personality, or conscience.

*Suttee:* Old Hindu custom in which a devoted wife is voluntarily cremated on the funeral pyre of her husband.

*Synovial fluid:* Lubricating fluid in the joints, a loss of which characterizes osteoarthritis.

*Tardive dyskinesia:* Involuntary movements of the tongue, lips, jaw ("chewing movements") and extremities resulting from excessive use of phenothiazine derivative drugs.

*Terminal drop:* Decline in intellectual functions (intelligence, memory, cognitive organization, sensorimotor abilities, personality), during the last few months of life; observed in many elderly people.

*Termination phase:* The last of Atchley's five phases of retirement, in which the retirement role is replaced by the sick or dependent role.

*Testamentary capacity:* The legally determined competency of a person to make a will.

*Thanaphobia:* An unreasonable fear or dread of dying and death.

*Thanatology:* A branch of knowledge concerned with the study of dying and death.

*Thrombosis:* See *Embolism*.

*Time-lag design:* Developmental research procedure for examining several cohorts, each in a different time period.

*Tranquilizer:* Psychotherapeutic drug having antianxiety or antipsychotic effects.

*Validity:* The extent to which a psychological or educational assessment instrument measures what it was designed to measure.

*Voluntary commitment:* Unforced submission of oneself to a mental hospital for examination and treatment (see *Involuntary commitment*).

*Wechsler Adult Intelligence Scale-Revised (WAIS-R):* An individual intelligence test designed for adults aged 16 years and over. It consists of 11 subtests grouped into Verbal and Performance scales, and yields three intelligence quotients: Verbal IQ, Performance IQ, and Full Scale IQ.

*Werner's Syndrome:* A condition of arrested growth occurring between the ages of 15 and 20; thought to be a later developing progeria.

# References

A better way to care for the dying. (1978, November). *Changing Times,* pp. 21–23.

Ad Hoc Committee of the Harvard Medical School to Examine the Definition of Brain Death. (1968). A definition of irreversible coma. *Journal of the American Medical Association, 205,* 337–340.

Adamowicz, J. K. (1976). Visual short-term memory and aging. *Journal of Gerontology, 31,* 39–46.

Adams, B. N. (1968). *Kinship in an urban setting.* Chicago: Markham.

Additional tips for Social Security recipients. (1988, April 11). *The Times* (Trenton, NJ), p. 2.

Agan, T., Casto, M. D., Day, S. S., & Schwab, L. O. (1977). Adjusting the environment for the elderly and the handicapped. *Journal of Home Economics, 69*(3), 18–20.

Age, heart attack no deterrent. (1981, October 18). *Los Angeles Times,* p. III–9.

Aging: Primitives handle it better. (1976). *Science Digest, 79*(3), 17–18.

Ahammer, L. M. (1973). Social-learning theory as a framework for the study of adult personality development. In P. B. Baltes & K. W. Schaie (Eds.), *Life-span developmental psychology: Personality and socialization* (pp. 253–294). New York: Academic Press.

Aiken, L. R. (1985). *Dying, death, and bereavement.* Boston: Allyn & Bacon.

Aiken, L. R. (1980). Problems in testing the elderly. *Educational Gerontology, 5,* 119–124.

Ainlay, S. C., & Smith, D. R. (1984). Aging and religious participation. *Journal of Gerontology, 39,* 357–363.

Alpaugh, P., & Haney, M. (1978). *Counseling the older adult: A training manual.* Los Angeles: University of Southern California Press.

Alsop, S. (1973). *Stay of execution.* Philadelphia: Lippincott.

American Association of Retired Persons. (1987). *A profile of older Americans.* Washington, DC: Author.

American Bar Foundation. (1976). Survey of legal needs: Selected data. *Alternatives, 3*(1), 1–23.

American College of Physicians. (1985). *Guide for adult immunizations.* Philadelphia: Author.

American Heart Association. (1985). *Heart facts.* Dallas: Author.

American Psychiatric Association. (1987). *Diagnostic and statistical manual of mental disorders* (3rd ed. rev.). Washington, DC: Author.

Anastasi, A. (1988). *Psychological testing* (6th ed.). New York: Macmillan.

Anders, T. R., Fozard, J. L., & Lillyquist, T. D. (1972). Effects of age upon retrieval from short-term memory. *Developmental Psychology, 6,* 214–217.

Anderson, B. B. (1979). *The aging game.* New York: McGraw-Hill.

Anderson, K. (1974). Science probes ways to prolong life. *Science Digest, 76*(3), 36–41.

Ansello, E. F. (1977). Age and ageism in children's first literature. *Educational Gerontology, 2,* 255–274.

Antonovsky, I. (1981). *Health, stress and coping.* San Francisco: Jossey-Bass.

Antunes, G. E., Cook, F. L., Cook, T. D., & Skogan, W. G. (1977). Patterns of personal crime against the elderly: Findings from a national survey. *The Gerontologist, 17,* 321–327.

Applebome, P. (1988, April 7). Fear rules the lives of some of Houston's elderly. *New York Times,* p. A16.

Arehart-Treichel, J. (1972). How you age. *Science News, 102,* 412–413.

Arehart-Treichel, J. (1976). Human reproduction and aging. *Science News, 110,* 297.

Arenberg, D. (1973). Cognition and aging: Verbal learning, memory, and problem solving. In C. Eisdorfer & M. P. Lawton (Eds.), *The psychology of adult development and aging* (pp. 74–97). Washington, DC: American Psychological Association.

Arenson, J. T. (1982). Inheritance. *Encyclopedia Americana* (Vol. 15). Danbury, CT: Grolier.

Aries, P. (1974). *Western attitudes toward death: From the Middle Ages to the present.* Baltimore: John Hopkins University Press.

Assael, H. (1987). *Consumer behavior and marketing action* (3rd ed.). Boston: Kent Publishing.

At age 75, chess master is still a blindfolded whiz. (1979, February 26). *San Francisco Chronicle,* p. 39.

Atchley, R. C. (1972). *The social forces in later life: An introduction to social gerontology.* Belmont, CA: Wadsworth.

Atchley, R. C. (1977). *The social forces in later life: An introduction to social gerontology* (2nd ed.). Belmont, CA: Wadsworth.

Atchley, R. C. (1980). Aging and suicide: Reflection of the quality of life. In S. Hayes & M. Feinleib (Eds.), *Proceedings of the Second Conference on the Epidemiology of Aging* (pp. 141–161). Washington, DC: U.S. Government Printing Office.

Atchley, R. C. (1987). *Aging: Continuity and change* (2nd ed.). Belmont, CA: Wadsworth.

Averill, J. H. (1979, November 15). Centenarians tell secret: Exercise mind and body. *Los Angeles Times,* pp. I–1, 17.

Axelrod, S., Thompson, L. W., & Cohen, L. D. (1968). Effect of senescence on the temporal resolution of somesthetic stimuli presented to one hand or both. *Journal of Gerontology, 23,* 191–195.

Back, K. W. (1971). Metaphors as a test of personal philosophy of aging. *Sociological Forces, 5,* 1–8.

Back, K. W., & Gergen, K. J. (1963). Apocalytic and serial time orientations in the structure of opinions. *Public Opinion Quarterly, 27,* 427–442.

Bahr, M. H. (1970). Aging and religious disaffiliation. *Social Forces, 49,* 59–71.

Baller, W. R., Charles, D. C., & Miller, E. L. (1967). Mid-life attainment of the mentally retarded: A longitudinal study. *Genetic Psychology Monographs, 75,* 235–329.

Baltes, P. B. (1968). Longitudinal and cross-sectional sequences in the study of age and generation effects. *Human Development, 11,* 145–171.

Baltes, P. B., & Kliegl, R. (1986). On the dynamics between growth and decline in the aging of intelligence and memory. In K. Poeck, H. J. Freund, & H. Ganshirt (Eds.), *Neurology* (pp. 1–33). Heidelberg: Springer.

Baltes, P. B., & Schaie, K. W. (1974). The myth of the twilight years. *Psychology Today, 7,* 35–40.

Barbenel, J. (1988, January 12). Tears for Kelly: An elderly man freezes to death. *New York Times,* pp. B-1, 3.

Barrett, J. H. (1972). *Gerontological psychology.* Springfield, IL: Charles C Thomas.

Barrow, G. M., & Smith, P. A. (1983). *Aging, the individual and society* (2nd ed.). St. Paul, MN: West Publishing.

Basseches, M. (1984). *Dialectical thinking and adult development.* Norwood, NJ: Ablex.

Batten, M. (1984). Life spans. *Science Digest,* 46–51, 98.

Bayley, N., & Oden, M. H. (1955). The maintenance of intellectual ability in gifted adults. *Journal of Gerontology, 10,* 91–107.

Beck, A. T. (1967). *Depression: Clinical, experimental, and theoretical aspects.* New York: Harper & Row.

Becker, E. (1973). *The denial of death.* New York: The Free Press.

Bell, A., & Zubek, J. (1960). The effect of age on the intellectual performance of mental defectives. *Journal of Gerontology, 15,* 285–295.

Ben-Yishay, Y., Diller, L., Mandelberg, I., Gordon, W., & Gerstman, L. (1971). Similarities and differences in block design performance between older normal and brain-injured persons. *Journal of Abnormal Psychology, 78,* 17–25.

Benet, S. (1974). *Abkhasians: The long-living people of the Caucasus.* New York: Holt, Rinehart & Winston.

Benet, S. (1976). *How to live to be 100: The life-style of the people of the Caucasus.* New York: Dial Press.

Benitiz, R. (1973). Ethnicity, social policy, and aging. In R. Davis & M. Nieswander (Eds.), *Aging: Prospects and issues* (pp. 164–177). Los Angeles: Andrus Gerontology Center, University of Southern California.

Bengston, V. L., Cuellar, J. B., & Ragan, P. K. (1977). Stratum contrasts and similarities in attitudes toward death. *Journal of Gerontology, 32*(1), 76–88.

Bengston, V. L., Kasschau, P. L., & Ragan, P. K. (1977). The impact of social structure on aging individuals. In J. E. Birren & K. W. Schaie (Eds.), *Handbook of the psychology of aging* (pp. 327–353). New York: Van Nostrand Reinhold.

Bennett, R. (1976). Attitudes of the young toward the old: A review of research. *Personnel & Guidance Journal, 55,* 136–139.

Berger, K. A., & Zarit, S. H. (1978). Late life paranoid states: Assessment and treatment. *American Journal of Orthopsychiatry, 48,* 628–637.

Berne, E. (1964). *Games people play.* New York: Grove Press.

Berne, E. (1966). *Principles of group treatment.* New York: Oxford University Press.

Biehler, R. F. (1981). *Child development: An introduction* (2nd ed.). Boston: Houghton Mifflin.

Birren, J. E., Butler, R. N., Greenhouse, S. W., Sokoloff, L., & Yarrow, M. R. (Eds.). (1963). *Human aging: A biological and behavioral study.* Pub. No. (HSM) 71-9051. Washington, DC: U.S. Government Printing Office.

Birren, J. E., Cunningham, W. R., & Yamamoto, K. (1983). Psychology of adult development and aging. *Annual Review of Psychology, 34,* 543–575.

Bischof, L. S. (1969). *Adult psychology.* New York: Harper & Row.

Blau, S. Z. (1961). Structural constraints on friendships in old age. *American Sociological Review, 26,* 429–439.

Blau, Z. S. (1973). *Old age in a changing society.* New York: New Viewpoints.

Blazer, D., & Palmore, E. (1976). Religion and aging in a longitudinal panel. *The Gerontologist, 16,* 82–85.

Bloom, B. L., White, S. W., & Asher, S. J. (1979). Marital disruption as a stressful life event. In C. Levinger & O. C. Moles (Eds.), *Divorce and separation: Context, clauses and consequences* (pp. 184–200). New York: Basic Books.

Bloom, K. L. (1961). Age and the self-concept. *American Journal of Psychiatry, 118,* 534–538.

Blue, G. F. (1978). The aging as portrayed in realist fiction for children. *The Gerontologist, 18,* 187–192.

Blum, J. E., & Tross, S. (1980). Psychodynamic treatment of the elderly: A review of issues in theory and practice. In C. Eisdorfer (Ed.), *Annual review of gerontology and geriatrics* (Vol. 1, pp. 204–234). New York: Springer.

Botwinick, J. (1966). Cautiousness in advanced age. *Journal of Gerontology, 21,* 347–358.

Botwinick, J. (1967). *Cognitive processes in maturity and old age.* New York: Springer.

Botwinick, J. (1977). Intellectual abilities. In J. E. Birren & K. W. Schaie (Eds.), *Handbook of the psychology of aging.* New York: Van Nostrand Reinhold.

Botwinick, J. (1978). *Aging and behavior* (2nd ed.). New York: Springer.

Botwinick, J., & Thompson, L. (1968). Age differences in reaction: An artifact? *The Gerontologist, 8,* 25–28.

Bower, G. H. (1966). A descriptive theory of human memory. In D. P. Kimble (Ed.), *Learning, remembering and forgetting* (Vol. 2). New York: New York Academy of Science.

Bowlby, J. (1960). Separation anxiety. *International Journal of Psychoanalysis, 41,* 80–113.

Brandt, E. (1987, December 13). Secrets of success after sixty. *Parade,* pp. 4–6.

Brim, O. G., Jr., & Wheeler, S. (1966). *Socialization after childhood.* New York: Wiley.

Brink, I. L. (1976). Psychotherapy after forty. *MH, 58*(3), 7–12.

Brodzinsky, D. M., Gormly, A. V., & Ambron, S. R. (1986). *Lifespan human development* (3rd ed). New York: Holt, Rinehart & Winston.

Brown, J. H. U. (1966). Physiological parameters of the human potential. In H. A. Otto (Ed.), *Explorations in human potentialities* (pp. 79–100). Springfield, IL: Charles C Thomas.

Brown, N. K., & Thompson, D. J. (1979). Nontreatment of fever in extended-care facilities. *New England Journal of Medicine, 300,* 1246–1250.

Bugen, L. A. (1977). Human grief: A model for prediction and intervention. *American Journal of Orthopsychiatry, 47,* 196–206.

Busse, E. W., & Blazer, D. G. (1980). *Handbook of geriatric psychiatry.* New York: Van Nostrand Reinhold.

Busse, E. W., & Pfeiffer, E. (1977). Functional psychiatric disorders in old age. In E. W. Busse & E. Pfeiffer (Eds.), *Behavior adaptation in late life* (2nd ed., pp. 158–211). Boston: Little, Brown.

Butler, R. N. (1971). Age: The life review. *Psychology Today, 5*(7), 49–55ff.

Butler, R. N. (1974). Successful aging. *MH, 58*(3), 7–12.

Butler, R. N. (1975). *Why survive? Being old in America.* New York: Harper & Row.

Butler, R. N., & Lewis, M. I. (1976). *Sex after sixty: A guide for men and women in their later years.* New York: Harper & Row.

Butler, R. N., & Lewis, M. I. (1982). *Aging and mental health* (3rd ed.). St. Louis: Mosby.

Buttenwieser, P. (1935). *The relation of age to skill of expert chess players.* Unpublished doctoral dissertation, Stanford University, Palo Alto, CA.

Byron, D. A. (1980, April 22). Was it all for naught? 46 years later, oldster tries to pay $1.50 bill. *Los Angeles Times,* p. I-20.

California Department of Justice, Office of the Attorney General. (1979). *Senior Crime Preventers' Bulletin, 7*(1), 2–3.

Campbell, D. P. (1965). A cross-sectional and longitudinal study of scholastic abilities over twenty-five years. *Journal of Counseling Psychology, 12,* 55–61.

Can oxygen fight senility? (1972, March 25). *Business Week, 2221,* 94.

Carey, R. G. (1976). Counseling the terminally ill. *Personnel & Guidance Journal, 55,* 124–125.

Carkhuff, R. R. (1969). *Helping and human relations* (Vols. 1 & 2). New York: Holt, Rinehart & Winston.

Carlson, R. (1981). Studies in script theory: I. Adult analogs of a childhood nuclear scene. *Journal of Personality and Social Psychology, 40,* 501–510.

Carson, R. C., Butcher, J. N., & Coleman, J. C. (1988). *Abnormal psychology and modern life* (8th ed.). Glenview, IL: Scott, Foresman.

Cartwright, A., Hockey, L., & Anderson, J. L. (1973). *Life before death.* London: Rutledge & Kegan Paul.

Center on Aging, San Diego State University. (1978). *A cross-cultural study on minority elders in San Diego.* (Grant Number AoA 90-A-317). San Diego: Campanile Press.

Cerella, J. (1985). Information processing rates in the elderly. *Psychological Bulletin, 98,* 67–83.

Charles, D. C., & James, S. T. (1964). Stability of average intelligence. *Journal of Genetic Psychology, 105,* 105–111.

Civia, A. (1967). Longevity and environmental factors. *The Gerontologist, 7,* 196–205.

Clayton, P. J., Hallikes, J. A., & Maurice, W. L. (1971). The bereavement of the widowed. *Diseases of the Nervous System, 32,* 597–604.

Cole, S. (1979). Age and scientific performance. *American Journal of Sociology, 84*, 958–977.

Comfort, A. (1964). *Aging: The biology of senescence.* New York: Holt, Rinehart & Winston.

Comfort, A. (1974). Sexuality in old age. *Journal of the American Geriatrics Society, 22*, 440–442.

Comfort, A. (1976). *A good age.* New York: Crown Publishers.

Comfort, A. (1980). Sexuality in later life. In J. E. Birren & R. B. Sloane (Eds.), *Handbook of mental health and aging* (pp. 885–892). Englewood Cliffs, NJ: Prentice-Hall.

Cook, F. L., Skogan, W. G., Cook, T. D., & Antunes, G. E. (1978). Criminal victimization of the elderly: The physical and economic consequences. *The Gerontologist, 18*, 338–349.

Cooper, A. F., Curry, A. R., Kay, D. W. K., Garside, R. F., & Roth, M. (1974). Hearing loss in paranoid and affective psychosis of the elderly. *The Lancet, 2*(7885), 851–854.

Costa, P. T., Jr., & McCrae, R. R. (1980). Still stable after all these years: Personality as a key to some issues in adulthood and old age. In P. Baltes & O. G. Brim, Jr. (Eds.), *Life span development and behavior* (Vol. 3, pp. 65–102). New York: Academic Press.

Cottin, L. (1979). *Elders in rebellion.* New York: Doubleday/Anchor.

Cottrell, F., & Atchley, R. C. (1969). *Women in retirement: A preliminary report.* Oxford, OH: Scripps Foundation.

Cowdry, E. V. (Ed.). (1939). *Problems of aging.* Baltimore: Walhams & Wilkins.

Cox, H. (1987). Living environments in later life. In H. Cox (Ed.), *Annual Editions: Aging* (5th ed., pp. 180–181). Sluice Dock, Guilford, CT: Dushkin.

Craik, F. I. M. (1968). Short-term memory and the aging process. In G. A. Talland (Ed.), *Human aging and behavior* (pp. 131–168). New York: Academic Press.

Cribier, F. (1981). Changing retirement patterns: The experience of a cohort of Parisian salaried workers. *Aging and Society, 1*(3), 12–18.

Cumming, E., Dean, L. R., Newell, D. S., & McCaffrey, I. (1960). Disengagement—a tentative theory of aging. *Sociometry, 22*, 23–35.

Cumming, E., & Henry, W. E. (1961). *Growing old: The process of disengagement.* New York: Basic Books.

Curtin, S. R. (1972). *Nobody ever died of old age.* Boston: Little, Brown.

Cutler, N. E. (1974). *The impact of subjective age identification on social and political attitudes.* Paper presented at the 27th Annual Meeting of the Gerontological Society, Portland, OR.

Cutler, S. J. (1976). Age differences in voluntary association membership. *Social Forces, 55*, 43–58.

Cutler, S. J. (1977). Aging and voluntary association participation. *Journal of Gerontology, 32*, 470–479.

Dancy, J. (1977). *The black elderly: A guide for practitioners.* Ann Arbor: University of Michigan Institute for Gerontology.

Davis, R. H. (1980). *Television and the aging audience.* Los Angeles: Andrus Gerontology Center, University of Southern California.

Dawson, D., Hendershot, G., & Fulton, J. (1987, June 10). Aging in the eighties:

Functional limitations of individuals 65 and over. *Advance Data,* Number 133. Washington, DC: National Center for Health Statistics.

de Beauvoir, S. (1972). *The coming of age* (P. O'Brien, trans.). New York: Putnam.

Denckla, W. D. (1974). Role of the pituitary and thyroid glands on the decline of minimal $O_2$ consumption with age. *Journal of Clinical Investigation, 53,* 572–581.

Dennis, W. (1966). Creative productivity between the ages of twenty and eighty years. *Journal of Gerontology, 21,* 1–8.

DeSpelder, L. A., & Strickland, A. L. (1983). *The last dance: Encountering death and dying.* Palo Alto, CA: Mayfield.

deVries, H. (1983). The physiology of exercise and aging. In D. Woodruff & J. Birren (Eds.), *Aging: Scientific perspectives and social issues* (2nd ed., pp. 285–304). Monterey, CA: Brooks/Cole.

deVries, H. A., & Hales, D. (1982). *Fitness after fifty.* New York: Charles Scribner's.

Dickens, W. J., & Perlman, D. (1981). Friendship over the life-cycle. In S. W. Duck & R. Gilmour (Eds.), *Personal relationships 2. Developing personal relationships* (pp. 91–122). New York: Academic Press.

Dingle, J. (1973). *The ills of man: Life and death and medicine.* San Francisco: Freeman.

Docs find geriatric difficulties (1978, March 19). *Stockton (Calif.) Record,* p. 19.

Doering, M., Rhodes, S. R., & Schuster, M. (1983). *The aging worker: Research and recommendations.* Beverly Hills, CA: Sage.

Doppelt, J. E., & Wallace, W. L. (1955). Standardization of the Wechsler Adult Intelligence Scale for older persons. *Journal of Abnormal & Social Psychology, 51,* 312–330.

Dowd, J. J., & Bengtson, V. L. (1978). Aging in minority populations: An examination of the double jeopardy hypothesis. *Journal of Gerontology, 33,* 427–434.

Dussich, J. P. J., & Eickman, C. J. (1976). The elderly victim: Vulnerability to the criminal act. In J. Goldsmith & S. Goldsmith (Eds.), *Crime and the elderly— challenge and response* (pp. 91–98). Lexington, MA: Heath.

Duvall, E. M. (1977). *Marriage and family development* (5th ed.). Philadelphia: Lippincott.

Eisdorfer, C. (1963). The WAIS performance of the aged: A retest evaluation. *Journal of Gerontology, 18,* 169–172.

Eisdorfer, C. (1969). Intellectual and cognitive changes in the aged. In E. W. Busse & E. Pfeiffer (Eds.), *Behavior and adaptation in late life* (pp. 237–250). Boston: Little, Brown.

Eisdorfer, C., Nowlin, J., & Wilkie, F. (1970). Improvement in learning in the aged by modification of autonomic nervous system activity. *Science, 170,* 1327–1329.

Ekerdt, D. J., & Bosse, R. (1985, August). *Period effects on planned age for retirement: 1975 to 1984.* Paper presented at the annual meeting of the American Sociological Association, Washington, DC.

Ekerdt, D. J., Bosse, R., & LoCastro, J. (1983). Claims that retirement improves health. *Journal of Gerontology, 38,* 231–236.

Elderly demanding equal TV time. (1977, August 10). *Los Angeles Times,* p. VI-1.

Ellis, A. (1962). *Reason and emotion in psychotherapy.* New York: Lyle Stuart.

Elsayed, M., Ismail, A. H., & Young, R. S. (1980). Intellectual differences of adult men related to age and physical fitness before and after an exercise program. *Journal of Gerontology, 35,* 383–387.

Epstein, L. J. (1976). Depression in the elderly. *Journal of Gerontology, 31,* 278–282.

Erikson, E. H. (1963). *Childhood and society* (2nd ed.). New York: Norton.

Erikson, E. H. (1968). *Identity, youth, and crisis.* New York: Norton.

Erikson, E. H. (1976). Reflection on Dr. Borg's life cycle. *Daedalus, 105*(2), 1–28.

Federal Council on the Aging, U.S. Dept. of Health & Human Services. (1979). *Policy issues concerning elderly minorities.* DHHS Pub. No. (HDS) 80-20670. Washington, DC: U.S. Government Printing Office.

Feifel, H. (1959). Attitudes toward death. In H. Feifel (Ed.), *The meaning of death* (pp. 114–130). New York: McGraw-Hill.

Ferrare, N. A. (1962). *Institutionalization and attitude change in an aged population: A field study and dissidence theory.* Unpublished doctoral dissertation, Western Reserve University, Cleveland, OH.

Fletcher, C. R. (1972). How not to interview an elderly clinic patient: A case illustration and the interviewer's explanation. *The Gerontologist, 12,* 398–402.

Fox, J. H. (1977). Effects of retirement and former work life on women's adaptation to old age. *Journal of Gerontology, 32,* 196–202.

Freiberg, K. L. (1987). *Human development: A life-span approach.* Boston: Jones & Bartlett.

Fries, J. F., & Crapo, L. M. (1981). *Vitality and aging: Implications of the rectangular curve.* San Francisco: Freeman.

Froehling, S. (1974). *Effects of propranolol on behavioral and physiological measures of elderly males.* Unpublished doctoral dissertation, Duke University, Durham, NC.

Gallup, G. (1977, December 25). To be happy is to be young, married, with a college background. *The Gallup Poll Release.* Princeton, NJ: Gallup Organization.

Gallup, G., & Proctor, W. (1982). *Adventures in immortality.* New York: McGraw Hill.

Galton, L. (1979, June 3). Best friend, best therapy? *Parade,* p. 20.

Garrett, D. N. (1978). The needs of the seriously ill and their families: The haven concept. *Aging 6*(1), 12–19.

Gergen, K. J., & Back, K. W. (1966). Cognitive construction in aging and attitudes toward international issues. In I. H. Simpson & J. C. McKinsey (Eds.), *Social aspects of aging* (pp. 322–334). Durham, NC: Duke University Press.

Gibson, M. J. (1982). Early retirement: A widespread phenomenon in Western countries. *Aging International, 9*(2), 15–17.

Gilligan, C. (1982). *In a different voice: Psychological theory and women's development.* Cambridge, MA: Harvard University Press.

Glaser, B. G., & Strauss, A. L. (1968). *Time for dying.* Chicago: Aldine.

Glasser, W. (1965). *Reality therapy: A new approach in psychiatry.* New York: Harper & Row.

Glenn, N. D. (1974). Aging and conservatism. *Annals of the American Academy of Political and Social Science, 415,* 176–186.

Glenn, N. D., & McLanahan, S. (1981). The effects of offspring on the psychological well-being of older adults. *Journal of Marriage and the Family, 43,* 409–421.

Glick, I. O., Weiss, R. S., & Parkes, C. M. (1974). *The first year of bereavement.* New York: Wiley.

Goldhamer, J., & Marshall, A. W. (1953). *Psychosis and civilization.* Glencoe, IL: The Free Press.

Gordon, C., Gaitz, C. M., & Scott, J. (1976). Leisure and lives: Personal expressivity across the life span. In R. Binstock & E. Shanas (Eds.), *Handbook of aging and the social sciences* (pp. 310–341). New York: Van Nostrand Reinhold.

Gorer, G. (1967). *Death, grief, and mourning.* Garden City, NJ: Anchor Books.

Gots, D. E. (1977). The long life diet. *Family Circle, 90*(9), 14, 20, 166, 168, 170.

Gove, W. (1973). Sex, marital status, and mortality. *American Journal of Sociology, 79*(1), 45–67.

Grad, S. (1987). *Income of the population 55 or over.* Pub. No. 13-111871. Washington, DC: U.S. Social Security Administration.

Granick, S., & Patterson, R. D. (1972). *Human aging, II: An eleven year follow-up biomedical and behavioral study.* Washington, DC: U.S. Government Printing Office.

Gratton, B., & Haug, M. (1983). Decision and adaptation: Research on female retirement. *Research on Aging, 5,* 59–76.

Gray Panthers of Greater Boston. (1985, January). *Media watch project.* Cambridge, MA: Author.

Gray, V. R. (1984). The psychological response of the dying patient. In P. S. Chaney (Ed.), *Dealing with death and dying* (2nd ed., pp. 21–26). Springhouse, PA: International Communications/Nursing Skill Books.

Greenberg, B. S., Korzenny, F., & Atkin, C. K. (1979). The portrayal of aging: Trends on commercial television. *Research on Aging, 1,* 319–334.

Greenwald, A. (1980). The totalitarian ego: Fabrication and revision of personal history. *American Psychologist, 35,* 603–618.

Gross, P. J. (1979). Crime prevention and the elderly. In A. P. Goldstein, W. J. Hoyer & P. J. Monti (Eds.), *Police and the elderly* (pp. 39–42). New York: Pergamon Press.

Gubrium, F. F. (1975). Being single in old age. *International Journal of Aging and Human Development, 6*(1), 29–41.

Gutmann, D. L. (1964). An exploration of ego configurations in middle and later life. In B. L. Neugarten (Ed.), *Personality in middle and late life: Empirical studies* (pp. 114–148). New York: Atherton Press.

Gutmann, D. L. (1967). Aging among the Highland Maya: A comparative study. *Journal of Personality & Social Psychology, 7,* 28–35.

Gutmann, D. L. (1969). *The country of old men: Cross-cultural studies in the psychology of later life.* Occasional Papers in Gerontology, No. 5. Ann Arbor and Detroit: University of Michigan and Wayne State University, Institute of Gerontology.

Gutmann, D. L. (1971). Dependency, illness and survival among Navajo men. In E. Palmore & F. C. Jeffers (Eds.), *Prediction of life span* (pp. 181–198). Lexington, MA: Heath.

Gutmann, D. L. (1972). Ego psychological and developmental approaches to the retirement crisis in men. In F. M. Carp (Ed.), *Retirement* (pp. 267–305). New York: Behavioral Publications.

Gutmann, D. L. (1974). Alternatives to disengagement: The old men of the highland Druze. In R. A. LeVine (Ed.), *Culture and personality: Contemporary readings* (pp. 232–245). Chicago: Aldine.

Gutmann, D. L. (1977). The cross-cultural perspective: Notes toward a comparative psychology of aging. In J. E. Birren & K. W. Schaie (Eds.), *Handbook of the psychology of aging* (pp. 302–326). New York: Van Nostrand Reinhold.

Hagestad, G. (1978). *Patterns of communication and influence between grandparents and grandchildren in a changing society.* Paper presented at the World Congress of Sociology, Upsala, Sweden.

Hall, G. S. (1922). *Senescence: The second half of life.* New York: Appleton.

Hambly, W. D. (1974). Funeral customs. *The world book encyclopedia* (Vol. 9). Chicago: Field Educational Enterprises.

Hansen, G. O. (1975). Meeting housing challenges: Involvement—the elderly. In *Housing issues. Proceedings of the Fifth Annual Meeting, American Association of Housing Education.* Lincoln, NE: University of Nebraska Press.

Hansen, J. C., Stevic, R. R., & Warner, R. W. (1977). *Counseling theory and process* (2nd ed.). Boston: Allyn & Bacon.

Hare, P. H., & Haske, M. (1984, January). Innovative living arrangements: A source of long-term care. *Aging Magazine,* pp. 3–8.

Harman, D., Heidrick, M. L., & Eddy, D. E. (1976, September). *Free radical theory of aging: Effect of antioxidants on humoral and cell-mediated response as a function of age.* Paper presented at the 6th Annual Meeting of the American Aging Association, Washington, DC.

Harris, L. (1981). *Aging in the eighties: America in transition.* Washington, DC: National Council on the Aging.

Harris, L., & Associates. (1975). *The myth and reality of aging in America.* Washington, DC: National Council on the Aging.

Harris, L., & Associates. (1979). *1979 study of American attitudes towards pensions and retirement.* New York: Johnson & Higgins.

Havighurst, R. J., Neugarten, B. L., & Tobin, S. S. (1973, August). *Disengagement and patterns of aging.* Paper presented at the meeting of the International Association of Gerontology, Copenhagen, Denmark.

Hayflick, L. (1977). The cellular basis for biological aging. In C. E. Finch & L. Hayflick (Eds.), *Handbook of the biology of aging* (pp. 159–186). New York: Van Nostrand Reinhold.

Hayflick, L. (1980). The cell biology of human aging. *Scientific American, 242,* 58–66.

Hayflick, L. (1984). The aging of humans and their cultured cells. *Resident and Staff Physician, 30*(8), 33.

Hechinger, G. (1977). Margaret Mead: Growing old in America. *Family Circle, 90*(8), 27–32.

Helsing, K. J., & Szklo, M. (1981). Mortality after bereavement. *American Journal of Epidemiology, 114,* 41–52.

Herr, J. J., & Weakland, J. H. (1979). *Counseling elders and their families.* New York: Springer.

Hertzog, C., Schaie, K. W., & Gribbin, K. (1978). Cardiovascular disease and changes in intellectual functioning from middle to old age. *Journal of Gerontology, 33,* 872–883.

Hickey, T., & Douglass, R. S. (1981). Neglect and abuse of older family members: Professionals' perspectives and case experiences. *The Gerontologist, 21,* 171–176.

Hickey, T., Hickey, L., & Kalish, R. A. (1968). Children's perceptions of the elderly. *Journal of Genetic Psychology, 112,* 227–235.

Hickey, T., & Kalish, R. A. (1968). Young people's perceptions of adults. *Journal of Gerontology, 23,* 216–219.

Hing, E. (1987, May 14). Use of nursing homes by the elderly: Preliminary data from the 1985 National Nursing Home Survey. *Advance Data*, No. 135. Washington, DC: National Center for Health Statistics.

Hinton, J. (1972). *Dying* (2nd ed.). Baltimore: Penguin.

Hochschild, A. R. (1973). *The unexpected community*. Englewood Cliffs, NJ: Prentice-Hall.

Hodgkins, J. (1962). Influence of age on the speed of reaction and movement in females. *Journal of Gerontology, 173*, 385–389.

Holmes, T. H., & Rahe, R. H. (1967). The social readjustment scale. *Journal of Psychosomatic Research, 11*, 213–218.

Horn, J. L. (1982). The theory of fluid and crystallized intelligence in relation to concepts of cognitive psychology and aging in adulthood. In F. J. M. Craik & S. Trehub (Eds.), *Aging and cognitive processes* (pp. 237–278). New York: Plenum.

Horn, J. L., & Donaldson, G. (1976). On the myth of intellectual decline in adulthood. *American Psychologist, 31*, 701–719.

Housing for the aging. (1977, May). *Architectural Record, 16*, 123–138.

Howell, S. C. (1980). *Designing elderly housing: Patterns of use*. Cambridge, MA: MIT Press.

Hoyer, W. J., & Plude, D. J. (1980). Attentional and perceptual processes in the study of cognitive aging. In L. Poon (Ed.), *Aging in the 1980s* (pp. 227–238). Washington, DC: American Psychological Association.

Hurlock, E. B. (1980). *Developmental psychology: A lifespan approach* (5th ed.). New York: McGraw-Hill.

Inglis, J., Ankus, M. N., & Sykes, D. H. (1968). Age-related differences in learning and short-term memory from childhood to the senium. *Human Development, 11*, 42–52.

Ingram, C. (1980, October 19). State panel to examine "sexual minority" issues. *Los Angeles Times*, p. I-1.

Ivester, C., & King, K. (1977). Attitudes of adolescents toward the aged. *The Gerontologist, 17*, 85–89.

Jacobs, E., Winter, P. M., Alvis, H. J., & Small, S. M. (1969). Hyperbaric oxygen: Temporary aid for senile minds. *Journal of the American Medical Association, 209*, 1435–1438.

Jacobs, R. H., & Vinick, B. H. (1979). *Reengagement in later life: Re-employment and remarriage*. Stamford, CT: Greylock Publishers.

Jacoby, S. (1974, March 31). Waiting for the end: On nursing homes. *New York Times Magazine*, pp. 13 ff.

Jarvik, L. F., & Bank, L. (1983). Aging twins: Longitudinal aging data. In K. W. Schaie (Ed.), *Longitudinal studies of adult psychological development* (pp. 40–63). New York: Guilford Press.

Jones, H. E., & Conrad, H. S. (1933). The growth and decline of intelligence. *Genetic Psychology Monographs, 13*, 223–298.

Kahana, B., & Kahana, E. (1970a). Changes in mental status of elderly patients in age-integrated and age-segregated hospital milieus. *Journal of Abnormal Psychology, 75*, 177–181.

Kahana, B., & Kahana, E. (1970b). Grandparenthood from the perspective of the developing grandchild. *Developmental Psychology, 3*, 98–105.

Kahn, R. L. (1969). From 9 to 5. *Psychology Today, 3*(4), 34–38.

Kahn, R. L. (1977). Excess disabilities in the aged. In S. H. Zarit (Ed.), *Readings in aging and death: Contemporary perspectives* (pp. 228–229). New York: Harper & Row.

Kalish, R. A. (1976). Death and dying in a social context. In R. H. Binstock & E. Shanas (Ed.), *Handbook of aging and the social sciences* (pp. 483–507). New York: Van Nostrand.

Kalish, R. A. (1977). Dying and preparing for death: A view of families. In H. Feifel (Ed.), *New meanings of death* (pp. 215–232). New York: McGraw-Hill.

Kalish, R. A. (1982). *Late adulthood: Perspectives of human development* (2nd ed.). Monterey, CA: Brooks/Cole.

Kalish, R. A. (1985). The social context of death and dying. In R. H. Binstock & E. Shanas (Eds.), *Handbook of aging and the social sciences* (2nd ed., pp. 149–170). New York: Van Nostrand Reinhold.

Kalish, R. A., & Reynolds, D. K. (1976). *Death and ethnicity: A psychocultural study.* Los Angeles: University of Southern California Press.

Kalish, R. A., & Reynolds, D. K. (1981). *Death and ethnicity: A psychocultural study.* Farmingdale, NY: Baywood.

Kallmann, F. J., & Jarvik, L. F. (1959). Individual differences in constitution and genetic background. In J. E. Birren (Ed.), *Handbook of aging and the individual* (pp. 216–263). Chicago: University of Chicago Press.

Kallmann, F. J., & Sander, G. (1963). Twin studies on senescence. In R. G. Kuhlen & G. G. Thompson (Eds.), *Psychological studies of human development* (pp. 124–130). New York: Appleton-Century-Crofts.

Kaplan, H. B., & Pokorny, A. D. (1969). Self-derogation and psychosocial adjustment. *Journal of Nervous and Mental Disease, 149,* 421–434.

Kastenbaum, R. (1964). The reluctant therapist. In R. Kastenbaum (Ed.), *New thoughts on old age* (pp. 139–145). New York: Springer.

Kastenbaum, R. (1966). On the meaning of time in later life. *Journal of Genetic Psychology, 109,* 9–25.

Kastenbaum, R. (1971). Age: Getting there on time. *Psychology Today, 5*(7), 52–54, 82–84.

Kastenbaum, R. (1981). *Death, society, and human experience* (2nd ed.). St. Louis: C. V. Mosby.

Kastenbaum, R., & Aisenberg, R. (1972). *The psychology of death.* New York: Springer.

Kastenbaum, R., & Candy, S. (1973). The 4% fallacy: A methodological and empirical critique of extended care facility population statistics. *International Journal of Aging and Human Development, 4,* 15–21.

Kastenbaum, R., & Durkee, N. (1964). Young people view old age. In R. Kastenbaum (Ed.), *New thoughts on old age* (pp. 237–250). New York: Springer.

Kavanaugh, R. E. (1974). *Facing death.* Baltimore: Penguin Books.

Kevles, B. (1986, August 27). Alzheimer's link to aluminum explored. *Los Angeles Times,* p. V-6.

Kimmel, D. C. (1978). Adult development and aging: A gay perspective. *Journal of Social Issues, 34,* 113–130.

Kimmel, D. C. (1979–1980). Life history interviews of aging gay men. *International Journal of Aging and Human Development, 10,* 239–248.

Kimmel, D. C. (1980). *Adulthood and aging* (2nd ed.). New York: Wiley.

Kinsey, A. C., Pomeroy, W. B., & Martin, C. C. (1948). *Sexual behavior in the human male*. Philadelphia: Saunders.

Kirchner, W. K. (1958). Age differences in short-term retention of rapidly changing information. *Journal of Experimental Psychology, 55*, 352–358.

Kivett, V. R. (1976). The aged in North Carolina: Physical, social, and environmental characteristics and sources of assistance. *Technical Bulletin No. 237*. Raleigh, NC: Agricultural Experiment Station.

Klein, R. (1972). Age, sex, and task difficulty as predictors of social conformity. *Journal of Gerontology, 27*, 229–235.

Kleinmuntz, B. (1980). *Essentials of abnormal psychology*. New York: Harper & Row.

Knopf, O. (1975). *Successful aging*. New York: Viking.

Kobrin, F., & Hendershot, G. (1977). Do family ties reduce mortality? Evidence from the United States, 1966–68. *Journal of Marriage and the Family, 39*, 737–745.

Kogan, N. (1961). Attitudes toward old people. *Journal of Abnormal Psychology, 62*, 44–54.

Kogan, N., & Shelton, F. (1962). Beliefs about old people: A comparative study of older and younger samples. *Journal of Genetic Psychology, 100*, 93–111.

Kubey, R. W. (1980). Television and aging: Past, present, and future. *The Gerontologist, 20*, 16–35.

Kübler-Ross, E. (1969). *On death and dying*. New York: Macmillan.

Kübler-Ross, E. (1974). *Questions and answers on death and dying*. New York: Macmillan.

Landis, J. T. (1942). What is the happiest period of life? *School and Society, 55*, 643–645.

Langer, E. J., & Rodin, J. (1976). The effects of choice and enhanced personal responsibility for the aged: A field experiment in an institutional setting. *Journal of Personality & Social Psychology, 34*, 191–198.

Lawton, M. P. (1975). *Social and medical services in housing for the elderly*. Philadelphia: Philadelphia Geriatric Center.

Lawton, M. P. (1979). Clinical geropsychology: Problems and prospects. In *Master lectures on the psychology of aging*. Washington, DC: American Psychological Association.

Lawton, M. P., & Yaffe, S. (1980). Victimization and fear of crime in elderly public housing tenants. *Journal of Gerontology, 35*, 768–779.

Lee, G. R., & Ellithorpe, E. (1982). Intergenerational change and subjective well-being among the elderly. *Journal of Marriage and the Family, 44*, 217–224.

Lefcourt, H. M. (1973). The function of illusions of control and freedom. *American Psychologist, 23*, 417–425.

Lehman, H. C. (1953). *Age and achievement*. Princeton, NJ: Princeton University Press.

Lehman, H. C. (1962). The creative production rates of present versus past generations of scientists. *Journal of Gerontology, 17*, 409–417.

Lehman, H. C. (1966). The psychologist's most creative years. *American Psychologist, 21*, 363–369.

Lerner, R. M., & Busch-Rossnagel, N. (Eds.). (1981). *Individuals as producers of their own development*. New York: Academic Press.

Lesser, J., Lazarus, L. W., Frankel, R., & Havasy, S. (1981). Reminiscence group therapy with psychotic geriatric inpatients. *The Gerontologist, 21,* 291–296.

Levinson, D. J. (1978). *The seasons of a man's life.* New York: Knopf.

Lieberman, M. A. (1965). Psychological correlates of impending death: Some preliminary observations. *Journal of Gerontology, 20,* 181–190.

Lieberman, M. A. (1973, April). Grouchiness: A survival asset. *University of Chicago Alumni Magazine,* pp. 11–14.

Lieberman, M. A., & Coplan, A. S. (1969). Distance from death as a variable in the study of aging. *Developmental Psychology, 2,* 71–84.

Lipman, V. (1979, July 8). How can artists rob elderly. *Parade,* pp. 22–23.

Lobsenz, N. M. (1974, January 20). Sex and the senior citizen. *New York Times Magazine,* pp. 8–9.

Loether, H. J. (1975). *Patterns of aging* (2nd ed.). Belmont, CA: Dickenson Publishing.

Lombana, J. H. (1976). Counseling the elderly: Remediation plus prevention. *Personnel & Guidance Journal, 55,* 119–121.

Long, J. B. (1975). The death that ends death in Hinduism and Buddhism. In E. Kübler-Ross (Ed.), *Death: The final stage of growth* (pp. 52–72). Englewood Cliffs, NJ: Prentice-Hall.

Longino, C. F., & Kart, C. S. (1982). Explicating activity theory: Formal replication. *Journal of Gerontology, 37,* 713–722.

Longworth, R. C. (1978, April 9). Soviets' geriatric sensations: They're old, but not that old. *San Francisco Chronicle,* p. 3.

Lopata, H. Z. (1973). *Widowhood in an American city.* Cambridge, MA: Schenkman.

Lopata, H. Z. (1979). *Women as widows: Support systems.* New York: Elsevier.

Lowenthal, M. F. (1964). Social isolation and mental illness in old age. *American Sociological Review, 29*(1), 54–70.

Lowenthal, M. F., & Haven, C. (1968). Interaction and adaptation: Intimacy as a critical variable. *American Sociological Review, 33,* 20–30.

Lowenthal, M. F., Thurnher, M., & Chiriboga, D. (1975). *Four states of life.* San Francisco: Jossey-Bass.

Lynch, J. J. (1977). *The broken heart: The medical consequences of loneliness.* New York: Basic Books.

Maas, H., & Kuypers, J. (1974). *From thirty to seventy.* San Francisco: Jossey-Bass.

Madden, D. J. (1985). Age-related slowing in the retrieval of information from long-term memory. *Journal of Gerontology, 40,* 208–210.

Maddox, G. L. (1968). Persistence of life style among the elderly: A longitudinal study of patterns of social activity in relation to life satisfaction. In B. L. Neugarten (Ed.), *Middle age and aging: A reader in social psychology* (181–183). Chicago: University of Chicago Press.

Maddox, G. L. (1970). Persistence of life style among the elderly. In E. Palmore (Ed.), *Normal aging* (pp. 329–331). Durham, NC: Duke University Press.

Manion, U. V. (1976). Preretirement counseling: The need of a new approach. *Personnel & Guidance Journal, 55,* 119–121.

Mannik, M., & Gilliland, B. C. (1980). Degenerative joint disease. In K. J. Issellbacher et al. (Eds.), *Harrison's principles of internal medicine* (9th ed., pp. 1894–1896). New York: McGraw-Hill.

Margolis, B., & Kroes, W. (1972). Work and the health of man. Paper commissioned by the Special Task Force, *Work in America.* Cambridge, MA: MIT Press.

Marshall, J. R. (1978). Changes in aged white male suicide: 1948–1972. *Journal of Gerontology, 33,* 763–768.

Masters, W. H., & Johnson, V. E. (1966). *Human sexual response.* Boston: Little, Brown.

Masters, W. H., & Johnson, V. E. (1970). *Human sexual inadequacy.* Boston: Little, Brown.

Mathieu, J. T. (1972). *Dying and death role-expectation: A comparative analysis.* Unpublished doctoral dissertation, University of Southern California, Los Angeles, CA.

Maugh, T. H. (1986, April 15). Firm hopes to market new "memory" drug. *Los Angeles Times,* p. I-3.

McCluskey, H. (1982). Education for older adults. In C. Eisdorfer (Ed.), *Annual review of gerontology and geriatrics* (Vol. 3, pp. 403–428). New York: Springer.

McCormack, P. (1979, August 15). Race tracks, bus depots: Social centers for elderly. *Los Angeles Times,* Pt. 1-B, p. 2.

McCormack, P. (1980, November 9). Elderly victims of abuse may be getting needed help soon. *Los Angeles Times,* pp. I-2, 24.

McCracken, J. (1976, August 7). The company tells me I'm old. *Saturday Review,* pp. 21–23.

McGee, J., & Wells, K. (1982). Gender typing and androgyny in later life. *Human Development, 25,* 116–139.

McPherson, B., & Guppy, N. (1979). Pre-retirement lifestyle and the degree of planning for retirement. *Journal of Gerontology, 34,* 254–263.

Medley, M. (1976). Satisfaction with life among persons sixty-five years and older: A causal model. *Journal of Gerontology, 31,* 448–455.

Meltzer, H., & Ludwig, D. (1971). Age differences in positive mental health of workers. *Journal of Genetic Psychology, 119,* 163–173.

Metchnikoff, E. (1908). *The prolongation of life.* New York: Putnam & Sons.

Minot, C. (1908). *The problems of age, growth, and death.* New York: Putnam & Sons.

Moberg, D. O. (1971). *Spiritual well-being.* Paper presented at the White House Conference on Aging. Washington, DC: U.S. Government Printing Office.

Mondale, W. S. (1975, November 6). Federal Employees Preretirement Assistance Act of 1975. *Congressional Record, 121*(164), pp. S.19393–4.

Moody, R. A. (1975). *Life after life: The investigation of a phenomenon—survival of bodily death.* Atlanta: Mockingbird Press.

Morgan, C. M. (1937). The attitudes and adjustments of recipients of old age assistance in upstate and metropolitan New York. *Archives of Psychology, 30*(214).

Morrison, M. H. (1983). The aging of the U.S. population: Human resource implications. *Monthly Labor Review, 106,* 15–19.

Mortimer, E. A., Monson, R. R., & MacMahon, B. (1977). Reduced coronary heart disease mortality in men residing in high altitude. *New England Journal of Medicine, 296,* 581–585.

Mowen, J. C. (1987). *Consumer behavior.* New York: Macmillan.

Nadelson, T. (1969). A survey of literature on the adjustment of the aged to retirement. *Journal of Geriatric Psychiatry, 3,* 3–20.

Nathanson, P. S. (1977). The necessity for legal services. In R. A. Kalish (Ed.), *The later years: Social applications of gerontology* (pp. 203–209). Monterey, CA: Brooks/Cole.

National Center for Health Statistics. (1987a, June). Advance report on final marriage statistics, 1984. *Monthly Vital Statistics Report, 36*(2), Suppl. 2.

National Center for Health Statistics. (1987c, August 28). Advance report of final mortality statistics, 1985. *Monthly Vital Statistics Report, 36*(5). Suppl. DHHS Pub. No. (PHS) 87-1120. Hyattsville, MD: Public Health Service.

National Center for Health Statistics. (1988a, March 21). Births, marriages, divorces, and deaths for 1987. *Monthly Vital Statistics Report, 36*(12). DHHS Pub. No. (PHS) 80-1120. Hyattsville, MD: Public Health Service.

National Center for Health Statistics. (1988b, July 29). Annual summary of births, marriages, divorces, and deaths: United States, 1987. *Monthly Vital Statistics Report, 36*(13). DHHS Pub. No. (PHS) 88-1120. Hyattsville, MD: Public Health Service.

National Institute on Aging. (1980, July). Age page. Accidents and safety. Bethesda, MD: Author.

National Retired Teachers Association, American Association of Retired Persons. (1978). *1978 Federal and State Legislative Program.* Washington, DC: Author.

National Safety Council. (1987). *Accident facts, 1987 edition.* Chicago: Author.

*National Tribal Chairman's Association.* (1976). Phoenix, AZ: National Indian Conference on Aging.

Nelson, L. P., & Nelson, V. (1973). *Religion and death anxiety.* Presentation to the annual joint meeting, Society for the Scientific Study of Religion and Religious Research Association, San Francisco, CA.

Neugarten, B. L. (1968a). The awareness of middle age. In B. L. Neugarten (Ed.), *Middle age and aging: A reader in social psychology* (pp. 93–98). Chicago: University of Chicago Press.

Neugarten, B. L. (1968b). Adult personality: Toward a psychology of the life cycle. In B. L. Neugarten (Ed.), *Middle age and aging: A reader in social psychology* (pp. 137–147). Chicago: University of Chicago Press.

Neugarten, B. L. (1971). Grow old along with me! The best is yet to be. *Psychology Today, 5*(7), 45–48 ff.

Neugarten, B. L. (1973). Personality changes in late life: A developmental perspective. In C. Eisdorfer & M. P. Lawton (Eds.), *The psychology of adult development and aging* (pp. 311–338). Washington, DC: American Psychological Association.

Neugarten, B. L. (1975, January 18). The rise of the young-old. *New York Times,* p. 29.

Neugarten, B. L. (1976). The psychology of aging: An overview. *Master lectures in developmental psychology.* Washington, DC: American Psychological Association. (Cassette tape).

Neugarten, B. L. (1977). Personality and aging. In J. E. Birren & K. W. Schaie (Eds.), *Handbook of the psychology of aging* (pp. 626–649). New York: Van Nostrand Reinhold.

Neugarten, B. L., and Associates. (1964). *Personality in middle and late life.* New York: Atherton.

Neugarten, B. L., Havighurst, R. J., & Tobin, S. S. (1968). Personality and patterns of aging. In B. L. Neugarten (Ed.), *Middle age and aging* (pp. 173–174). Chicago: University of Chicago Press.

Neugarten, B. L., & Weinstein, K. K. (1968). The changing American grandparent. In B. L. Neugarten (Ed.), *Middle age and aging: A reader in social psychology* (pp. 280–285). Chicago: University of Chicago Press.

New image for the old stereotype. (1977, August 11). *Los Angeles Times*, p. VI-1.

New York City Police Department-New York City Department of Aging. (1978). *Crime prevention for senior citizens*. New York: Police Dept. City of New York, Crime Prevention Section.

Newman, G., & Nichols, C. R. (1960). Sexual activities and attitudes in older persons. *Journal of the American Medical Association, 713*, 33–35.

Nisbet, J. D. (1957). Intelligence and age: Retesting after twenty-four years' interval. *British Journal of Educational Psychology, 27*, 190–198.

Nowak, C. (1974). *Concern with youthfulness and attractiveness in adult women*. Unpublished master's thesis, Wayne State University, Detroit, MI.

O'Rand, A., & Henretta, J. (1982). Delayed career entry, industrial pension structure, and early retirement in a cohort of unmarried women. *American Sociological Review, 47*, 365–373.

Offir, C. (1974). Old people's revolt—"At 65, work becomes a four-letter word." *Psychology Today, 7*(10), 40.

Overall, J. E., & Gorham, D. (1972). Organicity versus old age in objective and projective test performance. *Journal of Consulting & Clinical Psychology, 39*, 98–105.

Owens, W. A., Jr. (1953). Age and mental abilities: A longitudinal study. *Genetic Psychology Monographs, 48*, 3–54.

Owens, W. A., Jr. (1966). Age and mental abilities: A second adult follow-up. *Journal of Educational Psychology, 57*, 311–325.

Packer, L., & Smith, J. R. (1977). Extension of the lifespan of cultured normal human diploid cells by vitamin E. *Proceedings of the National Academy of Sciences, 71*, 4763–4767.

Palmore, E. (1969). Physical, mental and social factors in predicting longevity. *The Gerontologist, 393*, 103–108.

Palmore, E. (Ed.). (1970). *Normal aging*. Durham, NC: Duke University Press.

Palmore, E. (1980). The Facts on Aging quiz: A review of findings. *The Gerontologist, 20*, 669–672.

Palmore, E. (1981). *Social patterns in normal aging: Findings from the Duke Longitudinal Study*. Durham, NC: Duke University Press.

Palmore, E. (1982). Predictors of the longevity difference: A 25-year follow-up. *The Gerontologist, 225*, 513–518.

Palmore, E., Burchett, B., Fillenbaum, G. G., George, L. K., & Wallman, L. M. (1985). *Retirement: Causes and consequences*. New York: Springer.

Palmore, E., & Cleveland, W. (1976). Aging, terminal decline, and terminal drop. *Journal of Gerontology, 31*(1), 76–86.

Parkes, C. M. (1972). *Bereavement: Studies of grief in adult life*. New York: International Universities Press.

Parkes, C. M., Benjamin, B., & Fitzgerald, R. G. (1969). Broken heart: A statistical study of increased mortality among widowers. *British Medical Journal, 1*, 740–743.

Pascual-Leon, J. (1983). Growing into human maturity: Toward a metasubjective theory of adult stages. In P. B. Baltes & O. G. Brim, Jr. (Eds.), *Life-span development and behavior* (Vol. 5, pp. 118–156). New York: Academic Press.

Pastalan, L. A. (1974, October). The simulation of age-related sensory losses. A new approach to the study of environmental barriers. *The New Outlook for the Blind*, 356–362.

Pattison, E. M. (1977). Death throughout the life cycle. In E. Pattison (Ed.), *The experience of dying* (pp. 18–26). Englewood Cliffs, NJ: Prentice-Hall.

Paul, A. (1986, September 10). With rise in proportion of population above age 65, sociologists say study of aging is a growth industry. *The Chronicle of Higher Education*, p. 4.

Peck, R. C. (1968). Psychological developments in the second half of life. In B. L. Neugarten (Ed.), *Middle age and aging: A reader in social psychology* (pp. 88–92). Chicago: University of Chicago Press.

Pedrick-Cornell, C., & Gelles, R. J. (1982). Elderly abuse: The status of current knowledge. *Family Relations, 31,* 457–465.

Perry, P. W. (1974). The night of ageism. *MH, 58*(3), 13–20.

Peterson, J. A. (1971, January). Marriage and sex and the older man and woman. *Modern Maturity.*

Peterson, J. A., & Payne, B. (1975). *Love in the later years.* New York: Associated Press.

Peterson, J., & Rosenblatt, R. (1986a, March 23). Life past 85: Often sweet but painful. *Los Angeles Times,* pp. I-1, 26.

Peterson, J., & Rosenblatt, R. (1986b, December 30). 'Boomers' face a brave old world. *Los Angeles Times,* pp. I-1, 10, 11.

Peterson, L. R., & Peterson, M. J. (1959). Short-term retention of individual verbal items. *Journal of Experimental Psychology, 58,* 193–198.

Pfeiffer, E. (1977). Psychopathology and social pathology. In J. E. Birren & K. W. Schaie (Eds.), *Handbook of the psychology of aging* (pp. 650–671). New York: Van Nostrand Reinhold.

Pfeiffer, E., Verwoerdt, A., & Davis, G. C. (1972). Sexual behavior in middle life. *American Journal of Psychiatry, 128,* 1264.

Pfeiffer, E., Verwoerdt, A., & Wang, H. S. (1968). Sexual behavior in aged men and women. *Archives of General Psychiatry, 19,* 755–758.

Pfeiffer, E., Verwoerdt, A., & Wang, H. S. (1969). The natural history of sexual behavior in a biologically advantaged group of aged individuals. *Journal of Gerontology, 24,* 193–198.

Phillips, B. S. (1962). *The aged in a central Illinois community.* Urbana: University of Illinois Press.

Phillips, D. P. (1975). Deathday and birthday: An unexpected connection. In K. W. C. Kammeyer (Ed.), *Population studies* (2nd ed.). Skokie, IL: Rand McNally.

Phillips, D. P., & Feldman, K. A. (1973). A dip in deaths before ceremonial occasions: Some new relationships between social integration and mortality. *American Sociological Review, 38,* 678–696.

Piaget, J. (1952). *The origins of intelligence in children.* New York: International Universities Press.

Pillemer, K., & Finkelhor, D. (1988). The prevalence of elderly abuse: A random survey. *The Gerontologist, 28*(1), 51–57.

Pines, M. (1976). Age-ism . . . slashing our own tires. *APA Monitor, 7*(12), 7.

Plemons, J. K., Willis, S. L., & Baltes, P. B. (1978). Modifiability of fluid intelligence in aging: A short-term longitudinal training approach. *Journal of Gerontology, 33,* 224–231.

Population Reference Bureau, Inc. (1987). *1987 world population data sheet* (prepared by Carl Haub & Mary Mederios Kent, demographers). Washington, DC: Author.

Porter, S. (1977, August 17). Retirees' cost of living jumps. *Greensboro* (N.C.) *Daily News,* p. A-8.

Porter, S. (1980, July 31). Elderly face gaps in Medicare coverage. *Stockton* (Calif.) *Record,* p. 52.

Puner, M. (1974). *To the good long life: What we know about growing old.* New York: Universe Books.

Quirk, D. A. (1976). Life span opportunities for the older adult. *Personnel & Guidance Journal, 55,* 140–142.

Randall, J. L. (1988, February 25). Advertisers recognize senior citizen market. *The Times* (Trenton, NJ), p. B-6.

Raphael, S., & Robinson, M. (1980). The older lesbian: Love relationships and friendship patterns. *Alternative Lifestyles, 3,* 207–229.

Rawlings, M. (1978). *Beyond death's door.* Nashville, TN: Thomas Nelson.

Raymond, B. J. (1971). Free recall among the aged. *Psychological Reports, 29,* 1179–1182.

Reedy, M. N. (1983). Personality and aging. In D. S. Woodruff & J. E. Birren (Eds.), *Aging: Scientific perspectives and social issues* (2nd ed., pp. 112–136). Monterey, CA: Brooks/Cole.

Reedy, M. N., Birren, J. E., & Schaie, K. W. (1981). Age and sex differences in satisfying love relationships across the adult life span. *Human Development 24,* 52–66.

Reese, H. W., & Rodeheaver, D. (1985). Problem solving and complex decision making. In J. E. Birren & K. W. Schaie (Eds.), *Handbook of the psychology of aging* (2nd ed., pp. 474–499). New York: Van Nostrand Reinhold.

Reichard, S., Livson, F., & Petersen, P. G. (1962). *Aging and personality.* New York: Wiley.

Reichard, S., Livson, F., & Petersen, P. G. (1968). Adjustment to retirement. In B. L. Neugarten (Ed.), *Middle age and aging: A reader in social psychology* (pp. 178–180). Chicago: University of Chicago Press.

Reimanis, G., & Green, R. F. (1971). Imminence of death and intellectual decrement in the aging. *Developmental Psychology, 5,* 270–272.

Reisman, J. M. (1981). Adult friendships. In S. W. Duck & R. Gilmour (Eds.), *Personal relationships 2. Developing personal relationships* (pp. 205–230). New York: Academic Press.

Reports show decline in cardiovascular disease death rates. (1979, August 12). *Los Angeles Times,* p. A-13.

Rhodes, S. (1983). Age-related differences in work attitudes and behavior: A review and conceptual analysis. *Psychological Bulletin, 93,* 328–367.

Rich new market among nation's elderly. (1979, November 12). *U.S. News & World Report, 81,* 80–91.

Riegel, K. F. (1973). Dialectic operations: The final period of cognitive development. *Human Development, 16,* 346–370.

Riegel, K. F., & Riegel, R. M. (1972). Development, drop, and death. *Developmental Psychology, 6,* 306–319.

Riley, M. W., & Foner, A. (Eds.). (1968). *Aging and society.* New York: Russell Sage.

Robertson, J. F. (1976). Significance of grandparents: Perceptions of young adult grandchildren. *The Gerontologist, 16,* 137–140.

Robinson, J. P. (1969). Social changes as measured by time budgets. *Journal of Leisure Research, 1,* 75–77.

Rodin, J., & Langer, E. (1977). Long-term effects of a control-relevant intervention with institutionalized aged. *Journal of Personality and Social Psychology, 35,* 897–902.

Rodin, J., & Langer, E. (1980). Aging labels: The decline of control and the fall of self-esteem. *Journal of Social Issues, 36,* 12–29.

Roffwarg, H. P., Muzio, J. N., & Dement, W. C. (1966). Ontogenetic development of the human sleep-dream cycle. *Science, 152,* 604–619.

Rogers, C. R. (1965). *Client-centered therapy.* Boston: Houghton-Mifflin.

Rollins, B. C., & Feldman, H. (1970). Marital satisfaction over the life cycle. *Journal of Marriage and the Family, 32*(1), 20–28.

Romo, M., Siltanen, P., Theorell, T., & Rahe, R. H. (1974). World behavior, time urgency, and life-dissatisfactions in subjects with myocardial infarction: A cross-cultural study. *Journal of Psychosomatic Research, 18*(1), 1–8.

Rose, C. L. (1964). Social factors in longevity. *The Gerontologist, 4,* 27–37.

Rosenberg, M. (1964). *Society and the adolescent self-image.* Princeton, NJ: Princeton University Press.

Rosenblatt, R. A. (1986, July 6). 'Fountain of youth' eludes experts on age. *Los Angeles Times,* I-1, 24.

Rosenblatt, R. A. (1987a, June 9). Experts ask why women outlive men. *Los Angeles Times,* pp. I-1, 21.

Rosenblatt, R. A. (1987b, June 30). Inflation index for elderly studied. *Los Angeles Times,* p. I-12.

Rosenfeld, A. (1976a). *Prolongevity.* New York: Knopf.

Rosenfeld, A. (1976b). The Willy Loman complex. *Saturday Review, 3*(22), 24–26.

Rosenman, R. H., Brand, R. J., Jenkins, C. D., Friedman, M., Strauss, R., & Wurm, M. (1975). Coronary heart disease in the Western Collaborative Groups Study: A final follow-up experience to eight and one-half years. *Journal of the American Medical Association, 233,* 872–877.

Rosow, I. (1967). *Social integration of the aged.* New York: Free Press.

Ross, M. D. (1977). Effects of aging on otoconia. In S. S. Han & D. H. Coons (Eds.), *Special senses in aging. Proceedings of Symposium on Biology of Special Senses in Aging.* Ann Arbor, Institute of Gerontology, University of Michigan.

Rossiter, A. J. (1981, September 25). Technology brings need for new definition of death. *Los Angeles Times,* p. IA-3.

Ryan, R. (1978, January 22). Seniors want some surprising things. *Los Angeles Times,* p. VIII-1.

Sabom, M. (1983, January 16). "Clinically dead" patients reveal the peacefulness of dying. *Family Weekly,* pp. 11, 13.

Saleh, S. D., & Otis, J. L. (1964). Age and level of job satisfaction. *Personnel Psychology, 17,* 425–430.

Sargent, M. (1982, December 3). Researcher traces Alzheimer's disease eight generations back in one family. *APAMHA News, 8*(23), 3.

Sarton, M. (1978, January 30). More light. *New York Times,* p. A-21.

Sartre, J. P. (1957). *Existentialism and human emotions.* New York: Philosophical Library.

Saul, S. (1974). *Aging: An album of people growing old.* New York: Wiley.

Saunders, C. (1980). St. Christopher's Hospice. In E. Shneidman (Ed.), *Death: Current perspectives* (2nd ed., pp. 356–361). Palo Alto, CA: Mayfield.

Schaie, K. W. (1967). Age changes and age differences. *The Gerontologist, 7,* 128–132.

Schaie, K. W. (1977). Quasi-experimental research designs in the psychology of aging. In J. E. Birren & K. W. Schaie (Eds.), *Handbook of the psychology of aging* (pp. 39–59). New York: Van Nostrand Reinhold.

Schaie, K. W. (1977/1978). Toward a stage theory of adult cognitive development. *Aging and Human Development, 8,* 129–138.

Schaie, K. W. (1983). The Seattle Longitudinal Study: A twenty-one year exploration of psychometric intelligence in adulthood. In K. W. Schaie (Ed.), *Longitudinal studies of adult psychological development* (pp. 64–135). New York: Guilford Press.

Schaie, K. W., & Gribbin, K. (1975). Adult development and aging. *Annual Review of Psychology, 26,* 65–96.

Schaie, K. W., & Hertzog, C. (1986). Toward a comprehensive model of adult intellectual development: Contributions of the Seattle Longitudinal Study. In R. J. Sternberg (Ed.), *Advances in the psychology of human intelligence* (Vol. 3, pp. 79–118). Hillsdale, NJ: Lawrence Erlbaum Associates.

Schaie, K. W., & Labouvie-Vief, G. (1974). Generational versus ontogenetic components of change in adult cognitive behavior: A fourteen-year cross-sequential study. *Developmental Psychology, 10,* 305–320.

Schaie, K. W., & Parham, I. A. (1976). Stability of adult personality: Fact or fable? *Journal of Personality and Social Psychology, 36,* 146–158.

Schaie, K. W., & Strother, C. R. (1968). A cross-sequential study of age changes in cognitive behavior. *Psychological Bulletin, 70,* 671–680.

Schaie, K. W., & Willis, S. L. (1986a). Can decline in adult cognitive functioning be reversed? *Developmental Psychology, 22,* 223–232.

Schaie, K. W., & Willis, S. L. (1986b). *Adult development and aging* (2nd ed.). Boston: Little, Brown.

Schmale, A. H. (1971). Hopelessness as a predictor of cervical cancer. *Social Science & Medicine, 5,* 95–100.

Schmeck, H. M., Jr. (1987, November 17). Experts voice hope in Alzheimer's fight. *New York Times,* pp. C-1, 10.

Schonberg, W. B., & Potter, H. C. (1976). Friendship fluctuations in senescence. *Journal of Genetic Psychology, 129,* 333–334.

Schonfield, D. (1965). Memory changes with age. *Nature, 208,* 918.

Schuckit, M. A. (1977). Geriatric alcoholism and drug abuse. *The Gerontologist, 17,* 168–174.

Schultz, R., & Bazerman, M. (1980). Ceremonial occasions and mortality: A second look. *American Psychologist, 35,* 253–261.

Schwartz, A. N., Snyder, C. L., & Peterson, J. A. (1984). *Aging and life: An introduction to gerontology* (2nd ed.). New York: Holt, Rinehart & Winston.

Scott-Maxwell, F. (1968). *The measure of my days.* New York: Knopf.

Seefeldt, C., Jantz, R. K., Galper, A., & Serock, E. (1977). Children's attitudes toward the elderly: Educational implications. *Educational Gerontology, 2,* 301–310.

Select Committee on Aging. (1976). *Federal responsibility to the elderly.* Washington, DC: U.S. Government Printing Office.

Seligman, M. E. P. (1975). *Helplessness.* San Francisco: Freeman.

Selye, H. (1976). *The stress of life* (rev. ed.). New York: McGraw-Hill.

Senior citizens showing up for drug counseling. (1978, June 22). *Stockton* (Calif.) *Record,* p. 31.

Serock, E., Seefeldt, C., Jantz, R. K., & Galper, A. (1977). As children see old folks. *Today's Education, 66*(2), 70–73.

Shanan, J. (1985). Personality types and culture in later adulthood. *Contributions to human development* (Vol. 12). Basel: Karger. (Monograph)

Shanas, E. (1972). Adjustment to retirement. In F. M. Carp (Ed.), *Retirement* (pp. 219–244). Berkeley, CA: Behavioral Publications.

Shanas, E., Townsend, P., Wedderburn, D., Friis, H., Milhoj, P., & Stehouwer, J. (Eds.). (1968). *Old people in three industrial societies.* New York: Atherton.

Sheppard, H. L. (1979). Work and retirement. In R. H. Binstock & E. Shanas (Eds.), *Handbook of aging and the social sciences.* (pp. 286–309). New York: Van Nostrand Reinhold.

Shichor, D. (1985). Male-female differences in elderly arrests: An exploratory analysis. *Justice Quarterly, 2,* 399–414.

Shichor, D., & Kebrin, S. (1978). Criminal behavior among the elderly. *The Gerontologist, 18,* 213–218.

Shneidman, E. S. (1980). Death work and stages of dying. In E. S. Shneidman (Ed.), *Death: Current perspectives* (2nd ed., pp. 305–311). Palo Alto, CA: Mayfield.

Shneidman, E. S. (1983). *Deaths of man.* New York: Jason Aronson.

Shock, N. W. (1952a). Aging and psychological adjustment. *Review of Educational Research, 22,* 439–458.

Shock, N. W. (1952b). Aging of homeostatic mechanisms. In A. I. Lansing (Ed.), *Cowdry's problems of aging* (3rd ed., pp. 415–446). Baltimore: Williams & Wilkins.

Shock, N. W. (1962). The physiology of aging. *Scientific American, 206*(1), 100–111.

Shock, N. W. (1977). Biological theories of aging. In J. E. Birren & K. W. Schaie (Eds.), *Handbook of the psychology of aging* (pp. 103–115). New York: Van Nostrand Reinhold.

Shock, N. W., Greulick, R. C., Andres, R., Arenberg, D., Costa, P. T., Lakatta, E. G., & Tobin, J. D. (1984). *Normal human aging: The Baltimore Longitudinal Study of Aging.* Washington, DC: U.S. Government Printing Office, NIH Publication No. 84-2450.

Siegel, R. K. (1980). *Deaths of man.* New York: Jason Aronson.

Siegler, I. C. (1983). Psychological aspects of the Duke Longitudinal Studies. In K. W. Schaie (Ed.), *Longitudinal studies of adult psychological development* (pp. 136–190). New York: Guilford Press.

Siegler, I. C., McCarty, S. M., & Logue, P. E. (1982). Wechsler Memory Scale scores, selective attrition, and distance from death. *Journal of Gerontology, 37,* 176–181.

Signorielli, N., & Gerbner, G. (1977). *The image of the elderly in primetime network television drama* (Rep. No. 12). University, PA: Institute for Applied Communication Studies, Annenberg School of Communications, University of Pennsylvania.

Silverman, P. (1969). The widow-to-widow program: An experiment in preventive information. *Mental Hygiene, 53,* 333–337.

Simmons, L. (1977, November 20). Your chance of living to be 100. *Los Angeles Times,* pp. V-1, 14–15.

Simonton, O. C., Matthews-Simonton, S., & Creighton, J. (1978). *Getting well again.* Los Angeles: J. P. Tarper.

Simpson, M. A. (1979). *The facts of death.* Englewood Cliffs, NJ: Prentice-Hall.

Sinex, F. M., & Myers, R. H. (1982). Alzheimer's disease, Down's syndrome, and aging: The genetic approach. In F. M. Sinex & C. R. Merril (Eds.), *Alzheimer's disease, Down's syndrome and aging* (pp. 3–13). New York: Academy of Sciences.

Smith, B. B. (1979, July 22). Aging: What we'll be we'll be. *Los Angeles Times,* p. VII-4.

Smith, D. M., & Khairi, M. R. A., Norton, J., & Johnston, C. C., Jr. (1976). Age and activity effects on rate of bone mineral loss. *Journal of Clinical Investigation, 58,* 716–721.

Smith, M. E. (1963). Delayed recall of previously memorized material after forty years. *Journal of Genetic Psychology, 102,* 3–4.

Social Security programs in the United States. (1987). *Social Security Bulletin, 50*(4), Washington, DC: U.S. Dept. of Health and Human Services.

Soviets say work spurs longevity. (1977, August 22). *Greensboro* (N.C.) *Daily News,* p. A-11.

Spence, D. L., & Robinson, B. (1966). Patterns of retirement in San Francisco. In F. M. Carp (Ed.), *The retirement process* (pp. 63–75). Public Health Service Publication #1778. Washington, DC: U.S. Government Printing Office.

Spence, D. L., Feigenbaum, E. M., Fitzgerald, F., & Roth, J. (1968). Medical student attitudes toward the geriatric patient. *Journal of American Geriatrics Society, 16,* 976–983.

Stagner, R. (1985). Aging in industry. In J. E. Birren & K. W. Schaie (Eds.), *Handbook of the psychology of aging* (2nd ed., pp. 789–817). New York: Van Nostrand Reinhold.

Steinbaum, B. (1973). *Attitudes toward the aged in nursing students before and after a course in gerontology.* Unpublished doctoral dissertation, Columbia University, New York.

Step-up in fight on crimes against elderly. (1977). *U.S. News & World Report, 82*(23), 62.

Stephens, J. (1976). *Loners, losers, and lovers: Elderly tenants in a slum hotel.* Seattle: University of Washington Press.

Stephens, P. (1986, July 6). Some nations are obsessed with aging. *Los Angeles Times,* pp. IV-3, 5.

Storandt, M. (1983). *Counseling and therapy with older adults.* Boston: Little, Brown.

Streib, G. F., & Schneider, C. J. (1971). *Retirement in American society.* Ithaca, NY: Cornell University Press.

Streib, G. F., & Thompson, W. E. (1965). The older person in a family context. In E. Shanas & G. Streib (Eds.), *Social structure and family: Intergenerational relations.* Englewood Cliffs, NJ: Prentice-Hall.

Stroebe, M. S., & Stroebe, W. (1983). Who suffers more? Sex differences in health risks of the widowed. *Psychological Bulletin, 93,* 279–301.

Study finds underweight people have shorter life spans too. (1980, May 5). *Los Angeles Times,* p. I-17.

Sudnow, D. (1967). *Passing on: The social organization of dying.* Englewood Cliffs, NJ: Prentice-Hall.

Suran, G. B., & Rizzo, J. V. (1979). *Special children: An integrative approach.* Glenview, IL: Scott Foresman.

Sussman, M. B. (1976). The family life of old people. In R. H. Binstock & E. Shanas (Eds.), *Handbook of aging and the social sciences* (pp. 218–243). New York: Van Nostrand Reinhold.

Sussman, M. B. (1977, February 12). *Incentives and family environments for the elderly.* Final Report AoA Grant No. 90-A-316. Washington, DC: Administration on Aging.

Sviland, M. A. P. (1975). Helping elderly couples become sexually liberated: Psychosocial issues. *Counseling Psychologist, 1*(5), 67–72.

Symonds, M. (1978, Fall). New CJE counselor. *Criminal Justice and the elderly,* pp. 4–5.

Taves, M. J., & Hansen, G. O. (1963). Seventeen hundred elderly citizens. In A. M. Rose (Ed.), *Aging in Minnesota* (pp. 73–181). Minneapolis: University of Minnesota Press.

Tavris, C. (1987, September 27). Old age is not what it used to be. *New York Times Magazine,* Pt. 2, pp. 25, 26, 91, 92.

Teaff, J. D., Lawton, M. P., Nahemow, L., & Carlson, D. (1978). Impact of age integration on the well-being of elderly tenants in public housing. *Journal of Gerontology, 33,* 130–133.

Thomas, L. (1975). *Lives of a cell: Notes of a biology watcher.* New York: Bantam.

Tibbitts, C. (1977). Older Americans in the family context. *Aging, 270–271,* 6–11.

Tolstoy, L. (1960). The death of Ivan Ilych. In L. Tolstoy, *Death of Ivan Ilych and other stories.* New York: New American Library. (Originally published in 1886)

Torrey, B. B., Kinsella, K. G., & Taeuber, C. M. (1987, July). *An aging world.* International Population Reports Services P-95, No. 78. Washington, DC: U.S. Department of Commerce, Bureau of the Census.

Treas, J., & VanHilst, A. (1976). Marriage and remarriage rates among older Americans. *The Gerontologist, 16,* 132–136.

Trela, J. E., & Sokolovsky, J. H. (1979). Culture, ethnicity, and policy for the aged. In D. Gelfand & A. Kutzik (Eds.), *Ethnicity and aging: Theory, research, and policy* (pp. 117–136). New York: Springer.

Trelease, M. L. (1975). Dying among Alaskan Indians. A matter of choice. In E. Kübler-Ross (Ed.), *Death: The final stage of growth* (pp. 27–37). Englewood Cliffs, NJ: Prentice-Hall.

Troll, L. E. (1982). *Continuations: Adult development and aging.* Monterey, CA: Brooks/Cole.

Troll, L. E., Miller, S. J., & Atchley, R. C. (1979). *Families in later life.* Belmont, CA: Wadsworth.

Tuddenham, R. D., Blumenkrantz, J., & Wilkin, W. R. (1968). Age changes in AGCT: A longitudinal study of average adults. *Journal of Counseling & Clinical Psychology, 32,* 659–663.

Turner, J. S., & Helms, D. B. (1987). *Lifespan development* (3rd ed.). New York: Holt, Rinehart & Winston.

Turpin, D. (1986, September 28). 'Old is in' for pioneer developer. *Los Angeles Times*, pp. VII-1, 5.

Ullmann, C. A. (1976). Preretirement planning: Does it prevent postretirement shock? *Personnel & Guidance Journal, 55,* 115–118.

University of California Cooperative Extension (1978, March). Suggestions for giving psychological help to older people. *Human Relations, 3*(3).

U.S. Bureau of Labor Statistics. (1986, August). *Consumer expenditure survey: Interview survey, 1984.* Bulletin 2267. Washington, DC: U.S. Department of Labor.

U.S. Bureau of the Census. (1981). 1980 Census of population. *Supplementary Reports,* PC80-S1-1. Washington, DC: U.S. Government Printing Office.

U.S. Bureau of the Census. (1982, April). Voting and registration in the election of November 1980. *Current Population Reports,* Series P-20, No. 370.

U.S. Bureau of the Census. (1983, November). Voting and registration in the election of November 1982. *Current Population Reports,* Series P-20, No. 383.

U.S. Bureau of the Census. (1984). Financial characteristics of the housing inventory for the United States and regions: 1983. *Current Housing Reports,* Series H-150-83, Annual Housing Survey: 1983, Part C (December) and unpublished data. Washington: U.S. Government Printing Office.

U.S. Bureau of the Census. (1985). *Statistical Abstracts of the United States* (105th ed.). Washington, DC: U.S. Government Printing Office.

U.S. Bureau of the Census. (1986a, March). Unpublished data from the Current Population Survey.

U.S. Bureau of the Census. (1986b, March). Voting and registration in the election of November 1984. *Current Population Reports,* Series P-20, No. 405.

U.S. Bureau of the Census. (1986c, May). Projections of the population of the United States, by age, sex, and race: 1983 to 2080. *Current Population Reports,* Series P-25, No. 952.

U.S. Bureau of the Census. (1986d, June). Characteristics of the population below the poverty level: 1984. *Current Population Reports,* Series P-60, No. 152.

U.S. Bureau of the Census. (1986e, July). Household wealth and asset ownership: 1984. *Current Population Reports,* Series P-70, No. 7.

U.S. Bureau of the Census. (1987a, February). Estimates of the population of the United States, by age, sex, and race: 1980–1986. *Current Population Reports,* Series P-25, No. 1000.

U.S. Bureau of the Census. (1987b, July). Money income and poverty status of families and persons in the United States: 1986. *Current Population Reports,* Series P-60, No. 157.

U.S. Department of Health and Human Services. (1987). *Vital statistics of the United States, 1984. Vol. II. Mortality, Pt. A.* Hyattsville, MD: Author.

U.S. Department of Health and Human Services. (1988, January). *Social security: How it works for you.* SSA Publication No. 05-10006. Washington, DC: U.S. Government Printing Office.

U.S. Department of Health, Education, and Welfare. (1977). *Fact sheet.* DHEW Pub. No. (HDS) 77-20223. Washington, DC: U.S. Government Printing Office.

U.S. Department of Housing and Urban Development. (1983). Unpublished data from the 1983 Annual Housing Survey.

U.S. Department of Justice, Federal Bureau of Investigation. (1987). *Uniform crime reports for the United States—1986.* Washington, DC: U.S. Government Printing Office.

U.S. Department of Justice, Law Enforcement Assistance Administration. (1979). *A mutual concern: Older Americans and the criminal justice system.* Rockville, MD: NCJRS Document Distribution.

U.S. Senate Special Committee on Aging. (1985, February 25). Heinz says first DRG study flags potential hazards for older Americans. *News.*

U.S. Senate Special Committee on Aging. (1987). *Aging America: Trends and projections* (1987–88 ed.). Washington, DC: Author.

Valliant, G. E. (1979). Natural history of male psychologic health: Effects of mental health on physical health. *New England Journal of Medicine, 301,* 1249–1254.

Veatch, R. M., & Tai, E. (1980). Talking about death: Patterns of lay and professional change. *Annals of the AAPSS, 447,* 29–45.

Verwoerdt, A. (1973). Psychiatric aspects of aging. In R. R. Boyd & C. G. Oakes (Eds.), *Foundations of practical gerontology* (2nd ed., pp. 123–145). Columbia, SC: University of South Carolina Press.

Vinick, B. (1977, September). *Remarriage in old age.* Paper presented at the annual meeting of the American Sociological Association, Chicago, IL.

Volpe, A., & Kastenbaum, R. (1967). Beer and TLC. *American Journal of Nursing, 67,* 100–103.

Walford, T. V. (1983). *Maximum life span.* New York: W. W. Norton.

Wallace, D. J. (1977). The biology of aging. *Journal of the American Geriatrics Society, 25*(3), 104–111.

Ward, R. A. (1979). *The aging experience: An introduction to social gerontology.* Philadelphia: Lippincott.

Warped view of old folks. (1979, November 12). *Newsweek, 94,* p. 124.

Wass, H. (1979). Death and the elderly. In H. Wass (Ed.), *Dying: Facing the facts* (pp. 182–207). Washington, DC: Hemisphere.

Wechsler, D. (1958). *The measurement and appraisal of adult intelligence* (4th ed.). Baltimore: Williams & Wilkins.

Wechsler, D. (1981). *WAIS-R manual.* New York: The Psychological Corporation.

Weg, R. B. (1983). Changing physiology of aging: Normal and pathological. In D. W. Woodruff & J. E. Birren (Eds.), *Aging: Scientific perspectives and social issues* (2nd ed., pp. 242–284). Monterey, CA: Brooks/Cole.

Weinberger, A. (1979). Stereotyping of the elderly: Elementary children's responses. *Research on Aging, 1,* 113–136.

Weisman, A. D., & Kastenbaum, R. (1968). The psychological autopsy: A study of the terminal phase of life. *Community Mental Health Journal,* Monograph No. 4.

Weisman, A. D., & Worden, J. W. (1975). Psychosocial analysis of cancer deaths. *Omega, 6,* 61–75.

Welford, A. T. (1958). *Aging and human skill.* New York: Oxford University Press.

Wesman, A. G. (1968). Intelligent testing. *American Psychologist, 23,* 267–274.

Wilkie, F., & Eisdorfer, C. (1971). Intelligence and blood pressure in the aged. *Science, 172,* 959–962.

Williamson, J. B., Evans, L., & Munley, A. (1980). *Aging and society.* New York: Holt, Rinehart & Winston.

Willis, S. L., Blieszner, R., & Baltes, P. B. (1981). Intellectual training research in aging: Modification of performance in the fluid ability of figural relations. *Journal of Educational Psychology, 73,* 41–50.

Willmann, J. B. (1986, December 7). Developers target the well-off elderly. *Los Angeles Times,* p. VIII-12.

Willmann, J. B. (1987, July 19). Most U.S. elderly appear well-housed. *Los Angeles Times,* p. VIII-13.

Winokur, G. (1973). The types of affective disorders. *Journal of Nervous & Mental Diseases, 156,* 82–96.

Wood, V., & Robertson, J. F. (1978). Friendship and kinship interaction: Differential effect on the morale of the elderly. *Journal of Marriage and the Family, 40,* 367–375.

Woodruff, D. S. (1977). *Can you live to be 100?* New York: Chatham Square.

Yankelovich, Skelly, & White, Inc. (1977). *Raising children in a changing society: The General Mills American Family Report, 1976–77.* Minneapolis, MN: General Mills, Inc.

Yeasavage, J. A., & Rose, T. (1984). The effects of a face-name mnemonic in young, middle aged, and elderly adults. *Experimental Aging Research, 10,* 55–57.

Yerkes, R. M. (1921). Psychological examining in the U.S. Army. *Memoirs: National Academy of Science, 15,* 1–890.

Youmans, E. G. (1977). The rural aged. *Annals of the American Academy of Political and Social Science, 429,* 81–90.

Young, M. L. (1971). Age and sex differences in problem solving. *Journal of Gerontology, 26,* 330–336.

Younger, E. J. (1976). The California experience: Prevention of criminal victimization of the elderly. *The Police Chief, 43,* 28–30 ff.

Zatz, M. M., & Goldstein, A. L. (1985). Thymosins, lymphokines, and the immunology of aging. *Gerontology, 31,* 263–277.

# Author Index

# Subject Index